T0301675

Alternatives to Capitalism in the 21st Century

Series Editors: **Lara Monticelli**, Copenhagen Business School and **Torsten Geelan**, University of Copenhagen

---

Debates about the future of capitalism demonstrate the urgent need to envision and enact alternatives that can help tackle the multiple intertwined crises that societies are currently facing. This ground-breaking series advances the international, comparative and interdisciplinary study of capitalism and its alternatives in the 21st Century.

Forthcoming in the series:

Creative Construction: Democratic Planning in the 21st Century and Beyond
Edited by **Jan Groos** and **Christoph Sorg**

Out now in the series:

Prefiguring Utopia: The Auroville Experiment
By **Suryamayi Aswini Clarence-Smith**

From Capital to Commons: Exploring the Promise of a World beyond Capitalism
By **Hannes Gerhardt**

Alternative Societies: For a Pluralist Socialism
By **Luke Martell**

Politics of the Gift: Towards a Convivial Society
By **Frank Adloff**

The Future Is Now: An Introduction to Prefigurative Politics
Edited by **Lara Monticelli**

Find out more at

bristoluniversitypress.co.uk/
alternatives-to-capitalism-in-the-21st-century

Alternatives to Capitalism in the 21st Century

Series Editors: **Lara Monticelli**, Copenhagen Business School and **Torsten Geelan**, University of Copenhagen

---

Find out more at

bristoluniversitypress.co.uk/
alternatives-to-capitalism-in-the-21st-century

REMAKING MONEY FOR A SUSTAINABLE FUTURE

Money Commons

Ester Barinaga Martín

First published in Great Britain in 2024 by

Bristol University Press
University of Bristol
1–9 Old Park Hill
Bristol
BS2 8BB
UK
t: +44 (0)117 374 6645
e: bup-info@bristol.ac.uk

Details of international sales and distribution partners are available at bristoluniversitypress.co.uk

British Library Cataloguing in Publication Data
A catalogue record for this book is available from the British Library

ISBN 978-1-5292-2537-2 hardcover
ISBN 978-1-5292-2539-6 ePub
ISBN 978-1-5292-2540-2 OA PDF

Cover design: Liam Roberts Design
Front cover image: Coinage by Zualidro
Bristol University Press uses environmentally responsible print partners.
Printed and bound in Great Britain by CPI Group (UK) Ltd, Croydon, CR0 4YY

Sin prisa pero sin pausa – To all those communities that, without hurrying but without pausing, are showing us ways to build sustainable futures.

Contents

List of Figures and Tables

Figures

Tables

Acknowledgements

There is more than the author to any book, and this book is no exception. There is, of course, all the authors whose thinking and experiences inspire the argument developed in the book. These are visible in the references that sprinkle the text, appear in chapter notes and are listed at its end. Somewhat visible, too, are the monetary entrepreneurs and money users who made time for interviews and discussions, who generously shared experiences, lessons and frustrations and who warmly reacted to my questions and misunderstandings as an opportunity to teach – Mario Arias, Teresa Carrascal, Ton Dalmau, Miguel Ángel Figueroa, Giuseppe Littera, Danilo Piratello, Ramón Viader. Belén, Esther, Feliciana, Fuyu, Gloria, Joaquim, Jorge, Juan Luís, Manu, Salvador, Paca, Silvia. There are many, many more than I can recall now but my heart will always remember.

Less visible in the pages of the book are the institutions whose funding and infrastructures have enabled the possibility of writing it. This includes financial support from the Danish Ministry of Foreign Affairs, grant no. GFIIEG 18-11-CBS, for the action research project 'Community Currencies: Grassroots Financial Innovations for Inclusive Economic Growth' and from the Swedish Research Council Formas, grant no. 2020-00402, for the research project 'Special-Purpose Money: Complementary Digital Currencies and the Sustainable Development Goals', along with library support from Lund University and editorial support from the team at Bristol University Press – hidden actors without whom the book wouldn't have been possible.

Similarly important for the development of the book though somewhat invisible in its pages are all those events and settings that facilitate debate and those colleagues who liberally engage in it. My deepest gratitude goes to Lara Monticelli and Torsten Geelan, who coordinate the 'Alternatives to Capitalism' network at the Society for the Advancement of Socio-Economics conference and who encouraged me to write the book, and to the whole team behind the organisation of the Research Association on Monetary Innovation and Community and Complementary Currency Systems conferences of 2017, 2019 and 2022, in particular to Jérôme Blanc, August Corrons Giménez, Georgina Gómez, Jens Martignoni, Ricardo Orzi, Rositsa Toncheva and Masayuki Yoshida.

Smaller seminars, during which I could present the ideas in this book as they evolved, have also played a pivotal role in straightening the argument. Mario Aquino Alves, Eduardo Diniz, Lauro Gonzalez, Alf Hornborg, Alexander Paulsson, Mareli Pozzebon, Gabriella Spinelli and Paul Weaver have helped advance the argument in the book through seminars and online meetings organised within the framework of the 'Special-Purpose Money' research project. As part of the 'Community Currencies: Grassroots Financial Innovations for Inclusive Economic Growth' project, María José Zapata Campos, Michael Oloko, Richard Kiaka and Juan Ocampo contributed with questions, comments, critique and ideas that have been key for me to develop both thinking and research on complementary monies. Christian Gelleri and Isabel Feichtner kindly invited me to an international workshop on complementary currency design organised by the University of Würzburg in 2020. Although held online due to the ongoing COVID-19 pandemic lockdowns, the discussions during those two days were enlightening for the shape the argument in the book was to take.

Closer colleagues who have become friends thanks, among other things, to a shared interest in money have been essential to the process of learning and developing a theoretical and analytical framework. It can be said that we have developed together through a shared reading group that has been going on since 2017. Andreu Honzawa, Juan Ocampo, Queralt Prat-i-Pubill, Paola Raffaelli and Leanne Ussher – thank you for the joyful text discussions. Other colleagues whose encouragement from my initial steps into the world of money and whose patience during my obsessive periods has been a source of serenity are Christina Lubinski and again – I cannot thank her enough – María José Zapata Campos.

Giacomo Bazzani, Eduardo Diniz and Leanne Ussher thoroughly read earlier versions of one or all chapters, as did two anonymous reviewers, the very review process invisibilising them. Their comments helped me clean and refine the text. The choice and presentation of the monetary experiments unfolded in the book have also benefitted from ingenious questions from students in the 'Re-imagining Capitalism' course at the Copenhagen Business School and the 'Re-imagining Capitalism' and 'Re-imagining Money' courses at Lund University School of Economics and Management. Discussions with PhD students at 'Digital Monies for a Sustainable Future' at Lund University were particularly helpful.

Often ignored but always necessary are those small gestures that provide space, time and resources to actually sit and write. Thank you Nuria Agell for a timely invitation; Sergio from the Ecoliberia for the books; Juan Antonio for the desk; Juan Diego for the screen; Lidia, Jeroen, Eduardo and Julio for the apartment; and Ileana for the well-timed company (and the medicine).

Finally, family, often relegated to the end of the acknowledgements section and, in the process of bringing this book about, perhaps overshadowed by the whirlwind of writing. Erik, Elvira and Darío – the joy of my life – your support has been the anchor during the most intense moments of the journey. Thank you for helping me remain balanced.

Prelude

During the first half of 2016 my family and I found ourselves living in Málaga, Spain, where the economic crisis that started with the global financial collapse of 2007–2009 had been long and deep, unemployment figures reaching 26 per cent – up to 57 per cent for the youth. In the southern Spanish city, I met María, a young woman in her 30s with a double university degree, one in anthropology and another in social work.[1] Like many young people in that city, however, she had been without a stable paying job for several years. I met her in El Caminito, an abandoned urban plot that a group of citizens had taken over and started to cultivate. María told me that thanks to Málaga Común – a community group and its community currency – she was able to put food on her table and a roof over her head. She paid the rent in *comunes* which she earned by looking after other people's children and cooking for others. At the group's weekly lunches, I met others who, like María, were making their finances work thanks to Málaga Común: the physiotherapist who sold massages to the members; Oscar who repaired bicycles and built solar ovens; electricians and painters who repaired homes; or Raquel who taught me to dance *sevillanas*.

By 2016 I had studied and worked at various management and economics schools for over 25 years, specifically researching the social economy for nearly ten. And yet, I had never heard of local or community currencies. So I started looking into that phenomenon. Was it unique to social, outgoing, flamenco-dancing southern Spaniards? Were these currencies tools that emerged during major economic crises? How were such forms of money organised? Were they all alike or did they vary across groups, territories, technologies and times?

As so often happens when one starts searching with intent, I found a multitude of examples, several dozen local currencies in Spain alone. I found them in France, Great Britain, Italy and Germany. In the United States and Canada. In Switzerland and Japan. In Kenya and South Africa. Currencies of recent formation and currencies from the 1930s. I also started to understand that local currencies were not only created by citizens desperate for lack of conventional money. Among the currencies I was learning about there were several where private and public actors had taken a pivotal role.

Following the suggestion of my newfound friends in Málaga, I participated in that year's National Congress of community currencies, where I met community organisers approaching these currencies as local tools for building community, city officials testing them as novel instruments for social welfare delivery, activists pleading for a new understanding of money, and scholars suggesting the institutionalisation of a plurality of monies within the national territory. For someone like me, who had founded and was running a non-profit social venture to organise communities in stigmatised suburbs of Swedish cities and who had been researching social innovation for almost a decade, the mix of scholars, practitioners and activists present at the congress was exhilarating. The conversations blended intellectual debate with practical insights, abstract ideas with concrete advice, a critical stance with a hands-on approach. Unwittingly, those days were to mark a shift in the focus of my work as an academic and in the direction of my engagement as a citizen.

Indeed, seven years on, as I write these lines at the end of 2022, I can genuinely confess that money has taken over my life. More precisely, the *making of monies* commands most of my awake time: I study the organisation of alternative monies, teach about reimagining monies, and am actively involved in the introduction of complementary monies in both Kenya and Sweden. This has led me to realise that the practical work of remaking money necessarily goes hand-in-hand with the intellectual work of rethinking money. And conversely; the intellectual effort to understand local monies – as well as money in general – is eased by the practical specificities of organising money. Practical and conceptual involvement reinforce each other.

The form of the book pays heed to such practical–conceptual feedback. Chapters 3 to 8 unfold a variety of cases to elucidate what money is about, how it works, and how it is made to work. Theoretical elaborations concerning monetary value, monetary architecture and monetary governance build on real-world money initiatives. And vice versa, practical guidance on the design of monetary configurations and organisation of money initiatives derives from the theory developed through the cases in a sort of theory-informs-practice-informs-theory loop.

The result is a book that can be read following various reading strategies. The reader who is less interested in theory and more interested in the practical making of complementary monies can jump over Part I and go directly to Part II of the book. The reader who is already well-versed in diverse architectural configurations and governance institutions of money and is instead interested in understanding how those architectures and institutions can be geared towards the advancement of particular social and environmental goals may want to go directly to Part III of the book. Finally, for the more intellectually inclined reader, for the reader who is more curious about how ideas, concepts and theories materialise in money and shape our relationship to it, the advice is to conduct a deep reading of the book's Part I followed by the two interludes and concluding with Chapter 9.

Of course, the reader that reads all chapters following its numbered sequence will get a more profound and sophisticated comprehension of the theory–practice entanglement that constitutes money. Because the world of ideas and the world of practice are never far apart. Less so – as Keynes and Polanyi taught us and we will see throughout the book[2] – in regards a phenomenon, money, that is the foundation of the socioeconomic system.

PART I

Why Money?

1

Money and Sustainability: Really?!

'Remaking money for a sustainable future' – really?! Aren't money and greed what put the world in the unsustainable situation we are in? Is it not the search for profit for money's sake that has led to entrenched inequality and a life-threatening climate crisis? How could new payment technologies – fancy as they may be – change all of that? 'Money' and 'sustainability' can't simply go together.

We have danced to the tune many times: frolicked to Liza Minnelli's 'money makes the world go round', whirled to ABBA's dream of 'having a little money', gambolled to Dire Straits' 'get your money for nothing' or pranced to Pink Floyd's 'grab that cash with both hands and make a stash'. If in the heat of the partying you stopped to listen to the lyrics, you would have heard a much-repeated story. That we all want money; that we are anxiously ready to give up true love to marry rich; and that we may criticise greed yet readily submit to it for the sake of the good life money is supposed to bring about. 'For the love of money is the root of all evil' the priest cites the Bible from the pulpit.[1] Back on the dance floor, the O'Jays summon you: 'People! Don't let money, don't let money change you. It will keep on changing, changing up your mind.'

Money itself is neutral – or so the story goes. If anything, money is a magnifier of the person that you are. The Greeks knew this already. Who doesn't remember the myth of Midas our parents read as we fell asleep? The king from Phrygia who, granted his wish to turn everything he touched into gold, turned food and, in some versions of the legend, even his own daughter into the precious metal. Dionysus, the granting god, eventually reversed the curse but the lesson persists across the centuries: it is not gold per se that is damaging to the world, but our foolish relationship with it. Avarice, greed, unrestrained desire of wealth are human passions that need to be controlled, managed, contained for the health of the collective.

The understanding of money encapsulated in popular songs and childhood stories takes money as external, a thing one either has or doesn't have and that, in whichever case, one always wants more of, regardless of how much one manages to accumulate. Though a thing it may be, 'money changes everything' (Cindy Lauper); it *acts* on us, shaping our ambitions and giving form to our behaviour. It is, then, the passions money awakes that need to be governed. Pronouncing the lust for money a sin, the great religions of the world worked to govern individual passions through moral condemnation and prohibition. Usury laws may be the most emblematic of these prohibitions. The Catholic Church proscribed any form of interest charged on loans – or the making of money out of money – until the development of merchant capitalism in the Italian cities of the 13th century when usury laws were relaxed into a cap on interest.[2,3] Closely tied to religious prescripts, ancient central authorities governed the fieriness money awoke in creditors through institutions such as the Jubilee year – the cancellation of all debts every seventh year, the wiping out of all promises to pay back. In the Middle Eastern cities of Mesopotamia this was carried out through the destruction of the clay tablets recording financial obligations and the freeing of those held in debt bondage.[4]

To religious commands and central coercion, economists added the market for the government of human excess. Though inheriting the religious conception of human behaviour as driven by violent passions, in the 18th century, political economists – Adam Smith most notoriously – introduced the idea of 'countervailing passions',[5] the notion that some passions were less harmful than others, that they could counteract each other and that, most significantly, their interplay could be put to work for the benefit of society. As Smith put it in one of his most quoted passages:

> every individual … neither intends to promote the public interest, nor knows how much he is promoting it … he intends only his own security; and by directing that industry in such a manner as its produce may be of the greatest value, *he intends only his own gain*, and he is in this, as in many other cases, *led by an invisible hand* to promote an end which was no part of his intention.[6]

In the economics framing of the human model, there is no need for moral judgement, nor for a central authority to direct the passions. Free, self-regulating markets do that job. Economic thinking transformed the passion for accumulation – the lust for money – from a sin to be banned into an innocuous human trait which, paired with those of the many, led to the 'improvement of all'.[7]

In his defence of markets, Smith and fellow economists go even further. Not only did 'commerce and manufactures gradually introduce order and good government, [it also secured] the liberty and security of individuals, among the inhabitants of the country, who had before lived almost in a continual state of war with their neighbours and of servile dependency upon their superiors'.[8] The hand that invisibly governs 'the private interests and passions of individuals' became a mechanism in restraining the arbitrary wishes of the sovereign and in guaranteeing peace across nations. Money simply served to make the hand more agile, or 'to grease the wheels of commerce' as the expression usually goes. The Smithian view of human nature as excessive and of the self-regulating market as the natural mechanism to coordinate people and to free them from the whims of princes and sovereigns has informed mainstream economics and much policy making since the 1980s.

At this point, the critical reader would promptly jump on the seat. It is the lust for money that has brought a disregard of nature, extracting from it beyond its capacity to restore itself.[9] It is the search for profit for the sake of money that has led to exploitation of humans by humans – from the slave trade and forced labour driven by the Industrial Revolution to the coercive sweatshops that feed today's globalised economy.[10] It is the insatiable desire to accumulate that results in rising inequality, leading to increased political polarisation and the erosion of the social fabric.[11] The free market mechanism has proven incapable to align individual passions towards the service of people and planet. If anything, it seems to have exacerbated self-interested love of money.

Many an economist and political analyst agree. Exploitation of nature and peoples by other peoples searching for profit are not new phenomena. Nor are the criticisms new cries. Karl Marx's work was indeed a reaction to the social dislocations brought by unhinged industry and commerce. In his analysis of capitalism, Marx gave a central role to machinery, private property and money; in that sequence. The material conditions of large-scale machines demanded the division of labour into tasks that were ever more devoid of content, a process through which workers lost their freedom to determine how they worked, at what pace, for what purpose and at what rate. Labour-saving machines created a 'reserve army of labour' that helped the industrialist keep wages lower than the value workers added. Protected by the institution of property rights, the industrialist-capitalist – the legal owner of the means of production – appropriated the 'surplus value' when products were sold and 'exchange value' was realised in the market. In Marx's account of the capitalist process, money is again the standardised neutral measure of value that facilitates market exchange. It is also value in itself. Money can realise the value built into the products of industry only because money itself has value. Similar with labour. Labour's value is recognised as such only through its exchange against money in the labour market; the industrialist's ability to appropriate labour's surplus and accumulate capital rests on the transformation of labour into a product that is exchanged for money in a market.

For Adam Smith, it is the market that harnesses the human passions and aligns them towards the public good. For Karl Marx, it is the market that commodifies labour and submits workers to the capitalist's 'boundless drive for enrichment'. Those on Adam Smith's side see 'the capitalist process, not by coincidence but by virtue of its mechanism, progressively raises the standard of life of the masses'.[12] Followers of Karl Marx see in the capitalist mode of production a process that creates and continuously reproduces the antagonistic relationship between the working and the industrialist classes. 'It was in fact the cheapness of the human sweat and the human blood which were converted into commodities, which permitted the constant extension of the market.'[13] Differing understanding of the role of markets is, in a nutshell, the fault-line that has defined, and still defines, much political debate.

Accordingly, though economic and political analysts across the ideological spectrum agree on the numerous crises threatening civilisation, they disagree on the right way to address them. Liberalisation and the extension of markets say the first – advocating for the creation of markets for carbon emission rights and calling for further deregulation of labour markets. Regulation and taxation say the latter – supporting government intervention in markets and redistributive policies. Condition welfare benefits to work, the first counterattack; implement unconditional, universal welfare policies, answer the second.[14] As climate change increases the virulence of devastating natural phenomena, as ever more precarious work conditions turn 'the precariat' into a dangerous class,[15] as entrenched inequality dents social stability,[16] and as unpayable levels of private debt bring national and the world economy down, the debate across the ideological line becomes ever more polarised. Similarly acknowledging the urgency of the present historical moment, proponents on each side become more desperate to implement their solutions. Only, their solutions typically point in opposite directions. And so, countries see their political systems either deadlocked or threatened by sudden outbursts of discontent and violence.

Insurmountable as the divide may seem, the starting point of this book is the common ground that both sides stand on. Their views are based on grand narratives that put the market at the centre of historical development. The market is either good or bad – with a few in-betweens – but it is, in any case, a force driving human history. It either bridles individual passions towards collective progress, or it provides a place for the industrialist to capitalise on his 'werewolf-like hunger for surplus labour'.[17] Money acts but as a mere facilitator, extrinsic to the mechanism of the market, unrelated to the cogs of the economy and unconnected to the self-interested calculative nature of the entrepreneur and the capitalist. In Karl Marx, like in Adam Smith – as well as in their intellectual heirs – money is a *neutral intermediary* in market transactions. That is the blind spot both sides of the ideological debate share.

The blind spot: neither neutral nor intermediary

'Neutral intermediary' – this book argues otherwise. The view that money acts as a trade intermediary merely providing an outlet for self-interest is an oversimplification of what money is, how it works and how individuals *relate to* it (and, we will see, *in* it). Money may have become 'the end and aim'[18] of today's financial capitalism; yet money as an end hinges not on its supposed intrinsic value, but on its internal design, on the architecture of the monetary system. Money's value – how money works and the extent to which individuals use and trust it – is determined by the particular configuration of entities and agents that constitute money. The 'bills of exchange' common among European Middle Age merchants in the international fairs of Lyon accrued trust, and value, thanks to the tight networks of a small cosmopolitan elite of financiers sanctioning them. Precious metal coins embodied value thanks to the monarch's stamped badge on the coin and the imposition of tributes in that coin. The bill notes of private banks obtained (and, as we will see in Chapter 3, continue to obtain in today's digital form) their worth thanks to the sovereign's endorsement as legal tender and enforcement in payment of taxes.[19] When looking behind the token that most naïvely is mistaken for money – the paper bill, the silver coin, screen digits – when opening up the system of relations that undergird the token, we are able to see that, far from being neutral, the 'end' of money relates to the sectorial interests of the economic class that issues and governs it.[20] Money itself is interested, coloured by the loyalties of its masters.

Monetary technology also skews money. Or, as sociologists of technology would have it, the materiality of the token also shapes money's capacities. The precious metal content of the coins used for far-distance trade from Old Babylonia to the English Enlightenment sheltered a merchant from the vagaries of political power and the sudden impulses of kings. As the metal was appreciated in international markets, silver provided merchants with a material guarantee even if kingdoms failed or sovereigns decreed a reduction in the nominal value of their coinage.[21] Yet, the amount of the precious metal in possession of the legitimate authority limited the supply of money, a factor behind the repeated debasements of Roman currency, the pillages of the Crusades and the plunder of the Americas[22] – not to mention the difficulties in maintaining the gold standard in the 20th century.[23] Today's national monies are equally conformed by the technology supporting them. Digital technologies enhanced the possibility to package promises to pay – entries in the ledgers of commercial banks as we will see in Chapter 3 – slice and organise those packages into a variety of financial derivatives, and sell them forward through global financial networks of algorithmic trade. The 'distribution of risk' these technologies enabled quickly turned a wave of mortgage defaults in the US housing market into a financial crisis of global proportions.[24] Though, as we will see in Chapter 3, more than technology enabled the unbridled subdivision and distribution of promises to pay, the algorithmic speed and global reach of digital technologies were a sure enabler of it.

The system of relations that money is, then, is made of actors and technologies, loyalties and materialities, interests and objects. A final component of money crucial to consider is the imaginary integrated in its architecture. It is telling that both Adam Smith and Karl Marx held an understanding of money as a thing with intrinsic value, the universal commodity to be sold (or exchanged) in the market.[25] At the heart of such a commodity money imaginary is the tight mental connection often made between money and gold or silver. For Smith, the ease of transporting the precious metals facilitates market exchange; for Marx, the possibility to hoard the money commodity becomes the ultimate aim of the capitalist. The understanding of money as commodity prevails in today's financial markets where securities – a particular form of money[26] – are sold and resold, bought for its exchange value, not its use value; acquired for the ease with which markets can redispose of it, sell it forward, or, as the financial terminology would have it, purchased for its 'liquidity'.[27]

Even though the 'intrinsic value' of money was made insignificant on 15 August 1971, when Nixon took the United States off the gold standard, the *understanding* of money as commodity still shapes our relationship to it. Someone 'has' or 'doesn't have' money; money can be 'stocked' and 'stored' or it can 'flow' and 'circulate' at varying 'velocities'; money serves as a 'medium of exchange' to be 'traded' in a market for 'equally valued' goods or services. The popular understanding of money spread through songs and children's stories shines through the terms we use to describe how money works. It is an understanding of money that also permeates orthodox economics through theories of 'supply and demand' for money, 'marginal utility' of the money commodity, and the 'quantity theory' of money.[28] The gold standard may be dead, but the underlying conceptual pattern remains.

How money is understood is far from inconsequential intellectual philosophising. Writing in the mid-1940s, economic historian Karl Polanyi traced the root of the violent cataclysms of the first half of the 20th century to the enactment of three commodity fictions: human life had been turned into labour to be traded in a specific labour market; nature had been transformed into land that could be bought and sold; and money had been commodified through its tight association with gold. The liberal conviction that the market is the spontaneous and natural mechanism to organise economic life had led to the extension of the market principle to the organisation of the three elements of production: labour, land and money. Until the Industrial Revolution, Polanyi argued, markets had been mere accessories to social life, places where farmers and households met to exchange their produce surplus. Land, labour and money were organised along principles other than the market. Indeed, labour had been 'regulated by laws against beggary and vagrancy, statutes of labourers and artificers, poor laws, guild and municipal ordinances';[29] 'land stood under the custom of manor, monastery, and township, under common-law limitations';[30] and money came 'into being through the mechanism of banking or state finance'.[31] Yet, the advent of the complex industrial machine, with the large investment it involved, had made it necessary to secure large quantities of inputs as well as access to markets large enough to absorb the output and obtain sufficient income to recover the initial investment plus a return. The first – securing inputs to the machine – was made possible with the enclosure of common land and the Poor Law Reform. The enclosures drove common people out of the land they had lived on; the Elizabethan, misguidedly called, Poor Laws left them without the instituted support the most vulnerable had received from local parishes. Concomitantly, land was consolidated into compact private property and repurposed to produce cotton that fed the machine. Made indigent, the common people had no other choice than to move from their traditional communities, sell their labour and bear the inhuman conditions of the early factories.[32] The second – securing consumer markets that covered the investment of the business capitalist – was brought about through imperialism and the gold standard. Imperialism opened up foreign markets; the gold standard fixed exchange rates and guaranteed the international acceptance of that money. But fixing domestic money to gold meant flexibility in prices had to come from flexibility in wages – the price of labour – and in rent – the price of land. In other words, in order to keep competitive in foreign markets, workers and peasants bore the brunt of the social toll. Or, if you prefer, in order to attend to the interests of the business capitalist, the working and landed classes were the 'most immediately affected by the deleterious action of the market'.[33] This, Polanyi argued, was intervening in the money market – fixing the price of money to gold – in the name of self-regulating markets – for goods, labour and land.

The liberal response to the challenge of the expensive complex machine was to organise production under the market system. This required the commodification of human life, nature and money. First, human life and nature were 'subject to supply and demand … dealt with as commodities, as goods produced for sale',[34] 'treated *as if* produced for sale'.[35] But human life and nature are no other than the substrate of society and the environment in which it exists and so, in commercialising them into labour and land, the liberal creed was de facto subordinating society to the organisational principle of the market. This required the institutional separation of society into an economic and a political realm. In accomplishing this, 'hunger and gain – or, more precisely, fear of going without the necessities of life, and expectation of profit'[36] were the sole individual incentives acknowledged, satisfaction of which was mediated by a money that became understood as something that could be sold in a market. Money, then, was commodified into gold – and, therewith, thought to be apolitical, extrinsic to the functioning of the economy. And yet, neither labour nor land nor money are 'objects produced for sale on the market' – the empirical definition of commodity.[37] Their reduction to commodities had therefore the effect of reducing the 'rest' of society – that is, human life and nature – into accessories to the market economy. Or, in Polanyi's wording, 'instead of the economic system being embedded in social relationships, these relationships were now embedded in the economic system'.[38] The rise of fascism, authoritarianism and Bolshevism, Polanyi argued, were but the spontaneous reaction to the social ravages created by the organisation of society under the self-regulating market principle. In that, the 'collectivist countermovements' of the first half of the 20th century were similar; they aimed to protect society from the social dislocations and human suffering that the commodification of life, nature and money had led to.

In what concerns money and its relationship to the social body, Polanyi's analysis of market economy elicits the intensively political nature of money, even a money – gold commodity – conceived and organised *as if* a neutral intermediary in market transactions. The gold standard followed liberal ideology and accommodated to the interests of business capitalists. In this it was indeed no neutral intermediary. Nor was it a neutral intermediary when transmuting the pains of shifting international markets onto falling wages for workers and declining land-rents for farmer-peasants at home. Most insightfully, Polanyi's analysis attends to money as a relational phenomenon, shaped by the ideas and interests of the dominant economic class and shaping the social order to the image of those ideas and interests. As such, money becomes the crystallisation and tool of power arrangements across social groups.

What's money then?

If money is no neutral intermediary, what then is money?

To answer that question, an important distinction comes in handy; that between 'intermediary' and 'mediator'. The sociology of associations defines intermediary as 'what transports meaning or force without transformation: defining its inputs is enough to define its outputs'.[39] Intermediaries are entities which make no difference to whatever they connect. It is the computer that connects my fingers to these lines. The glasses with which you read these lines are also intermediaries. From the input – my fingers striking a keyboard, lines on a text – to the output – these lines, your reading – there is a straightforward connection, no interference. Intermediaries, that is, are passive, neutral, with no effects to the chains of associations they enable. Mediators, on the other hand, 'transform, translate, distort, and modify the meaning or the elements they are supposed to carry'.[40] If a computer virus transmutes the letters in my keyboard, these lines may become unreadable. If your son scratches your glasses and snaps one of their temples when playing with them, your reading may become less easy. There is not one output – these lines, your reading – from the input – my fingers, these lines. The circumstantial specificity of the input needs to be considered. In other words, mediators are entities that change that which they connect. They are active agents, provoking certain effects to the detriment of others.[41] They shape the behaviour of the components they connect and, thus, of the chain of associations they facilitate.

The difference between intermediaries and mediators is not one of ontological essences, but of performative effects. Computers and eye-glasses behave as intermediaries or as mediators depending on the particular circumstances, and it is often when the entities stop working that we realise that they were in fact mediators and not intermediaries. During break-downs, the intermediary that we had taken as a compact entity opens up. We are able to see that computers are complex systems made of electric signals, processors, memory, software, and a variety of connecting devices. Eye-glasses turn up to be made of soft surfaces, temples, nose pads and tiny screws. Break-downs open up the black-box the intermediary was made to be. The many components were there; it is only us who were not focusing on them. Break-downs direct our gaze, helping us to see anew the causal relation we assumed between input and output, to elicit the many elements forming the entity observed, and to trace the way these elements provoke the output we got. This is what happened to money – or rather, to our gaze – with the financial collapse of 2007–2009.

Money had been approached as an intermediary. It had gone so far as mainstream economics erasing it altogether from their economic analysis.[42] Similarly with much other scholarship. It was the greedy passion of entrepreneurs, businesses' insatiable desire to grow and consumers' conspicuous consumption that were found at the root of the multiple sustainability crisis we face today. From climate change and the loss of biodiversity to intolerable inequality and political polarisation, the cause was found in the vicious passions of people. Blame was individualised. Consumers had to become more aware, bankers less greedy, businesses more socially responsible.[43] Perceived as a veil, money was not part of the problem. It was black-boxed, its many constitutive parts hidden from the analysis. The financial collapse that started with the subprime mortgage crisis in the United States in 2007 and soon developed into an economic crisis of global proportions changed this unity of money. How could the misconduct of US bankers have consequences in other countries? Through what conduits did the actions of financial actors have effects on workers' everyday lives? And through what series of relations was the abundant money that had funded the housing market bubble suddenly become scarce? The monetary system was breaking down. At the edge of the precipice, many started asking questions. Our gaze was being redirected. Instead of unproblematic, many started to realise that money had been made opaque. The task was now to open up the established monetary system, recognise its components and the complex, layered relations among them. Commercial and central banks, hedge funds, pension funds, rating agencies and financial markets came to view, as did mortgage contracts and the possibility to pack, split, securitise and sell those contracts. Even the discipline of economics and its implicit imaginaries of what money was were scrutinised, for these, too, were found constitutive elements of the money system.[44] Monetary activists, grassroots entrepreneurs, civil society, scholars started to unpack money, to unfold the sociotechnical arrangements that configured it, and to point at its infrastructural effects on the economy and society at large. The cause–effect relationship between individual behaviour – of bankers, corporations, financial actors, consumers – and our sustainability challenges – economic despair, social dislocation and environmental devastation – was thus revised, blame transposed from profit-making ardour to a dysfunctional monetary system. Money had become a mediator.

Two fundamental insights follow when money becomes a mediator. One, as a mediator between parties, money contributes to constitute the collective. Two, as a sociotechnical arrangement, money is constituted by the collective. Herein lies a radical revelation, for, if money is constituted, collectively made through political, social, technological and conceptual practices, then it can surely be remade. A new form of hope is born and bred by the newly found sense of possibility. The awareness that money can be rearranged so as to harness its infrastructural capacity to advance a more fair, resilient and sustainable future started to open up novel horizons of thinking, doing and interacting.

Changing the question

Our creative limits start with the questions we ask: 'What is money?' 'Where does its value reside?' Historically, those questions have received two answers. The first defines money as a thing we exchange in the market for other things, the spontaneous creation of private businesses in order to solve the problem of the double coincidence of wants proper of barter trade. It is the understanding of money that dominates popular songs, children's stories and mainstream economics. The position is commonly known as Metallism for the tale it builds upon is the tale of gold, the value of the money-stuff residing in its precious metal content. The second answer defines money as a debt-relation, as credit granted with a corresponding promise to pay back. It places the origins of money in an economy of promises and social obligations, money-tokens simple debt records acting as mementos of social relations, IOUs (I-owe-you). We find this position most often among Keynesians and post-Keynesians, and it is often referred to as Chartalism from the Latin word *charta* – the token or paper recording the debt. In this understanding of money, the value of the debt-token resides not in the material object substantiating the debt-relation but in the trust placed on other human beings making good on their debts. Because of this need to trust many others, Chartalists often endorse Knapp's *State Theory of Money* according to which money is created by the state through the establishment of a uniform measure of value and enforcement of tributary debt.

Economic historians and anthropologists of money tell us that the factuality of these answers is historically contingent, different civilisations relying on commodity-money or debt-money at different times and for different purposes. That is, the accuracy of the answer to 'what money is', or 'what it was', depends on the specific time, place and people. It depends even on the specific type of trade merchants engaged in, silver money used for trade with foreign regions and debt-money for trade at home.[45] Money *is* not always the same, nor *was* it ever the same.

The confusion starts when such contextually determined answers are presented as ontological truths.[46] The question 'What is money?' pushes us to point at something in reply, yet we seem unable to point to any single thing. We feel compelled to point at historical referents – even if unfounded as the story of barter is[47] – and, abstracting from them, the answer indicates either towards a thing – commodity-money – or an accounting tool – debt-money. Each answer emphasises one aspect of particular monies: either the material elements – the precious metal the money-token is made of or is made to represent – or the immaterial component – the abstractions needed for recording debts. The problem is that what money is cannot be found solely in either the material world of objects nor the conceptual world of ideas. It has components from both worlds; simultaneously material and immaterial, a thing and an abstraction, a commodity and an accounting tool. The money-stuff and the money-of-account; the balance of elements depending on the particular money observed. To limit the answer to one single type condemns us to capture merely partial truths, shadows in either the material world or the world of abstract collective agreement, shared meaning and supposed trust. Pushed by the question to chase ontological shadows, each answer limits the realm of our imagination to either commodity-money or debt-money. I call these shadows 'imaginaries of money'. (We will read more about them and their diametrically divergent policy advices in Chapter 2 and Interlude 1.)

So, if we want to understand money to remake it, then the strategy may be as simple as reformulating the starting question. From a question that compels us to chase ontological essences, to one that directs our gaze towards descriptions of how money works and how it acts upon the world.

After all, our initial intuition is that, somehow, money is connected to the sustainability predicaments we face today. We then need a question that allows us to explore that intuition, a question that urges us to follow money's actions onto the world, one that propels us into tracing the paths through which the monetary system crafts the social and disrupts the environment. To understand money and its effects into the world we will need to elicit the circuits of action connecting money to the degradation of the environment, the polarisation of societies and the erosion of democracy. That question could be as plain as 'How does money work?' – a question that pushes us to explore 'the mechanics of money'.

Thus formulated, 'How does money work?' will help us understand the relationship between money and sustainability (or rather, for our conventional money, our unsustainable practices – as we will see in Chapter 3). It won't, however, help us remake money so as to enact more sustainable practices. To guide the work of remaking money for a sustainable future, we need to understand how money is made, its components and the relations among them, its internal architecture. 'How does money work?' helps us capture the insight that money constitutes the collective. The second insight gained by approaching money as a mediator was that money, in turn, is constituted. A slightly different question attends to the constituted nature of money: 'How is money *made* to work?' – a question that pushes us to look into the continuous 'work of infrastructuring and governing money'.

Now, in revealing that money is no neutral intermediary, anthropologists of money, economic historians and legal scholars have shown that there is no one money, but many.[48] If, as I have suggested, we approach money as 'a sociotechnical arrangement' which particular configuration depends on the entities and agents involved, and which particular infrastructural effects hinge on the specific rules and relationships it builds within, then we cannot ask about 'money' in the general. We need instead to ask about 'this' or 'that' money. About specific monetary architectures. The two previous questions will therefore be specified into 'How does this (X) money work?' and 'How is this (X) money made to work?'.

In attempting to answer these two questions for each monetary assemblage unpacked in the following chapters, I will be opening up the taken-for-granted 'thingness' of money. And, in doing so, several distinctions will surface: monetary tokens versus monetary system; imaginaries versus materialities; payment technologies versus governance rules. Analytically distinct, the two sides of these dichotomies are in practice inextricably merged, together configuring and arranging the sociotechnical composite that money is. As varied money composites are opened up, as several monetary experiments are unfolded, we will observe that the various monies are little like each other, at best bearing a mere family resemblance.

Even the value of money will become an illusory resemblance made possible by the use of the same term – 'value' – to refer to radically different *strategies to make money work* (elicited in Chapters 3–6, compared in Interlude 2, implementations for specific purposes contrasted in Chapters 7 and 8). Monies articulated around the imaginary of gold situate their value in the money-stuff itself, in its materiality or the materiality the monetary tokens are supposed to represent. Monies arranged along a debt–credit imaginary locate value in the trust creditors grant debtors will make good on their promises, in the legitimacy of the debtor or in the system guaranteeing debts will be paid. Radically different approaches to value as these are, what unites the entrepreneurs behind them is their effort to make money work by building value into their monetary system. And yet, whatever the quality of the value attributed to particular monies – value found in materiality or value found in the community of debtors – what makes a money work is not the particular place where value is supposed to reside. Rather, what makes money work is the mechanism that makes people accept the money-tokens in payment of their goods and services while inducing the same people to spend those tokens forward within the community of users; that is, a mechanism that provokes people to take and pass the money-tokens, to relate back so as to keep money-tokens in continuous movement. For no money works if its tokens are held still. For money to work, it needs a mechanism – which I have called *perpetuum mobile* – that imbues in its users a sense of obligation to relate forward. Only when money-tokens circulate, only when they are widely accepted and spent, does money work as medium of exchange and means of payment greasing the wheels of markets. The question 'How is this (X) money made to work?' is hence parallel to the question 'What makes this (X) money widely acceptable?' or, 'Why do merchants accept this (X) money in payment for their wares?' and 'What pushes them to spend it (X) further?' Wide acceptance is the empirical manifestation of a money's value.

In short, money is about people, just as it is about ideas, technologies, mechanisms, principles of social organisation, strategies of value, cultural habits of thought and relations; above all relations among all kinds of entities – between persons, between objects, between imaginaries, and between persons, imaginaries and objects. Standing on this approach, the book is not so much an economic study of money as a study of the sociology of the multiple relations that inhere in money. This is reflected in the somewhat eclectic corpus of readings the book builds upon, ranging from heterodox (and less heterodox) economics, to political economy, economic anthropology, economic history and economic sociology. As chapters confront different monetary arrangements with little in common but superficial family resemblances, the readings mobilised in each chapter will vary accordingly.

A monetary countermovement

For those interested in how money works, and in how it is made to work, these are lucky times. That money was key to the workings of the economy was widely acknowledged before the crisis of 2007–2009. Yet only a handful of economists – and possibly a few more bankers and financial actors – understood that the form money took shaped both the economy and society. Money, that is, was invisible for the majority of the population; its design and architecture taken for granted. The insidious economic and social consequences of what was called the Great Recession changed this naturalness of money. The concentration of wealth in 'the 1 per cent' in parallel to austerity policies, the increase of prices of financial assets parallel to a retrenchment of the welfare state resulted in a generalised realisation that the monetary system was not serving the interests of the population as a whole. This led to a revival in discussions of what money is, how it works and how it could be made to work. An increasing number of activists, citizens, entrepreneurs, practitioners, scholars and grassroots initiatives all around the world started to see money as a pivotal institution of capitalism, if not its most basic institution. The financial crisis brought with it destruction of our economic and social fabric. It brought, too, the denaturalisation of money. The mediating nature of money had been brought to light.

In the wake of this denaturalisation, a wave of agitators, engaged scholars and activist entrepreneurs[49] started to call for change in the way money works. Not contending the centrality of money for our economies, they focus instead on the form money takes: how it is created (and by whom), how it is designed (and along whose interests), and how it is governed (distributed and accumulated). From blockchain entrepreneurs redesigning payment infrastructures,[50] and grassroots entrepreneurial initiatives introducing local currencies into communities,[51] to bank money reformers crusading for sovereign forms of money,[52] these monetary initiatives seem to agree on the need to change the monetary system. Indeed, for many of these activists, tech and social entrepreneurs, scholars and communities, it is not money itself, but rather the way money is configured and made to work that is the root of all evil. If we want to move towards more fair, equalitarian, human and holistic economies, then, they argue, money needs to be changed.

In this newfound monetary awareness, three entrepreneurial spaces are particularly active: grassroots communities designing their own local currencies; local public administrations implementing city-wide currencies; and radical crypto-activists developing global payment infrastructures. These are, as it were, entrepreneurial spaces with diametrically distinct imaginaries of money and strategies to reorganise it. The first emphasise the centrality of *adapting* money to the needs and traits of the *local community* that is to use it; constrained by their institutional position, the second *tie* the new money to the national one and often prioritise the needs of *local businesses*; finally, the third often opt for a *standardised* money that can be scaled up *globally*. The first conceive economic relations as indistinguishable from communal relations; the second understand the economic and social realms as separate yet connected; the third devise money as divorced from the social relations among those that are to use it, and think of the economy as a sphere apart from the social sphere. The first work with well-defined community boundaries; the second build on legal definitions of who belongs to the city; the later assume a *homo oeconomicus* behaving free from communal norms.[53] Most often, the first implement monies designed along a credit understanding of money; the second and third endorse a Metallist understanding that locates the value of money on what it is made to represent (may this be a budgetary post in national currency or a basket of national currencies kept in a bank account). In line with their distinct understandings of money, grassroots currency practitioners, city administrators and crypto-entrepreneurs are assembling different monetary arrangements and developing divergent governance institutions. General assemblies to which all users are invited to decide on the rules for the creation and circulation of the currency are common practice among grassroots communities; participatory budgeting processes are being tested by city administrators. In the case of cryptocurrencies, it is often the crypto-entrepreneur and the developers deciding those rules and coding them into automatic algorithms. (Chapters 7 and 8 each compare three monetary arrangements developed for similar aims and yet arranged and governed along different organising principles).

Building on different imaginaries of money and embedded in different communities of practice, grassroots activists, city politicians and administrators, and crypto-developers are experimenting with a variety of monetary configurations ('how does this money work') and governance institutions ('how is this money made to work'). It is in this richness of experiments that we find our luck. As they experiment, tinker and remake money, they are showing us new ways to (re)organise the economy, suggesting new socioeconomic worlds, combining a novel mix of socioeconomic motives and, ultimately, envisioning new forms of living together. In a sense, these grassroots-, city- and crypto-entrepreneurial initiatives constitute an example of Polanyi's 'countermovement' – a spontaneous reaction to protect society against the consequences of economic liberalism and laissez-faire. Just like a Polanyian countermovement, the grassroots-, city- and crypto-entrepreneurs implementing new monies do not fit neatly into a socioeconomic class nor do they fall clearly under one ideological line, the instinct to protect society and the environment from the consequences of financialised capitalism present in all layers of the socioeconomic order and on both sides of the ideological debate.[54]

Whatever the organising principle they follow in the configuration of their monetary architectures, and whatever the outcome of their efforts, I argue that their monetary designs, emergent practices and governance institutions are contributing to develop a new imaginary of money – the money commons – an understanding of money as a public infrastructure that can be managed democratically to attend the evolving needs and priorities of the people using it. Grounded in the situated knowledges of communities, the book contends, the commons imaginary could contribute to a more sophisticated discussion and a more democratic organisation of the monetary system at large.[55]

The book is an attempt to better understand the efforts of communities, cities and crypto-entrepreneurs to reorganise money, thus making money a centrepiece in their work to build an inclusive and sustainable future. From looking at these monetary experiments, the book proposes a new imaginary of money – the money commons – as a framework that opens up the possibility for communities to adapt the architecture of money – and the ecosystem of monies – to the rich variety of actors, entities, technologies, ideas, relations and institutions constitutive of social life. In advancing the commons argument, the book challenges a hierarchy of knowledge in which economists alone are supposed to have anything to say about money and in which the management of money is left exclusively in the hands of established monetary experts. Ultimately, the argument in the book is that we need to identify new ways to reorganise money as well as to develop new knowledges to carry out the work of reorganising the economy. The many monetary experiments going on around the world today may provide a useful guide.

2

Imaginaries of Money

With characteristic provocation, French sociologist Bruno Latour approaches the Virgin Mary as an actor, whose existence may be in the realm of the imaginary, but whose performative effects are definitely found in the physical world of humans and objects.[1] A pilgrim embarking on a long journey 'because I was called by the Virgin Mary' is not to be taken as a delusional individual. The fact that the element that moved the pilgrim *to take action* adopts the shape of an invisible (to most of us) and illusory (to some) figure does not lessen that element's agency. Its ideational form does not detract performative capacity from the Virgin. In the way of the fabled invisible hand, the Virgin Mary *makes* the human actor *do* things, the illusion of her *makes a difference* onto the world. She is endowed with an agency with real world-making effects. John Maynard Keynes made a similar observation in reference to the performative effect of economic ideas onto the world:

> [T]he ideas of economists and political philosophers, both when they are right and when they are wrong, are more powerful than is commonly understood. Indeed the world is ruled by little else. Practical men, who believe themselves to be quite exempt from any intellectual influences, are usually the slaves of some defunct economist. Madmen in authority, who hear voices in the air, are distilling their frenzy from some academic scribbler of a few years back. I am sure that the power of vested interests is vastly exaggerated compared with the gradual encroachment of ideas. ... But, soon or late, it is ideas, not vested interests, which are dangerous for good or evil.[2]

This is particularly true for imaginaries of money.

The agency of imaginaries of money shines through stories about the origins of money. Money is there presented as either making markets more efficient, or making government more effective; as either transforming barter merchants into productive profit-maximising individuals or aligning a people towards the interests set by a central authority; as either a commodity freeing the merchant from the limits set by the double coincidence of wants or as an accounting record visualising quantified individual rights in relation to the social body. Ideas of money – about its source of value, about the original problem it addressed, about its inventors and its initial use – implicit in origin stories influence how money is made to behave, whether it is made to act as an instrument of markets or as an infrastructure of the state.[3]

Only, while the Virgin Mary (and the invisible hand for that matter) seem to speak with univocal voice, ideas about 'what money is' speak in two distinct voices. These voices are suggested in the set of 'either-or' pairs in the short list of agency performances in the previous paragraph: intrinsic versus extrinsic value, efficient markets versus effective government, its source exogenous versus endogenous to the economy. There are, as it were, two main origin stories and, alongside them, two main money imaginaries. The first sees in barter the precedent of money, conceives money as a thing – a commodity with intrinsic value – and markets as made of independent individuals exchanging things – one of them being money. The second sees money as originating in relations of debt between a central authority and its subjects, conceives money as a claim on goods based on those debts, and markets as organised by the central authority for the provision of needs to the social body.

The debate on the nature of money is very much contested, different understandings seemingly aligned to different designs of money, monetary policies and ideological inclinations. Money, that thing mainstream economists see as neutral to the workings of the economy, is impregnated with the beliefs, stories and political thoughts that accompany all ideologies and that *make a difference* on the world through specific monetary arrangements, policies and roles for the monetary actors. So to start understanding the ways in which money both is made and makes the world, it helps to unfold the origin stories of money. Learning how and why it is thought to have emerged will help us understand what problems it is thought to address, what actors are thought to be central, and where its value is thought to be located (or why it is thought to be generally accepted).[4] Origin stories will help us unveil where the infrastructural and social power of money is thought and, eventually, made to reside.

The barter story

In 1776, a professor of moral philosophy at the University of Glasgow brought the discipline of economics into being by inquiring into *The Nature and Causes of the Wealth of Nations*. In the chapter entitled 'Of the origin and use of money' Adam Smith placed the origins of money in imagined and distant societies that engaged in moneyless market exchange, or barter economies. With the division of labour, he argued, barter exchange must have become difficult, clogged by traders having more to offer than they were interested to acquire. With barter, traders could only offer the products of their own trade, but had no guarantee those products were interesting to the traders one wanted to buy from. Later phrased as the 'problem of the double coincidence of wants', the challenge barter economies posed was the 'difficulty … to find two persons whose disposable possessions mutually suit each other's wants'.[5] Smith exemplified with the challenges a baker, a brewer and a butcher may have had in agreeing to exchange:

> The butcher has more meat in his shop than he himself can consume, and the brewer and the baker would each of them be willing to purchase a part of it. But they have nothing to offer in exchange, except the different productions of their respective trades, and the butcher is already provided with all the bread and beer which he has immediate occasion for. No exchange can, in this case, be made between them. He cannot be their merchant, nor they his customers; and they are all of them thus mutually less serviceable to one another.[6]

Adam Smith continued:

> In order to avoid the inconvenience of such situations, every prudent man in every period of society, after the first establishment of the division of labour, must naturally have endeavoured to manage his affairs in such a manner as to have at all times by him, besides the peculiar produce of his own industry, a certain quantity of some one commodity or other, such as he imagined few other people would be likely to refuse in exchange for the produce of their industry.

In the barter story, money emerged *spontaneously* as a *private* innovation that overcame the limitations of barter exchange by making goods commensurable (directly comparable) in the same unit of account and exchangeable for the same type of tokens.

In the barter origins story, the 'commodity or other' that comes to ease exchange becomes money. What that commodity actually came to be – whether salt, shells or dried cod, whether tobacco, sugar, hides or leather – didn't really matter. What mattered was that, from then on, this thing came to be desirable not for its own sake, not for its specific utility, but for 'the power of purchasing other goods which the *possession* of that object convey[ed]'.[7] Whatever the thing exchanged for the goods wanted, it acted as a *medium of exchange* whose value was assessed as equal (commensurate) to the good bought. The barter story presupposes the existence of a *market* where *individuals* conduct exchange to satisfy their own needs and wants. It also presupposes the existence of a unit of account with which to measure and compare the value of the commodities exchanged. These two presuppositions are, as it were, the first of several logical incongruities in the imaginary of a money that starts with barter.

Nevertheless the story of barter continues. To avoid the loss of the *value intrinsic* to the good this property money was made of, and to circumvent the indivisibility of other money-commodities – oxen is a preferred example of Mr Smith – merchants eventually gave 'preference … to metals above every other commodity';[8] hence the name given to this school of thought, 'Metallism'. 'Rude' 'unstamped bars' of iron among Spartans and of copper in ancient Rome, the story goes, were used 'to purchase whatever they had occasion for. These bars, therefore, performed at this time the function of money'. Generalised acceptance of this form of money – whether made of iron, copper, silver or gold – hinged on the value granted to its metallic content; pointing at yet another presupposition of this origins story: that the specific metal has an intrinsic value of itself equally recognised by all, and that such value is therefore fixed for all.

In its 'rude state', however, the metallic content was difficult to assess. For one, metals were difficult to weigh, 'a small difference in the quantity makes a great difference in the value … proper exactness requires at least very accurate weights and scales',[9] something not only most merchants probably hadn't access to, but also something particularly troublesome for the small 'farthing's worth of goods'[10] commonly traded. Assaying the quality of the metal content was 'still more difficult, still more tedious, and … extremely uncertain'. Advocates of the barter origins of money introduce the state first at this point in the story. To solve the problem of identifying the quantity and quality of the metal content,[11] the public offices of the mint introduced coined money 'to ascertain, by means of a public stamp, the quantity and uniform goodness of those different commodities [metal monies] when brought to market',[12] the denominations of the coins initially expressing 'the weight or quantity of metal contained in them'. The role of the state in this story is limited to supporting the interests of the private sector by ascertaining the value of money which thus facilitates the smooth operation of the market.

But just as the state can use its authority to uphold the value of money for the benefit of the market, it can also misuse its authority by abusing its seignorage prerogative. '[T]he avarice and injustice of princes and sovereign states', Smith argues, 'abusing the confidence of their subjects, have by degrees diminished the real quantity of metal, which had been originally contained in their coins', allowing them 'to pay their debts and to fulfil their engagements with a smaller quantity of silver than would otherwise have been requisite'.[13] Smith's suspicions towards the practical ethics of the monetary authority reveal a conceptual distinction key to unveil two components of commodity money. The first refers to the nominal unit of value inscribed in the coin, the unit of account used to compare the value of goods traded in the market. The second refers to the precious metal content in the coin, the material stuff that gives money its value. An ideational/abstract component the first, a physical/natural component the latter; money-of-account versus money-stuff. Reducing the quantity of the metal content of coinage while keeping its nominal value enabled the sovereign to pay back more of his debts with the same amount of metal. Currency debasement has indeed been an operation rulers have resorted to throughout history, from the Roman emperors to Henry VIII's Great Debasement. Debased though they were, the currencies seemed nonetheless to have served well for the purpose of trade, thus begging the question of where the actual value of money resided. And yet, far from asking whether the value of the debased commodity-money did reside in its content or in the authority behind it, Adam Smith – along with Metallists – abhorred the idea of government's intrusion into the management of money by changing the quantity of its metal content. Emperors' and kings' payment of their debts with debased commodity money, he argued, was 'in appearance only; for their creditors were really defrauded of a part of what was due to them'. Seeing value as intrinsic to the money-commodity, advocates of this story argue against government involvement in monetary policy and for letting the value of money follow the natural 'principles which regulate the exchangeable value of commodities'. To be sure, many an advocate of commodity money argue for the price of money to follow the rules of free markets.[14]

Smith enunciates the larger sociopolitical implications of the management of money through the management of its quantity (and value). Not only did debasement (or devaluation) favour kings and emperors.

> All other debtors in the state were allowed the same privilege, and might pay with the same nominal sum of the new and debased coin whatever they had borrowed in the old. Such operations, therefore, have always proved *favourable to the debtor, and ruinous to the creditor*, and have sometimes produced a greater and more universal revolution in the fortunes of private persons, than could have been occasioned by a very great public calamity.[15]

It is an analysis that conceded the conflict of interests between the landed class of creditors and the debtor class of small farmers and trade entrepreneurs. It announced the opposing economic interests driving distinct imaginaries of money.

Though precious metals were in time substituted by paper notes, the barter line of reasoning continued to place the value of the notes in their metal *backing*. In *The Origins of Money* from 1892, the Austrian economist Carl Menger wondered about the fact 'that every economic unit in a nation should be ready to exchange his goods for little metal disks apparently useless as such, or for documents representing the latter'. His answer reproduced the logic of the barter story; people accepted intrinsically worthless paper as payment for their goods and labour because banks and states were ready to *convert* them for the precious metals in their vaults.[16] It was the link between the nominal value on the bills and the value granted to the metals backing it that made paper monies generally acceptable. When, as it happened from time to time, governments suspended convertibility of the notes into metal, the Metallists extended the logic into people's *expectation* of restored convertibility in the future.[17] For what concerns today's fiat, non-convertible, national money, advocates of the commodity imaginary have a difficulty to explain the source of its value.

The story of barter undergirds an imaginary of money as a thing valuable in itself, a medium of exchange emerging spontaneously in the private interactions of merchants, a commodity which natural properties make market transactions more efficient, an object merchants acquire for the general purpose of trading. The state plays no other role than guaranteeing the intrinsic value of this form of money, a guarantee needed for money to perform well as the 'universal instrument of commerce'. The agency of commodity money is supposed to reside in its assumed intrinsic value; it is the value of the metal that *makes a difference* in the trading capacity of the merchant.[18] Intruding in the management of money therefore risks 'disorder in the coin' and, with it, in the mechanism of prices and the functioning of markets.

Though logical incongruities run throughout the barter story – as we have seen, it assumes a monetary unit of account exists previous to the birth of money; it presupposes a society that accounts for value in monetary terms; it is unclear how merchants in a money-less society arrived to the division of labour; it cannot explain how individual merchants with various trading interests came to agree on a medium of exchange with a fixed value; and it fails to account for the wide acceptance of a money, like today's, made of intrinsically value-less paper and digits[19] – the barter story of the origins of money is a powerful one. It certainly has a strong pedigree. Both Aristotle and John Locke endorsed it; Karl Marx assumed it.[20] Open an introductory book in economics and chances are that its author takes you to an imagined barter economy;[21] today's central bankers repeat it.[22] Foremost, there is no historical nor anthropological evidence of a barter economy pre-existing money. In the years after Columbus' arrival to the American continent, no traveller or explorer reported discovering a land of barter.[23] Logically incongruent and empirically unsubstantiated, the barter story is nonetheless one of the foundational stories of the discipline of economics. A 'zombie idea' that is demonstrably wrong and yet continues to consume people's creative energy.[24]

The Babylonian story

In a letter dated 18 January 1924 and addressed to his fiancé, Russian ballerina Lydia Lopokova, the most reputed economist of the 20th century confessed to suffer from 'Babylonian madness'. Trying to locate the origins of money in the Ancient Near East, John Maynard Keynes had become 'absorbed to the point of frenzy'.[25] In the economic practices of the Mesopotamian civilisation, the British economist found evidence of the birth of money in hierarchical redistributive economies, of markets springing from a central political authority, and of the nature of money as an accounting device to record and discharge debts. Keynes never published a Babylonian origins story that would counter the myth of barter. Yet the insights he gained during his Babylonian frenzy were to influence his understanding of money, formulated most succinctly in the opening words of his *A Treatise on Money*: 'Money of account, namely that in which debts and prices and general purchasing power are *expressed*, is the primary concept of a theory of money.'[26] Keynes' imaginary of money as an accounting tool radically differs from the commodity imaginary stemming from the barter story. Its origins story necessarily follows a different line of thought.

The Babylonian story starts in the world's first large urban societies, those that emerged along the fertile lands at the confluence of the Euphrates and Tigris rivers.[27] The city of Uruk, the birthplace of Mesopotamian civilisation, was home to more than 10,000 people in its heyday during the third millennium BC. Agriculture and farming were the economic basis of these early urban economies. Independent as they were of rain to grow cereal, irrigation agriculture produced reliable harvests capable of feeding a growing urban population. Shepherds and farmers lived in the city, as did other specialised labourers needed for the provision and maintenance of urban life; bakers, brewers and weavers, merchants, teachers and temple officers, tool-makers, smiths and soldiers. Though rich in grain and livestock enough to feed its large population and attain a surplus to export, Babylonian city-states lacked timber and stones for building, as well as copper and tin for weaponry-making, and exotic prestige commodities, such as spices and precious stones, the possession of which was a symbol of economic, social and political status. To provision these, Babylonian cities relied on long-distance trade.

Today we take for granted that we will be able to find everything we need in the markets of our cities – from coffee beans and fresh pineapples coming from afar, to tools and fabrics produced closer to home. But in illiterate societies, with no money and no writing, it is difficult to conceive how urban production was organised in distinct trades, how food and other goods were distributed among its citizens, and how distant commerce was funded and coordinated. Fortunately, archaeological findings give us some cues.

Excavations of Southern Babylon in present-day Iraq offer testimony of the complex social and economic arrangements of these ancient city-states. The first surprising observation to the foreign eye is the non-existence of a marketplace; no open spaces have been excavated, nor are they named in contemporary literary records. Indeed, the ancient records that we have from unfamiliar observers of the day speak with equal surprise of the absence of markets in ordinary life. On the occasion of a visit to Babylon between 470 and 460 BC, Herodotus asserted that 'the Persians do not frequent market places and in effect, do not possess in their country a single market place'.[28] Instead, archaeological diggings reveal temples first, royal palaces later, at the centre of the urban space. It appears that early urban economies centred around these hierarchical public institutions.

Another archaeological finding that exposes much of the economic organisation of Babylonian city-states are the thousands of clay tablets found in the precincts of temples and palaces. With patient and systematic zeal, Assyriologists have decoded the tightly scribed cuneiform script that fill these tablets, displaying the economic relations between individual citizens and the city's central authority. Inscribed in clay, the tablets record the advances and rations distributed from the temple to individual citizens. Temple accountants and scribes listed the names and contributions to the temple expected from particular individuals: 'Lugid, the man of the levy, 864 liters of barley, Kidu, the man from Bagara, 720 liters of barley, Igizi, the blacksmith, 720 liters of barley.'[29] The tablets are, as it were, an archaic form of ledger registering citizens' individual debts to the central, crediting, public authority.[30] Individual debts to the temple were paid back come harvest time, at which occasion debts were simply cleared out. No need for commodity-money mediating between the parties; no need for coins to pay back the debt. All that was needed was the recording of the debt and of its cancellation through clearing.[31]

A system of equivalences was also needed for the temple to act as a storage-and-distributive centre of the incipient urban economy. Barley figures as the accounting unit quantifying the debts in the list of debtors to the temple. But advances by the temple took more than the barley form – raw materials to craftsmen to make tools, wool to weavers to fabricate clothes, rent of land to farmers, lending of animals to shepherds, or consigned goods to traders parting on sea voyages and caravan routes. How much barley was a fair counterpart for the advanced wool or lent tools? How much of the imported metals would repay the temple's consigned products? What was the barley equivalent to land rent and animals lent out? Commensurability is quintessential to any system of credit. In Old Babylon, barley provided the common denominator of debts and hence, of prices – a co-measure across distinct goods and services. Ratios of goods, products, services and labour to barley were fixed in terms of barley weight or barley grains. This system of a fixed unit of account and of administered prices kept the accounting of debts and their discharge simple.[32] Just as the source of the debt recorded in terms of barley may have been other than barley itself, the temples accepted the repayment of a debt in other commodities than the barley that served to measure that debt. Barley acted as the standardised unit of account and prices were fixed according to it, but a variety of commodities – barley, copper, wool, sesame oil are just some – were used as money.[33] Such a system facilitated the flow of resources between Mesopotamian central distributive authorities and the city's population.

Clay tablets from about 1,000 years later record debts in units of silver – another archeological finding key for understanding the evolution of money. It is unclear how silver became a unit of account for it had no practical utility in the Babylonian economy. Assyriologists find it plausible that it was silver's status as a prestige item that rendered it useful as a monetary unit. Its assigned value, however, was not connected to some form of assumed intrinsic 'natural' worth as the commodity imaginary of money would have it. Rather, just as a system of equivalences to barley had been developed across a wide range of commodities and services, so it was developed for silver. The shekel-weight of silver was made equal in value to the monthly consumption of barley per person, 240 barley grains, silver's value thus made as constant as the weight of barley. Though silver itself appears to have been seldom used to repay debts, debts could thereon be recorded and cleared out in terms of silver. All in all, we find the origins of money and monetary value in the temples' authority to proclaim a clear monetary dictionary consisting of accounting units and values.[34]

In fact, archaeological records witness this form of public money developed millennia before the invention of coinage and previous to the emergence of the first long-distance markets. It was the organisational monetary practices of temples and royal palaces that came to enable the specialised organisation of labour and the development of inter-city commerce.[35] Non-perishable and easy to divide, the cereal crops of the Mesopotamian valley lend themselves to storage, counting and distribution. Temples acted as 'holy storehouses', storing barley along with other products of daily need, and distributing them among the populace. This enabled the specialisation of labour, cereal growers being able to contribute to the temple with their crops and get other foodstuffs and items in return – all of which were, as we saw, recorded in clay tablets by the temple's scribes. The stability of abundant harvests and the centralisation of storage allowed for agricultural surplus to be exchanged for other products unavailable in the Mesopotamian region – not the least silver, which had to be brought from Anatolia, in what is now Turkey, and Susa, in modern Iran. It was the temples and royal palaces that organised the export economy. First, they coordinated the production of goods for export by employing women and other artisans to weave the fabrics and produce the commodities of interest to the people in the lands that produced or traded the coveted metals, stones, spices or building materials. Artisan labourers received payment in the form of rations and set hour equivalences in silver.

Temples, then, consigned merchants with the staples, fabrics, tools, and other commodities coveted by faraway populations, and merchants were to return with the metals, spices and other items needed for the urban economy of the city-state. The temple's consignment of goods to the trader was made against a security from the trader to the value of the goods consigned. Merchants' dealings in distant trading posts appears to have been conducted on the principle of 'cash delivery'; that is, trades were carried out on the basis of silver, which thus fared on both directions, to and from the city-state. On arrival from their trading ventures, merchants were paid on commission – a pre-set percentage of the value of the imported goods. Because, as we saw, prices took the form of equivalences fixed by the central authority, merchants did not risk the price changes common in supply-and-demand market economies. Their earnings derived not from price differentials between buying and selling but from the set commission earned from the turnover of goods. Trading activities were thus risk-free, both for the trader in regards price expectations, and for the commissioner temple in regards the debtor's – the trader's – insolvency, which was guaranteed by the security in hand.[36] In this way, trading ventures may have had an uncertain outcome, but they were devoid of risk. With no inflation of goods' prices, and with no interest charged on the debt to the temple accrued by the merchant, debtors were at a par with creditors, no one's interest prevailing over the other.

Although the Babylonian economy pivoted on the institutional framework of a storage-and-distributive authority, private business deals existed both in distant trading posts and at home.

> The trader needed capital to be provided in the form of short or long term loans, or of partnerships; associates, as members of the firm; employees to travel for him ... he was free to buy and sell non-consigned ware; to loan money to firms and to participate in their profits.[37]

Yet the public and private spheres of the trader's deals were always strictly demarcated. When acting on his public capacity for the procurement of government consignments, merchant activities were clearly formalised in documents written by public scribes. If acting as private business, trading activities were informal, contracts were agreed in terms of the money of account set by the central temple authority, and prices fluctuated around institutional price equivalences. In the Babylonian story, that is, markets are not previous to money and government. Rather, markets sprang out of the monetary and administrative practices of the centralised authority of temples and royal palaces.[38]

In the organisational economic practices of Mesopotamia's hierarchical public authorities we find an imaginary of money as credit from a central institution to its subjects; as the accepted means to redeem debt to the public authority; the money-token – or *charta* – the symbol of a debt–credit relationship between the individual and the authority that institutes the community, an IOU (I-owe-you). The key traits of Chartalism – as this school of thought is referred to – are succinctly summarised in the opening sentence of Georg Friedrich Knapp's opus *The State Theory of Money* (1924/1905): 'Money is a creature of law.' Law – that is to say, the state – defines the monetary unit of account, proclaims its standard value through a list of equivalences, and promotes it through acceptance at the public pay-offices. In this understanding of money the state is the foundation for money, for the markets that use it, and for the coordination of a specialised economy. The agency of this form of money, that is, hinges on the authority guaranteeing its administered value.

The English translation of Knapp's *State Theory of Money* appeared in 1924, 19 years after its original publication in German. It was translated and published on the behest of Keynes who, alongside his confessed 'Babylonian madness', translated those ideas into non-convertible 'fiat money' managed by the state.[39] The state credit imaginary of money is the basis for today's Modern Monetary Theory where taxes are the counterpart of tribute to the temple, fiscal policy the equivalent to temple's advances to the population, and monetary policy parallel to the temple's clay tablets.[40]

Two imaginaries with distinct agencies

The two origin stories reveal distinct patterns of thought in regards how money and markets are conceived and understood to work. Table 2.1 highlights the contrast between both modes of monetary thinking.

Such a clean separation of money imaginaries has characterised monetary discussions throughout Western history: from the Great Recoinage debate in 1690s England between John Locke and Isaac Newton – who both saw money in coinage itself, the value of the pound an objective reference to a fixed weight of silver – versus William Lowndes, Secretary of the Treasury with long practical experience and deep historical knowledge of English monetary history – who called for acknowledging the fall in value of the coin by raising the price paid for its silver content by the Mint;[41] to the Convertibility controversy on the occasion of the Napoleonic wars at the beginning of 19th century with Bullionists – led by David Ricardo – arguing that the government's 'too lavish issue of paper money' to fund war efforts was the direct cause of rising prices, versus the Bank of England – through its 'Real Bills' doctrine – countering that the bank 'never force a note into circulation, and there will not remain a note in circulation more than the immediate wants of the public require'. Rises in prices, the bank argued, were the result of poor harvests and Britain's subsidies to foreign war allies. In the 1840s, the debate was framed along the Currency versus Banking schools, the one side advocating a rigid supply of money by anchoring

Table 2.1: Comparing two main money imaginaries

	Commodity imaginary	**State credit imaginary**
Origin story	Barter market economies	Babylonian distributive economies
Nature of monetary units	A thing, an object, a commodity	A record/token of a debt–credit relationship between a central authority and the polity
Main original function	Medium of exchange	Means of payment (of an obligation/debt)
The individual's relation to money	As property, something one 'has' or 'does not have'	As a relationship, a promise to pay or its mirror, a claim for payment (George Simmel's 'claim upon society'); an IOU
Source of money	Exogenous: external to the doings in the economy	Endogenous: internal to the doings in the economy
Source of value (or, why would anyone accept it in payment of goods and services?)	Intrinsic/'natural': first in the metal content, then in the backing of the paper note. Advocates of this imaginary have a difficulty to explain the value of today's fiat money and tend to see its value as contingent on its scarcity	Political: central authority with the power to force the payment of tributes/taxes and to impose the means of payment
End goal of the monetary arrangement	Market efficiency: reduce transaction costs, make the functioning of markets more efficient	Social well-being: distribute a community's resources across its members for the well-being of the social body
Existence of markets	Markets exist previous to money	Sovereign's organisational power is a prerequisite for the existence of markets
Conceptualisation of: - Sale	Exchange of a good for an intermediate commodity acting as medium of exchange	Exchange of a commodity for credit
- Market	Place where goods are exchanged	A place for the clearing of debts and credits
Social organisation	Horizontal: community of traders in ideally competitive markets	Vertical: a centre that collects contributions from community members and redistributes these among them
Approach to the study of money	Individualist: money is the property of its individual holder	Public: money is a public tool to coordinate the economy

Table 2.1: Comparing two main money imaginaries (continued)

	Commodity imaginary	**State credit imaginary**
Economics of money	Supply of money economics (Quantity Theory of Money [QTM])	Demand of money economics (demand for credit/loans)
Monetary policy	Rigid supply of money in order to keep the value of money, and prices, stable	Elastic supply of money to accommodate it to the needs/demands of the economy
Whose interests it favours	Creditors	Debtors
Role of money in political economy	An instrument of trade neutral to the dynamics of the social body. Thus, money is, and should be, apolitical	An instrument to organise the social body. Money is thus inherently political
Economy–society dualism	The economy as a sphere separate from the political	The economy and the political are two aspects of the same phenomenon (society)
Most known proponents	Locke, Hayek, Friedman	Knapp, Keynes, Wray

money to gold; the other side advising an elastic supply of money that accommodates to the needs of businesses and the population at large.[42] The debate between Friedrich Hayek and John Maynard Keynes during the deflationary depression that followed Winston Churchill's decision to return Britain to the gold standard followed similar dividing lines.[43] Today, the debate runs along those that defend Milton Friedman's Monetarism and austerity policies in the midst of economic crisis against post-Keynesian economists advocating for active fiscal policies. Whatever form the debate has taken, its central questions have remained substantially the same: Where does the value of money reside? And who is to manage it?[44] Or, in the reformulation proposed in Chapter 1 of this book: How does money work? And how is it made to work?

'Hold on a minute', the reader may retort. Aren't we going astray in the midst of time? Aren't we digressing into intellectual abstractions of value and trust in the governance of money? What for? Does it really matter whether money comes from barter or from an obligation towards authority? Whether it is understood as a thing or as a relation of debt? After all, whatever its origins and whatever the imaginary, both stories tell us that money emerged as a way to organise the economy.

True. Money has been defined as a social technology for the coordination of the economy and society at large. The previous chapter argued that money should be approached as a sociotechnical arrangement with infrastructural powers – a mediator at once organised and organising. Still, origin stories are not to be dismissed as mere mythical tales or exotic histories of long foregone civilisations. Imaginaries of money are not to be disregarded as simply the stuff of intellectual debates. Origin stories and their implicit money imaginaries are of practical relevance because their answers to the two, historically persistent, questions – those of value and of governance; of how money works and how it is made to work – entail radically different performative effects concerning the roles assigned to the various actors constituting the monetary arrangement. The different locus of agency of the money imagined – intrinsic value versus central monetary authority – *make a difference* to how monetary actors are made to relate to the overall monetary arrangement.

First, the role granted to government. Proponents of the barter story often brandish it to argue for limiting the role of government in monetary affairs. After all, they contend, echoing Adam Smith, property, money and markets not only existed before any political institution, but were the very foundations of human society. It follows that insofar as government is to play any role at all, it is to protect private property and safeguard the soundness of the currency. Property, markets and money emerged naturally and governments should therefore limit their intervention in these issues not to interfere with their natural laws. By contrast, proponents of the state credit imaginary of money use the origins story in ancient Mesopotamia to argue the need for government to firmly intervene in markets, property and money. If money was an invention of political institutions for the organisation and coordination of society, then, surely, today's governments should play an active role not only in warranting the currency but in all matters of the issuance, distribution and governance of the monetary system.

Second, origin stories and money imaginaries shape the role accorded to banks. In the barter story, barter comes first, money comes later, and finally, once money has been created, comes debt–credit relations. In this story, the possibility to lend and borrow comes only after money has been invented, created and saved. This sequence defines the role of banks and other financial actors as mere intermediaries between those that have money and those that need it, between savings and the possibility to borrow, between creditors and debtors. In the Babylonian story, the sequence is reversed: first there is credit and debt; the stones, sticks, and paper where those credits are recorded eventually translated into money. Banks and financial actors are thus not so much intermediaries as the originators of debt–credit relationships represented in transferable tokens (bills of exchange then, digital bits today). Banks create loans by issuing debt which is, itself, money. They need not wait for savers to put their savings at the bank's disposal. Rather, financial actors create money and function as instrumental monetary mediators.[45]

Finally, stories and imaginaries condition the role bestowed on the public. In the barter story, a merchant either has money to restock her shop, or hasn't and thus cannot restock the shop; a member of the public either has access to the thing called money or doesn't. The public's relation to money is one of finding ways to accrue ready-minted money – either through selling labour power, renting or selling one's belongings. The public needs to find a strategy to make those with money willing to distance themselves from it. In the Babylonian credit story, money is virtual, an abstraction, a relation of credit and debt between economic agents, an account balance between two parties which promise to clear it out. As such, the quantity of money in circulation expands as agents agree to extend their debt–credit relations and contracts as debts are paid back. For the public, there is much possibility in this understanding of money as any citizen, any merchant, could pay through issuing debt given that other economic agents accepted her promise to clear that debt later on. The credit imaginary acknowledges the general public's role in the creation of money (this will be elaborated in Interlude 1).

In the distinct roles granted to the monetary actors, you have surely recognised a political divide. Indeed, the two origin stories take us to distinct political doctrines. The barter story builds on an understanding of money as commodity, a thing to ease trade, whose value is contingent on the scarcity of the material it is made of. Its advocates are therefore averse to government intervention in money matters and favour austerity policies to keep the money supply scarce.[46] The Babylonian story builds on an understanding of money as credit, account balances that expand and contract with the needs of trade. Its supporters hence recommend government intervention in monetary policies and an elastic supply of money. No wonder market libertarians tend to espouse the first line of thinking and those favouring developing the welfare state defend the second. In other words, propositions about how money is to be produced, how much of it is to be produced, and who is to produce it hinge on imaginaries that are ultimately political, not technical, in nature.[47]

Barter or state credit? Commodity or token of debt? Market or government? Horizontal or vertical? The debate has proven difficult to settle; possibly because money is both, at once commodity and IOU, the relationship between the two subject to continuous intellectual and power struggles.[48] For the argument in this book, whether one story is logically more plausible and empirically more substantiated than the other doesn't make a difference. As long as concrete imaginaries and stories are engineered into monetary arrangements and made to act through policies and mediators, the less historically accurate story may however be the one with the largest world-making effects. Just as the Virgin Mary and Adam Smith's invisible hand transform the agency of human actors, monetary ideas translate into monetary architectures with significantly distinct infrastructural effects on the economy and the polity.

Our conventional monetary system may be one of the best examples of a money that is at once a thing to be sold and a relationship of debt and credit. In today's national monies we do indeed find a dialectical synthesis of the commodity and state credit imaginaries of money. The next chapter turns to these, in an effort to open up the conventional monetary arrangement and unfold the way the credit and commodity imaginaries play out in the build-up of financial crises and our sustainability predicaments.

3

Sell It Forward: The Form and Reason of Today's Conventional Money

Until the financial implosion of 2007–2009, few among the general public stopped to wonder about money – where it came from, how it was created, who created it, what constituted its value, why some had so much whereas others had so little, or why the abundance of money during economic booms suddenly turned into scarcity during economic busts. Had you asked the common person – and more than one politician and financial money manager – the most probable answer you would have received was that money was created by government. The most knowledgeable among them may have nuanced the answer by introducing central banks into the money creation process. Few would have told you that the bulk of money circulating in the economy is created by private banks. Fewer would have acknowledged the key role borrowers – of any status, also you – played in the money creation process.[1] Money was normalised, unquestioned, taken for granted.

The global economic crisis that followed on the steps of the Great Financial Crisis of 2008 changed that normalisation of money. How could banks, that had been granting easy credit to subprime borrowers, suddenly ran out of money? Where had the money come from before and why was there so little of it now? And why had banks, whose market incentive was supposed to be to reduce risk, engaged in such risky forms of lending? Had the forces of self-regulating and self-stabilising financial markets not worked as supposed? Alan Greenspan – Chair of the Federal Reserve in charge of the US monetary policy during the easy-credit years – was himself at odds to answer the later question. At a congressional hearing on the subprime mortgage crisis on 23 October 2008, he declared 'those of us who have looked to the self-interest of lending institutions to protect shareholders equity, myself especially, are in a state of shocked disbelief. Such counter-party surveillance is a central pillar of our financial markets state of balance'.[2] This was a direct admission of the misconception at the heart of mainstream neoclassical economics that had guided Greenspan's policies, and an indirect admission that banks and other financial actors indiscriminately created the bulk of our money following short-sighted, self-interested calculations of profit maximisation with no regard to the real productive capacity of the economy.

As unprecedented monetary policies were implemented to avert the worst economic breakdown since the banking crisis of the 1930s, the public's questions concerning money piled up. Why were central banks around the world printing vast quantities of money and handing them out to the banks and financial actors whose practices had so obviously led to the ongoing crisis? What made private banks and financial actors so indispensable that central banks were willing to take over their toxic assets and governments chose to breach public deficit limits that had thus far constrained public investment?[3] Given the enormous injection of money into the banking system by the central banks that went on, the economics taught in most textbooks and endorsed by most economists predicted that bank lending would increase and high levels of inflation would occur. But following more than a decade of such easy monetary policies, economies remained in low growth and inflation remained low.[4] Was all we were taught about money and its relationship to the economy flawed?[5]

In Europe, quantitative easing (QE) – as the injection of vast amounts of money by central banks came to be called – was soon to be accompanied by austerity fiscal policies. We were told that to redress the large public deficits incurred to salvage the banks, governments had to 'tighten their belts'.[6] Public 'savings' were conducted on the healthcare sector, on the social welfare and pension systems, and on investment on infrastructure. Social services were cut down, leaving the homeless to fend for themselves on the streets, single mothers to struggle to feed their kids, and the elderly to turn down the heating.[7] During the years of austerity policies, inequality rose and labour conditions worsened, paving the path to political polarisation and risking the erosion of democracy.[8] Why were governments and central banks, who had so easily found the money to rescue private banks, now letting such levels of social despair happen? How could they find the money before but not now?

Another set of questions centred around the global dimensions of the crisis. A crisis that had originated in the irresponsible lending practices of US banks to willing US homeowners, how could it so quickly and virulently spread throughout the world? How had one's modest savings, placed in a supposedly safe pension fund, abruptly shrank?[9] How could financial actors in one corner of the world so affect savers in other corners of the world? What were the monetary arrangements and financial circuits that so tightly connected us?

Of the many money-related questions raised since 2008, Queen Elizabeth's is probably the most revelatory. During a briefing at the London School of Economics in 2008, she wondered, with blunt naïvety, 'If these things were so large, how come everyone missed them?'[10] How could economists – the experts who are to prevent us from such devastation – miss it? Indeed, only a couple of months before the crisis began, the Chief Economist of the Organisation for Economic Co-operation and Development forecasted 'sustained growth … strong job creation and falling unemployment'.[11] The optimism lasted until the momentous collapse of Lehman Brothers and until the subsequent unravelling of the globalised networks of financial actors and interconnected instruments into which our monetary arrangement had developed. The economic theories guiding these experts' predictions had been, it now came to full sight, blindfolded. Considering money an instrument to grease the wheels of markets yet neutral to the functioning of the economy, mainstream economic theories had ignored money altogether.[12] Academic and practising economists trained with textbooks filled with those theories knew therefore little – if anything – about how money actually worked; and how it was, actually, made to work. Without analytical tools to enable them see money, 'experts' had missed the warning signs.[13] This was all the more handicapping for predicting a crisis whose epicentre resided in the very way our monetary and financial system de facto works.

The response to the COVID-19 pandemic brought desperate urgency to these questions. Within days of the virus taking hold on the world, and to stave off the dawning economic crisis from lockdowns, central banks returned to the sort of loans and asset purchase programmes that characterised QE policies of the previous decade, introducing money through the buying of assets directly in open market operations or indirectly through, for instance, Special Purpose Vehicles.[14] Governments, too, implemented generous fiscal stimulus packages the size of which had not previously been seen in history. After years of austerity, once again, no dearth of money. The new money went to fund vaccine research, support state and local governments fight the virus, support struggling families, sick leave, unemployment insurance and, in the United States, direct cash payments to every citizen. The robust fiscal response in the United States resulted in, among others, the largest reduction in poverty on record.[15] Social welfare measures that had been impossible to agree on before for lack of funding, like child support, were now implemented without concern for national budgets. Where did all that money come from now and why was it not there before?

The COVID-19 pandemic evidenced another phenomenon worth questioning. Though countries were locked-down and economies contracted in 90 per cent of the world's countries in 2020, shrinking the global economy by 3 per cent and increasing global poverty for the first time in a generation,[16] the stock and money markets were, by all accounts, doing fantastic.[17] While curves visualising the health of the real economy pointed decisively down, financial markets pointed steeply up. The markets that are supposed to allocate money in the real economy, and derive their value from the real economy, showed to be, in actual fact, completely detached from the real economy. This translated into further inequality, the richest 1 per cent seeing their wealth increase during the pandemic while the bottom 20 per cent experienced the steepest decline in incomes.[18] Where were financial markets getting their money from? And why did market valuations go bullishly up even though economies were plunging?

Those who care to find responses to these monetary perplexities have to go beyond mainstream books. Almost 15 years after the financial crisis of 2008, economics university programmes continue to use textbooks that insist on some version of the Loanable Funds theory of banking – succinctly, that private banks act as mere intermediaries between savers and borrowers, savings (deposits) coming first and credit (lending) coming after[19] – with the consequent blindness to the crucial role banks play in money creation in the economy. The inadequacy of mainstream economics to explain what was happening became so manifest that students around the world organised to demand a renewal of textbooks[20] and prompted some professionals to redo their economics teaching and rethink the economics paradigm.[21]

To find answers, one needs to go to those few that did accurately predict the financial crisis of 2008. Their approach to money as a two-sided balance sheet phenomenon and their models of banking as a set of accounting practices enabled them to see the extent to which money creation through credit extension by private banks was at the heart of economic processes.[22] In common, these perceptive economists shared an economic analysis based on the distinction between financial and real-economy assets, an accounting approach to the relationship between the financial and real economy, a focus on the credit flows that finance financial assets, and a concern with the growth of private debt that accompanied growth in financial wealth.[23] From them, you will learn that the bulk of our money is created when private banks record newly created loans on their ledgers; that this accounting process consists of simultaneously marking up the assets and liabilities sides of the customer and bank ledgers; and that, as a consequence, lending (credit-creation) precedes deposits (savings). Putting banks' accounting practices at the origin of money, these models lead to more accurate descriptions of the rapidly growing levels of private debt and the consequent seesaw of booms and busts economies experience.[24]

You will also learn about how banks and other financial actors relate to the monetary assets they create through accounting. Through a process called securitisation, banks pack those assets (borrowers' promises to pay back their loans), split those packs transversally, and sell the repacked splits (now called 'securities') to willing investors. The asset that was created as one side of an accounting relationship is approached as a commodity (the bank's property) to *sell forward*. The bank gets a more liquid deposit, the investor – if s/he doesn't buy to further sell it forward – hopes for a regular stream of income (the borrower's payment of interest), and banks can 'democratise' credit.[25] Far from an 'originate [credit] and hold' model of banking, banks follow an 'originate to distribute' model,[26] spreading risk through the chain of financial actors that buy those 'securities' – including your pension fund. The repayment capacity of their customers is out of bankers' concerns for they can immediately monetise the loan by selling it forward in liquid financial markets. This is, in a nutshell, the monetary and financial arrangement at the origin of the swift global contagion of a crisis that started in the US housing market.[27]

Through this chapter, I hope to shed light on how the accounting mechanics of money creation alongside the relational governance practices towards that newly created money are at the root of our inequality, instability and unsustainability troubles. Tracing money has become critically important not only because instability is threatening our productive capacity and rising inequality is threatening the social fabric of our democracies. More relevant to the readers of a book that sets out to describe efforts to remake money for a more sustainable and inclusive future, understanding the relationship between how our conventional money works and our unsustainable predicaments can help us set the frame for different forms of money in at least two ways. The first concerns the design of money: to steer away from the type of monetary arrangements underpinning our multidimensional crisis. The second concerns the governance of money: to ground our relationship to the new monies on an imaginary that embeds them into the communities they are to serve. That is, in following the genesis, management and workings of today's money, the chapter hopes to set the stage for the possibility to reclaim, reimagine and reorganise money.

The mechanics of private bank money creation

A rare admission was published twice in the spring of 2014. Michael McLeay, Amar Radia and Ryland Thomas, of the Bank of England's Monetary Analysis Directorate, recognised in the bank's *Quarterly Bulletin* that the majority of today's money was created by commercial banks when extending loans; that contrary to popular conceptions, banks were neither mere intermediaries between depositors and loan-takers nor did they multiply central bank money; and that, in normal economic circumstances, central banks played a minimal role in determining the supply of money. Commercial banks, these economists conceded, created up to 97 per cent of the money circulating in the UK.[28]

Apart from an insight into the magnitude of the phenomenon, the article from the Bank of England provided a clear explanation of how the process of creating the majority of today's money works: banks create money in the form of new deposits recorded when making new loans and this, the extension of new loans, is done by expanding the two sides of the balance sheets – through double-entry accounting – of both the loan-taker and the loan-granting bank. The economists from the Bank of England included an illustration of money creation by an individual bank making a new mortgage loan (see Figure 3.1). For a step-by-step depiction of the balance sheet mechanics involved in extending a bank loan, see the Appendix.

Observing the process of creating bank money, Keynes concluded that, in principle, 'there is no limit to the amount of bank money that banks can safely create *provided that they move forward in step*'.[29] The mechanics behind Keynes' italicised words – 'provided that [the banks] move forward in step' – refer to the clearing of payments between banks. If banks settled all their inter-bank transactions through the transfer of reserves – as illustrated in the last panel of Figure 3.1 – 'the buyer's bank would have fewer reserves to meet its possible outflows' and thus, 'if it made many new loans, it would eventually run out of reserves'. Banks, therefore, 'seek to attract or retain new deposits'. If banks create money and transfer the newly created money to each other 'in step', then the marking up and down of deposits in the balance sheet of individual banks cancel each other out, as illustrated by the authors from the Bank of England in Figure 3.2.

The article's simplified illustration of money mechanics[30] helps us to unveil some common misconceptions concerning money. First, by extending a loan, deposits in the economy went up – the bank created money.[31] This is not a money someone – the bank – has and lends to someone else. In the popular and textbook descriptions of money and banking, banks act as intermediaries merely lending the savings of others. Influenced by a commodity imaginary of money, that view describes money as existing first, savings then being possible, and finally comes lending. The reality of money mechanics is however more closely related to a debt–credit imaginary of money: loans create deposits, and money is thereby produced. As the economists from the Bank of England write, '[m]oney creation in practice differs from some popular misconceptions – banks do not act simply as intermediaries, lending out deposits that savers place with them', and continue, '[w]henever a bank makes a loan, it simultaneously creates a matching deposit in the borrower's bank account, thereby creating new money'.[32] That is, money is created the moment the bank and its customer enter a relation of debt and credit. More precisely, new *money is created through the accounting process of banks when recording a debtor–creditor relationship.*

A second misconception similarly grounded in the commodity money imaginary is that the amount of loans a bank creates is limited by reserves or cash the bank holds.[33] The article in the Bank of England's *Quarterly* also

Figure 3.1: Mortgage creation by commercial banks: changes to balance sheets

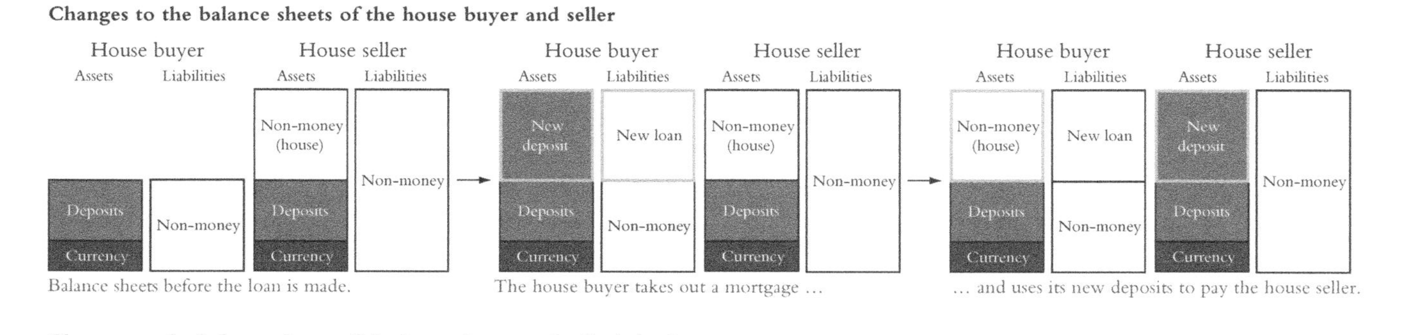

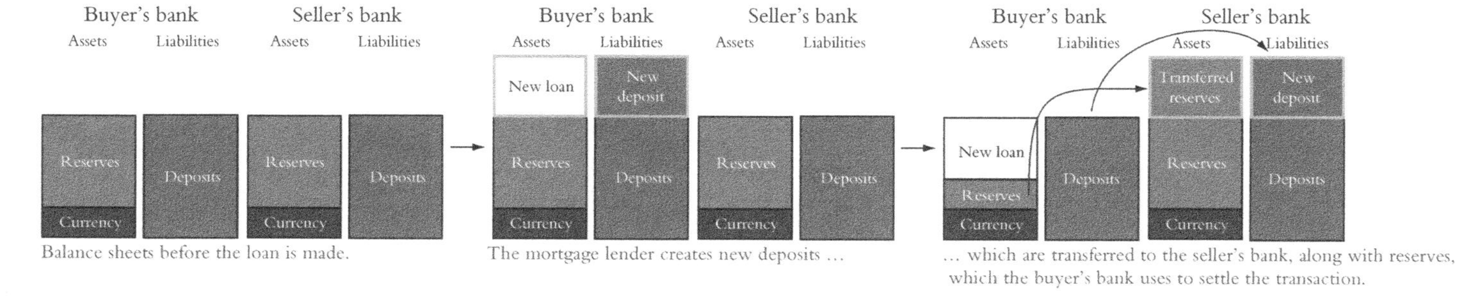

Source: McLeay, M., Radia, A. & Thomas, R. 2014. Money creation in the modern economy. *Quarterly Bulletin*, Bank of England.

Figure 3.2: Mortgage creation by commercial banks: changes to banks' balance sheets

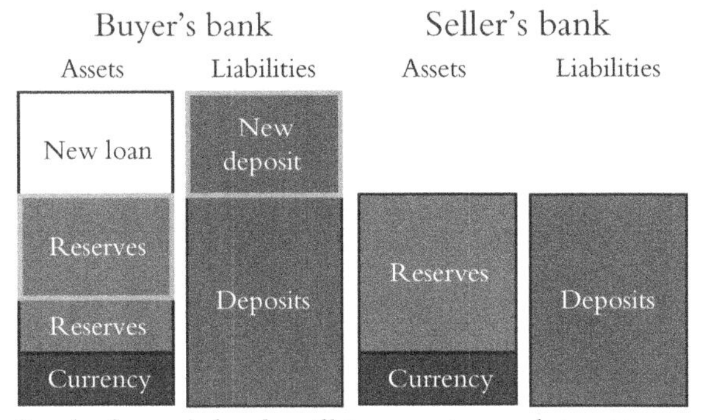

Source: McLeay, M., Radia, A. & Thomas, R. 2014. Money creation in the modern economy. *Quarterly Bulletin*, Bank of England

dismantles this conventional piece of knowledge, '*reserves are*, in normal times, *supplied "on demand" by the Bank of England to commercial banks* in exchange for other assets on their balance sheets. In no way does the aggregate quantity of reserves directly constrain the amount of bank lending or deposit creation'.[34] The article illustrates this through the aggregate balance sheets of the various actors before and after the money-creation process (see Figure 3.3).

In reframing money from a commodity to a relational phenomenon lies the key to understand yet another feature of its mechanics. In the first graph of the Bank of England's article, you may have already noticed that the buyer's payment to the seller for the house – the third set of balance sheets in Figure 3.1 – is conducted by marking down the buyer's new deposits and up the seller's deposits by the same amount.[35] The buyer's new loan remains though – the buyer's obligation to repay to the bank equal to the deposits the seller now holds. In other words, once the sale is conducted, the seller's bank account records the credit side of the debt–credit relationship money was created through, the debit side still recorded in the buyer's balance sheet. Because money is created through a debt–credit relationship, *someone's credit is always somebody else's debt*. This is important to put centre stage as, we will see in what follows, how creditors decide to use their money holdings will

Figure 3.3: Mortgage creation by commercial banks: changes to the balance sheets of central bank, commercial bank and loan-taker

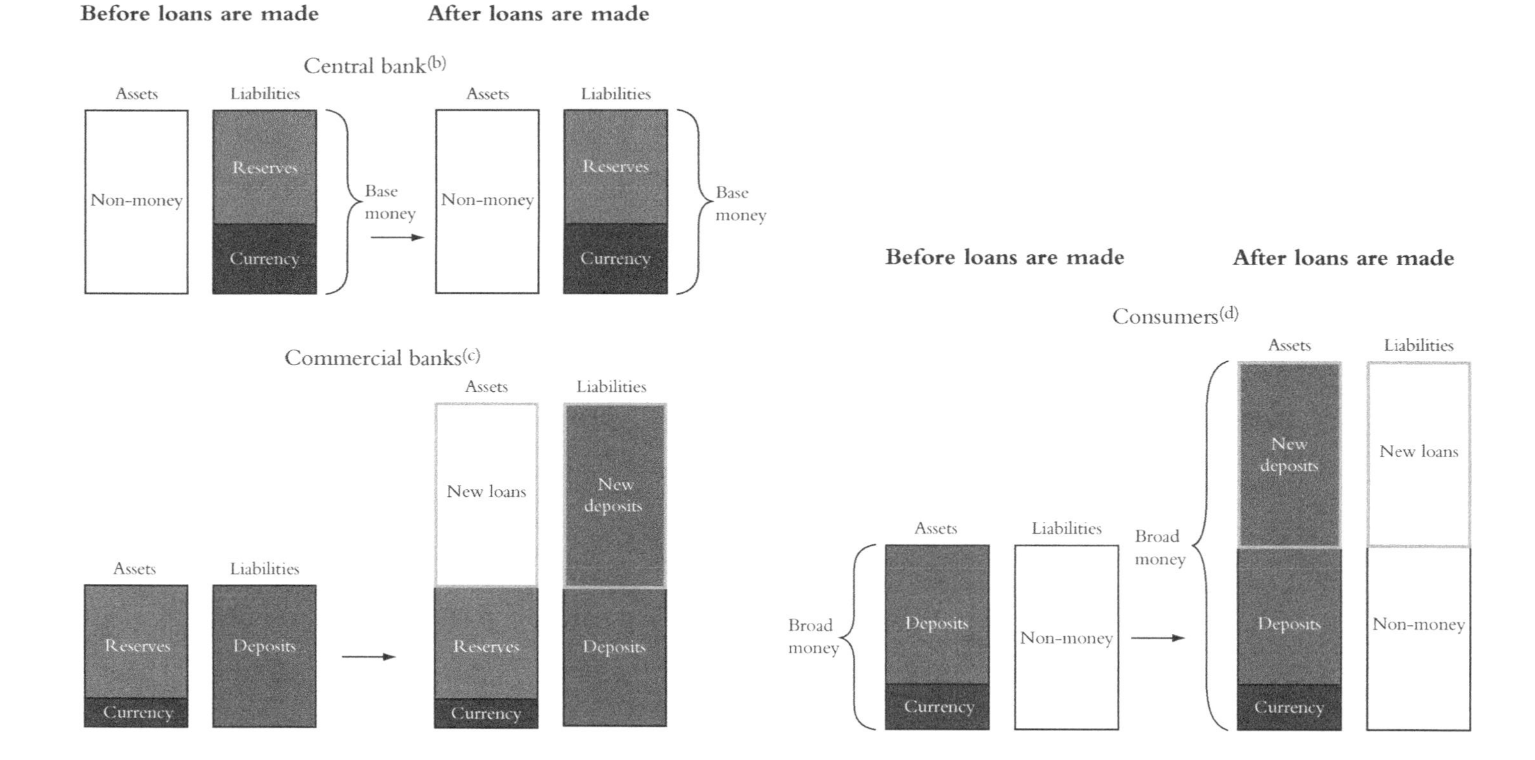

shape debtors' (in)ability to repay their debts, pushing them to incur further debt and forcing the systemic need for continual economic growth.

The unsustainable consequences of the process of private bank money creation

We have now seen the accounting mechanics: private banks lend money into existence. Socioeconomic relations underpin those mechanics: commercial bank money rests on debt–credit relationships individuals enter with banks. The creation of bank money rests on individuals borrowing,[36] and on *banks wanting to lend*. Herein, in banks' lending calculations, we find the source of some of our unsustainable predicaments.

While debt-based money has fuelled unprecedented rates of innovation, while access to credit has allowed many to own their homes, and while debt–credit relationships with banks have enabled small entrepreneurs to set up shop, the *reasoning private bankers follow when extending credit* strengthens inequality and intensifies economic cycles. First, through the form taken by bankers' trust in its customers. The debt–credit relationship anchoring the newly produced money (deposit) relies on the bank trusting the customer's ability to pay back the loan that originated it. Or, if you prefer, on the bank's assessment of the customer's *creditworthiness*. The collateral of a house ensures creditworthiness; record of a well-working business; a work contract that proves stable income – scarce blessings in the current environment of work precarity, inequality and instability.[37] Lacking these, the bank distrusts the prospective loan-taker's ability to repay her debt, and thus denies the loan. Bank money is *dispensed as selectively as unequal is the economy*: it goes to those that already have wealth (in the form of assets to put as collateral) and stable income, further entrenching inequality.

The second aspect of banker's reasoning related to our sustainability predicament relates to the performativity of their expectations of the future. Deeming the economy will grow, bankers see in the collateralised house an asset whose price will rise; in the entrepreneur's business plan they see the satisfaction of increasing consumer demand; in the work contract, sure employment. When hopeful of the future, bankers create money that strengthens consumer demand, secures employment and fuels price rises. And vice versa; when gloomy about the future, bankers reduce net lending. Falling consumer demand and rising unemployment worsen banks' creditworthiness assessments of its borrowers, eventually shrinking the money supply. In other words, *bankers' confidence over the future* steers money creation, glutting the sectors of the economy whose potential they presume – the building sector in the 1990s and 2000s – and starving those sectors whose chances they doubt – prioritising, for instance, fossil fuel over green energy projects.[38] This has two direct implications for the real economy. One, bankers' expectations of future profits set the direction of the economy. Two, lending when confident and tightening when fearful, the spirits, sentiments and partial calculations of financial actors seal the fate of the real economy (made of people of flesh and blood) into a pro-cyclical behaviour that intensifies booms and busts.[39]

Inequality is further entrenched by the mechanics of interest charged on bank loans. When loans are granted, the borrower commits herself to pay back the amount borrowed (principal) *plus* interest. Unpaid interest compounds on the principal, repayment obligations thus growing exponentially. Compound interest multiplies debt through a mathematical principle independent of the ability of debtors to pay back those debts, thus contributing to siphon wealth from those that had to ask for money towards those that could create it. Debtors have to work harder and longer to attend their growing debts. 'It is no accident', political economist Ann Pettifor observes, 'that the deregulation of finance led to the deregulation of working hours, and the abolition of Sunday as a day of rest. Instead, longer hours of work – '24/7' – with shops open 24 hours a day for 7 days a week – became an acceptable practice as the finance sector's values took precedence over other considerations.'[40]

In the exponential growth of debt that steams from compound interest some find the root of a monetary-driven imperative to constant economic growth.[41] To repay growing debt, businesses are coerced into continuous growth, with consequent intensification of natural extraction. The seas are over-fished; forests stripped; the soil degraded. Financing the productive economy through ever-growing debt squeezes nature's finite resources, effectively consuming the land that feeds us for the sake of honouring repayment to the world's creditors.

Others argue that the imperative to grow that so erodes nature comes not from interests themselves but from the hoarding of money. Because, as we saw, money is created through a debt–credit relationship, someone's credit is always somebody else's debt. It follows that what creditors do with the received interests and what savers do with their holdings affect debtors' capacity to repay their debts. For, when money accumulates and remains stagnant – for example, in the form of personal savings accounts and corporate cash holdings[42] – debtors experience increased difficulties to earn money with which to settle their debts.[43] This leads individual debtors to work an extra shift, compels businesses to produce and sell more to pay interests or dividends to their creditors, and locks the economy into an imperative to grow that traps humanity into incessant exploitation of nature.[44]

Summing it up in a Polanyian formulation, the creation of money through interest-bearing loans by commercial banks following a profit motive involves, in effect, 'no less a transformation than that of the natural and human substance of society into commodities' to sell in labour and commodity markets. The dislocation caused by the money creation process ensnares society into behaviours that threaten to subjugate people and nature to the interests of finance. Our sustainability predicaments, that is, are rooted in the very mechanics and entanglements of the process through which our economies create 97 per cent of their money. No need for moralistic critiques of corporate greed that exploits nature, oppresses workers and transforms citizens into consumers, nor for moralising discourses on the ignorance of the masses and the selfishness of individuals. The behaviour that leads to the exploitation of workers and nature is rooted in the internal mechanics and configuration of our conventional monetary system.

Commodifying a relationship to sell it forward

In the years building up to the financial implosion of 2007–2008, banks extended credit to people that would have traditionally been denied credit. In doing this, banks expanded their balance sheets with highly risky loans. And they did so to the tune of billions. Subprime loans in the United States totalled US$160 billion in 1999. In March 2007, they summed up to US$1.3 trillion. In 2006 alone, the year before the crisis began, over US$600 billion of subprime mortgages were issued, making 23.5 per cent of all mortgage originations[45] – a practice that left banks' balance sheets exposed to high credit risk. This risky monetary arrangement was made to work – at least for a couple of decades – by a novel approach to mortgage-creation. Securitisation, as the new approach was referred to, ignored the relational basis of debt-based money and instead approached the money thus created as if it were a commodity, property of the banks to hold or sell as they best deemed fit.

Testimonies in the Financial Crisis Inquiry Commission indeed witnessed that the growth in subprime lending was facilitated by this novel approach to mortgage-creation. As a way to reduce the credit risk built into their balance sheets, from the mid-1980s, banks and other mortgage-granting institutions started selling those loans to large investment banks. Wall Street security firms, such as Salomon Brothers and Merrill Lynch, pooled the loans and commodified them into financial securities they could further sell forward.[46] With the possibility to securitise subprime loans and sell them in financial markets, and deemed safe by credit rating agencies, the demand for securitised subprime mortgages grew in proportion. Securitisation grew in complexity too.[47] A wider variety of loans were packed and tranched into securitised assets and credit derivatives with ever more varied acronyms. MBS (mortgage-backed securities) were soon joined by CDO (collateralised debt obligations) and ABS (asset-backed securities), all of which were easily sold to willing investors all over the world. As Jim Callahan told the Financial Crisis Inquiry Commission, the question was not 'whether' you will get the money back (the initial credit risk) but 'when' you would get it back (a liquidity risk).[48] But liquidity risk can quickly turn into solvency risk, which is why central banks would do 'whatever it takes' to avoid the solvency risk of 'safe' banks.

All was well while financial markets devoured those securities. Banks thought they had ejected credit risk off their balance sheets, enabling them to grant more and easier loans. Individuals got access to easy credit for all sorts of needs. The housing construction sector saw the price of their product soar and homeowners relied on the increased valuation of their homes to refinance their original – already unpayable – debt. With the collateralised house continuously increasing in market value, so too did the size and risk of new mortgages, leading to more and riskier lending which fed higher prices all over again – a virtuous 'liquidity spiral'[49] where everyone gained. As late as July 2007, Citigroup CEO Charles Prince phrased the euphoria of the time with a visual metaphor: 'When the music stops, in terms of liquidity, things will be complicated. But as long as the music is playing, you've got to get up and dance. We're still dancing.'[50]

Banking – the making of money out of debt–credit relationships – had been transformed from an 'originate and hold' model into an 'originate to distribute' – or 'originate to sell' – model. Loan originators – not only banks, but other financial corporations too – competed fiercely, actively searching for borrowers among the most vulnerable groups and offering them mortgages with a low 'teaser' rate for the first two to three years after which it could be adjusted periodically. The goal was to 'increase our penetration into subprime'.[51] Borrowers were given the option to pick their payment each month, including compounding on the principal any shortfall in the interest payment.[52] The ability of loan-takers to make payments didn't really matter, for loans – and the money supply along with them – were created with an end to sell them forward. In the words of one of the biggest actors, their business focused on 'originating what was salable in the secondary market'.[53] Financial markets had transformed credit risk – the borrower's ability to repay – into high yielding securities; financial actors had commodified debt–credit relationships into mass-market financial products. Along with it, 'the definition of a good loan changed from "one that pays" to "one that could be sold"',[54] trust moved from the borrower's ability to pay onto liquid financial markets. The basis for the money-making banking practice of lending shifted from a strategy of concern and relational care towards the debtor to one of commodifying the debtor–creditor relationship to sell it forward. As long as the music lasted, there was no need to consider whatsoever the real, human relationship on which those financialised products were based. The everyday economic conditions of the families at the origin of the securities' promised cash flows could be, and were, ignored. In purpose, and in effect, the money-making machine had been detached from the real economy.

And then, the music stopped. Ownit Mortgage Solutions filed for bankruptcy on 3 January 2007, soon to be followed by American Freedom

Mortgage, New Century, American Home Mortgage, Ameriquest Mortgage, NetBank ... the list is long. Between 2008 and 2012, the Federal Deposit Insurance Corporation closed 465 banks in the United States alone. Contagion was global; Northern Rock in the UK, ABN AMRO in the Netherlands, UBS in Switzerland, Roskilde Bank in Denmark, Germany, Ireland, Latvia, Portugal, Spain, Australia, the Philippines, Venezuela. The speedy and virulent unravelling of the crisis brought to full sight the high leverage – debt-to-capital – ratios with which financial market participants had made the market liquid, vast debt taken to buy the mortgage-backed securities.[55] With little capital to absorb losses, and with toxic securities distributed globally, when borrowers started failing on their payments, financial actors fell down like domino pieces. A confluence of accounting practices, banking strategies, money imaginaries, profit projections and house dreams had built up a monetary edifice that was rapidly crumbling – a vicious liquidity spiral. The borrower's dream to own one's home, the bold projections of financial actors, the accounting practice of creating money by recording private loans, an 'originate-*to-sell*' banking strategy based on an imaginary of money as property, as a commodity that can be owned and indefinitely sold forward – all had come together to assemble a mercurial monetary and financial architecture with little oversight. When the reality of a relational money forced itself onto the intricate network of monetary practices and financial mediators that had so transformed it into a fictitious commodity, the assemblage disintegrated.

Some of the culprits drew the conclusion – rightful but understated – that 'we overdid finance versus the real economy and got it a little lopsided as a result'.[56] For some 30 years following the Second World War, banking was a boring business consisting of assessing customers one at a time, extending loans in local offices, and negotiating refinancing of those loans when the borrower met repayment challenges. A loan was a long-term contractual relationship through which the borrower committed to repay and the lender committed to facilitate repayment. Both parties bore responsibilities in that debt–credit relationship. The change from an 'originate and hold' to an 'originate to sell' banking strategy divorced bankers from all long-term commitment towards their clients. The original practice of lowering the costs of credit to homeowners may have democratised access to finance – as the argument went during the boom years. But the commodification of the debt–credit relationship implicit in the new banking strategy succumbed to issuing as much private debt (commercial bank money) as financial investors demanded. In doing so, the private money creation machine had been reorganised to serve the interests of financial markets.[57] Not only had it led bankers to shun responsibility towards the economic realities of their clients. Borrowers' commitments had been reoriented to feed the greed of an expanding financial industry, thereby disconnecting the creation of money from the realities of the real economy.

The mechanics of central bank money creation

Central banks do create money too. Their process, too, relies on double-entry accounting. Just like private banks do, central banks create money by expanding their balance sheets. Their purpose, however, differs from the purpose commercial banks follow when creating money. The later follow a profit motive that, as we saw, results in private bank money being created pro-cyclically, thus intensifying booms and busts. With a purpose to serve the overall economy, central bank money is – in the best of cases – created anti-cyclically, hopefully softening busts and economic recessions.[58] With the onset of the economic crisis following the Great Financial Crisis of 2007–2009, the Fed, the Bank of England and the European Central Bank engaged in so-called QE monetary policy. At the time, such policies were implemented to avoid the collapse of a banking and financial sector that would have brought a deeper economic depression onto the world economy. Unprecedented at the time, they were used again to support economies ailing from restrictions in human interaction imposed to cope with the COVID-19 pandemic.

QE monetary stimulus policies take the form of central banks buying a range of assets held in the balance sheets of various economic actors: from mortgage-backed securities held by commercial banks to corporate bonds, treasury bills, or sovereign, regional and local government bonds held by financial institutions, such as mutual and pension funds, as well as non-financial institutions, such as big businesses. The central bank pays for such asset purchasing programmes (APP – as QE policies are also called) by creating new reserves – or central bank money – and thus expanding its balance sheet. When the purchase is of assets held by an entity without an account at the central bank, commercial banks act as payment intermediaries, which similarly expand their balance sheet through the creation of new deposits. McLeay et al represent the impact on balance sheets of QE implemented by buying government bonds held by a pension fund (see Figure 3.4).

When QE is implemented by the central bank buying new assets created for the purpose – may this be by major corporate businesses or the government – QE results in the expansion of the balance sheets of both the central bank and the involved institution. Following the same visual representational style as the authors from the Bank of England, for sovereign bonds issued by government to fund pandemic stimulus packages, see Figure 3.5.

For newly created corporate bonds purchased through the intermediation of a commercial bank, all three involved actors expand their balance sheets (see Figure 3.6).

Figure 3.4: Impact on balance sheets of quantitative easing implemented by buying government debt from private actors

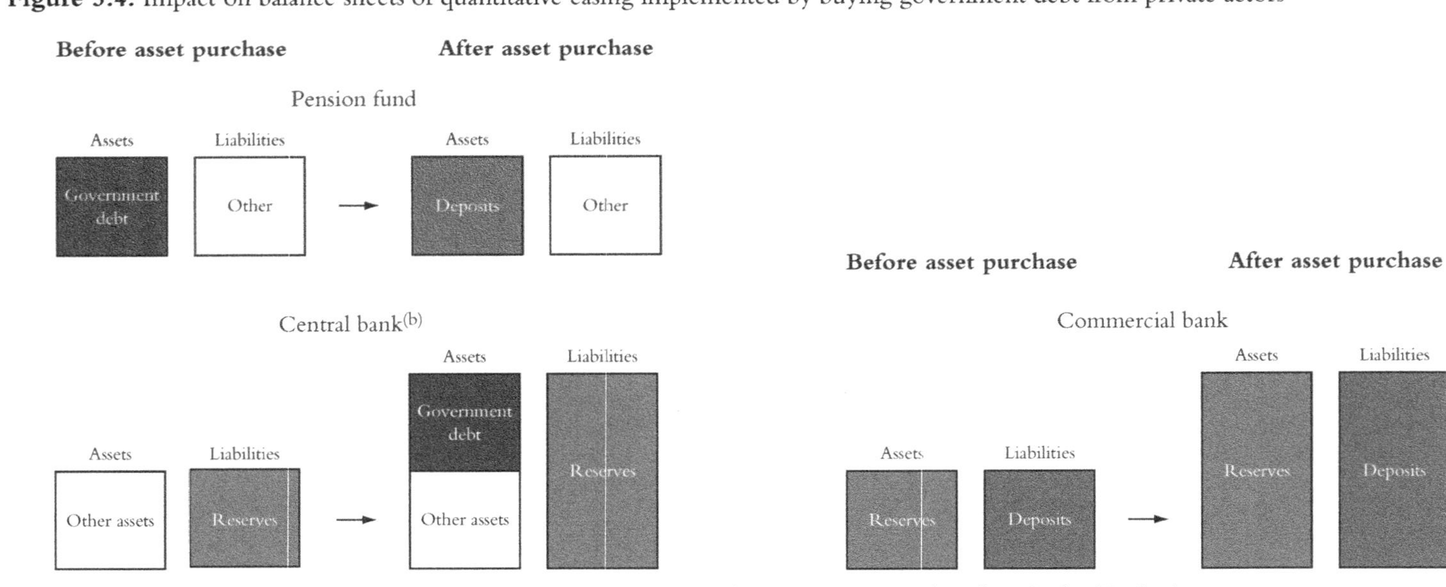

Source: McLeay, M., Radia, A. & Thomas, R. 2014. Money creation in the modern economy. *Quarterly Bulletin*, Bank of England

Figure 3.5: Impact on balance sheets of quantitative easing implemented through creating government debt

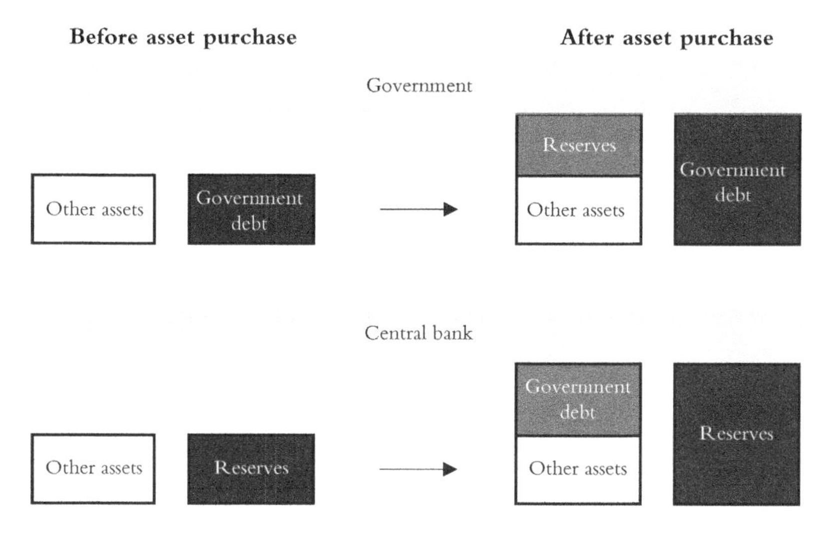

Figure 3.6: Impact on balance sheets of quantitative easing implemented through creating corporate debt

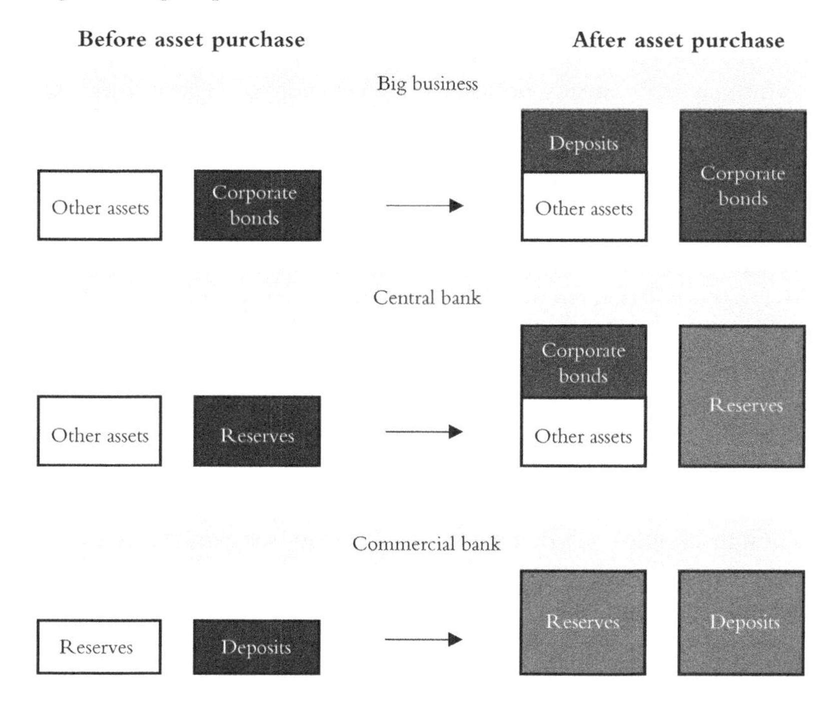

Figure 3.7: Impact on balance sheets of quantitative easing implemented through buying commercial banks' mortgage-backed loans

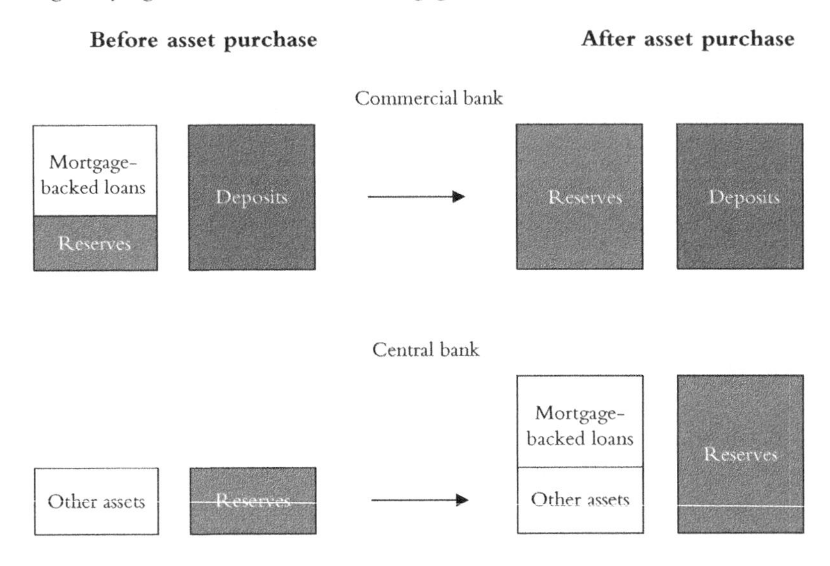

As for the support central banks gave to commercial banks to absorb the risk they had built in their balance sheets through subprime mortgage lending, the accounting operations involve the central bank expanding its balance sheet while the commercial bank substitutes its bad loans for central bank money (see Figure 3.7).

As you may have already noticed, in all instances of central bank money creation through QE, the central bank expands its balance sheet. It does so by creating reserves to fund the purchase of new or existing assets from another economic actor. It is, once more, a money based on a debt–credit relationship between the central bank and various financial and non-financial actors. How these other economic actors use their new monetary assets is decisive, for it will determine whether the new money will ultimately reach to the families, employees, small businesses and entrepreneurs the central bank was intent to support with its monetary policy.

Relevant to emphasise in a chapter on the monetary roots of our sustainability challenges is the central bank's *selective* introduction of money into the economy.[59] Democratically elected governments hopefully put that money to the service of the people they represent – as various governments did through stimulus bills that went directly to households, small businesses, self-employed and gig workers, hospitals, local governments and other institutions grappling with the effects of the COVID-19 pandemic, and that resulted in a sharp reduction in material hardship, food insufficiency and financial instability across the population.[60] Corporations and banks have, however, neither been democratically elected nor do they have a clear incentive to put the interests of the people first. Oftentimes, not even the well-being of its workers even while receiving government financial support.[61] Indeed, 'trickle down' expectations have not been realised; transmission of the monetary policy onto actors in the productive economy becoming increasingly ineffective. Instead, in an environment of low interest rates and QE, we have seen big businesses engaging in debt-financed corporate stock buy-backs that swell the market valuation of their companies and, along with it, the size of managers' bonuses (stock options);[62] we see insurance companies and mutual funds buying government bonds in financial markets; and in fear of lending to small businesses, we see commercial banks holding the new central bank money as reserves at the central bank.[63] Wall Street balloons, while main street withers away. The already wealthy get wealthier, while the poorest fall further down the poverty line.[64] Selectively granting easy access to money to actors ('big business' and the 'too big to fail') who do not pass on that money to the families, workers and entrepreneurs in the real economy, central banks' money creation process has been feeding rising inequality.

The monetary dysfunctions of the last 15 years have led to various calls to reform the monetary system. Depending on where the analyst puts the gist of the analysis, the reform proposed projects us into one or another direction. Those finding fault in the fact that the creation of money has been largely privatised suggest money should be solely created by public central banks subject to democratic control – so-called 'sovereign money' proposals. Those finding the main weakness in the creation of bank money *ex nihilo*, often propose banks' credit creation should be 100 per cent backed by reserves – the so-called 'Chicago plan' after a similar plan from the 1930s. Those for whom deregulation is the main culprit demand a stricter regulatory framework. Those condemning the 'originate-to-distribute' model guided by a liquidity paradigm that detaches financial markets from the productive economy call for banks to follow a logic of clearing that binds creditors to their borrowers. Those who despair about the selective injection of central bank money to the 'too big to fail' argue for central bank money being distributed as some form of dividend, or cash transfer, to all citizens – so-called 'helicopter money' or 'QE for the people'.[65]

The relatively recent interest in Central Bank Digital Currencies (CBDC) needs to be understood against such background. Though much of the discussion is framed as a technological upgrade of central bank money, the real transformative potential of CBDC is the restoration of the power to create money back to central banks. Further, a CBDC architecture that allowed citizens to have a bank account at the central bank would disintermediate the implementation of monetary policy facilitating its transmission onto the real economy.[66] There are, however, analysts that question whether CBDCs will be able to deliver on the hopes of recovered monetary policy independence central bankers put on them. The current entanglement of central banks with the commercial banking system, these analysts argue, effectively limits the possibility for the first to carry sovereign monetary policy.[67]

Money today: an infrastructural arrangement grabbed to serve a financial elite

Money is a sociotechnical assemblage with critical infrastructural powers. Its technical components may be most apparent for the common public: the notes, coins, ATMs and credit cards that people typically associate money with. Its social components include institutions – some more visible to the public, like central banks, commercial banks, and state insurance agencies; others less so, like the wide array of financial actors in the shadow banking industry. Other sociotechnical components include the legal code and double-entry accounting. In assembly, these components organise how money is created, how it works its way through the economy, and where it works (or who it works for).

While the infrastructure performs, its internal architecture is invisible to most users – a fact that is known to ethnographers of infrastructures since the 1990s.[68] When it doesn't perform, the network of components that make it up unfold to the eye. What was perceived as a passive intermediary becomes an active mediator. We become aware of the chips, circuits and devices that make up our computer systems when their connections fail. Those the infrastructure doesn't serve are acutely aware of its components. The person in a wheelchair sees the edge of the sidewalk not as another step on her path, but as a barrier to use. In a similar fashion, the financial collapse of 2007–2009 evidenced that money was not simply made of the digits in our bank accounts. The unravelling of the economic crisis that ensued brought to light the complex assemblage that money is.[69] It also made many aware that money had been arranged and governed to serve the interests of a financial elite.

Measures to lessen the economic effects of the COVID-19 pandemic, just like the unprecedented policy measures implemented after the financial implosion of a decade earlier, have reasserted the extent to which the monetary infrastructural arrangement caters to the elite. Historic reductions in poverty in the United States brought about by the robust monetary and fiscal stimulus of the Fed and US government notwithstanding,[70] a large size of central bank supported pandemic stimulus packages ended in the accounts of big corporations, shareholders, banks and financial institutions who kept the stimulus without transmitting it over to households, workers, small businesses and entrepreneurs.[71]

Under today's dysfunctional – at least for the many – monetary arrangement hides an approach to money as a thing that one can have and lose, a commodity that one can sell forward, a good that can be produced for sale, a property to keep. An imaginary of money as commodity transforms borrowers' promises to pay into assets, and coopts central bankers into the ultimate guarantee of the market value of those legally made-up assets; a commodity money imaginary incites big corporations and financial institutions receiving stimulus packages to hold on to the money thus slowing down the transmission of monetary and fiscal policies. That is, whether the actor creating money is private or public, the creation and distribution of the vast majority of our money attends the narrow private interests of the financial and corporate elite. Money, an infrastructure critical for the organisation of society, has been largely privatised. It no longer serves the interests of the communities, local businesses, workers, small entrepreneurs and citizens that make up the real economy.

But another money is possible.

A money that aligns the interests of those creating it to the interests of the many.

To reorganise money and put it at the service of people and planet, we need to ground the monetary architecture in a different understanding of money. In reassembling money, we need to move away from a cultural imaginary that constitutes subjects as either holders or debtors of a money-thing, towards an imaginary that enacts people's relationships as constitutive components of money. My argument in the rest of the book is that, to put money at the service of the many, we need, first, to recognise the many relationships that money builds upon, and then, to integrate those relationships in the making and governing of money. We need an imaginary of money as a commons.

INTERLUDE 1

Money Commons Imaginary

An origins story that can help us understand money as a commons is found on the island of Yap, the most westerly of the Caroline Islands, in today's Federated States of Micronesia. With Palau, its closest neighbour, some 300 miles southwest, Yap remained for the most part up until the early 20th century an isolated idyll of densely vegetated rolling hills and mangrove swamps surrounded by coral reefs. Upon losing the American-Spanish war for control of the Philippines in 1898, Spain, who had laid claim on the archipelago some 15 years previous, sold Yap for US$3.3 million to Germany. The episode led *Oceana*, a tiny German steamer 'plying between Sydney and The Marshall and Caroline Islands and Hong-Kong', to include Yap in its commercial route. It was thus that adventurer William Henry Furness arrived to the island on 1903 where he spent over two months enjoying 'the earthy perfume of damp groves of palm, the pungent odor of rancid coconut oil, and the scent of fires of sappy wood', lodging with 'the little colony of white people who live upon the island' and 'visit[ing] the natives'.[1]

Furness showed most interest in learning about the Yapese way of life. In his travel-book from the experience, he describes with anthropological sensitivity the cultural traditions, the social fabric and the economic organisation of a primitive people for which the term 'uncivilised [was] too narrow'.[2] Despite the small size of the island – 'whose whole length and breadth is but a day's walk' – and despite the few number of inhabitants – 'from five to six thousand' – Yap's was a curiously sophisticated society. There were fishing fraternities and bachelors' houses, a tribe system, and a rich tradition of singing and dancing; costumes and adornments clearly distinguished the passage of the ages as well as between freemen and slaves; men shared wives without any show of jealousy; there was a unique religion filled with genesis myths and elaborate burial rites. Surprisingly when compared to other contemporary primitive civilisations, Yap even had a decimal system with 'separate words for twenty, thirty, forty, fifty, but sixty is six-tens, seventy, seven-tens, etc.; and again uncompounded words for one hundred and one thousand'.[3] Fascinating as Furness' account of the Yapese is, the most remarkable feature, the aspect that has drawn most admiration, is its 'stone money' – a monetary system that has attracted the praise of economists as intellectually distant as John Maynard Keynes and Milton Friedman.[4]

And yet, the first visible aspect of Yap's monetary system, its stone quality, seems to retain us in a traditional gold imaginary of money.

> As the island yields no metal, the islanders have had recourse to stone, stone on which labour in fetching and fashioning has been expended, and as truly a representation of labour as the mined and minted coins of civilisation. This medium of exchange they call *fei*, and it consists of large, solid, thick stone wheels, ranging in diameter from a foot to twelve feet, having in the centre a hole varying in size with the diameter of the stone, wherein a pole may be inserted sufficiently large and strong to bear the weight and facilitate transportation.[5]

At the outset, Yap's stone money resembles the commodity money of fantasised barter economies – only, instead of salt, shells or dried cod, Yapese recurred to the limestone of 'Babelthuap, one of the Pelao Islands, four hundred miles to the southward', from where the stones were quarried, shaped and 'brought to Uap by some venturesome native navigators'. Indeed, Furness originally reasoned, 'the larger the stone the greater its worth, but it is not size alone that is prized; the limestone of which the *fei* is composed, to be of the highest value must be fine and white and of close grain'. Guided by the dominant gold imaginary, Furness' initial spontaneous reflection was to locate the value of the *fei* in the fineness of its stone-content along with the labour spent in 'fetching and fashioning' the stone.[6]

Furness however soon came to realise that the Yapese did not actually exchange their stone money when trading. It was not so much possession of the stone-objects as what was recorded on them that was essential to Yap's monetary system.

> The noteworthy feature of this stone currency is that it is not necessary for its owner to reduce it to possession. After concluding a bargain which involves the price of a *fei* too large to be conveniently moved, its new owner is quite content to accept the bare acknowledgment of ownership and without so much as *a mark to indicate the exchange*, the coin remains undisturbed on the former owner's premises.[7]

Yap's stone money does not simply challenge the conventional story about money's origins – as Furness himself noted:

> In a land where food and drink and ready-made clothes grow on trees and may be had for the gathering, it is not easy to see how a man can

> run very deeply in debt for his living expenses – for which, indeed, *there need be no barter, and if no barter, there is no need for any medium of exchange.*[8]

Intellectually most disconcertingly, Yap's stone money pushes us to rethink the constitution of a money that, to the lay eye, has the semblance of commodity. Yap's *feis* force us to look underneath its commodity appearance to uncover a system of credit balances recorded on the stone. The stone does not work so much as a good chosen for trading with other goods, as it does work as a ledger on which to record one's contribution to a member (or more) of the community. Marks on the stone are but net balances that discharge the community member who has taken (the buyer) from a personal obligation to the one who has given (the seller); a recognition of the seller's contribution to the buyer. The stones visualised the contributions the temporary owner marked on the stone had made to the community; the wealth of that member thus consisting on the favours she could legitimately claim from the community. Under a *fei*'s commodity appearance lies a 'truly philosophical' – in Keynes' appreciative words – understanding of money, one akin to Simmel's 'claim upon society'.[9] Or, if you prefer, the stone is merely the most palpable element of a system of credit and clearing of accounts that transforms a person-to-person credit–debt relation into a person-to-community relationship of credit.

Fatumak, Furness' 'faithful old friend', explained to the inquisitive adventurer that, in fact, the records, or the stone ledger for that matter, did not even need to be visible; that the stones acted as ledgers on the basis of a community that trusted its members and remembered its past. Furness recounted:

> [T]here was in a village near-by a family whose wealth was unquestioned – acknowledged by everyone, and yet no one, not even the family itself, had ever laid eye or hand on this wealth; it consisted of an enormous *fei*, whereof the size is known only by tradition; for the past two or three generations it had been, and at that very time it was lying at the bottom of the sea! Many years ago an ancestor of this family, on an expedition after *fei*, secured this remarkably large and exceedingly valuable stone, which was placed on a raft to be towed homeward. A violent storm arose, and the party, to save their lives, were obliged to cut the raft adrift, and the stone sank out of sight. When they reached home, they all testified that the *fei* was of magnificent proportions and of extraordinary quality, and that it was lost through no fault of the owner. Thereupon it was universally conceded in their simple faith that the mere accident of its loss overboard was too trifling to mention, and that a few hundred feet

> of water off shore ought not to affect its marketable value, since it was all chipped out in proper form. The purchasing power of that stone remains, therefore, as valid as if it were leaning visibly against the side of the owner's house, and represents wealth as potentially as the hoarded inactive gold of a miser of the Middle Ages, or as our silver dollars stacked in the Treasury at Washington, which we never see or touch, but trade with on the strength of a printed certificate that they are there.[10]

For the argument in this book, probably the most compelling aspect of Yap's money is that it forces us to revise the notion that money as a system of credit and clearing of balances needs of a central institution – such as the Babylonian temple, a central bank or a set of legally licensed private banks – to guarantee its functioning. Yap assuredly extends the credit imaginary to include the possibility of governance by the community of users. Though generalised trust is of the essence for monetary tokens to be widely accepted and, thereby, for the monetary system to work effectively, there is more than metal – the barter story – and central authority – the Babylonian story – to secure that trust. Fatumak's anecdote tells of a money whose value is guaranteed and managed by the community that trusts, responds and remembers.[11] A money commons created and run by its users.

Money commons

While for the untrained gaze money is what we hold in our wallets, see in our bank accounts or heavily stands outside a Yapese shack, having understood how money is created today, and reviewed various understandings of money, we may have already gained an intuition that money *tokens* – the coins in our wallets, digits in our bank accounts and *fei* on the island of Yap – are but one component of the monetary *system*. Ideas (on what money is and what it is for), actors (commercial and central banks, government, borrowers, financial actors and 'venturesome native navigators') and technologies (digital payment systems, watermarks on a bill or hefty limestones) are just as important elements shaping how monetary tokens actually function. Most crucially, the form of the relationships established between these ideas, actors and technologies define the rules of the money game, conditioning the direction and rhythm of economic activity and the dynamic and quality of the social fabric.

In this light, money is a sociotechnical arrangement with infrastructural powers, a 'social technology' for organising the economy,[12] an infrastructure coordinating our collective economic present and steering our shared future. When we open the black-box of money and learn to see its many components, we also start to see money as a form of commons, a *resource system* we not only depend on, but in whose existence, form and functioning we are deeply implicated. A commons imaginary of money elicits a collective that is part of making the infrastructure. It sheds light on the human-made rules that both constitute and govern money. Far from the commodity tokens of popular understandings of money, a commons imaginary of money helps us bring forward the community that undergirds monetary value and thereof co-constitutes money itself.

Now, as we saw in the preceding chapter, in allowing profit-seeking financial actors to create and manage the majority of our money, the conventional money commons has been largely privatised. For the part that central banks create and manage, our conventional money commons has been organised along a state governance principle. But private and public management of the money commons do not exhaust the alternatives of monetary governance. Communities, the Yapese showed us, can also satisfactorily act as stewards of money.[13]

An imaginary of money as a commons foregrounds that money has no independent existence apart from the community that trades, records and trusts. It emphasises that the value of money hinges on the community that interacts, accepts and remembers. A money commons revives the tradition that emphasised money as personal credit or acknowledgement of debt, only, this time, the debt is not towards a central institution but towards one's community of equals. In a thoroughly monetised society such as ours is, a commons understanding of money brings the potential to expand the lay-person's economic agency from today's limited possibilities of borrowing, consuming, saving and paying back to participating in assembling and managing the monetary infrastructure.

There is freedom and empowerment in seeing money as a commons that can be successfully managed by the community it is made to serve, because awareness of our constitutive role in the money system carves a space to reimagine ourselves from passive marionettes of the system to active remakers of it. Learning to see money as a commons offers a logical and anthropological alternative to both market and state, enabling us to broaden our sense of collective possibility and opening up for money to reflect the plurality of communities and forms of life.

Guarding from cooptation of the money commons

An event in Furness' travel-book warns us of the vulnerability of a money commons governed through fragile institutions.

> There are no wheeled vehicles in Uap and, consequently, no cart roads; but there have always been clearly defined paths communicating with the different settlements. When the German Government assumed the ownership of the Caroline Islands, after the purchase of them from

> Spain in 1898, many of these paths or highways were in bad condition, and the chiefs of the several districts were told that they must have them repaired and put in good order. The roughly dressed blocks of coral were, however, quite good enough for the bare feet of the natives; and many were the repetitions of the command, which still remained unheeded. At last it was decided to impose a fine for disobedience on the chiefs of the districts. In what shape was the fine to be levied? It was of no avail to demand silver or gold from the chiefs – they had none – and to force them to pay in their own currency would have required, in the first place, half the population of the island to transport the fines; in the second place, their largest government building could not hold them; and finally, *fei* six feet in diameter, not having been 'made in Germany,' were hardly available as a circulating medium in the Fatherland. At last, by a happy thought, the fine was exacted by sending a man to every *failu* and *pabai* throughout the disobedient districts, where he simply marked a certain number of the most valuable *fei* with a cross in black paint to show that the stones were claimed by the government. This instantly worked like a charm; the people, thus dolefully impoverished, turned to and repaired the highways to such good effect from one end of the island to the other, that they are now like park drives. Then the government dispatched its agents and erased the crosses. Presto! the fine was paid, the happy *failus* resumed possession of their capital stock, and rolled in wealth.[14]

Like it is the case for the natural commons,[15] the money commons are perpetually exposed to grabbing by the more powerful.[16] In the island of Yap, fragile governance institutions exposed Yap's stone money to cooptation by an alliance between foreign government and commercial interests. In Chapter 3 we saw that our conventional money has been grabbed by an alliance between a state-supported central bank and financial actors. In the following chapters we will see that each monetary arrangement is susceptible to being seized for interests other than those of the community it was initially meant to serve. Governance of money – like governance of other commons – we will see, is not decided once and forever secured. In reclaiming, reimagining and remaking money, it is important to build strong governance institutions that guard the continuous adjustment of the monetary assemblage to the evolving needs and priorities of the community, and that ensure those needs and priorities are set by the community itself.

PART II

Varieties of Monies

Beware idealisation of the money commons. Approaching money as a commons in whose making and management community members actively engage does not necessarily lead to a more just, more inclusive and more sustainable future. Implicit in some of the ideas shaping complementary monies, assumed in the roles assigned to the many actors, and codified in the algorithms of the underlying technologies, lie different delimitations of the community these monies are to serve as well as different understandings of the needs they are to satisfy. As we will see in the following chapters, variations in the implementation of a money commons are immense. On the one extreme of the spectrum, we find radical crypto-activists. Seeing money itself as the valuable resource and understanding their role as that of building a global payments infrastructure, crypto-activists tend to subordinate the idiosyncrasies and changing needs of local communities to the standardisation of governance rules. Community currency activists lie at the other edge of the spectrum. Seeing members' contributions in the form of goods and services as the valuable resource, and understanding their role as that of building resilient local economies, community currency practitioners subordinate scale to local needs. The risks run accordingly. The first risk eroding the democratic ideal of the commons; the latter forever remaining irrelevant.

Part II of the book looks into particular examples where grassroots groups, social entrepreneurs, elected politicians and crypto-activists are actively reclaiming, redesigning and reorganising money. Each chapter opens the black-box of one particular set of alternative complementary money initiatives, bringing out the ideas guiding them, the actors involved and the technologies built in. Each of the three chapters epitomise one of the three principles to govern a commons – community-based, state-based, private-based. As we will see, each governance mode follows the lines indicated by each of the money imaginaries – a commons imaginary underlies the community money of Sardinia unfolded in Chapter 4; a state credit imaginary shapes the city money of Wörgl analysed in Chapter 5; a commodity imaginary infuses Bitcoin's design and governance as described in Chapter 6. The imaginaries that influence these monies have direct consequences on their architecture, on how they work, on how individuals relate to them and, most acutely, on how they shape interaction among its users and, with it, the social fabric of that money's community of users.

4

Give It Forward: The Form and Reason of Citizen Money

> We usually have a relatively abstract view of money. With Sardex, the money I earn is the justification for my work which involves a person who is part of my own network, unlike euros which everyone is involved in. As a consequence, you establish a different relationship with that person, because it is as if Sardex is bringing you a little closer.[1]

How can money 'bring you a little closer'? Informants in Giacomo Bazzani's research on Sardex, a local mutual credit monetary system in Sardinia, Italy, repeatedly speak of Sardex money 'keeping them in touch', making it 'easy to have social goals'. They speak of an 'ethical code', a 'Sardex mentality', a 'philosophy'. During his many interviews to participants of the currency network, Bazzani listened to stories that told of a money that animated practices of solidarity and cooperation, a money that awoke 'curiosity' about the other and that enticed a 'common mission [to] develop our region through participation', from the unselfish giving of Sardex to victims of floods and earthquakes and the generous sponsoring of patron saints' festivities and children's shows to the collaborative organisation of promotional activities and market fairs.

Most surprisingly for businesses that had been put on the verge of bankruptcy by the Great Financial Crisis that began in 2007, Bazzani's interviewees delighted in profligate spending and indulgent investment they had postponed for years. Their fragile economic situation may have led banks to reject their loan applications, yet with Sardex, participating businesses had been able to set up shop, buy new computers, refurbish the restaurant or spend on novel technology that cut down the energy bill. They observed: 'Sardex customers usually spend a little more because they let themselves be tempted', admitting to not 'worry[ing] much about the price because you don't feel like you are spending'. They bought Christmas 'gifts much more willingly', went on holidays and renewed their wardrobes. For all their lavish investment and spending, and for all the doubts banks may have had on the viability of their businesses, they were nonetheless able to pay back in Sardex.

While conceding that 'earning money in Sardex [was] as tiring as it [was] in euros', participants in the Sardex monetary arrangement appreciated there was 'something "witty" and "inspiring"' about this local money that was lacking in the euro economy. Some reasoned that its wittiness rested on the values the local money instilled in its users – 'with Sardex our work is valued', 'people respect the dignity of my work without putting price as the number one problem'; it imbues 'trust, a desire for reciprocity, and to help the network grow'. Others contended its cleverness relied on the manner it 'obliges you to work at relationships'. 'Sardex unites us and this creates a closer relationship from the first meeting [because] Sardex allow[s] us to create new work and new opportunities'. It is 'as though we were a family', 'a brotherhood, a trade union, a private club', 'a clan'. 'You hug and greet each other warmly.' Others, still, argued there was more to it than ethical values and social relations. Interested individual gain was just as pivotal. 'The other factors remain, but now I use it because it is good for business.' Though with a definite purpose to save ('I joined … so I could spend Sardex and leave my euros in the cash-register'), access new clients, weather economic distress and 'make a living', participants' avowed self-interest could only be satisfied if aligning to the interests of the community. In their evaluations of who to buy from, impersonal economic calculations seamlessly mixed with communal care. 'By buying within the network, I am helping the network to operate well. This increases the number of my customers and also my spending capacity.' 'Giving others work' is also a way 'to obtain work', something they declared not to experience to the same extent in the euro economy.

Distant from the coldness of relations in conventional cash, oblivious to the precept to 'take the money and run', disdainful of the need to limit one's expenses and save, members of Sardex engaged in exchange forms impregnated with warmth, cooperation and liberality, while nonetheless mindful of 'helping yourself'. 'It is as if you entered a different dimension', a dimension that values the work behind what is exchanged and where debt grows the community. In the Sardex 'dimension', giving and debt seem to go hand-in-hand, spending and community-making two sides of the same phenomenon. Members of Sardex seem to be immersed in a web of relations and obligations similar to those in the tribal societies Marcel Mauss studied, abide by similar exchange-through-giving dynamics that Mauss argued made the collective, driven by a similar mix of generosity and self-interest that permeated the morality and practices of archaic societies.

In *The Gift: The Form and Reason for Exchange in Archaic Societies*, Marcel Mauss reviewed the anthropological literature on tribal and clan societies. Structured as relationships of obligation, he argues, gifts make society by continuously forcing economic exchange. In Marcel Mauss' hands, the logic of the gift is not one of altruism and free generosity, but rather one of reciprocity and forced generosity. Gifts, he finds, are structured as an obligation to give, an obligation to accept and an obligation to reciprocate. Think of the dinner guest who doesn't return the invitation, or of the friend who asks for favours but is seldom ready to return them. Not reciprocating the dinner invitation or the favour, the guest soon disappears from invitation lists and the friend quickly becomes a 'supposed friend'. And in Sardex, members indeed expected reciprocity in spending: '[Y]ou know that the people you buy from will come and spend Sardex at your [business].'

Whether the obligation to spend was self-interested – 'why should I keep them?' – or, as we will see, forced through formal governance rules, Mauss' observations on the reciprocal obligations of exchange-through-giving dynamics are relevant for understanding how mutual credit monies work and are made to work. Two of his observations are particularly relevant. One, the obligation to reciprocate makes exchange-through-giving relational in a deep sense, not as in mere objects passing from one tribe to another or between two individuals, but rather as acts that oblige the other to *relate back*, to give *forward*, to keep *doing community*.[2] And because society is partly being made as economic exchanges proceed, the economy is thusly steadily embedded into the community. A sense of obligation towards the communal other acts as a *perpetuum mobile*, continuously implicating individuals with each other and, in that constant activity, producing and reproducing the community economy. One Sardex participant expressed the tight connection between economic exchange and society performed by such gift-giving practices more mundanely: '[The] relationship between Sardex and society is strong.' Another member phrased the amalgamated community-cum-economy as 'the network has become a virtuously positive market'.

The second of Mauss' observations I want to highlight is that there is self-interest in giving, as much as there is generosity. Because of the obligation to reciprocate, gift-giving practices dissolve distinctions between 'liberty and obligation', between 'liberality, generosity, and luxury, as against savings, interest, and utility'.[3] Jumbling up together personal and communal interest, exchange-through-giving aligns the will of the individual to satisfy the needs of the community. 'Members are promoting their own interests and helping others at the same time', a Sardex member phrases it. A monetary arrangement that obliges to give back reconstitutes the interests of its users who learn to think of, and relate to, each other 'beyond [the interest of] making money'. 'There is not the coldness of an economic exchange that ends with the exchange of services for money, there is the curiosity to know what the other person does' feeding a 'strong sense of belonging when I give credit and let the others go away with a smile, I have also had the experience of being in debt to others in the network'. Through the lived experience of gift–debt relationships, community members further learn to think of, and relate to (and *in*), money differently.

> Sardex has helped me to understand the meaning of money. ... We always think we have too little money to feel good, but our well-being is tied to our satisfaction in what we do, and in satisfying our basic needs. Sardex has helped me to rediscover that there are more important things than money, we must not be slaves to money, we should work more at our relationships.

Mutual credit systems seem to provide spaces and relations that incite a different way of doing economy. And it is through the lived experience of different socioeconomic spaces and relations that these monies – local and small as they may be – sow the seeds of a vision for a different society.

Monies designed along mutual credit are firmly anchored in an imaginary of money as a credit–debt relationship, as a record of something given and something taken, simultaneously a right and a duty. Its mechanics are simple. They imply symmetrical obligations to give to, and take from, the community. This money is created, circulated and cleared out through the individual obligation to give (provide) goods and services to the community, the individual obligation to accept payment for the goods and services provided in the local currency, and the obligation to reciprocate by spending the money earned in goods or services from the community. Far from the commodity fiction of money that Polanyi despaired over, a money that is born out of relations of exchange and that is sustained through the continuous relational work of those that use it, steadily works at embedding the economy into the community. The very mechanics of mutual debt–credit relationships entice users to rearticulate their imagination, to relate symmetrically to each other, and to organise collectively for building a community economy. For their transformational potential to be realised, we will see, these local monetary systems require constant relational work to assemble the economy.

The chapter uses the stories of Sardex and Málaga Común – two mutual credit monetary arrangements – to make a twofold argument.[4] First, while relational work is pivotal to community currencies, it is not everything there is to them. As important as it is to understand the values and meanings that guide participants' interactions, such an analysis falls short of understanding how those motives and meanings are shaped by the very mechanics of the money they use. The meaning of money is not found in the cognitive interstices of people's minds; nor exclusively in the interpersonal relations of its users – intimate and caring as these relationships may be. The social meaning of these monies is firmly anchored in their architecture, in a design that transforms money users into money issuers and commercial relationships into contributions to the community. Second, just as it is key to appreciate the extent to which the internal mechanics of money shape individual and communal behaviour, if we are to understand the money–society twosome, we need to acknowledge the vital role sociality plays in the making of money. As many short-lived mutual credit groups have experienced, neglecting to lodge institutions to instigate and govern relations into the heart of these monies is a sure recipe for their failure to perdure.

So let's start with their beginnings, with the problem that incites these grassroots groups to reclaim, reimagine and reorganise money.

Absent (the connecting device of) money

'The problem with crises is that money doesn't move, and that jobs are lost', writes David Chapman, one of the founders of the local complementary currency Málaga Común in a blog post in 2010. And he continues, '[t]hat doesn't mean that people without a job do not have anything to offer to society. It means that there is no money to pay for their services'.[5]

The Great Financial Crisis of 2007–2009 hit Spain with force. The property-led growth of the previous decade was brought to a sudden halt, resulting in a strong economic downturn, bankruptcies of both major companies and small enterprises, a severe increase in unemployment and mass emigration. The speed and virulence of what was called the Great Spanish Depression took many observers by surprise. Total unemployment went from 8 per cent in 2007 to 18 per cent two years later, 20 per cent in 2010 and 26 per cent at the height of the depression, in 2013. Unemployment among the youth reached incomprehensible levels: from 18 per cent in 2007, to 38 per cent in 2009, 42 per cent in 2010 and 57 per cent in 2013. Málaga, a province in southern Spain heavily reliant on tourism, was hit particularly violently. Total unemployment reached 36 per cent in 2013 and youth unemployment went up to 67 per cent in 2013.[6] As Chapman very well observed in his blog entry, jobs were certainly lost.

Chapman's analysis of the crisis goes, however, beyond unemployment figures to suggest that what cripples the economy is not so much the lack of jobs as the lack of money. The chain of relations that transmuted the initial banking crisis in the United States into unsettling levels of unemployment in Málaga began with the central role commercial banks and other financial actors play in the creation of money through debt.[7] To the uncertainty created by the collapse of the housing market in the United States, banks reacted by suddenly stopping lending. In an economy where the market – with its liquidity principle – regulates the production of the majority of our money, banks' prospects of falling profits translated into a contraction of the supply of money (or credit) to businesses. Subsequently, businesses that often rely on bank credit for the management of their cash flow now worried not only about reduced demand and delayed payments from customers, but also about the credit crunch. As the network of relations of a globalised monetary system folded up, the result was soon felt across local economies: shutting businesses down, swelling numbers of people without employment, and intensified levels of poverty.

And yet, as Chapman indicates, regardless of banks' lending behaviour, people readily offered their services, while others would willingly secure those services; if only there was *money to connect* them both. One of the founders of Sardex illustrated the connectivity of money with an everyday example: 'I always give the example of the beggar who is hungry [because] he has no money and the restaurateur who has empty seats he would like to fill. There needs to be some mechanism for reaching an agreement.'[8] Such is the paradox of *money made scarce*. The less money there is, the less economic activity is supported, which in turn leads to even less money circulating, further crippling the economy. A vicious circle citizens find themselves submerged in because of a monetary system governed by the profit-making calculations of banking and financial actors.[9]

With the challenge framed as the absence of the connecting device of money, the solution gives itself: create links between producers and consumers, organise a payment system that enables willing labourers to connect with those with labour needs. To help construct trading ties, in Málaga, Chapman argued for a communications technology: 'Today, Internet helps us there. It is a great way to get goods and services without spending [conventional] money, and yet paying with all the good things that we can offer (our work, our abilities, our companionship …).' In Sardinia, the group of friends similarly aimed to build ties: 'The basic idea was to *put together* all the unsold items of Sardinian businesses: the un-expressed potential could not be expressed because the people who wanted those items could not afford them.'[10]

Absent money, grassroots groups and citizen initiatives mobilise to protect themselves. Málaga and Sardinia are but two places among many. In the aftermath of the economic crisis that ensued from the financial collapse of 2008, a wealth of citizen-driven initiatives set up to experiment with local complementary currencies.[11] Over 80 such monetary initiatives were documented in 2015 in Spain alone;[12] over 70 were recently mapped in France;[13] 49 were reviewed in Japan.[14] From Greece[15] to Germany,[16] from the UK[17] to Canada,[18] from Brazil[19] to Switzerland,[20] civil society has been hard at work redefining what it values and knitting communal ties with the help of local forms of monies. The phenomenon is not new. It happened in Argentina following that country's sovereign debt and banking crisis in

2001,[21] just as it happened both in Europe and the United States during the Great Depression.[22] To cope with the economic and social dislocations brought by recurrent crises, groups of citizens around the world take back the power to create money.

Complementary currencies come in many forms though, and many an attempt has been made to classify them. Attending to the purpose of the founders upon creation of the currency, they are classified as social, economic or environmental currency schemes. If attention is placed on the relationship of the complementary currency to the national currency, they are classified as convertible versus non-convertible. If focus is instead directed to the nature of the founders, they then will be classified as commercial, non-profit or state currencies, or private versus public. If the technology stands as the classificatory criteria, then they will be either paper, digital or cryptocurrencies. If the scalar reach of the currency is what matters, then they are boxed as local, regional, national or global currencies. If it is the nature of their backing that matters, then they will be labelled as fiat, time-based or backed (by another currency or by a basket of goods) currencies. If the imaginary of money they build upon is put at the core, then they will be addressed as token-systems (convertible or not) or credit systems.[23] Regardless of one's preferred taxonomy,[24] the variety of classifications gives a good idea of the many dimensions along which complementary monies are designed.

Within the large variety of civil monies, one design stands out: mutual credit systems. Found in citizen-driven Local Exchange Trading Systems (LETS), in commercial exchange circles and in time-banks, local monies following such a design are deemed 'among the most solid and promising projects on the CC scene'.[25] The longest-lived complementary currency, the WIR, a local business-to-business mutual credit system established in Switzerland in 1934 and still in operation, is indeed testimony that monetary systems structured along the clearing principle can be resilient to wars, booms and busts.[26] John Maynard Keynes similarly relied on the stability of such a design when, at the Bretton Woods Conference, he proposed a mutual credit scheme for remaking the international monetary system.[27] And while Keynes' *bancor* proposal was dismissed, Europe successfully implemented a similar scheme during the postwar period (1950–1958) under the European Payments Union – 'successful' in that it largely contributed to peacefully lift Europe up from the devastation of the Second World War.[28]

While the sheer scale of an international monetary arrangement makes experimentation at that level a historical luxury, we have much to learn from the many experiments going on at the grassroots level. How do mutual credit monetary arrangements work and how are they made to work? And what could we learn from local experiments that could be translated into the international scale? The chapter is an effort to answer those questions by following Oscar and Vanesa – from the Spanish Málaga Común – and by observing the activities of Sardex's brokers. Both initiatives shed light on the way the very mechanics of mutual credit monetary systems assemble the economy as well as on the relational work needed to make these monies work.

Can debt initiate the work of connecting a local economy?

Spring 2016. It is the weekly *Ecomedor* at El Caminito Real – an abandoned plot of land at the heart of Málaga reclaimed and transformed into a lush urban garden that produces fruit, tubers, spices and herbs. Like every Wednesday, members of the local complementary currency Málaga Común meet over lunch. Some 20 *commoners* – '*comuneros*' as they refer to themselves – sit around the table. María, a young woman in her late-20s who, despite her two university degrees – one in anthropology and another in social work – the labour market has never welcomed. Oscar, a wind power technician in his late-50s, unemployed for seven or eight years – first willingly, then forcibly. Vanesa, a woman in her mid-50s. She lost her job as a garden planner for the municipality when the crisis arrived and the colours in the municipal government changed. Jesús, who makes do selling a variety of trinkets – from sun cream to battery chargers. Pepe, in his mid-30s, whose birth handicap limits his possibility to get a stable and reliable job. Laura, a retired teacher; Esteban, a part-time programmer; Natalia, a woman in her mid-70s with no studies and coarse hands; Sara, a middle-aged woman who wears a pearl necklace; Andrés and Raquel, a couple with two daughters who struggle to feed their family. Each has a personal history of how the crisis left them in a precarious economic situation.[29] They learnt about Málaga Común through a variety of civic and neighbourhood associations. Few knew one another prior to joining the local currency network.

After lunch has been eaten, Oscar and Vanesa as well as the other *comuneros* around the table bring out of their backpacks home-made bread, cookies and kimchi, bananas and almonds from their own trees, or an artisan cloth-bag. These are either orders made in the days prior to the *Ecomedor* or offerings members price in *comunes*. Sara takes out her scissors and gets ready to give Esteban a much-needed haircut. Oscar lifts Vanesa's bike and sets to tune the gear. María, Jesús, Oscar and myself enlist to get our hair cut by Sara's expert hands. I joke about Sara making today the *comunes* she would otherwise earn in a couple of weeks. She laughs and tells that she earns much in the local currency. She spent 200 *comunes* (equivalent to 200 euros) at last month's complementary currency market alone. At that moment, María confesses that her account is in negative figures. Someone quickly interjects, "It doesn't matter; being in debt means that you have generated activity for the community." Oscar nuances the assertion: "Debt doesn't matter. Some have to be in debt for others to be in credit. Debt is not the matter. The problem is when you have been in debt for a long time."[30] To support María, someone suggests we could procure our lunch for the weekly Wednesday gatherings from her. "Sure!" María exclaims. Soon, five or six of us have ordered next week's lunch from her to be compensated in *comunes*.

During the half-year of fieldwork I conducted on the local monetary system Málaga Común, I witnessed many discussions on the meaning of debt. The tension always runs across the same individual/community line. Someone would admit feelings of shame about being in debt, with someone else then trying to reformulate individual debt into an action conjuring up the community. "Debt means activity, you generate movement and enrich the community."[31] Often, a member would distinguish between the emotional and the economic vectors of debt. "At the emotional level, one needs to realise that the debt in your account is not yours, that with it you are contributing to the community."[32] Negative feelings around one's individual debt in the local currency originated, the argument went, in our relationship to the official money. "I've been educated to pay back my debts. It is as if you were a bad person if you are in debt. I take pride in not having any debt. I owe nobody anything, and I don't like owing to people."[33] And yet, members insisted, a negative figure in one's account was a sign that the member had been part of a relationship that had contributed to make community.

While the newest members of Málaga Común struggled with their relationship to debt, some giving it as a reason for their reticence to join the local monetary system, those that had participated for a longer time were adamant that we needed to look at debt from a community perspective. Theirs was not a commodity imaginary of money in which debt visualises the value of commodities (money or other) someone has borrowed and now needs to pay back. Their understanding of money, and of the local currency in particular, rethought money as some sort of commons infrastructure and debt as the contribution of the individual to a community. Designed as a mutual credit system, the *comuneros* had grown to understand their monetised exchanges as essential activities weaving the tapestry of relations that enacted the community economy. For them, the economy was indistinguishable from the community, the local money indistinguishable from social relations, money's value indistinguishable from members' activities. Money was not something some had and debt a sign that you didn't have it. Rather, money seemed to be a web of relations and debt simply a position in that tapestry of relations.

The resignification of money was so complete that even those that had contemplated suicide admitted this form of debt had returned them hope in life. Raquel, who lived in the Palmilla neighbourhood where, at the time,

100 per cent of the young were unemployed and the general unemployment level reached 85 per cent, elucidated:

> 'Lots of people in the neighbourhood are already bored of smoking joints and drinking beer because that's all they do. Every Friday, for years, they gather together to smoke their three joints and drink their two beers. No thrill, no hope. Sometimes you hear how happy they get just because they managed to get some trifling employ. Nothing serious; but they have been without anything for years, absolutely nothing. They need something that gives them some hope, and I think Málaga Común could be it. It has been very good for me, it has given me hope back.'[34]

Practitioners and researchers of community currencies often point to the distinct social and cultural inclinations of the people involved in these parallel monetary arrangements. They speak of the values of care and solidarity nourished by its members, of their common understanding, and of the particular ethos of reciprocity they bring.[35] Much emphasis is placed in the immaterial dimensions of this form of money, in matters such as members' trust, social values, communitarian motivations and shared meanings.[36] This research elicits the social and human aspects that inhere, and shape, the meanings of money.

Zelizer's analysis is a good example of this line of argumentation. Economic sociologist Viviana Zelizer coins the term 'circuits of commerce'[37] to capture the many spheres in which markets are productively entangled with solidarity-sustaining personal relations. Challenging the assumption that impersonal markets and cold money corrupt relationships of care, intimacy and community, Zelizer identifies and sociologically dissects economies where monetised market transactions are woven together with solicitous personal relations. She finds that, across a wide range of socioeconomic spheres – from the caring labour of social workers to local monetary systems, from the world of sexual services to the domestic arena – 'people manage to integrate monetary transfers into larger webs of mutual obligations without destroying the social ties involved'. Mauss' gift economies, with their mix of self-interest and generosity, norms of reciprocal obligation, and a shared understanding of transactional relations, constitute another example of 'Zelizer's circuits',[38] 'bridging structures that facilitate the coexistence of intimate and impersonal social ties'.[39]

Zelizer's commercial circuits are characterised by the following:

- the existence of a well-defined boundary (those registered in the Málaga Común platform) with participants having some control over transactions crossing the boundary;

- transactions within the boundary are embedded in interpersonal ties (Wednesday's lunch being procured from María);
- are carried using a distinctive media (*comunes*); and
- enact a shared understanding of their dealings together ("you generate movement and enrich the community").

It is this 'shared understanding' along with the social norms and practices of the group that supposedly transforms these monies into something more than the cold matter money is portrayed to be in the stories of professional economists; the set of personal relations into which money use is embedded making it more than hard cash. In line with her previous work on the way people categorise (conventional) money depending on how they earn it, and how they earmark its use based on such differentiation of meaning,[40] Zelizer's analysis of local complementary currencies elicits the social dimensions of money. Money is imbued with meaning, we imbue it with meaning through relational work (categorising and earmarking it), and it is this meaning *we* imbue money with that shapes monetised interpersonal relations as well as our relationship to money. Zelizer introduced a much-needed sociological and cultural analysis to the phenomenon of money.

However, while economists' approach to money as a neutral intermediary is deeply under-socialised, this sort of analysis risks over-socialising money. Admittedly, students of money need to ground their understanding of how money works in the relational work into which money use is inserted (as we will see later in this chapter). Still, this relational work is not only of human origin. Money and money use relies on more than the immaterial realm of ideas, categories and abstractions; of relational values, interpersonal practices and social meaning. Insightful as this sort of analysis is concerning 'the social life of money',[41] it ignores that how money works is equally shaped by its mechanics. The knowledges that structure the design of particular forms of money in turn structure the meanings people charge money with. Put differently, values, norms and meaning need to be understood within the set of interactional patterns lodged in the architecture of money. Surely, this architecture includes actors and imaginaries, but it also includes technologies and accounting practices. That is, if we are to understand the peculiar performances of these local monies, we need to add the relational work conducted by non-humans to the relational work conducted by humans. The sliding meaning of debt members of the mutual credit currency system Málaga Común had points to meaning residing not in an individual's head, nor in the materiality of money, nor solely in interpersonal relations. Money's meaning and users' relationship to it are shaped, just as much, by money's very internal configuration. Just as people shape money use, so does money's form – its mechanics – shape people's understandings (and uses) of money.

The (connecting) mechanics of mutual credit monies: clearing

So, to the book's first question to help us unfold the mediating action of any monetary system: how do mutual credit systems work?

In technical prose: mutual credit systems distributed accounting systems that rely on a process of direct creation and clearing of credits and debits among buyers and sellers, where neither credits nor debits bear interest nor are they convertible into any other money. When a user sells one hour of work, rents out her car, repairs a bike, or sells home-baked bread, the amount agreed by buyer and seller is credited in the seller's account. The same amount is debited in the buyer's account, regardless of whether she had that amount or not in her account. The seller can then spend the accumulated credit in any service and product offered in the mutual credit network. If the buyer bought for more than she had credit for, then her account will show a negative figure. This is however no debt to the seller, whose account has already been credited for the services/products she offered. Individual debts are thus traces of a commercial relation, signs that the individual contributed to the economic activity of the network, and a promise to the community to offer services or products equivalent to the debt she has incurred. Symmetrically, credits are traces of a commercial relation, signals that the person contributed with goods or services to the community, and constitute a claim upon the community. In this sense, mutual credit systems are the epitome of Simmel's conception of money as a 'claim upon society'.[42]

Prosaic descriptions easily move into philosophical reflections that can feel removed from the experienced everyday operations of using money. Numerical descriptions may aid in this regard, as they take us through the step-by-step process of creating, using and clearing out this type of money. In a hands-on approach, the numbers registered in the process of accounting for a trade offer us a grip from which to grasp money as a claim and a promise, as a relation bearing rights and obligations.

The numerical description, stepwise, in a very simple community of three individuals is shown in Tables 4.1 to 4.4. At time 0 (Table 4.1), upon registration

Table 4.1: Accounts in a mutual credit system, time 0

Time 0	Account balance
Oscar	0
Vanesa	0
Sara	0
Total	**0**

Table 4.2: Accounts in a mutual credit system, time 1

Time 1	Previous account balance	Change	Current account balance
Oscar	0	+15	+15
Vanesa	0	−15	−15
Sara	0	0	0
Total	**0**	**0**	**0**

into the mutual credit platform, members' account balances equal 0 for members have yet not bought (taken) nor sold (offered) anything in the network.

Trading relations need first to be enacted for them to be recorded in the ledger. Mutual credit systems allow users to go overdraft with no added fees, to pay on credit at no interest. Let's look at what happens at time 1, when Oscar repairs Vanesa's bike for 15 *comunes* (valued equivalent to 15 euros).[43] Note that Vanesa starts with a balance of 0; she doesn't 'have' any monetary token. Yet, the defining trait of mutual credit systems is the possibility to spend first and earn later – or, as it were, 'buy on credit', procure goods/services on a promise to reciprocate in the future. When Vanesa pays Oscar for his work, the system credits Oscar's account and debits Vanesa's account with the amount agreed by the parties, 15 *comunes* – as shown in Table 4.2.

This most uneventful mechanical operation already hints towards a particular imaginary of money, one that propels us to rethink debt and communal relations. First, the nature of money. Observe that one single exchange – bike repair services for *comunes* – has resulted in two recording actions on the ledger – marking up Oscar's account for the value of the services he provided, and marking down Vanesa's account for the service she received. In the realm of money mechanics, this is what a transaction is, two records, one positive and one negative, a plus and a minus, at once someone's asset and someone else's liability. In the world outside the ledger, a transaction is a relationship between two persons – one providing and the other appropriating the service or good. Thus, to account for a transaction, both sides of the relationship need to be recorded. Money, this type of money, becomes a system to record that there has been a relationship of exchange; money, this money, is an accounting relationship. It is in this sense that some economists and anthropologists contend 'money is memory',[44] 'a giant spreadsheet where everybody makes contributions to society, which get added up, and give them a claim to the contributions of the rest of society'.[45] Or, putting it differently, the imaginary and mechanics of this money enact money as a debt–credit relationship that traces relationships of favours in the real economy.

Second, rethinking debt. What does the negative sign in Vanesa's account mean? She doesn't owe any payment to Oscar; Oscar has already received 15 *comunes* in the form of a credit record in his account. He could spend them immediately if he wanted to, even before Vanesa starts working herself out of her debit. So Vanesa's debt is not a debt towards Oscar. Vanesa's debt is a debt towards the community. She took a service Oscar offered to members of the community, and hence owes the community goods and services for the value of the services she took, equal the debt visible in her account balance. In these monetary mechanics, a debt becomes an individual promise to pay back to the community by providing goods and services to community members. Symmetrically, a credit becomes a Simmelian claim upon the community for goods and services provided by community members.

Third, such an imaginary and mechanics of money remakes one's role within the monetary system and, along with it, reconfigures communal relations. Vanesa started with no monetary tokens recorded in her account balance. Nor was there any token recorded in any of the members' balances. Formally, there was no money in the system; no one 'had' any money – as the commodity imaginary of money would phrase it. And yet, at the end of time 1 in our quotidian exercise, 15 monetary tokens (with both of their sides, the positive and the negative sides) are visible in the ledger. The moment Oscar and Vanesa agreed on and conducted the trade, they, together, created this mutual credit money. By Vanesa being willing to go into debt and by Oscar being willing to be paid through Vanesa's overdraft, the two have created 15 tokens. In using the possibilities inherent in a mutual credit system, the users of money become in effect the issuers of that money. This insight – the novel role of regular money users as also money issuers – lies behind Oscar's assertion at Málaga Común's gathering: "Debt means activity, you generate movement and enrich the community." Not only has Vanesa's debt allowed Oscar to earn some *comunes* that he can spend on other members' goods, Vanesa's debt has also enabled the flow of bike-repair services within the community. 'Both sides, the side that offers and the side that consumes, contribute [to the community]. Both contribute. What's important is the movement (circulation of the currency).'[46] Money for the community issued by community members. Vanesa rides away with her upgraded bike, Oscar is now able to consume without incurring debt, and the community has seen its economic activity increase.

At this moment in the explanation of mutual credit money mechanics, there is often someone objecting that if money can be created that easily by anyone at any point in time, it surely will end with inflation in the system, prices in the community economy rising above the level of prices in the conventional economy. The objection often brings up the key role central banks play in continuously managing the money supply. And here we have

Table 4.3: Accounts in a mutual credit system, time 2

Time 2	Previous account balance	Change	Current account balance
Oscar	+15	0	+15
Vanesa	−15	+10	-5
Sara	0	−10	−10
Total	**0**	**0**	**0**

Table 4.4: Accounts in a mutual credit system, time 3

Time 3	Previous account balance	Change	Current account balance
Oscar	+15	−10	+5
Vanesa	-5	0	-5
Sara	−10	+10	0
Total	**0**	**0**	**0**

a system where anyone can, indiscriminatorily, add to the supply! Here is where the operation of (multilateral) clearing comes in.

Back to our step-by-step exercise. At time 2 Sara rents Vanesa's bike for 10 *comunes*. The transaction is recorded as shown in Table 4.3.

Though Sara, just as Vanesa in the previous step, starts with no *comunes* recorded in her account balance, she, like Vanesa before, can spend *comunes* before earning them. Once again, monetary tokens are created the moment the two members conduct a trade. Yet, observe that the number of tokens in the overall ledger are the same at the end as they were at the beginning of time 2: 15. This is because mutual credit systems operate on clearing mechanics where debts and credits cancel each other out. The credit side of the trade between Sara and Vanesa clears Vanesa's previous debit. As a result, there are no more monetary tokens recorded at the end of the transaction, no larger supply of money.

Indeed, the automatic operation of clearing may even reduce the quantity of money in the system, with no negative consequences for economic activity in the community. Let's look at what happens at time 3, when Oscar gets a haircut from Sara for 10 *comunes* (see Table 4.4).

At the end of the transaction, there are 10 fewer *comunes* recorded in the ledger. This is observed in that the sum total of credit at the beginning of the period was 15, while at the end it is 5. It could be said that the monetary supply shrank, with no consequences for the economic activity of the community. There is no scarcity of money in a monetary system designed along mutual credit lines for users can spend money into existence when conducting a trade. Nor is there an excess of money (with the consequent risk of inflation), for debts clear when the debtor is paid for the services she offers. The supply of money adapts to the degree of economic activity in the community, increasing when needed, and decreasing when debts are cleared with credits. A system that works through credit and clearing self-regulates the supply of money to avoid the dual danger of inflation and deflation.

For citizens governing their own monies, the implications are revolutionary. Thanks to the mechanics of credit and clearing, a mutual credit system automatically adapts the quantity of money to the level of economic activity in the community or, if you prefer, the money supply adjusts to the economic relations members enact. Money and labour, finance and productive economy, are tightly embedded into each other. No need for complex algorithms (as we will see abound in the cryptocurrencies that build along an imaginary of commodity money). No need for expert economists. No need for a central monetary authority.

Well, that's at the mechanical level. If it were so easy as to let the recording system work its magic by itself, there would not be such a low rate of local mutual credit systems surviving the twin tests of adoption and time. On such a basis, many a commentators ridicule these local mutual credit monetary experiments as mere jokes, pie-in-the-sky idealism at best, gimmicks small local businesses resort to for cheap marketing at worst.[47] Or, as a story-teller that read and performed stories for children in the urban garden where members of Málaga Común met and ate every Wednesday put it: "I am already very old, and I have already grown tired of words. Those are just words. … Don't get me wrong. I tell stories. That's what I do. But what I want now is to do things, not just hear words."

Málaga Común was no exception to the challenges local mutual credit systems experience and, as it happened, the mutual credit network in Málaga eventually ceased to exist. At the time of my fieldwork, organisers and participants in Málaga Común regarded their challenges to reach out were due to a mix of bad incentives designed into the monetary system, a technology platform that was not user-friendly, and a dominant understanding of debt that shamed debtors. Their response was thus shaped along those lines. To align individual incentives to the needs of the community, the bi-monthly General Assembly decided to remunerate volunteers for their work in administering the system, in facilitating the meetings and in organising events – from local markets and communal lunches to workshops and presentations to organisations outside the network interested in the local money. They also set automatic fixed monthly charges on individual balances, introduced a standard entry bonus to welcome newly enrolled users, and started to more purposefully use the community account to 'create employment' within the community economy. Though there were no debit nor credit limits in Málaga Común, many a mutual credit network further sets such limits to align incentives, constantly negotiating their level depending on the earning and spending capacity of individual traders.[48] The technology platform was also actively managed in Málaga Común and 'ghost users' were cleaned and outdated ads removed; they moved to a platform with a more intuitive technical interface and considered paper ledgers for those users who felt less comfortable with an internet-based platform. By and large, what concerned them the most was however the shame those in a debt position often avowed to feel. To address this, the entry bonus was argued as a way to give newcomers the possibility to spend straightaway without incurring debt; the meaning of negative balances was discussed at workshops, seminars and lunches; the philosophy of the network was clarified in public presentations; and language use was discussed suggesting the playful rephrasing of terms, such as the 'eco-no-my' into 'eco-yes-ours'.[49]

There is, it seems, more to making a mutual credit system work than the adaptive issuance and disappearance of monetary tokens automatically performed through the operations of recording and clearing. Some scholars of local alternative currencies have, in fact, argued that it is the burden of management that accounts for the small size and poor diffusion of such systems.[50] Other scholars however look elsewhere, finding fault not in the social values and communal commitment of its members – as an over-socialised analysis would have it – but in the fact that the economic benefits these monetary schemes promise are simply not realised.[51] Or, as Rosa from Málaga Común explained, "basic needs are not covered [within the community]. The person who has *comunes* does not know where to spend them and the person who wants to get them doesn't know how to get them". She concluded with a resigned undertone, "What do we do?"[52] Sardex, a mutual credit system that has managed to establish and expand since its start in 2009, may provide some answers into how those systems that do work are made to work.

Sardex

Upon enrolling in university studies, five friends from the Sardinian town of Serramanna – brothers Gabrielle and Giuseppe Littera, Carlo Mancosu, Franco Contu and Piero Sanna – had dispersed across Italy and the UK to pursue various arts and humanities studies. They had kept in contact however and shared dreams of one day returning to the lovely island of their childhood. Piero and Giuseppe were both studying at Leeds University when they stumbled upon one of the local currencies in that country. This immediately awoke their interest and soon they were studying and debating today's monetary system with the other three friends. Enraged by the economic distress and inequalities they saw originating in the freedom of conventional money to move across national borders and leak out of regions peripheral to the global economy, the group researched deeper into complementary monies. This led them to the WIR in Switzerland. A trip to Basel convinced the friends about the potential of mutual credit monies to work as instruments for local economic development. In the WIR, they saw that another money and a more cooperative economy were possible.

When the crisis of 2008 reached Sardinia, the group of friends was ready to move back and eager to set up a local mutual credit currency system that would connect businesses on the island. To that end, in 2009 they started knocking on the doors of Sardinian businesses trying to persuade them to join the recently established Sardex. Dispelling the doubts of struggling businesses turned out to be strenuous work. Financially stretched by a crisis that had originated in the financial sector, small businesses mistrusted novel financial tools. Their accountants were similarly wary. During the first years, the team untiringly made calls, met every potential partner in person, and explained how such a currency network could work for them. By the end of 2010, they had managed to attract 200 businesses that were exchanging goods and services for 300,000 in Sardex. In 2011 the number of participating businesses had increased to 450 and the volume of transactions had quadrupled to 1,200,000 Sardex. By 2017, the network included about 4,000 businesses from all sectors of the Sardinian economy and the sum of all transactions amounted to the equivalent of 80 million euros.[53] By 2019, the value of all transactions reached some 220 million. The COVID-19 pandemic did not disrupt the trend and, in 2020, registrations of new businesses grew by 86 per cent.[54]

Sardex has attracted national and international media attention – with the *Financial Times* publishing a feature article in 2015 and ranking it among the thousand fastest-growing companies in Europe. Interest from other Italian regions and external investment capital have enabled the idea to spread and by 2021 15 similar currency networks operated throughout Italy, reaching out to some 4,000 additional businesses. The team of five friends had grown into a working force of over 100 employees including some 50 brokers.

Participants in the currency network as well as many an observer attribute Sardex's performance to the continuous relational work of Sardex's staff and brokers.[55] Indeed, when advising other local currency organisers, Sardex founders seem less concerned about the technology and the software and more attentive to building community. As Giuseppe Littera – one of the founding members – told a group of currency practitioners in Greece, 'focus on the impact you can have, work every day and try to build communities where there are none. … [In Sardinia] the social fabric was destroyed. And we started knitting'.[56]

Assembling the economy: 'knitting'

This brings us to the book's second guiding question for unpacking monetary systems: How is Sardex made to work? How does the team at Sardex Ltd govern the mutual credit monetary system? In looking at the continuous work of staff and brokers to run and manage Sardex, we will recognise the constant need to balance individual provisions to and appropriations from the community, to safeguard the possibility of reciprocity to the community, and to assemble the economy by securing the possibility of symmetrical relations.[57] We will also appreciate the extent to which, in doing this, they advance an imaginary of money as a commons infrastructure for the Sardex community economy.

There is first a strict selection of members based on criteria fit for the conditions of the mutual credit network. Sardex brokers carefully consider membership applications. Approval is based on 'buying and selling lists' the applying business needs to complete – lists of the products the business has bought and sold during the previous year. Sardex brokers compare those lists to the overall demand and supply in the network, thus assessing whether the particular business could benefit from what is already made available in the network as well as whether it could contribute with goods and services Sardex businesses need. Brokers decline applications if they deem the business would be unable to balance its earnings and spends in the network. In this way, the criteria defining membership boundaries are a first step to align the individual interests of traders to the collective conditions of the network, an effort to connect a trader's capacity to offer goods and services to the network with the network's capacity to appropriate goods and services from the individual.

Note that in the work of aligning individual and collective interests, the resources Sardex's brokers take care of are not monetary tokens per se – neither the conventional nor the complementary money – but the goods and services traders offer and need. Therein lies a particular understanding of the network's economy. The resource units that deserve the caring attention of brokers are the goods and services exchanged, what members contribute and appropriate, the gifts and takes. Credits and debts in Sardex are relevant for how they visualise individual members' contributions to and appropriations from the network. It is these goods and services that make the community economy; it is traders' productive activity that develop their economic commons.

Carlo Mancosu, co-founder of Sardex, hints towards this understanding of money and the community economy that inheres in mutual credit systems:

> Money [in the Sardex system] is a system of rights and duties. From the moment that I take from a community – as is the case in Sardex – I am

> in debt towards that community; when I settle that debt with the community, I have given what I have received. It's a beautiful thing.[58]

It is what 'I take from a community' that puts me in debt, and what 'I take' are the goods and services made available in the local currency. Symmetrically, for me to 'settle that debt with the community', I give 'what I have received'; that is, I offer goods and services and accept Sardex tokens in payment for them. The common resources which flow is regulated, taken care of, monitored and governed are the goods and services provided and appropriated by individual members. Sardex monetary tokens become simply a way to record the movement of those goods and services, one's account balance simply a visualisation of one's position in relation to the community; a creditor position when one has given more than taken; a debtor position when one has taken more than given. In other words, the Sardex monetary system becomes the infrastructure undergirding Sardex economic commons.

We saw earlier that the very mechanics of mutual credit monies implied a rethinking of money as a two-sided relational phenomenon, of debt as a promise to pay, and of credit as a claim upon the community. Here we see that it also implies a rearticulation of the goods and services individuals give and take as what ultimately makes the economic commons. In Málaga Común, we saw that the new thinking did not always reach the emotional level. Members of the local currency in southern Spain may have understood that for some to be on the plus side there needed to be others on the negative side, that their money was created when some agreed to be in debt and others credited such debt, and that central to the functioning of the community economy was thus members' willingness to offer in the local currency. Still, feelings of shame abounded, leading members to decline a trade. In Sardinia, brokers work to prevent the destructive aspects of the emotional disgust towards debt by, among others, requiring registration and annual fees in the official currency.

Upon approval of a membership application, the new member pays a one-off registration fee. There is also an annual membership fee ranging between 200 euros for small non-profit organisations to 3,000 euros for large companies.[59] Both the registration and the annual fees are to be paid in euros. While other mutual credit schemes do not require any fee – less so in an official currency – the Sardex team considers it sends an important signal to members of the mutual credit network; it is a way to coax members into trading in Sardex so as to make good of the fee cost. As one of the founders explained, the fee 'make[s] clear that membership entail[s] a small change in habits and that the member wish[es] to deal with this'.[60] The fee works as a strategy to induce traders to reach towards each other; it is hoped to act as an impulse to move goods and services through the Sardex network; a reason for the individual member to start giving and taking; an igniter to connect buyers and sellers and thereby assemble a local economy. And surely, the fees are, too, how Sardex covers the salaries of its much appreciated brokers.

'Buying and selling lists' as well as fees in conventional money set the boundaries of the Sardex community. They also incite members to the economic practices that nourish the network. Other rules remind members of the *symmetrical obligations* to give/offer and take/appropriate. Debtors have as much an obligation to repay their debts by offering produce to the network as creditors have to spend their credits by taking from it. Regarding creditors: according to the membership contract, positive balances that have gone one year without any expenditure can be withdrawn from the individual member's account. And those willing to leave Sardex though having a positive balance are given one year to spend their Sardex. The requirement to spend within one year rearticulates accumulated credit from individual wealth into idle spending capacity detrimental for the community economy. The requirement to spend within one year thus works as a strategy to compel trading connections that activate the local economy and make community.

As for debtors' obligation to pay back their individual debts to the community: if a member fails in her repayment commitment, Sardex's brokers look into the reason for the lack of payment. In the case of the death of the business owner, Sardex Ltd absorbs the debt. In the case of business bankruptcy, those businesses that have sold in Sardex to the now bankrupt business register the loss of that income without however getting back the goods or services they sold to the particular business. This practice is equivalent to the mutualisation of an individual member's losses. At times, Sardex Ltd has also absorbed the bankrupt business' losses. If, however, the lack of debt repayment is due to the member's particularly challenging circumstances, Sardex brokers help the struggling business to restructure its repayment plan. Finally, after one year, unpaid Sardex debts need to be paid back in euros.[61]

In the vein of keeping debt–credit relationships balanced, participating businesses are advised to sell in Sardex up to around 20 per cent of their revenues.[62] Not being convertible into euros – or any other currency, conventional or not – Sardex businesses ought to make sure they earn enough euros to buy supplies needed from outside the network, to cover utility costs and to attend tax obligations. This facilitates continued trade within the network. Further, the 20 per cent advised is a reminder that the stream of individual gives and takes – or, if you prefer, the communal web of gifts and debts – is kept in balance.

All these formal and informal governance rules notwithstanding, by far the work most appreciated by participants in the Sardex network is brokers' proactive 'knitting' of the trading community. For small businesses without resources to develop their own commercial channels, Sardex's broker team plays a crucial role. With an overview of all members' account balances and transactions, Sardex brokers are able to quickly single out those businesses that struggle to sell or accumulate without spending at the same pace. In those cases, brokers actively contact the struggling business to discuss their needs, suggest suppliers or put them in contact with customers. Further, keeping traders updated about new members and their offerings, Sardex brokering services actively contribute to extend traders' network and arrange economic exchange. As one member recounts:

> [S]ometimes my broker calls me and says: 'Look, such-or-such company has joined Sardex, have you noticed?' This means working together and offering me great service. I am an attentive entrepreneur, but I cannot monitor the 4,000 member companies to see who has joined and who has left. Knowing you can count on a person who calls you and tells you for example, 'Do you know that such-and-such stationery wholesaler has joined up?', is a great service. Or: 'Do you know you could rent this service?' This allows me to save time, expand my knowledge network, save money. If I don't have time to look through the list of members, I call my broker who gives me, say, six names. I get six quotes and I choose the cheapest one. … The brokerage service is crucial and fundamental within the network.[63]

In a monetary system that embeds the production of money into real economic activity, brokers' work at knitting the economy is more than an added service. Together with an imaginary of money as a debt–credit relationship, alongside a technological platform that mechanically records those relationships, and parallel to governance rules that safeguard the symmetry of the creditor–debtor relationship, brokers are constitutive of the Sardex monetary system. Actively connecting buyers and producers, brokers' relational work contributes to assemble the economy. Far from mainstream notions of self-regulating markets with money a neutral intermediary in market relations, Sardex brokers reveal that to be viable, markets need to continuously be brought together and money needs to be subordinated to the needs and relations of the community economy. With a comprehensive view over the flow of goods across community members, the central position of Sardex brokers is pivotal to assembling, governing and embedding the economy into the community.

A civil rearticulation of the money commons

Founders of mutual credit systems often start with the ambition to match excess capacity with unsatisfied needs, to connect the hungry person with the empty restaurant seat, to allow trade where working capital is scarce. A money designed along the principle of clearing overcomes the lack of connections between buyers and sellers due to lack of money by turning currency users into currency issuers who automatically create money when needed to complete a trade. Mutual credit systems work through mechanised credit creation and clearing operations. This may appear straightforward. Yet, as we saw, mutual credit monies need continuous and careful governance to be made to work. For any monetary system is a complex project, one that shapes and is shaped by imaginaries of money, constitutes and is constituted by members' relations to each other, frames and is framed by individuals' relation to monetary tokens, and configures and is configured by relational rules and institutions. Money, in other words, is co-constitutive of the community that uses it. Or, in Polanyian terms, when money's relational nature is acknowledged, *money acts as the infrastructure that helps embed the economy into society*.

Several lessons are packed into that insight. Unpacking the local mutual credit systems of Málaga Común and Sardex helped us unfold those lessons.

First, mutual credit money is relational for there cannot be money without a seller and a buyer, someone who gives and someone who takes, a creditor and a debtor. Constitutive of this relationship are imaginaries of money and debt as systems of rights and duties towards the community, an accounting practice – clearing – that distributes issuance and destruction of money to its users, a technical platform that records and visualises members' gifts to and takes from each other, and governance rules that insist on individual members' symmetrical obligations towards the community. Those are some of the non-human actors that make these local monies possible. But non-humans are not alone. Human actors are also needed for these monies to exist. Brokers' incessant work to bring markets together and the existence of a centralised authority with an overview over the flow of monetary tokens were key to making Sardex acceptable and thus to enact the monetary system. The ensemble of imaginaries, technical platforms, accounting practices, rules and institutionalised actors constitute money. It is in this sense that money is relational. It is made of a web of human and non-human actors.

There is a second sense to the relationality of this money. For money to work, for money to be accepted by a community, the relations that make it need to be continuously produced and reproduced. This incessant relational work is carried out by both the human and non-human components of monetary arrangements. Brokers' work may be the easier to observe. But a two-sided monetary design, platforms that visualise a member's debtor or creditor position towards the community, and rules that symmetrically sanction idle credit and unpaid debt do equally work to bring traders together and thus assemble the economy.

A third and last sense to the relationality of mutual credit monetary arrangements. The lived experience of creating money as one needs it transforms the way people relate to money and to each other. One is no longer anxious to save and keep something that is experienced as scarce and valuable in itself – as the commodity imaginary has it. With the possibility to create money as one engages in relationships of exchange, money is no longer scarce and one does good in relating to it prodigally. In Málaga Común members bought lunch from María and indulged in massages offered by a professional physiotherapist; in Sardex, they renovated their shops and went on holidays. User-issuers are 'able to do things [they] kept postponing'.[64] Conflating the roles of money user and money issuer also pushes processes of resubjectification. There is no shame in being a debtor, but a responsibility to give back to the community. One's willingness to trade transforms the sinful debtor into a catalyser of economic activity in the community, and the wealthy creditor into someone with an obligation to spend on the same community. That is, a money constituted through a relation of give and take configures in turn how people give and take.

Ultimately, the three relationalities of mutual credit money – money is made of relations; it is kept alive through relational work; and it configures the way people relate to money as well as to each other – articulate money as a commons infrastructure for the community economy. Created as a relation at the very moment of giving and taking, mutual credit monies become an arrangement that propels its users to give and take, to provide and appropriate goods and services to the community, to rethink themselves as stewards of an economy assembled together for the community by its members. Managed through unabating relational work, mutual credit monies impel its user-issuers to rethink themselves as communal members that generate resources for the community. They urge relational practices of commoning through which resources are offered to produce community. They nag its members to new economic habits that build on collaboration and engagement while maintaining self-interest. It is in this way that local mutual credit money is infrastructured by its members while itself acting as the infrastructure of the local economy. As mutual credit participants in one of these systems phrased it, 'wealth resides not in money, but in our healthy relationships',[65] relationships that are, in the last instance, constituted by the monetary arrangement.[66]

5

Tax It Forward: The Form and Reason of Municipal Money

The experiment was known as 'the miracle of Wörgl' for a reason. In the midst of the Great Depression, with unemployment figures soaring across Europe, businesses failing en masse, commercial banks reluctant to extend credit, and wretched public finances from falling tax revenues, the little Austrian town of Wörgl was, by all accounts, doing great. From 1 August 1932 to 1 September 1933, Mr Unterguggenberger, Mayor of Wörgl, paid for ambitious infrastructural programmes with depreciating money that circulated alongside the national legal tender. Inspired by the ideas of Silvio Gesell, a German-Argentinian businessman turned economist, Wörgl's new money was designed to lose value at a fixed date, thus incentivising its holders to spend it before it depreciated. During the 13 months the experiment lasted, the town managed to reduce its unemployment by 25 per cent, businesses averted bankruptcy and some even raised their turnover, the local savings bank was, once more, extending loans to businesses, and citizens were not only paying back past debts and tax arrears but even paying in advance tax dues in the future.[1] Roads, bridges and tourist attractions were built, drainage systems and street lighting expanded. The economic 'miracle' was readily visible to outside observers who pilgrimed to witness the experiment. A French observer reported:

> I arrived at Wörgl in August 1933, after exactly a year's experiment. It must be frankly admitted that we stand here before a miracle. The roads, once in a scandalous condition, resemble autostrades. The parish hall, cheery and smart looking, is entirely reconditioned and has the appearance of a lovely toy. A new bridge in reinforced concrete proudly bears the legend: 'Constructed in 1933, with free money'. One sees everywhere up-to-date lamp standards. Gesell, the little saint of the village, has himself benefited by the socialist burgomaster's loyalty to his principles: he has now a niche allotted to him. The workers engaged on

> the numerous relief works are all fanatical partisans of 'melting money'. I went shopping: 'relief money' was everywhere accepted, just as if it were legal tender. Prices have not risen. … When, towards the end of the month, an inhabitant of Wörgl does not know what to do with his 'money' which is about to lose 1% of its value, he bethinks himself of paying therewith his taxes. This alternative has not only led to the payment of the heavy tax arrears which had accumulated for years, but, what is unprecedented, to the payment of taxes in advance! … Here, the tax-payer does not protest at all. Indeed he enthusiastically favours the experiment and bitterly complains that the State Bank is attempting to stop new issues. This is because there is a general increase in well-being, the result of a new form of taxing. It does seem clear that, as the burgomaster claims, the new money fulfils its mission better than the old did.[2]

Tyrolese officials, opponents of the theories behind Wörgl's money, conceded that they saw 'a welcome sign of the revival of the collective spirit' and recognised 'its beneficial effects'.[3] Two of the most important economists of the time and possibly of the 20th century, John Maynard Keynes and Irving Fisher, would praise Silvio Gesell, the heterodox thinker whose ideas on money where implemented in Wörgl. In his *General Theory of Employment, Interest and Money*, Keynes described him as 'a strange, unduly neglected prophet', believing that 'the future will learn more from the spirit of Gesell than from that of Marx'.[4] Fisher would go on to recommend the issuance of Wörgl-like stamp scrip monies as a measure to 'prime the pump' and come out of the Great Depression.[5]

Neighbouring towns soon followed suit. By 1 January 1933 – a mere five months after the experiment in Wörgl started – the parish of Kirchbichel was issuing its own 'magic money' and four other Tyrolese municipalities had decided to do just as much. The invigoration of the local economy in the midst of deepening economic depression all across Europe attracted mayors from all over Austria and Switzerland and, in June 1933, Mayor Unterguggenberger held a meeting in Vienna with 170 mayors. All those present believed it was advisable to introduce the new money in their villages.

For all its popularity, Austria's central bank maintained that 'Wörgl broke the law'.[6] After several prohibition orders from the provincial and federal governments, on 1 September 1933 the office of the mayor withdrew the depreciating money it had issued. Wörgl quickly plunged back into economic depression. Though short-lived, the monetary experiment in Wörgl served as proof of concept of Gesell's ideas on 'free money'. And although almost a century old, the experiment holds lessons of relevance today. The first of these, often hailed by students of complementary currencies, is that it redirects the attention of monetary authorities from the quantity of money to its velocity of circulation. Two, it proves that in the management of public money, spending goes before taxing without necessarily creating inflationary pressures. The latter lesson goes today under the banner of Modern Monetary Theory (MMT) or, for its sceptical critics, Magic Money Tree. We will see the extent to which Wörgl's 'magic money' was a test of MMT ideas at the municipal level. Finally, the experiment in Wörgl teaches us the need to subordinate money to the needs of workers and citizens. Far from neutral and separate from society, money's infrastructural capacity shapes how we produce, exchange and consume and thus has an impact on the health of the economy and the fabric of society. As such, Wörgl is a reminder that money's architecture – how money works – and its governance – how money is made to work – need to be anchored into our collective institutions.

To start the work of unfolding Wörgl's scrip money, we need first to turn our gaze towards the challenge that moved its instigator, Mayor Unterguggenberger, and that informed its design.

Of flows and stocks: the contradictory uses of money

Most *Economics 101* books one gets hold of list three functions of money. Money serves as a unit of account, a medium of exchange (or means of deferred payment),[7] and a store of value. As a unit of account, money allows to visualise the economic value given to the goods and services so valued; it enables comparison of goods that would otherwise not be comparable on any other dimension. The fact that we use a standard unit of account to measure the economic value of, say, apples and shoes, is the reason we can compare those two goods. Having nothing else in common – one is a fruit, the other a piece of clothing; one is quickly perishable, the other can last years; once consumed, one cannot be consumed by any other person, the other can be reused by several consumers – they can nonetheless be compared in terms of their price. The visualisation of a good's economic value and the concomitant possibility to compare eases exchange and enables the organisation of markets.[8]

It is to the second and third functions that Keynes' and Gesell's insights apply. As a means of exchange, money allows to widen the networks of trade, to extend markets beyond small circuits of barter. If I am interested in swapping my shoes for your apples but you are not interested in my worn-out shoes, little will convince you to give away your apples for my shoes. In such an economy, trade stops when traders' interest for exchange is not reciprocal. Because money is *made* into the 'good' that everybody wants – we will later see one way to make money the object of everyone's desire – you would however accept to depart from your apples for money, for you are sure to be able to further exchange that money for shoes that you actually want.

In this way, money is said to solve the problem of 'the double coincidence of wants' inherent in barter trade[9] and 'grease the wheels of commerce'. In the parlance of economists, as 'a perfectly liquid good' money is universally accepted in exchange for everything else.

Money's third function is to serve as a store of value. Cautious of the vicissitudes of an uncertain future, we prepare for the proverbial 'rainy day' by saving money or other assets. Two traits of money make it a preferred venue to save in: one, its granted intrinsic value; two, its perfect liquidity – its ability to flow through circuits of trade; its perennial potential to be exchanged for any object of equal economic value; Menger's 'saleableness'.[10] That is, because we relate to money as a good with value in itself, and because that value can easily be realised in the market, we are inclined to stock money to brace for what the future may bring. Money saved promises its owner the ability to spend in the future; it allows the holder of money to meet expected expenses – our children's education, a bigger house, or the longed-for holidays – and unexpected contingencies – the loss of income due to sudden unemployment, an abrupt need to cover medical costs. As Keynes phrased it, money acts as 'a subtle device for linking the present to the future'.[11]

This is typically where *Economics 101* ends. Satisfied with listing and explaining the three functions of money, *Economics 101* evades expanding on the contradictory individual behaviours these functions require. For money to perform well as a means of exchange, the user of money needs to be willing to spend it, to *put it into circulation*, to buy so that the next holder can further use it for exchange. 'Your spending is my income; my spending is your income.' As a medium of exchange, money needs to flow from buyers to sellers and, again from these now buyers to new sellers. It is a function that rests on the interdependence between income and spending and that thus relies on people willingly and continuously entering relations of trade. Yet, for money to perform well as a store of value, the user of money needs to be willing to hoard it for its value. Its granted value inheres in everyone's perception of its preciousness, and thus on people's willingness to save it for another day, a behaviour that *takes money out of circulation*, stocks it up, and thus inhibits its performance as a means of exchange.

The contradictory individual behaviours the functions of money elicit are most visible in times of crisis. As expectations about the future worsen, individuals cut spending and, if they can, stock savings on the side. Sensing one's job is at risk, people stop dining at restaurants, postpone buying new gadgets, or decide they don't really need that gym-card. But what is rational economic behaviour for the individual works in detriment of the larger community. To illustrate the potentially devastating effects for the larger economy, during the first four years of the economic crisis that started with the financial collapse of 2008, some 50,000 small bars and cafés closed down in Spain, which amounted to 25 per cent of this type of small family business closing down.[12] Faced with the risk of losing one's income, Spaniards saved on the small luxuries of life – like the traditional mid-morning *cafetito* – slowing down the flow of money, inhibiting economic activity, weakening the tax base, and further worsening the economic crisis. No wonder politicians in Spain and around the world called for citizens to go out and spend. Keynes' insight on individuals' increased 'liquidity preference' – the propensity to hoard money – during harsh times is the monetary equivalent to Hardin's tragedy of the commons, where the sum total of individuals acting solely on the basis of self-interest results in the ruin of the resource system on which the community depends.[13]

The interest money accrues its holder exacerbates the tension between the functions of money in at least two ways: it entices speculation; and it gives money an unfair advantage over the goods it is traded for. Speculation first. Beyond precautionary saving for the rainy day, people also demand money for speculative reasons, for the financial advantage that expected changes in the rate of interest may bring the holder of money.[14] In this way, speculation effectively takes money out of circulation in the real economy and into short-sighted money markets. As more money goes into speculation, less money is put into long-term productive investment or used in productive endeavours, further hampering economic activity and further diminishing the level of employment.[15]

The second way in which the rate of interest on money increases the tension between the uses of money is by strengthening the quality of money over that of the goods it buys. In *The Natural Economic Order*, Silvio Gesell argued that the unequal condition of the wares to be sold in the market and the money to be used to buy those wares was at the root of economic crises. While items, from food to industrial products, deteriorate with the flow of time, the value of money increases in time thanks to the interest rate. To illustrate: to avoid tomatoes rotting in the shop, the merchant and the farmer are forced to lower the price of their produce at the end of the market day. Sellers are pressed to sell their wares. The owner of money, however, is compelled to wait because of the interest accrued on the money she holds. Interest-bearing money encourages hoarding and with it, Gesell argued, a slower circulation of money in the economy. During periods of financial stress, what is sound economic behaviour for the individual – waiting to spend one's money – further harms the community. The slower money circulates in a region, the more sluggish economic activity in that region, leading businesses to go bankrupt, banks to fail and unemployment to rise.

'Why', Gesell asked, 'must money, as a commodity, be superior to the commodities which, as medium of exchange, it is meant to serve? … In case of fire, flood, crisis, war, changes of fashion and so forth, is money alone to be immune from damage?'[16] The solution he offered went beyond the lowering of interest rates, beyond even the freeing of money from any form of interest. His solution was a form of negative interest rate. If money, he argued, was to depreciate like the wares it is supposed to buy, then both sides of the exchange relationship would be on a par. To prevent money from being hoarded and encourage people to spend, Gesell suggested charging a hoarding fee or carrying tax (also called 'demurrage'[17]). For notes to keep their face value, he proposed a stamp to be fixed weekly on the note, paid for by the holder of the bill. Hence the term 'stamp scrip' that the local monetary experiments of the 1930s received.[18] The periodic fee would make it costly to hold money, and thus would make people feel pressured to spend their money, just as producers are pressed to sell their wares – so as not to incur a loss. Gesell's suggestion was for a national money that lost 5–6 per cent of its value per year.[19] Irving Fisher would later advise a weekly fee of 2 per cent (equal to 104 per cent annually) for complementary monies of municipal reach. Such a fee would incentivise users to circulate money. It would also refocus monetary policy from quantity of money issued to velocity of money's circulation.

Velocity versus quantity

Both Keynes and Gesell were revolutionary thinkers. Keynes came to be the most prominent economist of the 20th century. Though fallen into oblivion today, Gesell's *Natural Economic Order* came to be reprinted in German several times, and translated to diverse languages already during his lifetime. Various English translations were made available between 1929 and 1934.[20] Keynes' and Gesell's suggestions spoke directly against the general laissez-faire spirit of their days and drew a path somewhere between British market liberalism and Marxist communism.

The dominant spirit of the 1930s was that the market, left to itself, led to full-employment equilibrium. Accordingly, laissez-faire advocates prescribed no state intervention in economic matters, deregulation of markets and free international trade based on the gold standard. Both Keynes and Gesell attacked such market fundamentalism[21] from the same direction: the equilibrium that the market reaches is not necessarily one of full employment. Markets may very well reach equilibrium at a socially suboptimal point where resources are left idle and unemployment is a scourge. Though using different vocabularies, both thinkers traced the reason for 'underemployment equilibrium' to the difference between *need* and *demand*: a man dying of thirst in the desert without money needs water, but deploys no demand. Demand for a good is not something that is given by the need or desire for that good. One may want something but, if one does not have money, that person won't exert any demand. Actual demand, that is, is given by access to money.[22]

A second point in common between both thinkers is that they traced the difficult access to money not merely to the quantity of money in the economy but – and herein lies the radicalness of their thought – to the slow circulation of extant money. Money was put to uses other than trade, precaution for an uncertain future and speculation driving money out of trade circuits and thus slowing down its flow in the real economy. Their solutions were attempts to speed up the velocity of money by inciting spending. Keynes' suggestions are the better known: in periods of crisis, monetary policies that reduce the interest rate in order to stir entrepreneurs into long-term investment, and fiscal policies that increase government spending into the economy. Keynes' are thus suggestions that consider the circulation of money while keeping a close eye on its quantity.[23] In contrast, focusing exclusively on the means of exchange function of money, Gesell's depreciating money related to the circulation of money alone. Keynes' solution implied state-driven management of the money supply and overall demand in the economy.[24] Gesell's solution implied redesigning the rules that govern the use of money so as to eliminate 'the superiority of money to goods'.[25] Keynes would praise such money reformers in his *General Theory*:

> Those reformers, who look for a remedy by creating artificial carrying cost for money through the device of requiring legal-tender currency to be periodically stamped at a prescribed cost in order to retain its quality as money, have been on the right track, and the practical value of their proposal deserves consideration.[26]

A clarification is due here. When telling of Gesell's depreciating money, there is always someone who regards it as identical to inflation. With inflation we already have a monetary phenomenon that decreases a currency's purchasing power, the argument often goes. Why, then, forcing money to depreciate? How is demurrage different to inflation?

The difference is vast. And critical for its influence in the monetary version of the tragedy of the commons. Inflation is an increase in the general level of prices in an economy. This means that it *affects everybody*, and that money ceases to work as an adequate measure of value. Demurrage, on the other hand, is a reduction in your account balance. This *affects only those with positive account balances*, those that accumulate more money than they are able (or willing) to spend. Prices need not be affected, nor the function of money as a standard of value. A demurrage fee charged to the hoarders of money aligns their individual incentives to the community's need for a smoothly circulating medium of exchange. This is not the case with inflation, for a general rise in prices does not discriminate between hoarders and spenders.[27]

The early 1930s in Europe were characterised by monetary disorder and social unrest. With unemployment ravaging the continent and countries devaluing their currencies in what became a de facto trade war, there was little access to money for the everyday citizen. Cities saw their tax revenues dwindle and the number of homeless rise. Not being able to count on support from central governments nor on expansionist monetary policies from central banks, some cities and private entrepreneurs took the issue of money into their hands. From the Wära in Germany to Hawarden in Iowa or Anaheim in California, these monetary experiments were local in reach and temporary in nature. According to some estimates, 118 local governments, 80 business groups and 60–75 self-help/barter organisations issued stamp scrip in the US alone.[28] In Wörgl, a little town in the Austrian region of Tyrol, Mayor Unterguggenberger put Gesell's ideas to the test.

Wörgl in 1932: unemployment and scarcity of money

Until the Great Depression of the 1930s, Wörgl, a town of some 4,200 inhabitants by the Inn River, had a bustling economy based on the cement and cellulose industries. However, what started as a stock market crash in the United States on 29 October 1929 soon spread throughout the global economy, with dire consequences for Wörgl. The cement plant, which had employed up to 60 workers in 1930, shrank to two workers by 1933. The local brewery fired 10–14 workers from the 33–37 it had employed only two years earlier. The cellulose factory went from 360–410 workers in 1930 down to four men in 1933, employed merely to guard the idle machines. The railway saw the number of employees go from 310 in 1930 to 190 in 1933. By the spring of 1932, the town of Wörgl counted 350 unemployed of which some 200, having seen their unemployment allowances from the federal government expire, were the target of municipal charity schemes.[29] Those with employment fared only somewhat better. Farmers – about a third of the population – had trouble selling their produce even if at depressed prices. Blue- and white-collar workers – about two-thirds of the working population – as well as small business owners feared faring a similar fate.

At the same time Wörgl desperately needed to repair its roads and develop its infrastructures. A local protest summed the critical situation: 'Wörgl, the worst of your vices is the pavement.'[30] But Michael Unterguggenberger, the newly elected mayor, couldn't count on taxes to fund such works. Declined production meant dwindling tax revenues for both the federal and the provincial governments. The first had fallen from 63,000 schillings in 1928 to 43,800 schillings in 1932; the latter had gone from 47,700 schillings in 1928 down to 17,100 schillings in 1932. With neither income nor revenues, people and companies not only couldn't pay taxes, but they also had outstanding tax debts with the town amounting to a total of 118,000 schillings.

With worsening public finances, Wörgl had to repay a mortgage it had incurred in 1927 to build the courthouse and a modern secondary school. The town owed 1,290,000 schillings – a mighty amount at the time – to the Innsbruck Savings Bank, whose interest rate had risen in July 1931 from 7 to 10 per cent and which Wörgl hadn't been able to find funds for, thus having an outstanding debt of 50,000 schillings from 1931's interests. For Wörgl, this resulted in empty coffers and the almost total suspension of operations of its local savings bank, the Raiffeisen Bank, as its assets, including those of the town, had been frozen.

The economic situation was aggravated by the disastrous deflationist monetary policy followed by Austria's Central Bank. According to contemporary observers, the bank 'reduced the total amount of notes in circulation from a yearly average of 1,067 million in 1928 down to 997 in 1932 and 872 in 1933'.[31] The reluctance of commercial banks to extend credit to the private sector further reduced the supply of money from 4 billion schillings in 1928 to 2.2 billion in 1934.[32] That is, not only were unemployment rampant, tax revenues feeble and public debt uncontrollable, but the money supply had been reduced by 45 per cent, leading to a debilitating scarcity of money in the economy.

Mr Unterguggenberger's experiment with depreciating money

Having lived through the economic crises of 1907–1908 and 1912–1914 as well as through the catastrophic hyperinflation of the post-First World War period,[33] Mr Unterguggenberger was disheartened by how poorly intellectuals from the right and the left alike understood the situation. Striving for social justice, he had joined the Social Democratic Party. Yet, while he agreed with the central tenet of socialism – 'freedom of exploitation of men [*sic*] by men' – he disagreed with the method promoted at the time – nationalisation of the means of production. Mr Unterguggenberger was also similarly critical of the social relief measures suggested by the middle class, from unemployment insurance and federal housing agencies to laws for the protection of tenants. These, he reasoned, did not tackle the underlying causes of unemployment, housing shortages and poverty. They were only palliatives that couldn't possibly change a system that led to economic despair and social dislocation.

In Silvio Gesell, Mayor Unterguggenberger found an analysis of the root cause of the depression. The trouble was surprisingly simple yet catastrophic for the overall system – a 'magneto trouble' as Keynes called the technical malfunctioning at the root of the depression;[34] a 'software crash' in Krugman's updated formulation.[35] The trouble wasn't to be found in workers' lack of competence nor in a reduced productive capacity. The economic engine was just as fit, '[f]or the resources of Nature and men's devices are just as fertile and productive as they were'[36] before the crash. The trouble was in the poor understanding of that engine, a 'colossal muddle, having blundered in the control of a delicate machine, the working of which we do not understand'.[37] For Gesell, as for Mayor Unterguggenberger (and Keynes), the problem laid on a muddled imaginary of money,[38] which could easily be tackled through the rearticulation of the monetary arrangement. Echoing the German-Argentinian thinker – and pre-scientist of Keynes' analysis in *A Treatise on Money* – the mayor argued money circulated too slowly and that interest rates had something to do with it.

> Slow circulation of money is the principal cause of the faltering economy. Money as a medium of exchange increasingly vanishes out of working people's hands. It seeps away into channels where interest flows and accumulates in the hands of a few, who do not return it back to the market for the purchasing of goods and services but withhold it for speculation. As money is an indispensable wheel in the machine of production, accumulation of great sums in a few hands means a gigantic danger for peaceful production. Every time the flow of money is interrupted, so is the exchange of goods and services, with a consequent fall in employment. Uncertainty about the state of the economy makes the owner of money careful, causing him/her to hoard it or to spend it reluctantly. He or she distrusts investment. Money circulation is thus slowed down, the turnover of goods and services shrinks and jobs disappear. Such a situation denies incentives to the population, threatening peace and wealth with destruction. Whole nations and states are under the threat of ruin.[39]

As soon as he took office, the 'mayor with long name' – as Irving Fisher referred to Mr Unterguggenberger – met with businessmen, farmers, bankers and local authorities, with workers, wives and the local priest, and organised them into Wörgl's Welfare Committee. He was not in search of charity, but after job creation. In coordinating representatives for a wide array of economic interests and from all social classes, Mr Unterguggenberger was after a broad support for a money that periodically lost value; a stamp scrip with a hoarding fee/tax (Figure 5.1).

Desperate about the situation in Wörgl and overcoming divisions, all members of the Welfare Committee unanimously accepted the mayor's proposal. In July 1932, the town printed paper notes for the value of 32,000 schillings in denominations of 1, 5 and 10 schillings. Twelve boxes, one for each month, were printed on the side of each note. For the note to keep its face value, a stamp worth 1 per cent of the note's face value was to be glued at the end of each month in the corresponding box. That meant

Figure 5.1: Front of Wörgl scrip

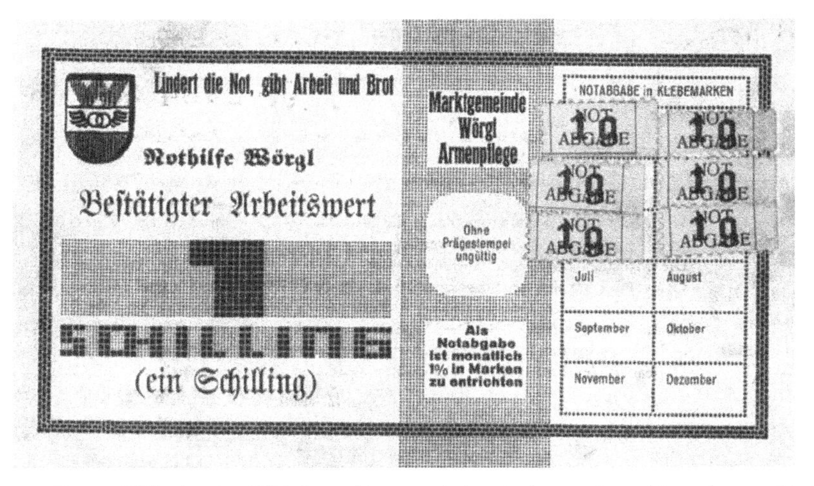

Source: Front of Wörgl scrip, 1934. https://www.mindcontagion.org/worgl/worglmoney.html

Wörgl's money depreciated 12 per cent annually, double the rate Gesell had suggested but much lower than Fisher's recommended 104 per cent annual rate. Stamps were bought at the town hall.

Aware of the risk that Austria's central bank would consider the new currency an infringement on its exclusive right to issue money, the new currency was called 'Wörgl Labour Certificates' and the stamps 'Relief Contribution Stamps'.[40]

The scrip was injected into the economy through an ambitious work relief programme. Workers coming from the ranks of unemployed received their wages fully in stamp scrip in payment for an extensive upgrade of Wörgl's infrastructures. The scrip was also introduced in the form of wages to the town's manual workers and clerical employees, even to the mayor – between 50 and 75 per cent of the salary of those who voluntarily agreed was paid in the new money.

As to withdrawal of the scrip, this happened in two ways. One, the town hall committed to convert Wörgl's currency into national schillings at a deduction/redemption rate of 2 per cent. Conversion was covered by trustees, among whom the parish priest, who agreed to back the new currency with a deposit in the legal national currency equivalent in value to that issued in local money. The Raiffeisen Bank used this money to grant loans at 6 per cent interest to local merchants in need of restocking goods from outside the region. The local bank offering this service for free, the entirety of the interest paid on such loans went to Wörgl's treasury office. Though witnesses suggest not much of Wörgl's money was converted into the national Austrian schilling, the mere possibility to convert seems to have facilitated trust in the local money. In the words of a clergyman, 'there was no doubt about security, because one knew it to be fully covered'; in those of the shoemaker, 'that way one had money for some maintenance … and one did not lose with that money because the municipality readily changed it back'.[41]

Taxes seem however to have been by and large the main route to withdraw monetary tokens from circulating in the town's economy. 'Before I was skeptical', the pharmacist avowed, 'but was surprised afterwards at how taxes were paid despite the difficult times'. Indeed, the possibility to pay one's unpaid taxes and other municipal fees in the local money seems to have been the main reason for businesses to accept Wörgl's notes. Figures are suggestive: in the first six months alone, 79,000 out of the 118,000 schillings in residents' overdue taxes were paid to the town, 90 per cent of it in depreciating money,[42] and payment of that year's taxes compared to the previous year increased by 67 per cent.[43]

The tailor in Wörgl nicely described Wörgl's monetary circuit. 'The workers on the maintenance projects begun by the municipality needed clothing. They came to me, paid with relief money, and with that I paid for taxes, lighting and water.'[44] Within a few days, Wörgl's labour certificates had circulated at least three times: first, from the town to the workers; second, from the workers to the tailor; and third, from the tailor back to the town. For a simple visual representation of how the monetary arrangement Mayor Unterguggenberger organised worked, see Figure 5.2.

On 1 August 1932, the first wages, amounting to 1,800 schillings, were paid out. They returned to the town's coffers on the same day to pay off old taxes. The town hall recirculated these in the form of new wages. By the third day, a total of 5,100 schillings of overdue taxes had been paid. The velocity exceeded initial expectations and, at its peak, 7,443 schillings were issued, barely one fourth of what had been printed. While Austria's

Figure 5.2: Wörgl's municipal monetary arrangement

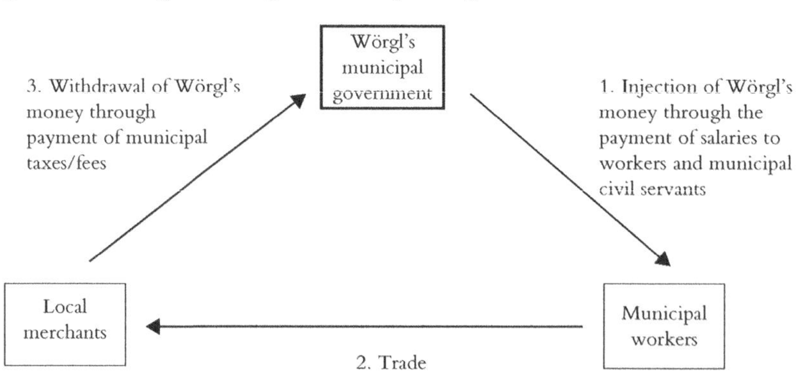

central bank kept 914 million schillings circulating for a population of six million – that is, 153 schillings per person – Wörgl issued less than two schillings per person.

Thanks to the new money and a grant of 12,000 schillings from the provincial government for the purchase of materials from outside the municipality, the town was able to embark on a far-reaching employment and construction programme. The road leading to the railway station was reconditioned and asphalted, sidewalks and 11 street lamps added; a reinforced concrete bridge was built; the inn was demolished and rebuilt elsewhere; several roads were widened and extended, the water reservoir was concreted, forest paths several thousand metres long were constructed and provided with some 300 seats; the farm roads were repaired and gravelled; the up to then inaccessible Aubach gorge was opened through blasting, the construction of an access road and the building of several bridges; the drainage system was improved; reparations of the town square and the mayor's offices were carried out; a new ski jump in the southern end of the town and a new water reservoir for the fire department were built. Observers attributed a noticeable increase in local tourism to such comprehensive revamping of Wörgl's infrastructures.

All in all, a 'ridiculously small'[45] quantity of local money succeeded in funding about 100,000–120,000 schillings in renovation and upgrading of Wörgl's public infrastructures during the second half of 1932 alone. According to critical observers, this amounted to about 7 per cent of the overall generated trade, which added up to 2.5 million. That is, once the mayor introduced the new money to pay for new works, Wörgl's certificates were spent rapidly, supporting further trade. In the words of a local merchant, 'I have clearly noticed the upsurge in business. I used more than half of these Bills to buy goods and other expenses.' The urge to spend also contributed to reduce the degree of private indebtedness. 'With official money it often happened that people who actually had enough to pay their debts let the merchant wait, just to cash in on the interest from the savings bank.'[46] The mayor concluded that 'private enterprise benefitted to the experiment as much as [public] enterprise'.[47]

Despite the increase in trade, no rise in prices seems to have occurred. Von Muralt, assisting the American economist Irving Fisher, travelled to Wörgl to observe the experiment first-hand. He witnessed no other price increase than the price of milk in a nearby small village was two groschen cheaper,[48] a fact he attributed to purely local conditions. During the 13 months the experiment lasted, the issuance of new money did not lead to inflation. Designed to force spending, Wörlg's money circulated rapidly, reinvigorating the economy and generating employment without the inflationary pressures attributed to monetary policies that, narrowly following some version of the Quantity Theory of Money, focus on the quantity of money issued instead of on its velocity of circulation.[49]

So stark was the rush to spend the new money that tax dues were even paid in advance, individuals thus reducing their degree of indebtedness towards the municipal office. As a contemporary observer reasoned:

> This eagerness to pay taxes may be, in my opinion, simply owing to the fact that the business man who finds at the close of the month that he holds a considerable amount in relief money, can dispose of it with the greatest ease and without loss by meeting his parish obligations. A change of attitude has manifestly taken place. If formerly the paying of taxes was deferred to the last, now it occupies first place.[50]

The mayor quickly reintroduced those taxes in the form of new wages, thus further contributing to Wörgl's economy.

The municipality of Wörgl was however unable to pay back debt or interests on the 1,290,000 loan from the Innsbruck Savings Bank despite the bank granting a reduction of 50,000 schillings in overdue interests. The mayor's refusal to pay back the interests of the debt was however in line with his ideas on money. He considered the level of interest (10 per cent) and the compounding of it 'a form of slavery'.[51] Instead, he found an ingenious settlement. The mayor forwarded to the savings bank various town claims, mainly a debt of 50,000 schillings from 1927 the provincial government had to the town for construction of roads; which, including overdue interests, raised to 70,000 schillings.

Modern Monetary Theory in a municipal key

Why was anyone willing to accept a money that was twice worse than the national money? Not only was its circulation geographically limited to Wörgl and its surroundings; its value was made to decrease monthly through the demurrage fee. Why were merchants, who could access the widely acceptable (more liquid) national money, willing to accept Wörgl's stamp scrip in payment for their goods and services? In other words, how was Wörgl's relief money made to work?

Brought up as a practical implementation of Silvio Gesell's ideas, Wörgl's money is most often discussed mainly for its hoarding fee/tax.[52] Such a fee effectively detached the local money from its store of value function, thereby facilitating its flow and enhancing its function as medium of exchange. A money that 'attracts a penalty when idle'[53] incites its holder to pass it over. While our established monetary systems comprise transaction-based tax that disincentives spending by making transactions more expensive, a time-based tax incentivises spending by making holding onto money costly. A hoarding fee – or carrying tax – charged monthly potentially fuels the continuous flow of money; it propels users to part from their money before the fee's due date; it drives money users to pass the fee/tax forward.

And yet, though the fee surely shaped the reception and recirculation of the local money, a hoarding fee cannot have been the reason why the money was widely accepted in the first place. Making money 'worse' (in the sense that it could 'only' work as a medium of exchange, not a store of value), such a fee restrains acceptance of the local money, and thus its possibility to work. We know for instance that some merchants were initially reticent to accept the new money even though they had the possibility to convert it into the national schilling. What moved them to start accepting the new money? Those that never accepted the money in payment for their services tell us a good deal of what in fact made the money acceptable – or, in other words, how it was *made to work*. The rail station and the post office, both government institutions with primary interests outside the town and *without any municipal tax obligation, did never accept* the local currency.

Taxes. Taxes made Wörgl's money acceptable.

More precisely, Wörgl's money worked because of Wörgl's residents' obligation to pay taxes alongside the possibility to pay those taxes in the new money. And this, in turn, was possible because the municipality acted simultaneously as currency issuer and tax enforcer. Taxes created a demand for the money those taxes could be paid in, and the currency was made available in the economy through the municipality spending it into circulation. The mayor of Wörgl orchestrated municipal fiscal and monetary policies to work in tandem – for these coordinate the flow of money in and out of the economy.[54] Mr Unterguggenberger put this relationship succinctly; 'new relief works were started, for it was found that the depreciating money issued for wage payments would certainly be returned in the form of tax and arrear payments by the time that the next pay date arrived, and would be thus always available for fresh payments'.[55] Municipal spending in conjunction to municipal taxes constitute money into a *perpetuum mobile*. Public spending and taxes drove Wörgl's money back and forth between the town's residents and the municipal office; tax obligations and continued public investment kept the stamp scrip flowing. The time set by the stamping of the scrip marked the rhythm of the *perpetuum mobile*'s oscillation.

Observe the origin and causation of Wörgl's money. Money was spent first, only to be taxed afterwards. Money needs first to be made available for taxpayers to be able to then redeem their debt to the public office. The accounting reason is clear: one cannot pay with a money one cannot access and so money needs first to be injected into the economy. The role of fiscal policies such as those implemented by Mayor Unterguggenberger is thus to spend money into circulation, to make money available to merchants and workers who can then further spend it to satisfy their needs and, eventually, return it to the authority that issued it. In the meantime, between the mayor spending the money into circulation and tax-payments withdrawing it from circulation, money has hopefully flowed through a variety of economic actors and supported economic activity. Wörgl is merely an empirical case leading to what Keynes taught us in *The General Theory*, that the direction of causation goes from spending to income, from injection to leakage (taxes), from (public) investment to savings.[56]

Having recognised the origin and direction of this form of state money, we have the conceptual and practical tools to enhance its flow so as to contribute to advance particular purposes. Concerned by the high number of unemployed, many of which had been idle for such a time they were no longer entitled to unemployment benefits, the mayor directed public spending to the creation of jobs. The initial spending was targeted to mobilising the (labour) resources that the lack of conventional money had turned idle. In that pursuit, Mayor Unterguggenberger embarked on a formidable infrastructures programme, which provided employment while building lasting public goods. Bringing fiscal and tax-raising authority together with monetary sovereignty, the mayor could productively implement counter-cyclical fiscal policy and facilitate the attainment of full employment.

Most empowering of all, all municipal spending was self-funded. Given Wörgl's wretched public finances, such extensive public spending wouldn't have been possible had the mayor not started to issue Wörgl's own currency. A condition enabling to spend first and tax later is that the spending and taxing agent also takes the authority to create the money it spends and taxes in. Monetary sovereignty is the prerequisite to self-fund locally adapted public investment.

Together, these traits of Wörgl's monetary arrangement – a government agent that issues and spends in its currency, can force payment obligations on its citizens, and can impose the payment of those obligations in its own currency – carve policy space for the municipality to actively support the local economy. When at the national level, such a monetary arrangement has been described as MMT.[57] As the case of Wörgl's 'labour certificates' shows, MMT is not so much a theory as it is a description of a monetary arrangement that coordinates fiscal and monetary policies in territories with monetary sovereignty. Along with MMT scholars, the 'miracle of Wörgl' advances the argument that monetary arrangements are not neutral, that they can be governed towards the attainment of the common good, and that there is much to gain from bringing the governance (including its issuance) of money closer to the territory which economy that money is to support.

A municipal rearticulation of the money commons

Historically, financial crises are followed by economic slumps. The Great Depression that trailed on the heels of the Stock Market Crash of 1929 is similar in many ways to the Great Recession that followed the financial collapse of 2008. Credit dried up, businesses went bankrupt, private demand from households vanished, banks had to be saved and unemployment exploded. Money-tokens ceased flowing. The economy, which had been working at full speed up until then, suddenly regressed. What starts in a malfunctioning of the financial infrastructure has repercussions across the gamut of economic actors. And yet, workers still have the competences, factories the machinery, and consumers the needs. 'We are as capable as before of affording for everyone a high standard of life', Keynes argued of economic crisis.[58] The problem is not the economy's productive capacity. The problem is simply that money gets stuck. Uncertain about the future, banks restrict credit, businesses wait on planned investments, households save – all these prudent and virtuous individual decisions that, in aggregate, have a negative effect on the social body. Individual interests, that is, are not aligned to the interest of the collective. A tragedy of the commons in its monetary version.

At the root of the misalignment there is a simple 'magneto problem' (in Keynes' words), a 'software crash' (in Krugman's update), a 'colossal muddle' as to how we understand the 'delicate [economic] machine' (Keynes again), a confusion in the imaginaries of money (in the language of this book). For an ambivalence structures our conventional money, that between money as an instrument to coordinate collective action – a means of payment – and that of money as a vehicle to store private wealth; between money thought as the record of a debt–credit relationship – a relational phenomenon – and money conceived as a thing with intrinsic value – a property phenomenon. Depending on what valence takes over, money will be put to work for either the community or the individual hoarder; money-tokens will continuously flow through economic agents or stock up in immobilised savings and speculative money markets; it will nourish relations of exchange or serve individual gain. When single currencies have to fulfil the contradictory functions of money, we end up in situations where the level of individual hoarding inhibits the coordination capacity of the money instrument, 'excessive saving … causing under-employment of capital and labour in periods of bad trade'.[59] That is to say, when one single currency system embraces inconsistent imaginaries of money, individuals turn towards the commodity fiction resulting in a misalignment between the individual interest to save and the interest of the collective to continue relating and trading.

Wörgl's solution successfully unstuck the flow of money-tokens in three ways. One, the fulfilment of the functions of money is separated into different currencies. The 'labour certificate' is used for spending, 'consumption money' as Jérôme Blanc describes it;[60] the national schilling for saving. As a result, the first can perform as a medium of exchange without harming citizens' capacity to save in the national currency. Two, adding a hoarding fee not only worsens the capacity of the local currency to act as a store of wealth; it also incentivises the user to spend it before the fee's due date thus further accelerating its flow. Third, public spending and taxing in the local currency pushes the currency in, through and out of the economy only to be injected back in again – a *perpetuum mobile* enabled by the underlying relationship of obligation between the community of currency users and the taxing authority issuing the currency. Spending and taxing in unison, both with uninterrupted regularity, ensured the perpetual flow of money-tokens through the local community.

Wörgl's rearticulation of the money commons into a municipal money requires a centralised authority with jurisdiction to issue currency and impose taxes. This is no different to the way MMT scholars describe how our conventional monetary system actually works. Wörgl's monetary arrangement brings however the MMT articulation of money closer to those which it is to serve. This facilitates the adaptation of spending and taxing to the particular needs and circumstances of the territory. It brings the governance of money closer to those who use it, hopefully making it more responsive to local priorities and challenges. As the relational distance between currency users and the currency issuer is shortened, money is more easily embedded into the community. The municipality becomes a central piece in the local monetary arrangement, as it itself both represents and enacts the money–society twosome.

The end of Wörgl's 'miracle' provides us with an additional argument in favour of bringing currency issuance and taxing in a complementary currency down to the municipal level of elected public officials. Despite its success, and despite the fact that the whole of Wörlg's population – from manual and clerical workers to shopkeepers, school principals, doctors and the clergy – supported the new money, Austria's National Bank deemed that 'Wörgl broke the law' and shut down the monetary experiment, the town swiftly plunging back into economic depression. If money is a relational arrangement with infrastructural powers for the community, then we need to subordinate the governance of money to the community which it so constitutes. In other words, we need to subordinate money to democratic politics. The proximity of municipalities to its constituencies make them an ideal level from which to organise the money commons.

6

HODL It Forward: The Form and Reason of Algorithmic Money

Today's monetary experiments are as much driven by a frustration towards the financial system as they are by an excitement about new technological developments. This double motivation is most apparent in the so-called 'crypto space', where much hope is placed on the blockchain technology and the cryptocurrencies based on it.

Advocates proclaim 'the dawn of a new revolution' powered by an 'extremely disruptive technology that would have the capacity for reconfiguring all aspects of society'. Melanie Swan, founder of the Institute for Blockchain Studies, argues that 'blockchain is in a position to become the fifth disruptive computing paradigm after mainframes, PCs, the Internet, and mobile/social networking'.[1] Alongside the novel technology, cryptocurrency enthusiasts ground their optimism in 'the bitcoin standard' programmed into the original blockchain. Blockchain technology enables moving the making of money from the bank system and 'into the hands of individuals', 'offer[ing] us the tantalizing possibility of a world where money is fully extricated from politics and unrestrained by borders', a 'decentralized, apolitical, free-market alternative to central banks' with an 'unstoppable and globally-accessible hard money' that abides to a 'stable' monetary policy.[2] A money without politics; a money governed by predictable algorithms free from the whims, passions and excesses of an elite of bankers and financiers. A monetary standard, bitcoin, that can overcome the troubles of 'the fiat standard' followed by our conventional monies.[3] Nothing more; nothing less.

These predictions may sound wild to the novice. Yet their advocates see them already unravelling in the ushering of a completely new family of startups. DeFi – decentralised financial technologies, many based on blockchain developments – has certainly emerged as an industry challenging the power balance of the established banking and financial actors.[4] Look only to El Salvador that, in an effort to promote financial inclusion, made bitcoin legal tender in September 2021 and is planning to build a Bitcoin City. The crypto-crash of May–June

2022 that wiped out 58 per cent of bitcoin's market value does not deter these bitcoin enthusiasts, nor El Salvador's president who eagerly retweeted Bitfinex's and Tether's CTO's judgement on the matter: 'Imagine in 1904 call Ford cars a failed industry because less than 1% of the population had a car. (First car produced in 1903) There are some that are brave and have a vision. Others live to criticize. El Salvador is brave.'[5] Their recurring mantra, 'just HODL and wait'. Other countries will soon follow suit. If not bitcoin, then any of the other thousands of cryptocurrencies may well become that stable global currency.

The disruption brought by the technology and some of the new cryptocurrencies is indeed reason of concern for many an economist and central banker. Admitting the potential of the blockchain, the European Central Bank (ECB) nonetheless lists the downsides of cryptocurrencies, from the privatisation of seignorage and the challenge to capital controls, to the facilitation of illegal activities and the unsustainable levels of energy consumption.[6] More high-pitched voices warn for the 'lawless frenzy of risk-taking' in cryptocurrencies, Ponzi schemes 'using an illusory narrative of ever-rising crypto-asset prices to maintain inflows and thus the momentum fuelling the crypto bubble'.[7] In a similar vein, International Monetary Fund economists alert El Salvador of the 'significant risks to consumer protection, financial integrity, and financial stability' that using bitcoin as legal tender poses.[8] Others seem less worried for, given their monetary design, cryptocurrencies have no chance to become an established medium of exchange – they are in fact no currency at all[9] – and the 'blockchain has no economic future'.[10] Suffice as proof the 15 years that have gone by since bitcoin's introduction into the world – an infinity in the age of fast-paced technological adoption. Still, these 'blockchain dreamers'[11] augur their monetary predictions are yet to be realised.

Whatever they may become, bitcoin and its sister currencies are provoking a rethinking of money, not only from actors inside crypto-land, but also from central actors in today's monetary field.[12] As Lael Brainard, member of the Board of Governors of the Federal Reserve System, phrased it on December 2019 at a colloquium organised by the ECB on the challenges to monetary policy posed by these technological and monetary innovations, these currencies

> are leading us to revisit questions over *what form money can take, who or what can issue it, and how payments can be recorded and settled.* While central bank money and commercial bank money are the foundations of the modern financial system,[13] non-bank private 'money' or assets also facilitate transactions among a network of users.[14]

So, what is all the fuss about? A neutral technical solution to our collective coordination problems, as crypto-entrepreneurs argue? A religion of liberation, as some economists contend?[15] The harbinger of an economy that is really free from entrenched power structures, or yet another craze in the latest variety of financialised capitalism? In this chapter, I will make no claim to being able to foresee the future, less so in what refers to monetary matters. After all, gold has had no practical use for centuries and its status as currency backing collapsed over 50 years ago; and yet, its standing in financial markets and its role in the monetary imaginary remain strong. Instead, in unfolding bitcoin, in looking at how bitcoin works and how it is made to work, the chapter unravels the connection between, on the one hand, the 'intended but unrealised effects'[16] that guided the technological and monetary decisions coded in bitcoin's algorithm and, on the other hand, its erratic development.

Nakamoto's intended effects

On 31 October 2008 Satoshi Nakamoto – the renowned yet unknown inventor, or group of inventors, of bitcoin – sent a message to an obscure cryptography mailing list. It contained a nine-page document with the title 'Bitcoin: A Peer-to-Peer Electronic Cash System' explaining a 'purely peer-to-peer version of electronic cash', 'an electronic payment system … allowing any two willing parties to transact *directly* with each other *without the need for a trusted third party*'.[17] Some two months later, on 3 January 2009, Nakamoto created the first block of the chain – the genesis block – containing 50 bitcoins and the message 'The Times 03/Jan/2009 Chancellor on brink of second bailout for banks'. Nakamoto's texts give us an insight into the monetary frustrations driving the invention.

In the White Paper and in the message inscribed in the genesis block, Nakamoto pointed to two challenges he saw in the existing payment infrastructure and that he intended to address with bitcoin. First, and most explicit in the White Paper, the mediation conducted by banks and other financial actors when we pay electronically – may this be with a credit card or through platforms such as PayPal. Second, and implicit in the message in the first block, the instability in the creation of money in our conventional monetary system, an instability that had led to the financial collapse of 2008 and to the need for the central banks to issue money on a hitherto unparalleled massive scale in order to save the banks.[18] The first problem was to be addressed with the creation of Bitcoin, the blockchain. The second with the mining of bitcoins, the currency. That is, the blockchain infrastructure went hand-in-hand with a new form of money. In remaking the payments infrastructure, Nakamoto was also remaking money. 'Electronic payment system' and 'electronic cash' are, in bitcoin, two components of the same invention.

'Mediation increases transaction costs'

First, to the most explicit challenge, that related to the payment mediation conducted by banks and other financial institutions. A good way to understand this challenge is to look into the recent conflict between two powerhouses, Amazon and Visa, over the processing fees Visa charges for credit card transactions in the UK. Now, I am no fan of Amazon – and the ways in which it squeezes workers, displaces small retailers and empties cities.[19] Yet, with its push-back on 'swipe fees', Amazon echoes Nakamoto's vexation with 'the cost of mediation [that] increases transaction costs'.[20]

So what is that work of mediation that Visa performs? Or, more mundanely, what goes on when you pay with your credit card?[21]

Imagine you go for a stroll and end up happily lost in a tiny, dust-covered, filled-to-the-ceiling bookshop. In one of the over-packed shelves, you find a book you had been searching for a while and do not hesitate to buy it. You reach to your pocket, take out your credit card, and swipe it in the terminal the book-seller puts in front of you – a gesture that was repeated 47.8 billion times by residents in the euro zone in 2020 to pay for items valued at a total of 2 trillion euros.[22] A routine gesture with a heavy economic weight. You wait for a few seconds – three, four, five – after which the terminal informs you that your card has been accepted and prints a receipt. You walk light-hearted out of the shop with the book in your hands. What happened during the three, four, five seconds you waited for the approval of your card?

While you waited for approval, the little terminal contacted the *front-end processor* – a platform that handles the authorisation of the payment. If you instead bought the book online on Amazon, there would have been an extra intermediary, the *online payment gateway*, that routes your transaction to the front-end processor. When you swipe your card or type your card number with your keyboard, you give your personal data to the front-end processor: account number, expiration date, billing address' zip code and the secret CVV code found on the reverse of your card. That information is stored in the magnetic band of your card. The front-end processor can then recognise what type of card you own, if it is a Visa, a Mastercard or any one of the others. It then contacts the *card association* and asks whether there is enough money in that credit card to cover for the book. Mark that it is not asking whether it is you who have the money, but whether there is money in the bank account associated with the card. The card association forwards that question to your bank – referred to as the *issuing bank* as it typically issues the card to its customer, you – and your bank makes sure there is enough money in that bank account. Again, the bank does not yet check if it is you who actually swiped the card. The bank acknowledges that there are indeed enough funds in the card's associated bank account, in which case it answers back through the *payment processor*. The payment processor is sometimes a division within the bank or, again, an external company the bank outsources its payment processing to. With the approval from the bank, the payment processor communicates it to the card association, the card association communicates the approval to the front-end processor and the front-end processor communicates it to the bookshop's owner through the terminal on the counter. You have now become the happy owner of the book. Observe though that no payment has yet been done. In fact, you haven't yet paid for the book you are already enjoying.

You may have noticed that when you open your internet bank account your most recent payments are coloured in a different shade. In mine, it is greyish. This greyish colour indicates that, though recorded in your account, the payment has yet to be conducted. It often takes two to three banking days for the colour to disappear. What happens during those two days?

During that time the front-end processor has accumulated a number of receipts owed to your now favourite bookshop. The front-end processor contacts the bookshop's bank – generically called the *acquiring bank* – to request payment for the book you are already reading at home. The bookshop's bank pays the bookshop's owner for the total of the receipts. Notice that the money has not yet been transferred from your bank account to the bookshop's bank. So having paid to the merchant, the bookshop's bank now contacts your bank and requests reimbursement. It is now that your bank checks that the person swiping your card was really you and not somebody else. It is at this point that your bank may suddenly contact you to certify that it was you who ordered the payment. You may have had a similar experience to the one I had when I first travelled to Kenya, an area of the world I had never been to before, and paid with my Visa card. A couple of days later I received an email from my bank wondering whether it was indeed me who had been in Kenya and used that credit card to pay for a coffee. This is my bank's antifraud team making sure that it was me paying for that cup of coffee in a Kenyan coffee-shop. When the antifraud team is certain that it was you who bought the book, it communicates so to the bookshop's bank. The payment is, however, not conducted directly. Instead, all payments made in both directions, from the bookshop's bank to your bank and from your bank to the bookshop's bank, are cleared together and settled by an *automatic clearing house*, yet another actor in the conventional payment processing infrastructure.

Let's take a step back and look at the whole payment process (visually synthesized in Figure 6.1). At least seven financial entities stand between you and your book (those marked in italics), six of which have access to your identifying information in your credit card. Each one of them demands a percentage for its role in processing the payment, adding up to total transaction fees between 1 and 3 per cent of every single sale. Amazon's argument with Visa takes aim at the charges going to the card association. But some of the mediation charges go to the banks, for whom payment processing fees are a major source of profits.[23] All those fees are charged to

Figure 6.1: Drawing of payment process

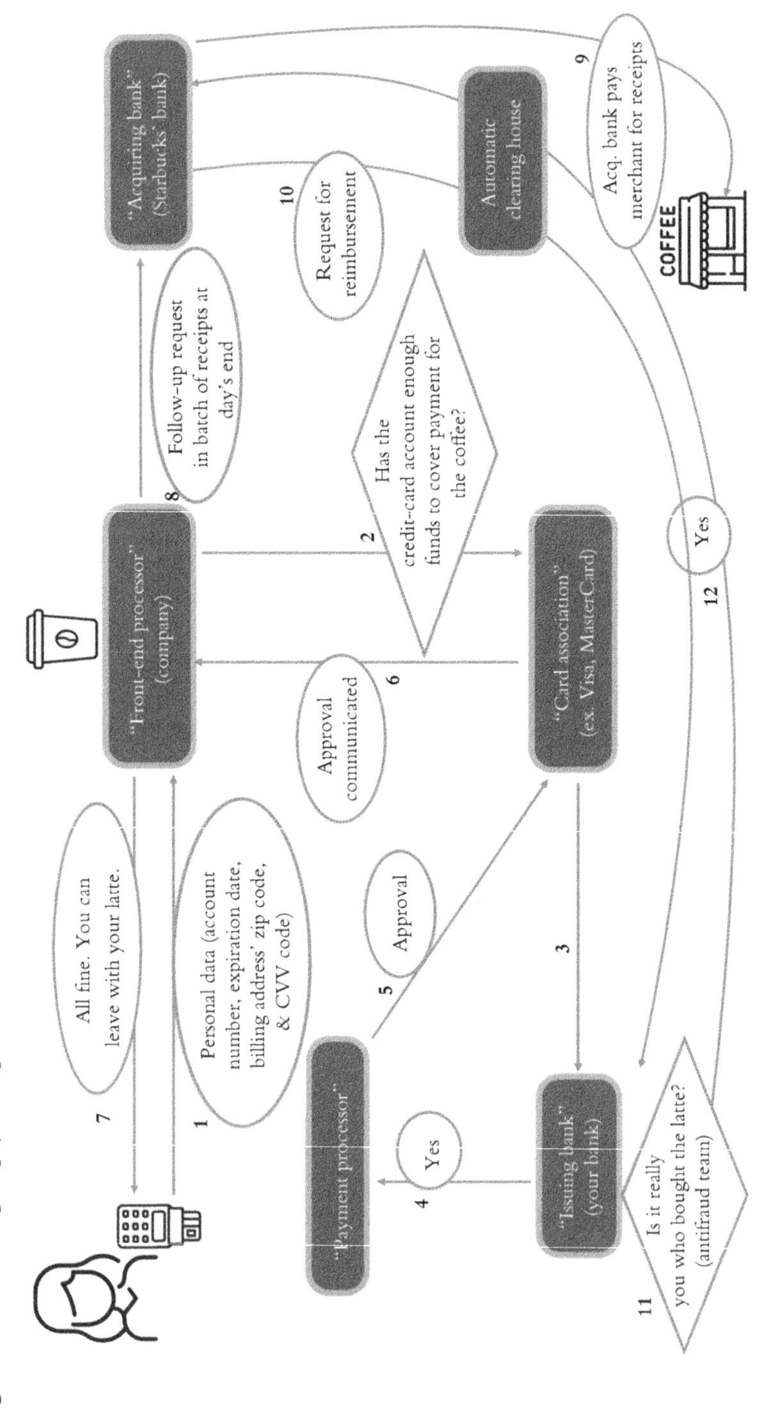

the bookshop owner, in addition to charge-backs the bookshop's bank will impose if a customer disputes a charge, depriving the merchant of both the money and the good sold. To cover its costs, the bookshop owner passes them to the customer through a higher price tag.

Other bank mediation charges are further levied upon the customer, like card issuance fees, checking fees and the interest charged to the millions of customers that don't pay their balances in full each month. Not to speak of the charges occurring when you buy your book when travelling abroad, in which case, there will be a host of other mediators to carry the exchange of currencies: Foreign Exchange Trading Banks and Brokers, Foreign Currency Settlement and Clearing House, and currency messaging services such as SWIFT. These costs will this time be imposed directly on you through foreign transaction fees, adding to the unfavourable foreign-exchange 'spread' between the price you are charged for acquiring the foreign currency and the price it costs your bank to acquire it. These costs can add as much as 7–8 per cent to the price tag, costs that are covered by you on top of those paid by the book-seller.

In 2020, those bank charges, card processing fees and foreign exchange costs amounted to US$1.9 trillion, 5 per cent down from 2019 due to COVID-19 pandemic-related lockdowns, compared to 7 per cent growth rate between 2014 and 2019[24] – in any case, a huge burden on the overall economy. In its recent challenge to Visa, Amazon is only taking aim at the fees charged by one of the various financial mediators in the payment infrastructure: the owners of card payment networks. The ECB similarly aims at card payment mediators – its concerns, however, go beyond that of costs to include the oligopolistic structure of an industry dominated by non-European businesses and the concomitant loss of European sovereignty in an infrastructure that is key to a market economy. As it writes in a report from 2019: 'Increasingly, payment service providers only issue cards from international card schemes. Such an arrangement calls into question market efficiency in terms of costs, competition and governance, as European payment service providers have little or no influence on the market's development.'[25]

Nakamoto aimed larger. The intention stated in Bitcoin's White Paper was 'to make payments over a communications channel *without a trusted party*'.[26] He aimed to circumvent all mediators: card associations and banks, payment processors and clearing houses, foreign exchange agents and messaging services. Nakamoto invented a technology that bypassed extant banking and financial mediators in a transaction. The radical disintermediation of the payment process: from you directly to the bookshop owner, from wallet to wallet, just as when we pay with physical cash. Only, with bitcoin digital; 'digital cash'.

Digital payment mediators fulfil important functions though. They may be expensive, have access to your personal data, and privately own an infrastructure that enables the provision of a public service. Yet, they ensure that the payment is safe, that the money is there, and that it is you and not a swindler buying that book. Being digital, there is also a need to secure that the payer does not double-spend the monetary units by simply copying and resending them to someone else – think of the ease with which you send multiple copies of the same document digitally compared with the impossibility of you and your friend holding the same physical book at the same time. These 'trusted third parties' Nakamoto wanted to do away with prevent double-spending. If he was to successfully dodge them, he needed to develop a system that was efficient, secure and trustworthy. A system that could guarantee the two questions the conventional payment infrastructure was guaranteeing. One, has the credit-card account enough funds to cover payment for the book? And two, is it really you who bought the book? Being digital there is a third question Nakamoto needed to address: How do I make sure the person sending me a digital token hasn't sent a copy of it to someone else? These are, as it were, the three questions Nakamoto's technology had to solve if it was to enable direct payment between buyer and seller, from person to person. How does blockchain technology manage to address all three questions?

Thus far we have understood Nakamoto's challenge. To understand Nakamoto's solution we need to understand two key concepts. The first one has to do with the imaginary of money undergirding the payment infrastructure. In the book-seller example, no money moved across actors, and even before payments were settled between banks, due payments in both directions were first cleared out. In our conventional payment infrastructure, money is a system of debits, credits and balances. The second key concept to understand Nakamoto's solution relates to where these debits, credits and balances are recorded. They are recorded in banks' private centralised digital ledgers (accounting databases, or accounting books when on paper). The banks act as mediators keeping copies of our ledgers.

Satoshi Nakamoto's solution involved moving from a system of centralised ledgers kept by private banks to one single distributed public ledger kept by a multitude of individuals. The network difference is best represented with Paul Baran's visualizations of decentralized and distributed communications (in Figure 6.2).

Image B represents today's dominant payment infrastructure where banks constitute central nodes in the network, each maintaining its own ledger. Image C represents Nakamoto's solution: one ledger maintained by many individuals. In the image at the centre, nodes represent private banks. In the image on the right-hand side, nodes represent individuals – or rather, Central Processing Units (CPUs) run by individual actors. In image B you see several centralised private ledgers; in image C, one single public distributed ledger.

Figure 6.2: Paul Baran's decentralised versus distributed networks

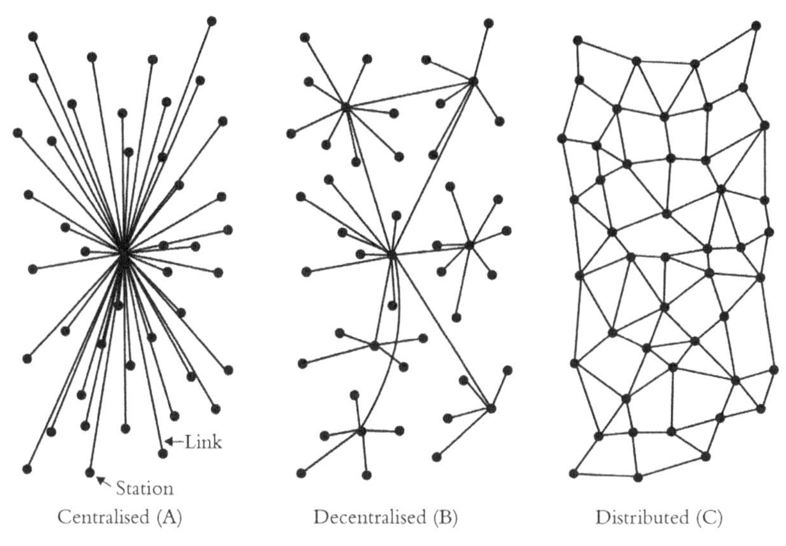

Source: From P. Baran. 1962. *On Distributed Communications Networks*. The RAND Corporation. Used with permission. https://www.rand.org/content/dam/rand/pubs/papers/2005/P2626.pdf

Nakamoto's blockchain is but a database of transactions stored and updated by a multitude. This is, in essence, the geniality of Bitcoin, and the locus of its disruptive potential on a scale similar to that achieved by the internet.[27]

In a lattice-like distributed network such as the blockchain, each and every node keeps a copy of the single ledger – the blockchain – containing a record of all transactions made. Further, each node validates new transactions and updates its ledger copy with the new validated and agreed-upon set of transactions. The result is that every node has an updated copy of the ledger,[28] making it very difficult, if not impossible, to tamper with the data stored in it. For a dishonest node or a malicious hacker to change the information stored in the ledger, s/he would have to alter all nodes at the same time. It is this specific feature that allows Nakamoto to circumvent financial intermediaries, for 'trusted third parties' are no longer needed to ensure the veracity of the recorded data. In the blockchain, the multitude of nodes and validators do that work. The distributed character of the network moves trust from financial and banking entities onto the network technology.

Apart from moving the locus of trust, another advantage of the lattice-like structure is that it cannot fall down. An attack on one node in a centralised network can be disastrous for that network. The messages that were sent to a node and forwarded by that node do not have another route, thus disconnecting a section of the network. In contrast, an attack on a node in a distributed network does not affect that network's capacity to continue connecting nodes. Messages are simply rerouted. Authorities may seize one or several nodes, but it cannot possibly seize all nodes. As Nakamoto expounded on in an email to Jon Matonis – an early collaborator – '[a]s long as there are users, it survives'.[29]

But validating transactions takes computing time. And energy. To implement the blockchain, Nakamoto had to find 'an incentive for nodes to support the network', a system to motivate individuals to contribute with their CPU time and electricity.[30] This is where bitcoin, the currency, came in. Validators would be remunerated with newly created 'coins' issued by bitcoin's algorithm – basically an algorithm to reward the infrastructural work of validating. To decide which of all validators to remunerate for each set of transactions validated – and put together in a block – validators would also have to solve a difficult cryptographic problem. The first to solve it – a process called 'proof-of-work' – would receive the newly 'mined' bitcoins, and the block of the winning validator would be appended – chained – to the ever-growing blockchain. When the energy costs of validating and solving the crypto challenge was to exceed the value of the coins distributed, Nakamoto foresaw covering the difference with transaction fees charged to the payer.

Nakamoto's incentive was however far more than a technical solution to a motivation problem. Sending new coins to validators was also more than 'a way to initially distribute coins into circulation'. Just as much – and above all for many of today's crypto-anarchists – launching bitcoin-the-currency was a pronunciation of discontent with the current monetary system. It was Nakamoto's solution to their/her/his second challenge.

'Chancellor on brink of second bailout for banks'

The White Paper does not make any reference to our conventional monetary system, nor to the monetary troubles that were unravelling in 2008 when the paper was sent to a cryptography mailing list. In Nakamoto's various written postings, however, many read a second, just as far-reaching and disruptive intention behind the creation of bitcoin. *The Times*' headline the inventor included in the genesis block is for many a rather direct cry of war against the tremendous issuance of money central banks were conducting in order to save private banks from bankruptcy. The message Nakamoto wrote on the board of the P2P Foundation – a non-profit organisation focused on supporting development of peer-to-peer technology – was more explicit:

> The root problem with conventional currency is all the trust that's required to make it work. The central bank must be trusted not to debase the currency, but the history of fiat currencies is full of breaches of that trust. Banks must be trusted to hold our money and transfer it electronically, but they lend it out in waves of credit bubbles with

> barely a fraction in reserve. We have to trust them with our privacy, trust them not to let identity thieves drain our accounts. Their massive overhead costs make micropayments impossible.[31]

A system where private banks could create money by extending credit at will and where central banks could further expand the monetary supply to save the banks that had created the financial chaos of 2008, could simply not be trusted. Beyond the matter of costs and data privacy, the issue of trust in the banks was problematic at the level of the creation of money. Able to create money at will, private and central banks were risking the value of the money they created and, Nakamoto seems to have argued, making our monetary system unstable.

Satoshi Nakamoto's solution was to eliminate all human factors from the creation of bitcoin money. He fixed the number of bitcoins that could ever be created, determined the rhythm of their creation, hardcoded it all into the algorithm and, with no other human mediation possible, let the algorithm do the work of money creation. An apolitical, trust-less, neutral mechanism was to control the money supply, which was set to reach the maximum of 21 million by the year 2140.

As they say, the rest is history. Bitcoin succeeded in attracting enormous attention. As of September 2022, there are 11,757 nodes providing their computer power to validate transactions and to process payments;[32] over 19 of the 21 million bitcoins have been created; and the value of one bitcoin hovers around US$20,000 (down from over US$45,000 in March 2022). As some argue, bitcoin has proven that the infrastructuring work of processing payments can be secured by individuals running their own computers and servers. In passing such a test, they continue, bitcoin and its sister cryptocurrencies have become a serious challenge to the oligopolistic power of the financial establishment.

Bitcoin has also failed ostentatiously. Over 15 years since its launch, bitcoin has yet to become Nakamoto's dreamed currency for small casual transactions. Instead, it has become an asset for speculators. Not only do the financial and banking mediators Nakamoto wanted to outcompete remain just as strong; a myriad of new actors have emerged that mediate payments in bitcoin and other cryptocurrencies: from cryptocurrency exchanges and electronic wallet providers, to cryptocurrency lending platforms and cryptocurrency remittance services.[33] Remunerating the infrastructuring work of validating with bitcoins has indeed, as Nakamoto planned, attracted actors into it; yet the increasing value of the cryptocurrency is associated with such an increase in the efficiency and cost of the validating technology that only a handful of investors have the resources for it. This has resulted in the centralisation of validation into a few major nodes and the concentration of bitcoins into a few hands.[34]

If bitcoin has managed to attract such remarkable level of attention, why has it then failed to live up to Nakamoto's intended dreams? Some locate the reason for this failure in the low speed of the validation process. With about three transactions validated per second,[35] bitcoin can't simply compete with Visa's 3,674 transactions per second. Another reason is found in bitcoin's massive energy consumption, currently comparable to that of a country like the Netherlands.[36] None of these reasons however answer why other similar cryptocurrencies, with smaller energy consumption and faster payment processing,[37] have not reached the day-to-day use bitcoin was imagined for either.

The reason resides in the two dimensions this book sets out to unfold in any monetary system: design of the monetary architecture – how money works – and its governance institutions – how money is made to work. I will be straightforward: neither bitcoin's internal monetary design nor its algorithmic governance are conducive to wide, daily, casual, common use. Indeed, it is these two traits that make bitcoin a phenomenon that is far from the apolitical, trust-less, neutral money that Nakamoto intended it to be.

HODL property money

'How does bitcoin, the currency, work?' – the book's first analytical question to unfold a monetary assemblage. How do the monetary design decisions Nakamoto took and hardcoded into the bitcoin algorithm shape individual use of the currency and impact on its systemic behaviour? How do the form of issuance and distribution incite speculation by individuals and price volatility in the system? And to what extent are those monetary decisions conducive to the non-use of bitcoin as an everyday medium of exchange?

Spelling out Nakamoto's design decisions on the internal architecture of bitcoin-the-currency:

1. the quantity of money issued is fixed;
2. released at a predetermined rhythm; and
3. distributed as property (an asset) to the validating nodes.

These design characteristics derive, as it were, from a particular political economy, one that disguises obsolete monetary ideas with a veneer of utopian technological disruption. 'Digital metallism', as some scholars of money refer to it,[38] naturalises an imaginary of money as a commodity which value resides in its very scarcity. Its effects – as we will see – are far from apolitical and neutral. From users, it demands trust in the supposedly inherent value of the currency as well as in a market that will realise that value.

Fixed quantity of money released at a predetermined rhythm

Asked for the choice of 21 million as the maximum number of bitcoins that were ever to be issued, Nakamoto's answer already pointed to the political effects of the choice. In an email to Mike Hearn, the pseudonymous inventor wrote:

> My choice for the number of coins and distribution schedule was an educated guess. It was a difficult choice, because once the network is going it's locked in and we're stuck with it. I wanted to pick something that would make prices similar to existing currencies, but without knowing the future, that's very hard. I ended up picking something in the middle. If Bitcoin remains a small niche, it'll be worth less per unit than existing currencies. If you imagine it being used for some fraction of world commerce, then there's only going to be 21 million coins for the whole world, so it would be worth much more per unit. Values are 64-bit integers with 8 decimal places, so 1 coin is represented internally as 100000000. There's plenty of granularity if typical prices become small. For example, if 0.001 is worth 1 Euro, then it might be easier to change where the decimal point is displayed, so if you had 1 Bitcoin it's now displayed as 1000, and 0.001 is displayed as 1.[39]

In choosing 'something that would make prices similar to existing currencies', Nakamoto points to a desire to hold prices stable. At the time of bitcoin's release, central banks of major economies were engaged in an unprecedented monetary policy that involved buying toxic assets nobody wanted as a way to inject money into the failing banking and financial system.[40] Quantitative easing, as the policy is called, resulted in the total assets of the Federal Reserve Bank increasing from US$882 billion to US$4.473 trillion (a fivefold increase) from December 2007 to May 2017,[41] the Bank of England buying £645 billion worth of bonds between August 2009 and March 2020,[42] and the ECB's growing from 1.338€ trillion in December 2007 to 4.7€ trillion in early March 2020.[43] Mainstream economists and those following a Quantity-Theory-of-Money type of reasoning feared the enormous injection of money would result in hyperinflation – or, as Nakamoto suggested in the P2P Foundation's blog previously quoted, in a debasement of the currency. Hence bitcoin's solution: to such fears fixing the money supply.

By definition, fixing the quantity of money in an economy means the amount of money cannot possibly adapt to the changing needs of that economy. Whether the economy requires new investment (and thus injecting money to fund it) or whether it overheats (and thus requires pulling money out), the supply of money does not budge. Nor does it respond to the potential growth in the number of people using bitcoin. Nakamoto created only some space for adaptation to an increase in the demand for bitcoins by programming a slow but predetermined growth in the number of bitcoins released. But as supply slowly reaches its 21 million and as demand dramatically increases with the increased demand for bitcoin in crypto-markets, the eventual adaptation is thought to happen through the movement of prices characteristic of free markets. 'There's plenty of granularity if typical prices become small' means that between 1 bitcoin and the 100,000,000 satoshi that make up that bitcoin, there is plenty of room for prices to move. Physical cash does not allow for such granular division. Imagine the shop-keeper having to give you change for one euro in those small amounts. With digital cash however, it is just a matter of the numbers recorded, and these are neither heavy nor do they take space.

This is a monetary design that completely relies on the idealised market mechanism where money is but a neutral instrument to communicate the value of goods and services exchanged. But imagine that, to adapt to the increased demand for money in a world with fixed money supply, prices did indeed accommodate. As the value of bitcoin increases in dollars/euros, the same good would have to be tagged with a lower bitcoin price tag. Instead of my book costing 31 satoshis (about 10€ at the moment of writing) like it did last month, it may cost 24 satoshi (about 8€) this month. This is what deflationary money means in practice. Adaptation to the monetary needs of the economy is done through prices. What a great deal for me!

Maybe not such a great deal. For I know that since the general level of prices is falling because there is not enough money in circulation to buy goods and services, prices will necessarily continue to fall. Which means that my book may cost 18 satoshi (about 6€) in one month and maybe 15sat (5€) in two months time. Expecting prices to decrease, I will postpone my purchase for as long as I can, holding onto my money, and thereby keeping it out of circulation. It is, that is, a monetary design that encourages individual users to hold it – or Hold On for Dear Life (HODL), the preferred idiom in the crypto world.[44]

This thought exercise was already played at the beginnings of bitcoin. Hal Finney alighted on the idea already on 10 January 2009:

> As an amusing thought experiment, imagine that Bitcoin is successful and becomes the dominant payment system in use throughout the world. Then the total value of the currency should be equal to the total value of all the wealth in the world. Current estimates of total worldwide household wealth that I have found range from $100 trillion

> to $300 trillion. With 20 million coins, that gives each coin a value of about $10 million.
>
> So the possibility of generating coins today with a few cents of compute time may be quite a good bet, with a payoff of something like 100 million to 1! Even if the odds of Bitcoin succeeding to this degree are slim, are they really 100 million to one against? Something to think about.[45]

No wonders crypto-enthusiasts take a HODL long-term approach to keeping their bitcoins – according to some estimates, 80 per cent of bitcoin owners have never sold.[46] The fixity and scarcity programmed into bitcoin incites currency users to hold it forward, to speculate on its future value. A monetary design feature – fixed scarcity – that unambiguously shapes individual behaviour.

Meanwhile, on the other side of the trade relationship, the book-seller is not only unable to sell the book today or tomorrow, she most probably is unwilling to sell it to such a depressed price. For she incurred a cost when buying it, and probably also incurred a debt she hoped to repay by selling the book with a margin. Selling the book at a lower price than she bought it would make her unable to pay back her debt. As the fall in prices is generalised, she has no other way to repay her debt than to sell goods and services she fully owns – even from outside her regular business operations. And who would buy them? If anyone at all, it could be those that have wealth and money to such a level they are unencumbered by prices going down tomorrow. Deflationary money, that is, implies a transfer of wealth from those who do not have to those that already have.

A deflationary design also implies that adaptation of the money instrument to the needs of the economy is carried through forcing economic distress and social dislocation onto businesses with small savings capacity – typically small and medium businesses. Nakamoto's answer to Sepp Hasslberger's suggestion to adapt the money supply to the number of nodes in the network indirectly suggests the burden of adaptation being carried by those that would be forced to accept fewer bitcoins in payment for the same goods:

> [T]here is nobody to act as central bank or federal reserve to adjust the money supply as the population of users grows. … In this sense, it's more typical of a precious metal. Instead of the supply changing to keep the value the same, the supply is predetermined and the value changes. As the number of users grows, the value per coin increases. It has the potential for a positive feedback loop; as users increase, the value goes up, which could attract more users to take advantage of the increasing value.[47]

In other words, owners of bitcoin see the value of their 'hodlings' go up, which means they can buy more with fewer bitcoins. That is equivalent to saying that those in need of bitcoin money – to, say, pay back their bitcoin-denominated debts – see the price of their products go down. As prices fall, so does their capacity to repay their debts, turning them into slaves of their creditors. I may walk away with a cheaper book, but my favourite book-seller may not be there tomorrow. Nor any other of my favourite merchants. As Krugman succinctly summarises the chain of effects of the bitcoin monetary model, 'hoarding, deflation, and depression'.[48] In focusing on igniting individual speculative drive, it seems Nakamoto ignored that deflationary money is unfitted to the task of aligning individual interests to those of the collective.

We may agree with Nakamoto's analysis of the discretionary monetary policy central banks were conducting to save the financial and banking system; we may also agree with Nakamoto's critique of the extractive fees charged by financial mediators in the payment process. But endorsing his solution implies encouraging a system which effects strengthen those very actors bitcoin was designed to weaken. Satoshi Nakamoto's analysis may be correct; Nakamoto's solution – the monetary design hardcoded into the blockchain – is destructive of the real economy and of the social relations underpinning it. It is a hardcoding of the tragedy of the commons.

An asset with no liability

In direct opposition to our conventional fiat money, the creation of bitcoin follows the reason of property. You either get it, or you don't – and nobody else has anything to do with the bitcoin you get to own. It is created as an asset which is no one's liability, a right to use it – most often HODL it – without anybody having a corresponding obligation to accept it nor earn it. One-sided money that only exists in the asset side of the balance sheet. Commodity money.

In Chapter 3 we saw that our conventional money was created as a debt–credit relationship. Private banks issue money the moment they grant a loan and deposit it in your bank account. That deposit is recorded in your bank account as an asset which brings on the bank the obligation to convert it to cash upon request. Central bank money – coins, notes and reserves – are similarly created as a debt–credit relationship where the coins, notes and reserves are assets to their holders yet liabilities – obligations – to the central bank.[49] Chapter 4 discussed Sardex, a mutual credit system where money is created, once again, as a debt–credit relationship at the moment buyer and seller conduct a trade; the seller's account records the proceedings of the sale as an asset while the buyer's account records them as a liability, an obligation to give back. Wörgl's money in Chapter 5 was of a similar nature; only, the liability associated to the asset materialised in the 'labour certificates' was only indirectly connected to these. Local taxes were the obligation that balanced the right to use Wörgl's scrip money. These are all relational monies, two-sided monies that exist simultaneously in the asset and liability sides of the balance sheets of distinct monetary actors.[50]

Relational two-sided monies connect creditors with debtors, contributors with appropriators, public (monetary and tax) authorities with taxpayers. The obligation associated to the monetary tokens so created works as a mechanism that instigates money to move, to circulate, if only to respond to that genesis obligation. On someone's ledger there is a recorded liability that needs to be attended, and thus an incentive to accept that money in payment for one's goods and services if only enough to attend the liability incurred. As the asset side has no other value than that of the goods and services it can buy in the real economy or the local taxes it can requite, creditors' incentive is to spend it forward on those goods, services and taxes. Relational monies, that is, build into their very architecture a *perpetuum mobile* mechanism.

A *perpetuum mobile* is altogether absent in bitcoin. Nowhere is there in bitcoin a mechanism triggering holders to move their money, to spend it forward. Bitcoin is 'mined' and given to the 'miner' as property. No one else but the lucky node is related to that newly minted bitcoin token. At the moment of creation, no one incurs an obligation to return it, nor to accept it in payment for anything. Without a built-in Maussian obligation to give, take and reciprocate,[51] and with no tax obligation within its system, bitcoin provokes an extreme form of Keynesian liquidity preference. Without *perpetuum mobile* designed into the monetary assemblage, nothing to induce circulation of the currency.

In fact, without *perpetuum mobile*, no currency at all. Just an asset. Etymology can help us here. 'Currency' comes from the latin *currens*, the present participle of the verb *currere*, 'to run, move quickly'. The function of money to serve as a means of exchange requires, as we saw in Chapter 5, that money circulates. Without it moving, nothing that *currens*, and thus no currency. With the HODL mentality induced by a deflationary money alongside the lack of a built-in mechanism to provoke its flow, all we have left is a store of value function. As such, it may perform better or worse, but left to its own devices, deflationary property money certainly won't work for the 'small casual transactions' Nakamoto intended bitcoin to support.

In this, bitcoin is comparable to gold, a preferred money imaginary of Nakamoto and crypto-followers. Gold and bitcoin share a number of traits: the final supply is fixed, either by the natural world or by the man-made algorithm; addition of the quantity supplied is slow and determined by the labour of miners, either humans or machines; their creation is exogenous to the network of transactions they are meant to support and thus, both gold and bitcoin dissociate money creation from relations of production. Both are created as assets that are no one's liability. And neither flow to support the real economy; rather, they are stocked mainly for financial gamble. Neither a currency, both financial assets serving no other interests than those of individual speculators.

In the name of financial and monetary 'stability', Nakamoto adhered to an obsolete gold mentality – a 'barbarous relic' as Keynes phrased it[52] – that translates 'stability' into monetary rigidity – an 'inelastic' money supply as economists would phrase it. Such a gold imaginary means flexibility comes not from the supply of money ('the printing press' has been algorithmically fixed), but from an adjustment in the value of money, which translates into an adjustment in prices – first those of goods, soon after those of labour. In other words, merchants and workers take the toll of keeping the money supply hardcoded. Further, created as property dissociated from any relation of production is tantamount to disembedding money from the productive economy. In other words, this is a monetary arrangement that is unable to serve the economy and, by extension, the community and social relations that make the economy. Instead, merchants and workers, social relations and communities are put at the service of money – and the moneyed interests.[53]

At the risk of being overly explicit, in the form of its internal architecture, bitcoin money is far from apolitical and neutral. If bitcoin 'becomes the dominant payment system in use throughout the world' its programmers dreamt of, its hardcoded Quantity-Theory-of-Money mentality would have far-reaching economic, social and political consequences. Deflationary property money hides a sociopolitical totality that precipitates the concentration of digital and material wealth into the hands of the few, turns everyday citizens into the slaves of creditors, and potentially destructs the productive capacity of the economy.

Governing the algorithm

Well, some argue, if the root to the low acceptance of bitcoin for small everyday transactions is located in the rules coded in the algorithm, why not simply recode it? It is just about enabling adaptation of the money supply to the number of nodes in the network, as Sepp Hasslberger argued in an email to Satoshi Nakamoto.[54] Bitcoin money may be governed by the algorithm – Lessing's 'code is law'[55] – but the code could certainly be continuously updated to fit the changing circumstances of its growing user base. This leads us to the book's second question to any monetary arrangement: How is it made to work? Or, adapted to algorithmic monies: How is the algorithm upgraded and maintained?

In 2015 a seemingly insignificant technological disagreement on the size of the blocks of bitcoin-the-blockchain divided the bitcoin community. The division was so sharp and virulent that some described it as a 'civil war'.

The dispute and its subsequent resolution tell a good deal of the invisible dynamics of governing the algorithm.[56]

Block size has been an issue of concern as far back as 2010, when Nakamoto set the limit to one Megabyte. With relentless increase in the number of transactions in bitcoin, the size of the blocks became the object of heated contention that eventually led to hostility, threats, censorship and ostracism towards some of the original members of the bitcoin community. The size of a block determines how many transactions can be stored on the block. The rhythm to which blocks are appended to the blockchain is set by the rhythm to which bitcoins are programmed to be created and distributed, every ten minutes. By 2015, the dual limit to block creation – in time and size – was causing a long queue of transactions awaiting validation, thereby prolonging validating time at random from ten minutes to several hours and increasing transaction fees above those charged by credit cards. If the system aimed to become a real alternative to financial mediators such as Visa – as Nakamoto had suggested in the White Paper – it most certainly needed to perform better.

A few of the Bitcoin core developers suggested increasing the block size. The technical argument was that larger blocks would enable processing more transactions per second. With small blocks, users are required to pay transaction fees for nodes to prioritise confirmation of that transaction. Following the surge in the number of bitcoin users and transactions, transaction fees were rising sharply, arresting global adoption and thwarting the possibility of bitcoin becoming a currency for small casual exchanges. A small block size limit was impinging on the capacity of bitcoin to scale up.

Opponents contended that larger blocks would prompt centralisation of the network. More computer power would be needed to complete the work of validation, thereby deterring many from validating and potentially concentrating the infrastructuring work into a few well-funded nodes with the capacity to invest in the necessary equipment. Smaller blocks make it cheaper to run a node, and thus ensured that smaller validators could run full nodes, increasing the number of people conducting validation work and, through that, strengthening security in the network. A large block size would risk the distributed nature of the network and with it, Satoshi Nakamoto's original intention.

In short, if the community aimed to become global, it needed to shorten the validating time – technically, this translated to larger blocks. If the community instead aimed to remain secure, it needed to make sure as many nodes as possible contributed to the validation work – technically, this translated to smaller blocks. From the technological perspective, a scalability versus security debate. Stalemate.

In 2010, Satoshi Nakamoto had singlehandedly decided on, and coded, the block size limit. But in 2015, the inventor was not there to resolve the conflict. Nakamoto had vanished on December 2010 to 'ventur[e] into more complex ideas' and transferred control over the source code repository to Gavin Andresen – a main contributor to the bitcoin code since its beginnings. Not wanting to become the sole leader of such a project, Andresen shared control over the code with four other developers – Pieter Wuille, Wladimir van der Laan, Gregory Maxwell and Jeff Garzik. The team of five came to be known as the 'core developers'. A couple of years later, in 2012, the Bitcoin Foundation[57] was created to act as the institution that could speak on behalf of the bitcoin community. With no single figure making decisions, with no 'benevolent dictator' guiding the community, the contentious decision would have to be solved via the tiny group of core developers and debated through the Bitcoin Foundation.

But the technical disagreement cut across the team. Gavin Andresen supported increasing the block size; Gregory Maxwell claimed larger blocks would compromise decentralisation and thus security in the network and trust in the technology. Meanwhile the number of bitcoin transactions was steadily increasing, blocks more frequently edging the limit of transactional data, with consequent delays in the processing of transactions and growing transaction fees. It did not take long before an online statement signed by major mining (validating) pools[58] was requesting the introduction of blocks eight Megabytes in size.

In an effort to overcome the stalemate, on 16 August 2015, Gavin and Mike Hearn – another early contributor to the bitcoin code – activated the Bitcoin Improvement Proposal (BIP 101) implementing a vote process on the issue. Practically, voting was to be done by miners opting (or not) for the newly introduced Bitcoin XT which had a block size limit of 8 Megabytes. Upon 75 per cent of the miners moving onto Bitcoin XT, the BIP 101 would activate, adjusting bitcoin rules to allow bigger blocks and hard-forking the blockchain.[59]

The second half of 2015 saw the bitcoin community viciously divided against itself. Those in the big-blockers faction testified to systematic censorship of any of their posts defending Bitcoin XT in bitcoin.org – the official Bitcoin website run by the Bitcoin Foundation – as well as in the two largest community forums – Reddit and Bitcointalk.org. Even Coinbase, the leading bitcoin startup in the United States, was removed from the bitcoin.org website for its support for Bitcoin XT and received a 'denial of service' attack that forced it offline for several hours. Miners reported suffering targeted attacks upon adopting the new bitcoin software.[60] Mike Hearn and Gavin Andresen – the developers proposing the vote – were accused of forcing a 'tyranny of the majority' and 'democratically coerc[ing]' bitcoin users[61] – a startling oxymoron that reveals more about the accuser's approach to democracy, power and governance than about the accused.

Though Bitcoin XT initially garnered support from miners, with over 1,000 of them running the software in the late summer of 2015, they soon abandoned it. It is unclear why Bitcoin XT failed to assemble enough support. Censorship, cyber attacks on big-blockers and miners' fear of the conflict lowering confidence in bitcoin and thus its price – the moneyed interests – have been argued to have played their role. Yet, though Bitcoin XT was abandoned, other efforts to increase the block size followed quickly – Bitcoin Classic and Bitcoin Unlimited – Bitcoin Cash eventually making it in 2017. And today, though the size limit of blocks in the original bitcoin remains, the technical challenges have been temporarily circumvented through Segregated Witness, an off-chain solution that decreases the amount of transactional data stored in blocks and thus enables more transactions to be stored in each block.[62]

The incident speaks volumes about how algorithmic money such as bitcoin is made to work; it tells about what De Filippi and Loveluck call 'the invisible politics of bitcoin'.[63] It tells of a money that is governed by a a few self-named expert technical developers, some of whom have questionable views on democratic decision-making. Far from Nakamoto's utopia of a self-governing money free of social and political relations, bitcoin epitomises money's sociotechnical nature. An engineer's dream of a driver-less money blatantly ignores that someone has to continuously make decisions about the self-driving technology. Both the outcome of those decisions and how they are made are socially and politically loaded.

So yes, bitcoin may indeed be created free from the political interventions of central bankers; yes, it may indeed be exempt of the need to trust established financial mediators. But neither of those detachments makes it apolitical nor trust-less. What bitcoin-the-blockchain has achieved is simply a shift in where politics and trust are located. In bitcoin, and algorithmic monies more generally, political impulses and the need to trust have moved from central and private bankers to developers and their code. Instead of a financial elite taking decisions on the money supply and the payments infrastructure, we got a much smaller tech-caste hardcoding decisions on the same. Neither of them, neither the financial elite nor the tech-caste, have the real economy and the communities making it at the heart of their monetary doings.

A privatised articulation of an intended money commons

It is easy to sympathise with Satoshi Nakamoto's original intention. The economic crisis that reverberated in the aftermath of the financial collapse of 2008 left many unemployed, without homes, and with unpayable debts.

At the epicentre of the economic disaster were the financial and banking actors that had lent money into existence 'in waves of credit bubbles'.[64] Despite that, central banks were being forced to feed the culprits with repeated rounds of massive asset purchasing programmes – an improvised non-standard monetary policy that came to be named 'quantitative easing'. Austerity measures were imposed soon after as central banks demanded governments to return the debt they had incurred to save the financial and banking sector. And austerity measures, with cuts to funding of welfare benefits and public services, eroded the already degraded public commons, further impoverishing the many.[65] The Occupy movement, with its demands for socioeconomic justice for the 99 per cent, emerged as a popular response. Though austerity policies or Occupy had not yet happened when Nakamoto launched bitcoin into the world, the anger that pervaded among the many helps explain why many joined the pseudonymous inventor's crusade to do away with banks and financial mediators. If they were 'too big to fail', the reasoning went, then we'll need to make do without them.

From a commons perspective, it is far more difficult to agree with Satoshi Nakamoto's solution. If nothing else, because after 15 years it has utterly failed to deliver on its double promise of a commons payment infrastructure running a currency that can be casually used for everyday transactions. Beyond the intended effects that never happened, there are signs of unintended consequences that are outright dangerous. During the pandemic, a bitcoin fever put many in the situation of potentially unpayable debts, exactly the same situation that led to the 2008 debacle. For Fear Of Missing Out[66] on the exponential rise of bitcoin's price, a growing number of young unexperienced investors put their meagre savings as well as rolled over credit card debt to buy the crypto-asset.[67] Dwellers in the slums of Kenya and residents in the marginalised suburbs of major Western cities told me with excitement of their latest crypto-investment, which they acquired with borrowed money. They are being told to buy and HODL for the long-term and to ignore bitcoin's volatility in the meantime,[68] instigating a behaviour that is at the root of bitcoin's very failure to act as a currency for everyday exchanges. Because, why would they use it to buy and loose out on the potential to 'get rich off this'?!

The 'intended effects' that never realised did however shape bitcoin monetary configuration and, with it, the behaviour it induces on individuals. First, the currency. With an intent to avoid ad-hoc monetary policies, Nakamoto took those monetary decisions and coded them into the algorithm. The ambition was to leave the creation of a predetermined quantity of money to the algorithm. No possibility for any human entity – central bank, private bank, or other – to intrude. Fixed money supply. But rigidity in the money supply implies the adaptability to accommodate a growing number of users inevitably comes through variation in the market value of this currency. And so, we see bitcoin's price grow alongside the number of HODLers. The increasing market value of bitcoin translates into, first, decreasing prices nominated in bitcoin (fewer bitcoins/satoshis are needed to buy the same amount of goods and services) and, second, speculative behaviour of those getting into the system (buy and hold onto bitcoin to get on the price rally). Both decreasing prices of goods nominated in bitcoin (deflation) and the speculative motive steadily drive individual owners of bitcoin to remove the cryptocurrency from circulating in the real economy, hampering its ability to act as a medium of exchange. In other words, individual interests are not aligned to the collective need for a means of exchange. A seemingly neutral monetary decision – fixing the monetary supply – with fierce political effects – individual speculative desires are prioritised over the social good. The monetary version of the tragedy of the commons is hardcoded into the Bitcoin algorithm.

Second, the payment infrastructure. With an intent to detach the payment process from financial mediators, Nakamoto distributed the infrastructural work of validation to a collection of nodes. But nodes are made of servers ruled by the algorithm, and servers and algorithms need investment, maintenance and upgrading, all of which involve people, relations and negotiations. And when there is money to gain, as in bitcoin, competition drives petty investors out, concentrating the work of infrastructuring into a few nodes with financial muscle. In what concerns upgrading of the algorithm, few have the sort of technological expertise needed to do the coding, once again concentrating infrastructural development work into a tech elite that have shown no tolerance for democracy. It may be open to any to start a node or take part of the code, but with such financial, technical and democratic entry barriers, the articulation of bitcoin-the-infrastructure is trusted to, and privatised into, the hands of a tiny few. There is a good dose of sociality – and with it of politics – even in the supposedly most automatic of technologies.

Succinctly, bitcoin's inability to deliver on its intended effects – serve as cash for small casual transactions and disintermediate the payment process – hinges on a series of conceptual confusions driving its design. It confuses money for property, currency for asset, stability for rigidity, predetermination for apolitical, and disintermediation for trust-less-ness. A gold imaginary undergirds this muddled web of notions. The money imaginary of gold translates into property money that prompts its users to hold it as an asset, for its value is supposed to reside in its scarcity (rigidity) which is determined (by nature if gold, by the algo if bitcoin) previous and independently of any trusted third party.[69] But property money is by design detached from the relations of production and dissociated from any obligation to reciprocate, and so, it has no built-in mechanism – no *perpetuum mobile* – to force its movement into and through the economy.

Probably the most important lesson we can draw from the bitcoin experiment is that we cannot design society out of money; nor is it possible to govern money through automatic pilot. More directly, money is always organised which involves politics, social practices and cultural imaginaries. Contrary to the arguments of their supporters, bitcoin-like money does not manage to extricate money from a network of financial mediators, political institutions and cultural imaginaries. Rather, bitcoin-like monies *re-embed* money into a different assemblage of mediators, institutions and cultural assumptions. As the sociotechnical infrastructure of the economy that money is, money is necessarily designed and governed, and ineluctably requires continued adaptation to the community it is to serve. If we want to reclaim, reimagine and reorganise money for a sustainable and inclusive future, then, we need to put social relations and political institutions at the heart of the new money arrangements.

The persistence of the gold imaginary into the new crypto-monies is rooted on the seductive idea of a money free from power and politics. This is understandable; yet blind to the social, relational and political nature of money. Utopian calls for autopilot neutral money are bound to end up expanding the scope of politics. The twin questions of 'what rules are designed into the money' and 'who those rules are made to serve' will continue to be central regardless of the technology supporting the monetary assemblage.

INTERLUDE 2

Perpetuum Mobile

'How do we make it work?' ask many a money entrepreneur.[1] Whether the person asking is a community organiser setting up a local currency or a developer coding a global cryptocurrency, whether the technology supporting the new money is old-fashioned watermarks on paper or algorithms and a mobile app, whether the imaginary guiding the efforts is that of commodity-money or of debt–credit relational money, the anxiety behind the question is that neither intended reach, nor technology, nor cultural understanding are, by themselves, no matter the combination, conducive to a money that people are willing to take and spend. Hyman Minsky phrased the problem elegantly: 'Everyone can create money; the problem is to get it accepted.'[2] Under the pragmatic question lies a sociological curiosity: What makes sufficiently enough people accept – and use – a particular money-token?

The answer provided typically goes something like this: 'people accept money because of its value'. And so money entrepreneurs endeavour to imprint in their monies one or another form of value – be it through the metal content of the money-token and the scarcity of its supply, as in those monies guided by a commodity imaginary; be it through the coordination of communities that commit to provide goods and services in exchange for the money-token, as in those monies guided by a credit imaginary. But, if you think about it, 'value' is a muddled term. Asking about value pushes us to look for where it resides – intrinsic or extrinsic to money? It forces us into impossible ontological discussions – is its essence objective, subjective or intersubjective? It presses us to define a sphere of action – does value have an economic or social valence? The term 'value' compels us to look at the shadows of the mechanism that makes money work. Focusing on 'building value in money' traps the entrepreneur into labyrinthine un-ending philosophical questions because the answers to what is value and what makes a community value certain elements and not others are, in the last instance, a matter of civilisational configurations.[3]

Approaching money as a sociotechnical arrangement offers a pragmatic way out of the muddle. If money is a relational phenomenon, then the question of what makes it work is really a question about the relationships that constitute money. We then need only to describe those relationships, wonder about what makes people *relate forward and back* in perpetual give-and-take interactions that keep money-tokens moving through interactional circuits. And we need to identify those interactional patterns that keep people interacting. For it is continuous interactions that bring life to money; money, we saw in the previous chapters, works through constant relational work. The reverse is also the case: for money's capacity to infrastructure society inheres in the activity of the social interactions folded into it. No interactional activity, no monetary infrastructure that works for the community of users, no tool with which to craft society.

For the monetary entrepreneur, the shift in approach carries a clear strategic recommendation: insert in the monetary architecture a mechanism that impels people to interact with each other; a mechanism that compels individuals to accept and spend the money-tokens, a mechanism that incites money users into recurrent back-and-forth interactions with each other. Thereof the take on interactional patterns: to identify which of them has a built-in *perpetuum mobile*; for those that have it carry the potential to bring money, and its constitutive community, into life.

Patterns of interaction

Reciprocity, solidarity and mutuality present themselves as three interactional patterns variously folded into the social relationships in which money is entangled.

Reciprocity is the pattern proper of person-to-person exchange. It builds on a notion of equivalence that demands a tit-for-tat independent of individual abilities, resources and needs. Reciprocity assumes equality between the interacting actors, symmetry in their engagement with each other. The seller offers her goods and the buyer her money-tokens both expecting corresponding worth for what they exchanged. It is the pattern characteristic of barter, a give-and-take of goods and services commensurate on a one-to-one basis,[4] 'vice-versa movements taking place as between "hands" under a market system',[5] 'a back-and-forth process involving two sides in which each side gives as good as it gets'.[6]

Solidarity, or rather 'vertical solidarity', is the pattern of interaction between the individual and the hierarchically organised collective in which she functions and lives. It operates through 'appropriational movements toward the center and out of it again'.[7] There is asymmetry between the interacting parties, for the individual is obliged towards an entity representing the totality of the social body. The instituted center collects from members, stores and redistributes goods and services throughout the social body. As an interactional pattern, vertical solidarity builds on inequality and dependence between the parties. It is the pattern characteristic of redistributive societies, found in large-scale economies from Hammurabi's Babylonia to today's welfare states.

Mutuality is a pattern of interaction found in horizontal collectives. It operates on the principle of 'from each according to their abilities, to each according to their needs'.[8] As in the previous pattern, there is asymmetry of interaction for not all members of the collective are equally able to contribute to it. Members pool together whatever each of them can contribute, mutualise the pooled resources, and collectively decide who and how to grant access to those now collectivised resources. Yet, unlike the previous pattern, asymmetry is not grounded on inequality and dependence, but on equity and interdependence, on sharing the burden and the benefits of labour. This pattern – which could also be called 'horizontal solidarity' – characterises cooperative, communal economies.

To understand how these interactional patterns differently compel actors to relate to each other, it is necessary to understand the sort of obligation inserted in the pattern. In reciprocal relations, the obligation is individual-to-individual, discharged at the very moment the exchange is completed. With the interacting parties having given each other equivalent offerings, none of them is obliged to continue interacting. There is nothing forcing any of them to relate back to the other nor to the community within which they trade. Indeed, with the exchange completed, each party can choose what to do with her new possession independently from any other consideration but her individual interests; she can choose to keep it and hold it forward, or to get rid of it and sell it forward. No longer under any form of obligation, the interacting parties are free to part ways and dispose of their belongings as they may so wish.

For (vertical) solidary and mutual interactions, the obligation persists even after the exchange has concluded. It is never a one-time obligation to give like under reciprocal interactions. Instead, being a *social* obligation, an obligation towards one's community, the obligation persists as long as the community exists. In hierarchical communities, the obligation is towards the centre, towards the legitimate entity that represents and enacts the group, the recurrent completion of the obligation guaranteed by more or less formal regulations and tools of coercion. Think of seasonal tributes to the Babylonian temple or of annual taxes today. In horizontal communities, the obligation is towards the aggregated members in the abstract, and is guaranteed by peer pressure, by the groups' social institutions and cultural norms, as well as by a variety of governance rules and sanctions the members may have agreed upon. Think of the savings-and-loans groups formed by citizens in many countries around the world.[9]

All three interactional patterns involve reciprocal expectations and responsibilities. But while in patterns of reciprocity all individual responsibility ends with the accomplishment of the person-to-person exchange, in (vertical) solidary and mutual interactions the obligation towards the collective remains and recurs. The continuation, or not, of a sense of obligation towards a larger collective Other – society, the community – necessarily shapes individual interactional behaviour.

The 'forward', then, in the various strategies shaping and organising the monetary assemblages seen in the book so far imply very different mechanisms. The forward-strategy in those monies aligning to a commodity imaginary – 'sell it forward' of conventional money; 'HODL it forward' of algorithmic monies – signifies 'forward freely', a prompt to the individual to act in her self-interest without regards to the interests and priorities of the larger community. In contrast, the forward-strategy in monies aligned to a credit imaginary – 'give it forward' of citizen monies; 'tax it forward' of municipal monies – signifies 'forward to the community', a prompt to the individual to relate back to the collective. The first set of forward-strategies separate economic practices from the social sphere; the later embed economic practices within the heart of the social. The first is based on an economics of material individual self-interest; the latter on an economics of social obligation. The first builds upon the reduction of human motives to those of *homo economicus*; the latter takes a more comprehensive approach to human drive, one that acknowledges the coexistence of impersonal market transactions with interpersonal intimacy and dissolves the distinction between individual and social interests. Unavoidably, the first, commodity-based monies, can hardly work for the community; while for the latter, credit-based monies, there is possibility to work for the community and thus become a true commons. (For a comparison between the three interactional and institutional patterns, see Table I2.1).

In fewer words: monetary architectures designed along an imaginary of credit translate obligation into a system of relational accounting and the sense of social obligation into a *perpetuum mobile*. It is the continuous movement of the pendulum, the repetitive interaction between members, the perennial sense of community-*oblige* that ultimately crafts, maintains and develops the collective.[10] Abandoning the fiction of commodity money confronts us to the reality of social obligation, opening up the possibility to found new ways of living together.

Way too neat

The book has elicited three imaginaries of money – commodity, state credit and commons mutual credit; three principles to organise money – market, central authority and communal democracy; and, now, three interactional patterns to insert into the monetary architecture – reciprocity, vertical solidarity and mutuality. Moreover, the argument points to imaginaries, principles and patterns nicely mapping onto each other. This is all very neat!

Table I2.1: Comparing interactional and institutional patterns

Interactional pattern	Mutuality (horizontal solidarity)	(Vertical) solidarity	Reciprocity
Economic dynamic	Pooling and sharing	Collecting, storing and redistributing	Equivalence/ substitution
Institutional arrangement conditioning the pattern	Communities with a well-defined boundary	Centrality	Markets
Relation among individuals/parties	Interdependence (complex web of relations)	Dependence (of individual to the centre)	Independence
Topology of the network of relations	Asymmetrical and horizontal	Asymmetrical and hierarchical	Symmetrical
Underlying social principle	Equity	Inequality	Equality
Organisational principle	Commons	State	Self-regulating market
Imaginary of money	Commons credit	State credit	Commodity

Maybe too neat?

Sardex, a local money guided by the commons credit imaginary and aligning individual and collective interests along relations of mutuality, was however coordinated by a central authority. Not a state-based entity, granted, but centralised in the social venture nonetheless. In Wörgl, with a central municipal authority coordinating money along lines of vertical solidarity, a commodity imaginary flickered when the mayor imposed a demurrage tax on money holdings to put them on a level with wares. Bitcoin is, possibly, the most consistent of the monetary experiments unfolded thus far. Its design is guided by a commodity imaginary, the interests of its HODLers coordinated by currency and financial markets, and the validation work done for the network duly reciprocated in bitcoins. But even in bitcoin we find entanglement of the three trios. For the Bitcoin Foundation conjures up a central authority that manages the algorithm steering the monetary arrangement.

Maybe we simply need to embrace the fact that human societies are never a neat assemblage. And since money is an infrastructure configuring society and constituted by society, it follows that money can never be as neat as the mapping of cultural imaginaries, coordination principles and interactional patterns may incline us to believe. Even when there is a clear, well-defined purpose to the newly implemented monetary system. To attest, many of the monetary experiments in the two chapters that follow.

PART III

Developing the Money Commons

Real utopias, as American sociologist Erik O. Wright calls ideals that are grounded in practical experiments of humanity, build on a combination of idealism and realism, of vision and implementation, of political imagination and action orientation. Real utopias feed on the tension between dreams and practice.[1] As we have seen in the second part of the book, in money matters, the tension between the utopia carved out by a new monetary arrangement and the practice of enacting it centres around two main questions: what are the rules governing money and who gets to decide those rules – or, more broadly, how does money work, and how is it made to work; the architectural design and the governance institutions of the particular money. As we have also seen through the various complementary monies unpacked thus far, this tension is resolved differently depending on the cultural, political and economic arrangements in which the actors coordinating the experiments embed the new monies. The architecture of a specific money, that is, hinges on the relational restraints of its designers and managers. Finally, and key to the implementation of any monetary utopia, the shape money takes shapes in turn dynamics in the community that uses it. The form and reason money took – whether a 'sell it forward', 'give it forward', 'tax it forward' or 'hold it forward' – made a difference on how the individual related to that money and thus shaped the social reality where individuals lived and acted. In a nutshell, as money is constituted, it constitutes community. As it is shaped, it shapes the social fabric. As it is embedded in socioeconomic relations, it embeds the economy into society.

The third part of the book further develops that line of argument. Chapters 7 and 8 each unfold three complementary monies sharing a similar real utopia – the advancement of more inclusive societies through the implementation of a universal basic income, in Chapter 7; the promotion of economies based on a relation of care towards nature, in Chapter 8. Each of the three monies unfolded in each of those two chapters follows a distinct principle for organising the monetary arrangement – community democracy, central authority, self-regulating market. In the money–society co-constitutive manner we have now learnt to discern, the principle organising the particular money comes to similarly organise the community of users of that money. What social dynamics eventually evolve inhere in what socioeconomic relations are organised within money – with direct implications, we will see, for the nature of the markets that come to dominate and the depth of the democracy that comes to be exercised. In other words, the effective realisation of the utopias intended with the monetary arrangement ultimately depends on the specific articulation of the monetary configurations. The reclaimed, reimagined and reorganised money works as it is made to work. Chapter 9 translates such lessons into a set of guidances for organising monies that have the potential to advance more inclusive and sustainable societies.

7

Freeing Monies: Remaking Money for Inclusive Economies

Universal basic income (UBI) is an idea whose time has come. Or so it would seem from the multitude of voices clamouring for it. Major tech-industry figures are converging with popular movement activists in demanding this particular form of progressive politics. From the likes of Silicon Valley entrepreneurs Jack Dorsey, Mark Zuckerberg and Elon Musk to more anarchist crusaders Yiannis Varoufakis and David Graeber, from politicians of the establishment such as Richard Nixon to political reformers such as Martin Luther King, from economists on the right such as Milton Friedman to those on the left such as Guy Standing, UBI is increasingly heralded as a form of welfare that is to project us into a more economically, socially and politically sustainable future. Their arguments differ along with their ideological inclinations: to address the rise in unemployment brought about by enlarged automation contend the techies; to take aim at the politically dangerous levels of inequality reason the moderates; to democratise the economy advance the activists. The common mantra, to give everyone the possibility to live a dignified and fulfilling life.

The general idea of a UBI – that the government should make a regular payment to every citizen sufficient to guarantee her material existence as a right with no strings attached – directly addresses some of the most pressing aspects of precarity and inequality that so trouble many observers today. The regularity and unconditionality of payments take immediate aim at the uncertainty that so limits the precariat. The level of payment – high enough to cover basic needs – is meant to guarantee the right to subsistence so as to grant a dignified life. For scholars and activists, like for an increasing number of renowned supporters,[1] the certainty of having one's material needs covered is a fundamental requirement for deepening democracy. The Greeks realised this already, when they instituted rewards to citizens to enable their participation in political and cultural life.[2] A basic income detaches income from employment and thus enables people to have more control over their time so that, if they so wish, they can engage in work that is not remunerated but that nonetheless builds the polity: from participating in political debate to caring for family, friends and neighbours; from volunteering for one's community to enrolling in education and retraining. In liberating the individual of the need to endure excruciating labour conditions and to perform jobs that go against one's ethical principles to be able to barely survive, and in freeing citizens from the constraints that determine reception of welfare benefits, a UBI becomes an essential component in efforts to build societies where people enjoy the moral freedom to act as they think is right, and the republican freedom to speak back to power. A more egalitarian, democratic and emancipatory system, it is argued, requires that everyone has their subsistence secured.[3]

While pilot studies show the promises UBI in national currency offers for recipients,[4] and while UBI ideas are slowly infiltrating the programmes of political candidates in several national and local elections,[5] the objections to move from pilot studies to institutionalised UBI programmes are still many. One set of concerns refers to its financing. A regular basic income paid to everyone in a country would simply be unaffordable, this objection goes. The second set of concerns relates to cultural and ideological assumptions of worth and human nature. Providing 'something for nothing', basic income is said to promote laziness, reducing the supply of labour; scarcity is needed to make people work. The gigantic stimulus packages governments put together to confront the COVID-19 pandemic has proven the first set of objections is a matter of political will, not of lack of funding. The second set of objections has been proven wrong in many UBI pilot studies, which show recipients resolve to keep jobs that give them an occupational identity or to retrain for future participation in the labour market.[6] That is, both objections have more to do with politics and our assumptions about human nature than with the technical and economic merits of the proposals. And so, while UBI is increasingly defended as a necessary intervention to change the politico-economic system and bring about a more inclusive future, because its approval requires of the established institutions, UBI advocates are rendered powerless by the very system they aim to transform.

Instead of waiting for change to come from established institutions, a variety of actors are taking the lead by creating complementary monies through which to implement their UBI vision. From grassroots groups anchored in local communities to digital entrepreneurs with global ambitions and regional public authorities in partnership with civil society organisations, UBI has become a policy ideal mobilising shifting interest groups in what Polanyi may have called a countermovement. United by a recognition of the need to protect themselves and others from the destructive sociopolitical effects of intense inequality, and infused with the sense of real possibility new technologies have awakened, these groups varyingly call on the commons, the state or the market to design, organise and realise a different socioeconomic order. Each following its own organisational principle, grassroots groups, local public authorities and the private sector are, independently of each other, assembling their own monetary arrangement to put their UBI utopias into practice.

The actors behind Demos, Mumbuca and GoodDollar all share a dream for a different economy, for an economy that is more equal, caring and fair, an economy inclusive of the most fragile. They all conceive UBI as the policy tool that would allow society to realise that dream. They all take a hands-on learning-by-doing approach to the concrete realisation of the UBI utopia. Yet they advance different practical answers to the twin questions of money's architectural design and governance. Informed by distinct cultural and ideological imaginaries and standing on distinct power structures, Demos, Mumbuca and GoodDollar follow distinct organisational principles to remake money. The chapter asks the book's two analytical questions – how does this [X] money work, and how is it made to work – to unfold the three complementary monies. The answers found show that though these monetary experiments may be presented under the same UBI story-line, though they may cater to the most fragile in our societies, the different set of relations they assemble into the new monies has far-reaching consequences for the form of the economy and the depth of democracy these monies enact in the communities using them. This lesson holds beyond the particular experiments studied. Attending to how the relationship between money creation, economic interests and sociopolitical groups is designed and organised into the monetary assemblage can help us appreciate the extent to which that particular money truly has a chance to align individual interests towards inclusion of the many in the common good.

Demos

'Este sistema no nos representa' ['This system does not represent us']. On 15 May 2011, tens of thousands of young citizens took to the streets all over Spain to denounce a political system that, they felt, did not represent their economic realities. The economic crisis that followed the financial crash of 2008 had left many in unstable, insecure jobs with declining real wages and no clear occupational narrative. The austerity policies governments were implementing worsened the situation, leaving this 'new dangerous class' with little or no benefits, with poor public welfare services and in a situation of chronic debt.[7] A generation better educated than any previous in history, they faced however a future of precarious, badly paid jobs for which they were overqualified. A few days previous to regional elections, the manifestations quickly grew into a movement – known as 'the Spanish revolution' or the 'movement of the outraged'[8] – demanding 'real democracy now!' Thousands of 'youth without future, no home, no job, no pension, no fear' camped in the squares of cities across the country, resisting official calls to empty those public spaces and enduring police violence. Under cries such as 'we are not merchandise of politicians or bankers' and 'traitor politicians, culpable bankers', the outraged voiced their discontent with the traditional political powers seen by the many as supportive of an economic system – global capitalism – that took their future away from them. They condemned a financial system of 'economic terrorism', in which established political parties promulgated the interests of capital – 'State = Capital' – condemning citizens to 'give [their] souls for a mortgage' and to 'become slaves for a roof and a job'.[9] The Spanish revolution had been inspired by the Arab Spring and would soon inspire similar outraged movements in various countries of the North Atlantic in what became known as the Occupy movement.[10]

Campsites on city squares developed into small urban laboratories for the kind of direct democracy and economy of solidarity and mutual care the young activists were clamouring for. They self-organised in groups that attended the children, collected, cooked and distributed food, gathered books and lent them freely, educated for non-violent struggle, informed new arrivals, continuously updated media communication, and organised shifts to guarantee sanitation and security in the camp. For all the febrile activity, for all the lack of sleep, they lavished time and energy in various forms of horizontal decision-making processes. They held daily general assemblies to discuss technical issues of organising the camps, developed hand-signals to conduct consensus-based direct democracy, and collectively studied the latest labour market reform. The intense months of experimentation with direct participatory democracy and horizontal social coordination created both a community organised without market or state, and an enraptured sense of boundless possibility. The experience opened the horizons to a more exciting world. It catalysed a 'transformative outbreak of imagination'[11] that not only projected a vision of another organisation of society but that had also realised that vision in the relatively small heterogeneous and inclusive communities that coalesced in the squares.

Aware that 'nobody is going to come to save us', tired of 'feeling like the donkey forever chasing the carrot', yet armed with a new sense of possibility, activists from La Isleta, a mixed neighbourhood of the capital city of the island of Gran Canaria, went on to try to realise their collective utopia. They took their demands for a caring economy and dreams of a deepened democracy forward into action by designing an 'economic system along different rules which radically change how the economy works'. At the heart of the economic system they were engineering they put a new monetary system; and at the core of that new money they put UBI. They aimed to organise an alternative monetary arrangement that not only implemented a UBI but whose rules for the creation and governance of money also followed the values of mutual care, equality and direct democracy they had experienced in the square.

The form and reason of their community currency was made clear from its very name. 'Demos' was chosen for its triple signification. First, it makes direct reference to the Greek *demos* – the common people, plebeians with civic status and rights, commoners – to foreground those 'who give money its value' and 'who money should really serve'. The double reference to the *demos* as both the basis of value and the purpose of money encapsulated some of the lessons the outraged of La Isleta had learnt as they contributed to organise the camp on the square: one, the extent to which *individual contributions* constituted the communities shaping up on the square; and, two, the centrality of the *relationship between rights and obligations* for a community to work. Thereof the second signification, a collective exhortation to give explicit through the collective imperative form of the verb '*dar*' (Spanish for 'to give'), '*demos*' (literally 'let us give'), as in 'let us give a monthly payment in complementary currency [so as to] guarantee everyone can satisfy one's most basic needs', as well as in 'the need for every one to give' if the community economy is to work.[12] Finally, 'Demos' made for the acronym of what the grassroots group stood for, 'Democracia Económica en MOneda Social' or 'Economic Democracy in Community Currency'.[13] Two pillars of Demos were, from its very start, key to the sort of deep economic democracy the group was intent to realise: the universality of a basic income in the local currency and the governance of the monetary arrangement through a general assembly.

How does Demos work? Or, the initial design features of Demos' internal architecture:

1. the quantity of money issued is proportional to the number of users;
2. released at a monthly rhythm through the payment of a UBI to all active individual members; and
3. a fixed proportion of each member's account balance is automatically withdrawn monthly and transferred to the Common Fund.

First, the issuance of demos. Every time a new member registers, an amount equal ten times the basic income is created and placed in the Common Fund. The purpose is to 'mirror the human value of participants in the monetary system by making this human value equivalent to the existing quantity of money'.[14] There is a direct relationship between the amount of demos and the size of the community, an implementation of the designers' twin premises that money is to serve the community and that money derives its value from the community. In a second step, demos is automatically introduced into the community at the beginning of every month through the transfer of basic income from the Common Fund to each member account. Concerned about the 'sustainability of the basic income over time', the third step consists of automatically charging to every member at the end of the month a 'cooperative tax' equal to 10 per cent of the member's account balance. It is, that is, a time-based tax similar to the demurrage we saw accelerated Wörgl's money in Chapter 5. In the words of one of demos' co-designers:

> '[T]he basic formula of incomes and taxes is really simple. In the end, you have money circling around. It feels like the easy trick of a street magician but it results in many positive effects. It allows you to distribute money [as well as] to discourage its accumulation in individual accounts for, why would you contribute [sell] too much? You would end up paying more taxes than the income given to you. So you end up being more interested not in contributing yourself but in teaching someone else to do what you contribute with.'[15]

From the outset, it seems, Demos was engineered so as to encourage individual users to balance their economic activity with their level of consumption; to provoke a behaviour in line with the collective vision of a caring and more equal economy. The call to align individual behaviour to the requirements of the real utopia they were building was condensed in the maxim 'Give as much as you can receive', a direct call for individual members to balance their contributions to and appropriations from the community, their obligation to give with their right to take. In its form and reason, the Demos monetary arrangement combines the *perpetuum mobile* mechanism of 'tax it forward' we saw in Chapter 5 with the form and reasoning of the gift we saw in Chapter 4 – to recall, an obligation to give, an obligation to take and, most crucially, an obligation to give back.

Demos' demurrage tax mechanism soon proved inadequate to induce reciprocate giving to the community ('give it forward'). The first basic incomes in demos were paid in June 2012. Though a small amount, initially fixed to 50đ per month (equivalent to 50 euros), Demos' commoners soon observed some users – 'ninja users' – were taking from the community without contributing to it. On receipt of the Demos basic income at the beginning of the month, they would go to the Demos markets – '*mercademos*' – spend it all on products commoners readily offered in the local currency, and leave with an untroubled 'I don't have any more demos left, so I'll come next month once I've received my basic income'. For an economy that was being organised from scratch by the grassroots, the monetary arrangement needed to incite members to contribute with their goods and services, to provide for the community-in-the-making, to produce for there to be a real economy outside of the established euro. Yet dependent as individual members were on euros, some of them were producing in the conventional economy alone and consuming in the emerging complementary economy;

they were taking from the local community without giving back to it. The tragedy of the commons was playing out from the very start of the local currency. True, a cooperative tax was withdrawn from the accounts of ninja users, but this made no productive contribution to the community economy. For monetary tokens alone do not make an economy – an insight ignored by many a crypto-entrepreneur and that we will see happen again in GoodDollar's UBI. The *pendulum mobile* of the tax mechanism that had been built into Demos was not triggering the obligation to reciprocate with real goods and services that so builds community and economy.

By January 2013 the General Assembly was discussing changes to the rules that governed the monetary arrangement. And they decided to deal with their own version of the tragedy of the commons the same way communities around the world have dealt with similar tragedies for centuries: with a graduated system of sanctions and rewards.[16] The basic income was to remain universal, yet the level of payment was conditioned in two ways. First, the basic income to be paid each month was to vary with the total volume of trade in the community two months previous – a monetary design that strengthened the relationship between the amount of demos in circulation and the size and activity of the community. The more members in a community, and the more active these members were, the higher the monthly basic income. Second, the basic income paid to each individual member was to vary with the degree that member had contributed to, relative to taken from the community. Those members that had taken more than they had contributed received a basic income somewhat lower than the average. Those members that had contributed more than taken received a basic income somewhat higher than the average. A universal basic income whose level is conditioned to one's contribution to the community, they hoped, would remind users of the importance of giving for both building community and developing the economy. The two design features aimed at aligning individual interests to the interests of the collective.

Once such system of sanctions and rewards was decided in the General Assembly, the calculations were automated through the code, whereupon individual behaviour adjusted swiftly, promptly strengthening the community economy. Members who had not found members interested in the products they offered quickly set to learn about other members' interests and adapted their offerings accordingly. Goods most in demand – mainly local food, lodging and transportation – were readily offered. "We started to see ourselves under the key of 'what can I give'." As they gave, earned, spent and took, members became aware of the value others granted to skills and competencies they had themselves been blind towards. The middle-aged unemployed woman whose bakery unfailingly sold out as did the elder woman's marmalades. In realising the value of their offerings, some members found a springboard to imagine their lives differently and to start up their own small businesses. Today, the middle-aged woman sells home-made cakes to local cafés who pay her in euros, the elder woman runs a marmalade business that sells, in euros, to grocery stores on the island, and Lali has dared to realise the dream of her youth, "earn a living as a herbalist". As one member proudly assessed, "[I]t is the dream outcome of any labour-market programme".

Most notably, the experience taught the community the enormous infrastructural capacity well-arranged money can have – even such a local and young money as Demos was. As a Demos user phrased it, "[I]t started as a response to government inaction but that soon was forgotten in favour of what we were observing. Demos was organising us!" Or, "[T]he rules you implement change behaviour." Among those rules, Demos' General Assembly identifies those related to taxes, rewards and sanctions as the most determinant. Connecting taxes to the level of one's wealth – one's account balance in the Demos economy – 'makes selfishness unprofitable'. As for rewards and sanctions, they concede, they help educate members about the reciprocal obligation to take and give back, about the relationality of this money; it teaches members to move away from an imaginary of money as property – a commodity to dispose with at will – and onto an imaginary of money as a relation of credit and debt towards one's community; it teaches them to relate back, to give forward, thus contributing to co-develop commoners and commons in the process.

As the COVID-19 pandemic winds down, Demos markets are being spontaneously organised. "We have missed each other" – an indication of the enduring sense of community and of individual responsibility towards each other Demos-money has contributed to develop.

Mumbuca

Located some 40 kilometres north of Rio de Janeiro, along the Brazilian Atlantic coast, Maricá is home to over 160,000 inhabitants. A satellite city to Rio, a mere 23 per cent of Maricá's working-age population work in the municipality. With no industrial or productive capacity within its territory, the largest majority of Maricá's working population commutes to Rio and other neighbouring cities to earn a living. Maricá's economy is further characterised by a large number of families living under the poverty line, an extensive informal economy, and a youth with little hope in the future.[17]

The City of Maricá receives a large sum of royalties from the oil fields in Bacia de Santos. In an effort to support the most vulnerable families, in 2011, the mayor of the city decided to distribute part of these royalties as a social benefit added to the federal government's welfare programme, 'Bolsa Família' – a national income transfer programme conditioned on keeping children vaccinated and in school. The mayor was however aware that the royalties transferred as welfare to citizens in the form of Brazilian reals soon leaked out of Maricá as residents and merchants used it to buy from outside the city or to pay debts owed elsewhere. That is, paid in Brazilian reals, the extended welfare programme was strengthening Maricá's economy and its families only to a very limited extent.

Determined 'to develop the city's economy … trade in particular',[18] in December 2013, Maricá introduced a local currency, mumbuca, through the Mumbuca Community Bank.[19] Oil royalties backed the new currency on a one-to-one basis. Mumbucas were injected into the city's economy as welfare benefits – again, on top of the regular benefits in the national currency – to the city's low-income families. Introduced as a strategy for local development, merchants had no obligation to accept the currency in payment of their goods. To attract them to the city currency network, however, merchants were given the possibility to convert their earned mumbucas into Brazilian reals, these coming from the royalties backing the currency. To keep it local and constrain money leaking out of the municipality, convertibility was restricted to merchants that were registered in the municipality. Conversion was also charged at 2 per cent, which went to fund the operations of the Mumbuca Community Bank.

From its inception, the Mumbuca monetary arrangement developed organically, following a trial-and-error process of sorts through which the local public authority and the community bank learnt together. Starting small at first, the city gradually increased the size of the welfare benefits paid in mumbucas, enlarged the range of beneficiaries and developed the underlying technology. In late 2014, one year after its inception, 14,000 families received a complementary family benefit of 85 mumbucas/month – equal to 85 reals – which eventually grew to 130 mumbucas per family and month, and later transformed into 130 mumbucas per family member and month – a family of four thus seeing its total allowance increased from 130 to 520 mumbucas. New welfare programmes, catering to other precarious citizens, were added in 2015: a 'youth solidarity minimum income' – 100 mumbucas monthly for young persons aged 14 to 29 – and a 'pregnancy minimum income' – 85 mumbucas per month paid to mothers during pregnancy up to the child's first birthday.

Distrusting yet 'another political initiative', merchants were initially reticent to accept mumbucas, the number of merchants in the Mumbuca network barely growing beyond the 100+ that first registered in 2014. To promote acceptance, the city cancelled the 2 per cent redemption fee for those merchants converting mumbucas into Brazilian reals before the 5th of the month. Another key development during these initial years was the city's decision to support the digitalisation of the infrastructure. In 2018, mumbuca went from a paper- and card-based currency onto a digital currency supported by the e-Dinheiro payment platform alongside a Mumbuca plastic card.[20] The e-Dinheiro platform allowed beneficiaries not only to receive and spend their mumbucas, it also gave them access to regular banking services, including a savings account, a checking account, or the possibility to obtain a smaller line of credit. A previously unbanked and vulnerable population could now pay their bills, make P2P transfers, or buy a phone on credit. In this way, the expansion enabled by a monetary technology driven by a community bank embedded Mumbuca deeper into Maricá's economy.

The continuous tinkering with Mumbuca's monetary arrangement – from its rules and beneficiaries to its technology and partners – meant that by the time the COVID-19 pandemic hit Maricá, the city was well prepared to quickly roll out an encompassing UBI programme.[21] First, it enlarged, simplified and unified its various welfare benefits under two programmes: a '*renda básica e cidadania*', literally 'citizen's basic income', handing 300 mumbucas per person per month to all registered citizens unconditional of their means, and a '*renda minima*' or 'minimum income' of about 1,000 mumbucas handed to precarious micro-entrepreneurs in the gig economy as well as to employees companies retained despite the economic downturn brought by the lockdowns. Second, the fact that the technology was already in place and citizens were versed in its use enabled the immediate implementation of the UBI-like emergency benefit programmes.

Indeed, while implementation of the emergency basic income approved by the Brazilian Congress on the onset of the COVID-19 pandemic faced challenges in outreach, in April 2022, the Mumbuca-based UBI successfully reached to 42 per cent of Maricá's population.[22] With a large informal economy, many Brazilian citizens are not registered in the federal government's registry, and even if registered, many of them do not have a bank account. During a time of increased health risk, agglomerations formed at the entrances of government agencies and bank offices across the country as citizens queued to register, renew their national identity cards, and start a bank account through which to receive the emergency basic income they were eligible to. In Maricá, instead, registered citizens eagerly downloaded the Mumbuca app to claim their rightful basic income, the city easily transferring the Mumbuca basic income to its citizens.[23] The number of Mumbuca bank accounts grew from 37,550 in December 2019 to 65,374 in September 2021 – a 74 per cent increase. Most tellingly, the volume of trade in mumbucas in local businesses grew from 36 to 254 million mumbucas in 2021 – a 603 per cent growth in local trade, guaranteeing money served the local economy.[24] The results of the last municipal elections in November 2020 are telling of the satisfaction of Maricá's population with the outreach of the municipal welfare programmes: 94 per cent of citizens renewed their confidence in the Workers' Party that governs the city.

If you think about it, it is not at all surprising. A monetary system anchored in local government brings the infrastructural capacities of money to empower public development policies at the city level. And conversely, anchoring the monetary architecture on a centralised, if local, authority, enhances the infrastructural capacity of money by amplifying its reach and speeding up the rate at which city-dwellers embrace it. We saw this in the case of Wörgl in Chapter 5; we see it again in Maricá. A welfare policy that benefits the population at large directly addresses the concerns for inequality, precarity and poverty that dominate the day. When delivered in a currency organised to work for the region a little longer – by constraining its use to the local territory – the public welfare policy not only supports low-income citizens but has the potential to further strengthen local businesses and the local economy. As money remains circulating in the territory, it remains working for the territory. The local nature of the monetary architecture and its articulation through local public policies are both key features to understand the rapid change the currency effected on the economic dynamics of the local business community.

Mumbuca's monetary architecture includes however a design feature that weakens its ability to work for the territory, its economy and its people. The possibility for local businesses to redeem mumbucas in Brazil's national currency opens up a gate for money to leak out of Maricá. What's more, convertibility risks the long-term sustainability of any local currency. Such dynamics were readily observable in the complementary-currency-based UBI-like programme implemented in Barcelona between 2018 and 2019. After 13 months, once the backing in euros was exhausted, the programme necessarily ceased.[25] In Maricá, in 2018, businesses redeemed 85.5 per cent of the mumbucas injected into the economy, big businesses redeeming to a much larger extent than small businesses. Had Maricá not had a stable and secured source of national money in oil royalties, the possibility to redeem would have consumed the backing of the local currency and, with it, mumbucas would have ceased to exist. Such a high conversion rate was a sign of the, then, limited trust – or use, or both – local businesses had for the local currency.

Yet, as local businesses gained trust in the commitment of public authorities and as the mumbuca economy developed, conversion ratios went down. In 2019, 67.88 per cent of mumbucas were converted into Brazilian reals, and 60 per cent in 2021.[26] Over 12,600 businesses accept the local currency in payment for their goods and services, 67 per cent of which trade at least once a month in the local currency, and 26 per cent of which pay for all their supplies exclusively in mumbucas.[27] With mumbucas not being accepted for payment of taxes (the 'tax it forward' strategy of a monetary architecture anchored in a city government, as we saw in Chapter 5) and with mumbucas distributed as a right with no required counter-obligation (the 'give it forward' strategy we saw in the community-based monies of Chapter 4), there is no clear *perpetuum mobile* mechanism built into Maricá's local monetary arrangement.[28] As the number of merchants not converting mumbucas into reals grows, the answer to the question 'how is mumbuca made to work' – or 'why would merchants accept mumbucas in payment of their goods and services' – necessarily hinges on the size and variety of the real economy that gradually articulates into the monetary arrangement. The larger and more varied possibilities merchants have to spend their mumbucas, the more willing they are to accept them in payment for their goods. The so-called 'network effect' as it plays out in monetary arrangements – the more and more varied the merchants associated to the local money, the more valuable the monetary tokens. Or, in a formulation more attuned to the commons perspective of the book, the value of a currency for an economy rests on the community of users behind it. Mumbuca is evidence of the key role local governments play in catalysing the network effect, even in the absence of a *perpetuum mobile* designed into the monetary assemblage.

GoodDollar

The 'flagship CSR [Corporate Social Responsibility] of eToro'[29] – a multi-asset investment platform – GoodDollar is a cryptocurrency designed to channel impact investment into a UBI of global reach. The premise of the GoodDollar UBI experiment is uncontested: wealth inequality is 'one of the biggest problems in the world today', leading to 'populist movements, instability and violence',[30] a problem the founders of GoodDollar argue is bound to get worse as artificial intelligence, machine learning and automation result in the further disappearance of jobs. GoodDollar team's discontent with the mainstream solution to inequality is widely shared:

> [T]rickle-down economics has proved a failure. The wealthiest 10% of the globe's population now earns 52% of its income, whereas the poorest 50% takes home just 8% of that total. The gap is even more pronounced when it comes to wealth. Of the world's total assets, the poorest half of the population owns just 2%, while the top 10% hold three-quarters.[31]

GoodDollar's suggested solution: '[UBI as a] new approach to capital and liquidity distribution'; 'get one GoodDollar a day and keep the banker away'.[32] GoodDollar's drive for change is inserted within the seemingly attractive trend to incentivise investors to put private money to work for people and planet: '[W]e have a fundamental belief that there are enough people who care not just about doing well for themselves, but also about doing good for others … there is a large and growing appetite to invest in impact-driven initiatives that seek human and/or environmental wins alongside financial gains.'[33] An appeal 'to do well while doing good' that underscores a form of reasoning that juxtaposes finance with the common good. GoodDollar's technical infrastructure and organisational arrangement is professedly apolitical: 'take blockchain technology and create a non-profit', dodge the 'political discussion' that comes with UBI when conceived at a national scale and when implemented through 'government-led currencies', and write UBI scheme into 'computer code that cannot be manipulated or changed' thus making it 'independent of one's specific politics or government'.[34]

Fundamentally, GoodDollar's ambition to 'righting the balance of economic equality'[35] through a global UBI distributed by means of the GoodDollar cryptocurrency builds simultaneously on the logics of financial rewards and social good. These otherwise contradictory forms of reasoning[36] are brought together through a perceived apolitical arrangement that is 'much a part of laissez-faire, of market structure. … It's really about just changing mechanics to create something that's fairer but could be as free and as open'.[37] In short, GoodDollar's efforts to build a UBI utopia are simultaneously grounded on the profit motive that drives actors in financial markets and the notion of monetary automation enabled by the code.

In the supposedly apolitical mechanics of GoodDollar – I apologise for the barrage of crypto-jargon – investors *stake* – hold forward – their assets in the GoodDollar Trust. These yield interests which are deposited – *yield farming* – in the form of DAI – a decentralised *stablecoin*[38] – into the GoodReserve to back the *minting* – issuance – of GoodDollar tokens (G$). Users can further back the minting of GoodDollar by depositing cryptocurrency in the GoodReserve in exchange for new G$s. Finally, G$s are also minted daily as the reserve ratio – the ratio between the G$ minted relative to the value of interest locked in the GoodDollar Reserve – is set to reduce gradually. Once minted, G$s are distributed partly to investors – 'supporters' in the GoodDollar ecosystem – as return for their investment, and partly to UBI recipients – 'claimers' – as a basic income they receive when they log into their GoodDollar *wallet* and actively request the payment, a request they can claim daily. Though 'no one guarantees the liquidity or market price of the G$ to any extent at any time',[39] in theory, anyone holding G$s can convert them into any of the cryptocurrencies held in the GoodReserve. The conversion rate varies according to a *bonding curve* – an *automated market-maker* mechanism that facilitates the liquidity of GoodDollar or, in lay-language, a computer programme that automatically prices cryptocurrencies against each other thus removing mediators when buying and selling G$s. This results in the total supply of G$s varying alongside the assets staked in or removed from the GoodReserve: 'when a user buys G$s, the tokens are minted, when they sell, the tokens are burned'.[40] If not through the GoodReserve, G$

holders can always try to exchange their G$s for other cryptocurrencies at *decentralised exchanges* (DEX) – peer-to-peer marketplaces enabling crypto-traders to exchange their crypto-holdings without the mediation of banks, brokers or any other financial intermediary.

Already here, in the rules that govern the creation and distribution of G$s, we can observe the political nature of the GoodDollar monetary arrangement. How many G$s are created and at which frequency they are created is contingent on investors and investors alone: on their willingness to put their assets to work for the GoodDollar global utopia, on how long they are willing to hold their assets in the GoodDollar Trust, and on the degree of returns they demand from their investment in GoodDollar. There is a direct relationship between the amount of G$s issued and the financial disposition of investors; the supply of G$s completely detached from the number of UBI claimers GoodDollar is supposed to serve. The level of UBI paid daily is similarly dissociated from the economic needs of recipients. Instead, daily UBIs vary alongside the interests generated by the assets of the investors and the degree of distribution of these interests back to investors relative to UBI claimers. That is to say, the rules for the creation and distribution of GoodDollar money are designed along a financial market principle that prioritises the moneyed interests of investors. Whatever trickles down to UBI claimers – in September 2022, around 105 G$/day, at a price of 0.000176 US$/G$ equivalent to 0.0185 US$/day or less than two cents a day[41] – depends on the benevolence of investors to stake their assets and forgo financial returns. It is difficult to see how a monetary system that puts the profit calculations of the wealthy at the heart of its monetary rules is to free money from politics. The sanctity of financial returns gives space to a denial of responsibility on the part of the well-off for the condition of the world's poor. In the case of GoodDollar, it reproduces wealth and power disparities at the heart of money creation. Instead of a money free of 'changing governments', we got a money and accompanying social welfare scheme organised around the whims and changing bets of investors, leaving the poor GoodDollar is supposed to serve exposed to the uncertainty and instability of financial market forces.

Another important component articulates into the GoodDollar monetary assemblage: markets where users can spend their G$s, thus conferring use value on G$s. To this end, GoodDollar has set up its own dedicated online marketplace in which users can advertise the goods and services they want to sell and find the goods and services they want to buy. As for the development of on-the-ground markets in G$s, the assumption of the GoodDollar team is that, as users accumulate the complementary currency, 'local vendors and merchants will face growing pressure to accept it in exchange for goods and services'.[42] The ease with which G$s can be converted into other currencies (or, as phrased in the White Paper, 'as G$ will be liquid from day one'), it is hoped, would also attract merchants to accepting the cryptocurrency in payment for their goods. In other words, two cultural assumptions guide the articulation of the new money with the productive economy where the poor live and work: pressure from users holding commodity money (or demand exerted in G$s) and ease of conversion (or locating the value of money in money itself). Building on these assumptions, the GoodDollar team expects the free introduction of G$s into the economy will lead to the spontaneous emergence of online and on-the-ground trade relationships. As we saw in Chapter 2, such cultural beliefs are in line with the economic orthodoxy of the barter myth, which conceives markets develop spontaneously and money as a neutral intermediary that eases relationships of trade.

With barely two years in existence, it may be too early to deem whether markets do end up developing spontaneously in the GoodDollar economy. So far, transaction figures seem to point in a different direction. Twenty-two months after its inception, in June 2022, with the total number of active UBI claimers 75,800 and the total number of unique claimers 444,358, only 4,540 transactions had been conducted.[43] If we assume active claimers carried those transactions – an assumption that results in the largest possible percentage of users actually conducting trade – we obtain 6 per cent of them did so – down to 1 per cent if we take the total number of unique claimers. G$ UBI claimers, the figures show, are holding (or maybe HODLing) to their G$s. And lively markets have therefore little chance to emerge spontaneously.

As we learnt through the monetary experiments in the book, the effectiveness of a currency for trade hinges not on its ease of conversion (liquidity), nor on its presumed intrinsic value. For a currency to actually serve as a medium of exchange and means of payment, it needs of a mechanism that provokes its holders to be willing to part from it, to spend it, to put it into circulation. In the crypto-space, dominated as it is by an approach to money as a commodity whose market value development brings dreams of easy capital earnings, it is however unclear what would break the preference of investors and claimers to hold to their G$s. A money imaginary that prompts users to relate to it as property to hold on to and eventually sell for a financial gain inhibits the movement of G$s into real markets. It is a money disembedded from relationships of trade in the productive economy. When, as it is the case with the GoodDollar initiative, markets for real goods and services do not exist prior to the launch of the complementary currency, the question that monetary designers need to ask is 'Why would participants in the monetary system be willing to spend the currency?' The ease of conversion – thanks to the 'automated market-maker' – alongside a cultural expectation in the crypto-space of increases in currency values, risks inclining G$ users to hold their crypto-money forward. And with no, or little spending, no emergence of a market for real goods and services where the poor receivers of UBI could put their G$ to use. A money assembled along the 'hold it forward' reasoning serves the speculative drive of investors and crypto-claimers without the possibility to satisfy the economic needs of the poor.

The final component in the GoodDollar monetary assemblage is its governance institution: the GoodDAO. A DAO, acronym for *decentralised autonomous organisation*, codes the crypto-fantasy of a money free of politics into a set of *smart contracts* – computer programs that execute automatically when predetermined conditions are met. Man-made as they are, those programs can be updated, recoded and continuously adjusted to the evolving needs of GoodDollar users. Monetary variables such as the reserve ratio or the expansion rate of the GoodDollar supply, the conversion rate between G$ and the collateral in the GoodReserve, the minting rate of G$s when interests are deposited in the GoodReserve, UBI spending plans or the number of G$s rewarded for marketing referrals, can be re-programmed if the team maintaining the GoodDAO so decides. Decisions are taken through participation and vote by members in the GoodDAO community. Membership in the GoodDAO governance institution and individual voting rights are determined by one's holdings of GOOD – 'a non-transferable token [that] therefore has no market value'[44] – at the equivalence of 1 GOOD = 1 vote. GOOD governance tokens are distributed regularly to investors and UBI recipients as these 'interact with the protocol'.[45] In short, the purpose of embedding the GoodDAO into the GoodDollar arrangement is to democratise decision-making concerning the management of money. 'DAOs are governed by the community, for the community.'[46] The GoodDAO is an effort to transfer the control of money from the GoodDollar Foundation to the overall community and thus 'safeguard against the wealthiest in the community capturing the lion's share of power'.[47] A commendable ambition if the governance of money is to attend the common interest.

Now, two aspects bear a central import on GoodDollar's version of monetary democracy. One, how GOODs are distributed across the GoodDollar community. Two, the conditions and point of time at which the voices of the many are given entry into the decision-making process. Concerning the first dimension, the distribution of voting power across the community. The one-GOOD-one-vote rule springs from the proof-of-stake reasoning that dominates the crypto-space, where voting rights hinge on the individual proving genuine interest in the particular cryptocurrency. The more cryptocurrency an individual holds, the stronger the commitment in the currency that individual is taken to have. The larger one's stake in the specific cryptocurrency, the more sincere the individual's interests on the good functioning of the currency is supposed to be. Proof-of-stake democracy – one-cryptotoken-one-vote rule – is based on individual wealth; the more you own, the more voting possibilities you have. It is the amount of crypto-possessions that grant you voting power – a form of democracy that is far from the liberal democratic ideal of one-person-one-vote. In grounding the strength of individual voting rights on individual holdings of the governance token, one-GOOD-one-vote fails to recognise the equal worth of each community member. An Athenian democracy of sorts, where non-proprietors – slaves, freed slaves, foreigners, women and children then, the have-nots in GoodDollar – are excluded from voting.

Such form of democracy begs the question of how unequally GOODs are distributed across members. It also raises the question of whether UBI claimers that do succeed in spending their G$s to satisfy their economic needs do retain the GOODs that may have been granted to them. Central as they are to assess the depth of the GoodDollar democracy, those two questions remain however unclear in the White Paper. From a blogpost by GoodDollar HQ, we learn that 'beyond the initial and ongoing annual distributions of the token' – unclear to whom and in what proportions – there are two ways to earn more GOOD. 'One is by *staking* G$ claimed through the app to the GoodDollar Trust. The other is by *staking* to the protocol (currently, in DAI), which will earn rewards in both G$ and GOOD.'[48] That is to say, GOODs, and with them voting rights, are handed out to stakers, investors in the GoodDollar economy, putting staker-investors at the pinnacle of decision-making. This skews decision-making towards the wealthy, risking further bending the monetary arrangement towards the investors whose interests the G$ architecture already prioritises. It is all but certain that the interests of investors align to the interests of the poor the global UBI initiative aims to serve.

Let's imagine that GOODs are distributed evenly, and that poor UBI claimers are therefore given a fair chance to voice their interests and shape the future of GoodDollar. A second vector relevant in the design of real inclusive democracy concerns the conditions and point of time at which one is allowed to raise one's voice. Members who want to submit a proposal for change to the GoodDAO are required to have a minimum of 240,000 G$s in their wallets,[49] about US$42 at the time of writing. Though the figure may seem low for today's UBI claimers, it is a sizeable amount for those GoodDollar intends to serve, 'populations [who] currently live on less than US$10 a day'.[50] At any rate, conditioning the suggestion of ideas to one's savings is yet another wealth constraint perverting the GoodDollar democracy.

It is also about timing. Imagine, again, that the G$s savings requirement was to be voted away, and that no other form of wealth – whether in GOODs, G$s or stakes – was to condition the strength of one's voting rights. Inviting the community to participate in the governance of money *after* the monetary arrangement has been designed, organised and implemented weakens the extent to which the community can effectually influence the monetary architecture. Investors have already been placed as the anchor of money creation, their interests at the centre of money distribution. Poor members of the community are only invited *ex post*. Other monetary architectures,

architectures that would have placed the poor at the core of money creation, are left out of the decision process opened up with the transfer of control to the GoodDAO. Designs that anchor money creation in the economic needs of users – like those we saw in the Sardex chapter or in Demos earlier in this chapter – are not possible any more. Those decisions have already been taken, coded and executed. And yet, those are the primary decisions affecting the level of UBI payment and thus the extent to which the poor will be able to cover their basic needs. *Ex-post* democracy is but a chimera of democracy.

Crypto-dreams of autopilot money free from politics, governments and bankers are rooted in a laissez-faire market principle that re-embeds money in a different set of political and cultural arrangements. Given money's capacity to infrastructure economic and social life, we cannot escape the need to arrange and continuously manage money. As GoodDollar shows, efforts to end politics in money are likely to end up shifting money's constituencies and displacing politics to spheres where fewer have the possibility to effectively raise their voice.[51]

Rearticulating money, markets and democracy

'What should the relationship between economics and politics be like to ensure that everyone has what is necessary to live a fulfilling life?' Pope Francis' question to young progressive scholars resonates with those raised by UBI advocates. Independently of background and ideological inclination – from the right and the left, from tech entrepreneurs and political candidates, from activists and scholars – UBI demands are refocusing the discussion of the economy on reaching the most fragile, on including those living on under US$10 a day, on providing stability to present and future precarious workers. Not for the sake of charity; not because of a suddenly woke philanthropic generosity. But because of a profound insight that the future of all, later generations included, hangs on the future of the weakest. Recent political and social instability has obviated that a sustainable future requires an economy oriented towards the common good, an economy that ensures 'everyone has what is necessary to live a fulfilling life'. UBI demands conjure up a diverse Polanyian countermovement calling for an economy that provides for the welfare of all.

Driven by a sense of urgency and an action-oriented attitude, some dreamers-doers have taken digital technologies into their hands to start experimenting with monies to build new inclusive economies. A UBI that reaches all is ultimately their collective goal. The understanding of 'inclusive economy' they code into their monetary rules is however differently framed depending on the social, economic and political position they act from. For the community grassroots group, an inclusive economy is about economic democracy; for the local public authority, it is about regional economic development; for the fintech entrepreneur, it is about doing well while doing good. Different framings lead to different monetary designs, to different organisation of economic relations and to different governance arrangements. They result in monetary assemblages that piece together the economy–society twosome differently. Such difference manifests most obviously in the role given to markets and the depth granted to democracy.

Markets play a pivotal role in all three complementary monies. They are however differently embedded into the monetary architecture. In Demos, the market is the place where members give and take, where participants exercise their right to appropriate and execute their obligation to give. It is a place of reciprocity, a place where debts and credits are cleared out, a place in which to 'give forward' and make community. Markets are simultaneously economy *and* community. Recognising the intense work required to set up markets that work effectively, Demos' monetary rules anchor the creation and distribution of money into the activity members carry out to develop community markets. In Mumbuca, markets are equal to the economy. The state is the institutional setting within which markets function. Traders, markets, economy are made synonymous; local state policies to strengthen the economy thus directed to traders and the markets they work in. Markets are the object of local government's economic development policies. Rules concerning the creation and distribution of money are contingent on local government, its budget and its assessment of citizens' economic need. In GoodDollar, markets of a particular type constitute the very rules coded into algorithmic money. Through the interests they generate, financial markets determine the rhythm at which money is created; through the price they accord, financial markets determine the value of the new money. Neither a community, nor an object of policy, in GoodDollar financial markets are the very principle organising money. The other markets, markets where the poor can attend their real needs, are assumed to emerge spontaneously; no need to embed the monetary arrangement into them.

The three complementary-currency-based-UBI schemes epitomise, as it were, three distinct principles for the design and organisation of economic and social relations – community-centred, state-centred, market-centred. Decision-making in monetary governance similarly follows the distinct principles. In Demos, the monthly General Assembly, open to all community members, makes monetary decisions through direct vote. In Mumbuca, the local government, elected every fourth year, makes those decisions in association with the local community bank. In GoodDollar, monetary decisions have been made by the developers and automated through smart contracts. The rules of Demos democracy and of its money are co-designed with users from before its implementation – *ex-ante* direct participatory democracy. In Mumbuca, citizens elect those that decide and re-elect them, or not, every four years – representative democracy as we know it. In GoodDollar, developers decide, code and launch before users are invited to any decision-making process. Having put the interests of one group at the core of the money creation and distribution rules, the possibility to make decisions that radically change the system are limited for the other group – *ex-post* democracy skewed towards the moneyed interests of financial actors. In both Demos and Mumbuca, money and the economy are subordinated to democratic politics, direct and continuous democracy the first, and indirect and intermittent democracy the latter. In GoodDollar, democracy and the economy are subordinated to the financial market organisational principle coded into the monetary algorithm.

Apart from eliciting the wide range of architectures and governance institutions welfare programmes under the same scheme may follow, Demos, Mumbuca and GoodDollar offer lessons that go beyond themselves. One, money is necessarily political in at least two senses: whose interests it serves; and how social groups with varying economic interests are included into its design and governance. Two, if money is to reach the most fragile, it needs to be articulated into state institutions that confer it legitimacy, scale and trustworthiness. Three, if it is to put the economy at the service of society, money needs to be embedded in communal relations of reciprocal rights and obligations. In other words, we need to make sure the design and governance of money are subsumed to democratic control, and directed to meet our individual and collective needs.

Money is a phenomenon with the capacity to infrastructure the economy and the polity. If we aim beyond giving the poor a means of subsistence, if we aim towards everybody having the means to live a free and fulfilling life, if we aim towards building an inclusive, just and equitable future, then we need to make sure the relationships we articulate into the money assemblage are just, inclusive and impartial. We need to subsume money and the economy under a renewed vision of democratic politics. Markets are to be embedded as forums where community is made, the state as the partner that leverages community, investors as yet another component on equal footing to the have-nots. From the recognition that real value is created together follows the need to include, on equal terms, the voices of the many into the making of money. As we reclaim, reimagine and reorganise money to build an inclusive and sustainable future, we can take the opportunity to insert its constitutive relations in a deepened form of democracy.

8

Greening Monies: Remaking Money to Service Nature

'Blah, blah, blah.' No translation needed. With those three simple sounds Greta Thunberg, the young Swedish climate activist, effectually conveyed the frustration many feel over the inaction of international agencies, governments and corporations over the ongoing environmental crises. Reports rapidly follow one another, the latest invariably making for more petrifying reading than the previous one.[1] An overwhelming majority of scientists agree climate change and biodiversity loss are caused by human activity.[2] Together with poverty and inequality, the World Bank identifies climate change as one of three 'defining issues of our age'.[3] The International Monetary Fund pronounces it 'a major threat to long-term growth and prosperity';[4] the United Nations, 'a global emergency that goes beyond national borders'.[5] Meanwhile, international summits fall short in their agreed ambition to tackle climate change,[6] governments fail to implement the measures and reach the targets they have committed themselves to,[7] and big corporations continue to engage in outright deliberate environmental crimes, greenwash practices at best, ecocide at worst.[8] Small and medium enterprises play also their part in the environmental disasters, '80% of pollution incidents and 60% of the commercial and industrial waste produced in England and Wales' coming from them.[9] Ongoing environmental collapse is but a manifestation of the extent to which the fate of the environment is interwoven to the way we organise society. Nature and society are but two sides of the same coin. In baptising our time the 'Anthropocene Epoch',[10] scholars recognise the constitutive relationship between human activity and the health of the planet. It is, too, a recognition that tackling the environmental collapse and restoring healthy ecosystems requires reorganising our economies. Indeed, to highlight the extent to which the dominant organisational form of our economies is at the root of our global environmental challenges, some scholars suggest the term 'Capitalocene' to refer to our present epoch.[11]

While those at the top keep deferring action to deliver on their insufficient promises, those at the bottom are organising to build resilience at the local level – restoring wetlands and mangroves, mobilising for the planting of trees, engaging in urban guerrilla gardening, grabbing land and giving it to the landless, building community economies and eco-villages for low-impact living, testing cooperative forms of democratic leadership, recuperating indigenous knowledges, developing novel grassroots educational programmes that have people and the planet at their core, revising notions of 'growth' and visions of the 'good life'.[12] The hope guiding the manifold efforts is common: to galvanise the multitude into civilisational transformation through prefigurative change of economic, social and political everyday practices.[13] Having given up on attempts to mitigate and frowning at attempts to adapt incrementally, they instead undertake transformative adaptation 'for and by ourselves'.[14] Their focus is on developing new ways to integrate the organisation of human society into the natural world, and test new civilisational forms that merge humans and nature in relationships of mutual care.

Within such varied bottom-up mobilisation, complementary monies are being implemented as sociotechnical instruments to move individuals into action and ignite ecological collaboration. Their starting point is the recognition that *we have never been modern*;[15] that human society and nature, the economy and the environment, have never been separate spheres. Modernism may have conceptualised them as distinct fields, organising the sciences in separate faculties, experts in independent groups, policy resolutions in distinct agencies. Yet, what the climate predicament tells us with apocalyptic strength is that nature and society go hand-in-hand, that the natural environment is indistinguishably enmeshed in the economic and political fabric of communities, and that we therefore need to heed nature in the way we organise our societies. Attending such insight, some monetary entrepreneurs attempt to embed nature into socioeconomic practice by articulating the environment into the very rules making and governing money.

The chapter looks into three complementary monies designed to infrastructure a healthier relationship between nature and society. Each of them is designed and governed to deal with their own specific environmental predicament – that is, the monetary configurations have been made greener. Conversely, each of them induces individuals and communities to care for their natural environment – in other words, these are monetary assemblages that nudge individual agency and collective action towards green behaviour. Hence the double meaning intended in the chapter's title: money has been made green; it, in turn, greens the behaviour of its users.

In each of the three complementary monies studied in the chapter – Turuta, Vilawatt and Plastic Bank – we will be able to recognise a money that is both constituted by, and constituting of, an economy committed to the stewardship of nature. Each following its own organising principle, the three monetary assemblages transform actions of care for nature into monetary tokens, and then organise the larger infrastructure so that those tokens can be transferred across persons and exchanged for goods and services. The designs of their monetary architectures line-up actors, ideas, interests and materials so as to make a difference on the individual motive of action – from pure gain to care for nature – and thus on the capacity to organise collectively towards respecting and caring for nature. The difference between the principles organising these monies does however differently shape their strategy to mobilise for global transformation and, with it, to advance civilisational change.

Turuta

Vilanova i la Geltrú is a city of some 65,000 inhabitants located in the Mediterranean coast about 45 kilometres south of Barcelona. Inspired by the principles of the *Earth Charter*,[16] in July 2009 a group of citizens started to meet regularly to research and debate how they could organise collectively 'to transition towards another model of society'. Over a year later, in October 2010, the citizen group launched the Turuta currency. They considered that a local complementary currency could be an effective instrument to 'spur new actions', mainly those that could 'promote the production of local products and maximum energy savings, in a word: local resilience'.[17]

The choice of name speaks of the commitment to the territory and its peoples of the initiators. Turuta refers to one of the most emblematic and lively events in the local carnival festivities, where participation is massive. From its inception, this territorial and participatory commitment translated into efforts to 'integrate the local currency fully in the local economy, people and culture' because, they argued, 'real strength is in the people and in our cooperative capacity to do things, to transform our world, to promote the transition from the current exclusive, unsustainable and aggressive model to a model that is respectful of diversity, sustainable, and peaceful'.[18] They therefore opted for a monetary design that allowed for the articulation of local merchants, individual citizens and public authorities on equal terms and that assumed and imbued care for nature as *the* motive of action. The tree was the metaphor that guided their work of building relations of community with people, territory and nature.

Turuta is designed along the lines of a mutual credit system, such as those in Sardinia and Málaga we saw in Chapter 4, and imbues in its members the same form and reason of the gift, the mutual give-and-take we saw in those two local monies. Only, with a creative tweak: individual members are not allowed to go into debt; instead community land-recuperation projects record the debt of the collective. The time individual commoners invest in reclaiming urban land for collective urban farming is remunerated at ten turutas (Tt) per hour, equivalent to ten euros. These are credited into the individual account and debited into the account of the particular land-recuperation project. Individuals can then spend their Turuta balances in associated local merchants as well as buy the produce of the land they have worked to recover. As a current board member describes the Turuta system, "it is a mutual credit system where debt–credit relationships are between members and the association; a system through which we socialise member's negative balances in the form of transformational projects". A monetary arrangement that articulates in its very design the human motive not of gain but of "wanting to participate in social evolution and change by promoting relationships of proximity, cooperation and mutual help".

To illustrate, let's take two community members, Carmen and Ton, who each work in a community land recuperation project. Carmen supports the ecological improvement of the Community Vineyard for two full working days; Ton participates in one clean-up and reconstruction day of the historical transhumance paths of the Garraf Massif.[19] The accounting sequence is shown in Table 8.1.

The rules governing the creation and distribution of turutas are decidedly entangled with local nature, and so is the human motive modelled into the monetary rules. Turutas are created through work to improve the environment, and are distributed to those carers of the local natural commons. These can be spent with local merchants but, ultimately, turutas are withdrawn from the system as the land gives back to the commoners – in our example, when Ton and the local merchant buy produce from the

Table 8.1: Example of changes in Turuta account balances

Accounts	**Account balances**				
	Time 0: Initial account balance	**Time 1: Carmen and Ton work on recovering the land**	**Time 2: Ton spends 50 Tt from his balance on produce from the recuperated land**	**Time 3: Carmen spends 30 Tt from her balance on produce from the local merchant**	**Time 4: Merchant spends 30 Tt on produce from the recuperated land**
Carmen	0	+ 160	+ 160	+130	+130
Ton	0	+ 80	+ 30	+ 30	+ 30
Project: Garraf	0	– 80	– 80	– 80	– 80
Project: Community vineyard	0	– 160	– 110	– 110	– 80
Local merchant	0	0	0	+ 30	0
Total	**0**	**0**	**0**	**0**	**0**

community recuperated land (times 2 and 4 in Table 8.1). In other words, what time and care individual commoners dedicate to regain nature in the local territory, is taken back in the form of herbs, fruits and vegetables. The state of the balance of that exchange-through-giving is visualised in turutas. Turutas, that is, are accounting records tracing relationships of care between humans and nature, which can be cleared out once nature has healed and become productive. In this way, the Turuta monetary arrangement integrates nature with the environmental concerns of those who inhabit it.

Apart from anchoring the mutual credit system in relationships of care for nature, the relational design of the Turuta adjusts to the fears of community members. Early into their efforts, the grassroots collective found out the extent to which the negative experience of debt dominant in conventional money was a limit in attracting fellow commoners.[20] The solution was simple: to impede individuals going into debt. This differs from many mutual credit systems. "If I have euros, I can buy", the grassroots group reasoned, "if I don't, I can't". Similar in the Turuta. They wanted a monetary system "that was easy and resilient". The collective took the decision and coded it into their digital system, individual accounts fitted to record figures on the positive, never on the negative. This implied, however, that members had to work before being able to buy and experience the material benefits of the Turuta. Aiming to attract and mobilise citizens into action towards the environment, a second feature was therefore designed into the monetary arrangement. To enrol, individuals are required to pay a fee of 10 euros for which 10 Tt are immediately credited to their new individual account, enabling them to start buying local and ecological produce from the recuperated gardens without, for that, first having worked in those gardens. These turutas are debited to the Cooperative Fund account, which further collects individual donations in turutas. Note, however, that although euros can be converted into turutas – whenever one wants – with a 5 per cent bonus, the reverse is not possible.

Community projects are approved, and the use of euros and the Cooperative Fund are decided through direct participatory democracy. The General Assembly is open to all members and meets two or three times a year. Collectively, attendants to the General Assembly deliberate on the viability of the land recuperation or other community projects members have proposed to the board prior to the assembly, on the availability and assignment of working groups for the projects, or on the running of the Local Exchange Office that supports Turuta members and informs the wider citizenry about the local currency.

Slowly but surely, through small-scale but organised continuous action, conducted by grassroots working groups of individuals integrated in the civic, commercial and administrative fabrics of the city, the Turuta has become a common sight in the urban landscape. Regular Turuta markets, stickers on the front doors of local merchants announcing acceptance of turutas and, in

July 2014, the City Council's unanimous approval of the turuta as the local currency of Vilanova i la Geltrú. The City's Environmental Department became another member, on an equal footing to that of some other 565 members, 66 of whom are 'professional providers (businesses, commercial establishments, legal free-lancers, etc.)'.[21]

Merchants accepting turutas witness reaching a new customer profile. A baker who offers the possibility to pay 25 per cent of the price of their products in the local currency observes that

> 'a very interesting new clientele is coming with values of ecology, cooperation and lovers of local products, all of which I share. This means that I have a lot of turutas, but I am already beginning to be able to exchange them for other products or services, and ... [these new clients] also mean I get [more] euros.'

Further, merchants do not need to fear for their perishable goods any more. Come the end of the week, the fishmonger whose fresh products do not last over the weekend started to offer her fish 100 per cent in turutas. Soon she had no problem with unsold produce, and had to limit payment in turutas to 50 per cent of the fish's price.

Despite the citizen group's advances in recovering and commoning urban land – some urban land sites have been reclaimed and recuperated by citizen groups, others have been donated by the city – they do not aspire to grow beyond a communal scale: "500 to 1,000 inhabitants at most, because relationships of proximity, knowledge, trust and, above all, participation are very important." For the members, it is active participation in the general assemblies, in the working groups, in the approved projects, that makes community and spurs individuals into environmental action. The local currency is a tool that incites, organises, visualises and remunerates participation. Growing too big risks diluting the sense of social obligation that moves individuals to action. "If there would be too many, we would create another tree [association], and another, and another. The Turuta would be the same for everyone, but the projects would be the responsibility of the respective trees." An organisational logic, that is, centred in the everyday, in the small, in cooperation, in constant and slow action, in the capacity to adjust to the "dynamics and singularities of each territory [and people]" – in all but name, the organising principle of the commons. Their motto: "We go slow because we are going far." Their hope: "The sum of all these initiatives is what will lead to great change."

Vilawatt

Forty per cent of energy consumption and 36 per cent of greenhouse gas emissions in the European Union have their origin in buildings. Those figures make the built environment – homes, offices, schools, hospitals, libraries and other public buildings – the single largest energy consumer and one of the largest emitters of carbon dioxide in the EU.[22] Those figures also put buildings at the centre of policies and public initiatives that aim to reduce greenhouse gas emissions by at least 50 per cent by 2030 compared to levels in 1990 and no-net emissions by 2050, both goals set out by the European Commission in its European Green New Deal.[23] With over 70 per cent of Europe's population – some 359 million people – living, working and studying in cities,[24] there is an increased awareness of the key role cities play in pushing the transition towards energy-efficient zero-emission buildings and a climate neutral future. It is against this background that Viladecans, a city in the outskirts of Barcelona, launched Vilawatt.

A city of some 67,000 inhabitants in just 20.4 square kilometres, Viladecans grew in the 1960s and 1970s to become a service city to the Catalan capital. Some of its most densely populated neighbourhoods were constructed with poor building techniques before the Spanish legislation on building insulation of 1976 and consume, as a result, above average levels of energy.[25] Those neighbourhoods are home to low-income residents, likely to suffer from energy poverty and unable to afford the retrofitting of their residential buildings for energy efficiency. Viladecans City Council conceived Vilawatt to usher citizens, merchants and public institutions into collaborating 'to promote and ensure a secure, clean and efficient use of energy' in the city. The four key instruments used to ignite the transition to 'a new energy model at the local level'[26] were 'energy supply, energy culture, retrofitting of buildings and a local currency linked to energy savings'. Vilawatt refers to the public–private–citizen consortium behind the initiative as well as to the currency propelling the new network of actors and capacities to 'lead the process of energy transition in the city of Viladecans'.

Vilawatt monetary arrangement follows a 'tax it forward' form and reason – such as that in the Wörgl of the 1930s we saw in Chapter 5 – with issuance firmly entwined to the energy savings goal that so guides the initiative. As in Wörgl, public spending is focused in the territory and precedes the payment of local taxes in the local currency. Again, as in Wörgl's municipal money, the authority to issue the currency and the authority enabling tax-payments in it are united under the City Council. To recall, the origin and direction of municipal monies goes from public investment to private spending to tax payments – a 'tax forward' strategy that both makes the money more easily acceptable and constitutes its *perpetuum mobile* mechanism.

In Viladecans, the initial public investment was largely funded by the EU programme Urban Initiative Actions and focused on reducing the energy consumption and on developing the energy production capacity of buildings. Windows, doors, fences and blinds were changed, internal and external insulation was installed, and solar panels were placed on rooftops. Citizen communities were created with the capacity to share energy with other neighbourhoods even if these are not directly connected to the Vilawatt network. An information office was set up to advise citizens on their contracts and bills, and bulk-buying of renewable energy was coordinated by the Vilawatt Consortium. Half of the energy savings thus accrued are then issued in Vilawatts and automatically transferred to citizens in the Consortium. The other half are reinvested in retrofitting other buildings through direct public investment or through subsidies to citizens. On a voluntary basis and in the near future, civil servants will be able to apply for a minor portion of their salary to be paid in Vilawatts. The more than 3,500 citizens that take part in the initiative find use for their Vilawatts in the more than 200 local merchants associated to the network who, in turn, can spend the local complementary money in goods and services among themselves and, as of 2022, to pay municipal taxes and services. In this way, Vilawatt's monetary architecture, by design, entangles the city's fight for climate neutrality and against energy poverty into the city's local economy.

Anchoring the issuance of Vilawatts on accomplished reduction in energy consumption and introducing them into circulation through rewards for, and further investment in, energy saving measures, the Vilawatt monetary architecture is decisively articulated to the energy-production needs of the territory. The monetary arrangement thus aligns the interests of individual citizens with the interests of nature. Beyond aligning interests, Vilawatts monetary tokens visualise energy savings. At the intersection of government bureaucracy and scientific objectivity, numbers – more so when they constitute rewards for the behaviour they visualise – act as vehicles for igniting democratic debate;[27] in this case, a broad discussion among citizens and local businesses of everyone's role in the energy transition and the recognition of the need to update one's know-how and skills for advancing a climate neutral future – a re-skilling that the Vilawatt Consortium has facilitated through the creation of learning communities, the offering of training programmes to small businesses, and active labour market interventions that prioritise the most vulnerable citizens. In this way Vilawatt not only aligns the interests of residents in Viladecans with those of the planet. Most importantly, in underscoring every single one's energy use, Vilawatt heightens self-reflection on one's energy practices in relation to those of one's neighbours – personal meditations that nudge the individual motive of action from monetary gain to care for the environment. To put it simply: a money integrated in energy savings cultivates, by design, awareness of our collective responsibility for the Earth that we all share.

To heighten the democratisation of energy-awareness and knowledge, the institution governing Vilawatt – the Vilawatt Consortium – includes local merchants and citizen associations alongside local public entities – the City Council most notably. Because issuance and circulation of the local currency is grounded on energy savings accomplished by residents and local businesses, the energy behaviour of residents and local businesses plays a central role in the functioning of the Vilawatt monetary assemblage. This requires actors in the network to continuously listen to residents' and businesses' concerns, practices and situated knowledges in matters of energy consumption and production. In their dual role as providers of renewable energy and as energy users – or, if you prefer, as backers of the currency's issuance and as entry points for the circulation of the local money – the behavioural patterns of residents and merchants can determine the success of the city's climate neutrality efforts as well as the stability of the Vilawatt green money. It is to heed attention to their voices, doubts, challenges and learnings that the Vilawatt Consortium inserts merchants and residents in the very constitution of the Consortium itself. The Consortium, a public–private–citizen partnership, brings together all the local stakeholders to the climate predicament. Collaboratively, local residents, local businesses and local elected public authorities decide on the development of Vilawatt, the currency and the energy projects charging it. Jordi Mazón, deputy mayor of Vildecans, argues that the governance model is 'the greatest strength of Vilawatt Project … a well-established structure, the PPCP [public–private–citizen partnership] Consortium, which manages energy differently and is leading to the change of the energy model'.[28]

The impact of an initiative based on the wide participation of citizens and local merchants is visible in the number of dwellings retrofitted (55), the aggregate energy savings in the city (about 30 per cent), the ubiquity of energy debate, which has become part of citizens' everyday life, the expansion of the project from the initial district to include the whole city, and the persistence of the initiative beyond the initial EU funding. The optimism generated is such that the year targeted for the city to achieve climate neutrality has moved from 2050 to 2030.

The focus of the environmental efforts of Viladecans City Council is squarely on their local territory; on their constituency. The climate challenge is however a global one. To organise for global transformation, those behind Vilawatt argue for the sum of many city-led efforts, a movement of cities working along similar lines. Jordi Mazón, deputy mayor for ecological transition and leader of the Vilawatt project, uses the metaphor of atoms to describe the worldwide movement of cities required to reach global climate neutrality.

> The most amazing materials currently being developed – the ones that are changing fields such as urban planning, engineering, and measurement, transforming our way of life in a radical way – are based on nano-science. … These innovative materials are based on

> manipulating atom by atom and putting them in optimal positions, to achieve a better material. The macroscopic properties of a material are the result of an optimal microscopic structure. ... Likewise, small-scale innovation on a small municipal-scale must make it possible to build a better society and planet. Municipalities are what atoms are to materials, and politicians are the equivalent of nano-science engineers. We aim to create a better planet by improving our municipalities.[29]

Vilawatt organises money along a state principle where a central authority, though municipal, has the capacities to both issue and accept the complementary money in payment for the provision of a public good (energy). Although uncompromisingly local, such radical municipal initiatives envision global change by inspiring one municipality at a time. To this end, Viladecans has already started collaborating with the cities of Seraing (Belgium), Nagykanizsa (Hungary) and Trikala (Greece) to share knowledge, transfer practices and keep the momentum of an emerging municipality-driven city-based polycentric movement.[30]

Plastic Bank

Plastic is one of our most pressing environmental challenges. With some 400 million tons of plastic produced each year and only a smaller percentage being incinerated or recycled,[31] the majority of plastic either ends up in landfills or leaks out into the environment. When breaking down, plastic trash turns into micro-plastics that are easily transported by the winds to the most remote, uninhabited corners on the planet – from the heights of Mount Everest to the depths of the Mariana Trench, from the Grand Canyon in the United States to the Kavir and Lut deserts of Iran.[32] Micro-plastics and the toxic chemicals they release contaminate the soil, poison our lakes, pollute the seas, fall from the sky with rain and snow, and ultimately make it to our food plates.[33] Experts agree that to address this suffocating plastic glut, we need to change our behaviour concerning the production, consumption and waste management of plastic. They also agree on the urgent need to galvanise collective action at a global scale.[34]

Waste-pickers are among the most stigmatised and vulnerable groups of society. They offer, nonetheless, an invaluable service to people and the Earth. In gathering plastic waste from river banks and beaches and in bringing that waste to collection centres, waste-pickers discontinue waste's path towards fields and valleys and onto rivers and oceans, and connect the trash with the recycling centre. In performing such disconnecting and connecting work, waste-pickers constitute the human component of waste-collection infrastructures.[35] With an estimated 21 million metric tons of plastic entering the earth's oceans every year,[36] and with low-to-middle-income countries in coastal areas being its main entry points, waste-pickers in these countries could play a key role in the sort of waste-recycling global circular economy international agencies and think-tanks call for.[37] And yet, the value of their labour is seldom recognised, their waste economy remains largely informal, their living conditions undignified. Dissociated from the value of waste-pickers' stewardship of the environment, our monetary arrangement maintains the illusion of nature as separate from society.

David Katz saw the connections between the two and recognised that making explicit the nature–society relationship could help galvanise collective action. Finding peace where the sea meets the shore, over the years, Katz had 'just seen it degrade. Every year it gets worse and worse. What we see on the water's edge is what the ocean spits back at us'.[38] A 3D printing seminar helped him appreciate the economic value of plastic and associate the plastic debris that litters beaches to the living conditions of the poor.[39] If only there was a paradigmatic change in how we understood plastic, what today is one of our utmost environmental disasters could be transformed into an economic opportunity that mobilised the many towards its management. In Katz's own words, 'if we could change how people see plastic, that will be part of the solution'.[40] Plastic Bank, the initiative David Katz set up in 2014, was born from the insight that such a cultural change could be catalysed by articulating plastic waste to major brands that use plastic in their production process through the mediation of waste-collectors, plastic disposal-and-recycling centres, and the provision of money, goods and services against collected waste. Plastic Bank was to organise a monetary assemblage to infrastructure a waste-based economy.

Plastic Bank's monetary configuration is designed in parallel to the circular waste economy it aims to instigate. In the regions where it works, the venture sets up a network of 'storefronts where people can return the material' and provides these stores with equipment to weigh, clean, shred, bale and ready the plastic for export. For the plastic waste they bring to the store, collectors are credited at 'a consistent above-market rate … in a blockchain-based banking application'. Collectors can then use their credit to acquire basic goods and services offered at the store or can keep the credit in the form of 'blockchain-secured digital tokens'. In essence, David Katz admits:

> [W]e are a global chain of stores for the ultra, ultra poor, where everything in the store is available to be purchased using plastic garbage. And we offer school tuition, medical insurance, communications, power, sustainable cooking fuel, high efficiency stoves, sanitation, communication, and a whole product range, all available to be purchased using plastic garbage.[41]

In this way, the poor and vulnerable in the communities Plastic Bank works in are mobilised to clean beaches while earning 'a stable, liveable income'.

Similar to the Turuta and Vilawatt monetary arrangements, by integrating care for the environment into the rules deciding the creation and distribution of monetary tokens, Plastic Bank directs individual self-interest to attend the needs of nature.

> What we've really done is we've created Candy Crash of recycling, an application for the world so that the more they use it, the more they earn ... the more that you clean it, the better credit rating we can provide you, the more access to financial tools you can receive, the more reward ... when our collectors receive certain levels, when they've achieved and collected ... they can be recognised for their contribution to society and to humanity. An ability for the unseen to be seen. A stewardship of all people and all things.[42]

Reportedly, Plastic Bank's monetisation of waste has mobilised individual agency and resulted, by September 2022, in 3.04 billion plastic bottles and over 60 million kg of plastic waste being stopped from ending up in the seas.[43]

Alongside waste-collectors, another central actor that needs to be brought into the nature–society twosome is major companies using plastic in their products. Plastic Bank manages to articulate them into the monetary assemblage by selling not only treated, upcycled plastic waste to them, but Social Plastic – plastic that 'provides a social benefit: impoverished communities gain access to stable income, local economies are boosted, and life necessities, such as food, water, and electricity, become more accessible'. Plastic Bank's Social Plastic attaches the poor into its value, for which it can charge above market prices for the plastic waste it sells to brands – such as Marks & Spencers or Henkel – 'who reuse social plastic in their products'. In this way, David Katz concludes, 'we've created a globally recognisable and traceable currency that is waste'.

In placing plastic waste at the heart of the monetary arrangement undergirding a waste-based circular economy, Plastic Bank forces us to reconceptualise value and money. In Plastic Bank's arrangement, value consists neither of the objective value assumed intrinsic to materials such as gold (as the commodity imaginary of money has it); nor does value consist of the subjective desire expressed at markets.[44] Rather, value becomes a sociomaterial relational phenomenon that derives from connecting a variety of actors (collectors, stores and brands), recycling equipment (to weigh, clean, shred and bale plastic) and understandings (waste as a resource and waste-pickers as stewards of the environment) to an accounting system that visualises relations of value. Money becomes the configuration of actors, equipment and understandings; the actor-network enabling the performance of waste's value, visualising it through figures, and remunerating actors for their infrastructuring work. Collectors accept the credit (in the form of tokens) recorded in the blockchain application in payment for the waste they have collected because the totality of the monetary assemblage allows for the circulation of the value represented by the token. Neither the credit nor the token are value in themselves. Collectors accept the credit-token because it can move through a network of actors that transforms it into goods and services they need. With a more visual metaphor, David Katz compares waste to diamonds to highlight the way value hinges on the configuration of many heterogeneous components. 'It's not different to walking over acres of diamonds. If Lise [a waste-collector] was to walk over acres of diamonds but if there was no store, no bank, no way to use the diamonds, no way to exchange them, they'll be worthless too.'[45] As a result of the arrangement, '[t]he value of Social Plastic goes beyond the commodity price of plastic: a ladder of opportunity is created for the world's impoverished and our oceans are protected from pollution'.[46]

To adapt to local specificities, Plastic Bank embeds its collection-and-recycling-value-creating-network within extant local actors. To illustrate, in Haïti, Plastic Bank collaborates with 'small grocery stores and lottery centres [that act] as collection locations'; in the Philippines, it works 'with a cooperative of junk shops which represent 150 junk shops to unify them'; in urban Brazil, it organises a 'social franchising model … to make it a more viable business venture for local entrepreneurs' as well as 'includes congregations, the Church, where parishioners are encouraged to not just bring their offerings on Sunday but to bring in their recycling'.[47] Though the price of Social Plastic is still set by Plastic Bank, organising it as a network of stores each with capacity to decide how it engages its waste-collectors decentralises and localises governance of some of the components of the waste-based monetary arrangement.

Plastic Bank illustrates the infrastructuring work needed to assemble and manage monetary configurations as well as the infrastructural capacity of money. Plastic Bank reveals money as a sociotechnical infrastructure that catalyses individual agency and structures fields of action (a plastic waste ecosystem). And vice versa. The changed individual behaviour that the new money catalyses changes, in turn, the monetary arrangement itself: new waste entrepreneurs set up shop, congregations join the effort and communities coalesce, thus steadying the value of the plastic-currency for major brands. Money assembles and is assembled by devices (digital platforms), cultural understandings (of waste and value) and actors whose interconnection continuously effect an influence in money itself.

The stability of Plastic Bank's sociotechnical monetary arrangement hinges on the price paid to collectors for the waste they gather. At the moment, that is a fixed price set by the social venture. Yet, there seem to be plans to introduce variability in that price by extending the free market ideal to the organisation of collectors' waste-gathering labour. In a fact report from 2019, David Katz writes: '[O]ur ambition is to let the open market determine the price of Social Plastic, while today we have a fixed price. It will be a great success if Social Plastic can become cheaper than virgin plastic.'[48] With social plastic cheaper than virgin plastic, the hope is that more 'agree to use social plastics in [their] manufacturing and that on its own will influence tens of thousands of people'.[49] Since the price paid for the plastic collected decides the amount of complementary money issued, letting that price be determined by the free market necessarily implies anchoring the rules governing the issuance of Plastic Bank's tokens in the ideal of a self-regulating market price mechanism. David Katz is right in foreseeing that the decision would influence tens of thousands of people, most notably, the many vulnerable waste-collectors. It is, however, doubtful such influence would be positive alone.

In Plastic Bank's monetary arrangement, the price of social plastic constitutes the remuneration paid to collectors for their labour, for their work caring for the beaches and the fields. Imposing variable market prices on collectors' stewardship of nature would involve no less a transformation than that of the stewards into commodities. The implication could be the immediate deterioration of collectors' living conditions. Karl Polanyi warned us against the dangers of commodifying labour. Because labour does not behave like a commodity, because its supply cannot simply adjust to the vagaries of markets, using the market price mechanism to organise the supply and demand of social plastic risks resulting in the most vulnerable – waste-collectors – taking the toll of adjustment.[50] Lower prices for social plastic means lower remuneration for the labour of people already living under the poverty line. Subordinating humans to the market, Polanyi showed, led to the dislocation of society itself. It is in this respect that the three monetary assemblages analysed in the chapter differ the most. To organise widely, Turuta's strategy goes through the mobilisation of many communities that give forward care to nature; while Vilawatt's strategy goes through the mobilisation of many local governments that tax forward investments in nature. In contrast, Plastic Bank's strategy goes through selling collectors' labour forward to major brands. The fairness and sustainability of such a strategy is subject to the mechanism determining the price of collectors' care labour. When monetary arrangements move in the direction of subsuming labour to the market, workers and their families are forced to bear the labour costs that are no longer rewarded by the lower price. They are forced to get by with reduced remuneration for the same amount of labour. Lower prices satisfy the interests of big brands without attending to the needs of the poor – a monetary rule, that is, that prioritises the demands of capital over those of an informal unprotected and unorganised global proletariat. While the alliance between corporate capital and entrepreneurs with a liberal humanist agenda is a requirement for articulating diverse actors into a global fight for nature, we need to be attentive to the way such an alliance, if organised through the ideal of a self-regulated market mechanism, organises bare life in the poor coastal areas of the planet.

Articulating nature into the money assemblage

Naming the present epoch the 'Anthropocene' is a recognition of the interdependent fate of nature and humanity. Mainstream economists may build their models on the assumption of a nature divorced from the economy, they may regard the environmental consequences of the market-based organisation of societies as mere 'externalities' to be ignored. And yet, whatever economic models depict and predict, nature speaks back at them with apocalyptic force. The land has been impoverished, the air polluted, the waters made poisonous. Droughts, heatwaves, precipitations, hurricanes have intensified. Life on Earth – the life of plants, animals and us – is threatened with extinction thanks to the very form we have organised ourselves. Nature and economy are not, after all, independent from each other. Increasingly, we are becoming aware of the need to build new civilisational forms that unhesitatingly put the economy at the service of nature.

Designing and implementing new civilisational forms is no small task. Nor is the outcome of the civilisations prefigured necessarily that intended. When the transformation required is, as this one is, at the global scale, the implications, if the efforts go awry, are potentially too large. Fortunately, there are many small actual initiatives experimenting with novel ways of organising the economy–nature twosome. Some of these put the reorganisation of money at the core of the novel civilisation-making efforts. In order to articulate the economy – that is, the system through which we, us all, individuals, communities and societies at large, organise the production and distribution of goods and services – into nature itself, in an attempt to mobilise individuals to take care of nature, these new monies are designed to reshape individual agency, to move people into new trajectories of action.

Indeed, the issuance rules of all three currencies link the supply of money directly to performed acts of care for nature. In Turuta, monetary tokens are issued to remunerate the labour involved in cleaning, preparing and cultivating previously abandoned and dilapidated land. In Vilawatt, the monetary tokens are issued to subsidise citizens' investments to lower the energy consumption of their homes as well as to reward accomplished energy savings. In Plastic Bank, monetary tokens are distributed in exchange for plastic waste collected and brought to Plastic Bank storefronts. As these monies remunerate land renewal, energy savings and plastic waste collection, individuals are moved to renew land, save energy and clean the beaches of plastic waste. As the monetary configurations transform a dilapidated plot into productive land, decrease energy use, and turn collected plastic into transferable value, individuals are guided towards caring for those specific dimensions of the local habitat. In short, the monetary rules governing the creation and distribution of money fundamentally shape how people act towards the environment around them. Connecting the creation of money directly to the care of nature thus necessarily mobilises people to caring for nature. Anchoring the supply and initial distribution of money in acts of natural care is the first step to put the economy at the service of nature.

The next step seems still in need of resolution: how to mobilise widely, how to go beyond the smaller local community, how to organise collective action at the global scale. Following a community-based organisational principle of collective action, those behind Turuta call for many small communities of citizens organising locally. The focus is on instigating an individual sense of responsibility towards each other and towards one's territory – a sense that is best cultivated through relations of proximity. Vilawatt's suggested answer similarly focuses on the territory and similarly places the locus of organisational efforts at the local level; in Vilawatt, however, the driving actors are not organised citizen communities but elected municipal councils. As in Turuta, Vilawatt proposes global transformation needs to happen through the mobilisation of many localities each adapting their efforts to their own priorities and circumstances. Plastic Bank's answer is instead global from the outset. Herein resides the main strategic difference between the three monies. In Plastic Bank the organisation of collective action requires connecting actors that already have a global reach – major corporations – to the many hyper-local efforts of waste-collectors through the creation of a global commodity market – a global market for social plastic, a material produced with human labour. While its price remains fixed and higher than other forms of plastic, there is little risk for the deterioration of the living conditions of the collectors. But if the global price of social plastic is allowed to vary alongside the supply and demand of the material, the globalisation of Plastic Bank's prototyped waste-based-economy risks benefiting big corporations at the expense of vulnerable waste-pickers and their families. To remain inclusive, fair and resilient, we therefore cannot leave the organisation of global collective efforts in the hands of profit-seeking capitalists nor subordinate the income of waste-pickers to the self-regulating price mechanism of free markets. And yet, the dilemma remains. If we are to reach globally, it may be too slow to wait for communities and cities around the world to take action. In the face of global climate and environmental catastrophe, our very survival hinges on tight global cooperation between dense clusters of local action. How can local action and global cooperation be catalysed and organised simultaneously?

The answer advanced in this chapter is that organising glocally can effectively be done by rethinking and remaking money. It is through the reconstitution of money that we are to start a transformation of our civilisation's relation to nature. Indeed, the actors behind the three complementary monies seen in the chapter are leading the creative efforts by working on intentionally articulating society to nature. Their strength lies in having understood the entangled relationship between monetary configurations and civilisational forms. Their canniness resides in having seen that it is impossible to distinguish nature from society and society from the form of that society's money. A lay-person may think she is holding a 'funny money' in her hands, whereas in fact she is holding a small-scale infrastructural prototype of a new civilisational form, a model that directs individual agency towards caring for nature in order to enable the organisation of collective action towards changing the way the economy and nature interact. As soon as we dive into the configurational design of the monetary infrastructure behind the money-token we hold in our hand, we are able to identify all the actors, cultural ideas, interests and material artefacts that have been lined up so as to incite us to get hold of that token. Money, once more, is framed by human design, and pre-formats individual action. If we are serious about addressing our environmental predicament, it is therefore imperative to realign money to cater for the health of nature.

9

Learning to Live Together Anew: Money Commons That Serve People and Planet

Money has undeniably become a weapon of war. In the early hours of 24 February 2022, Russia ramped up its invasion of Ukraine – ongoing in Crimea since 2014 – by launching dozens of missile attacks across the country. Four days later, the EU imposed a ban on transactions with the Russian Central Bank. Eight days later, on 8 March, Western countries cut major Russian banks from the SWIFT international payments system and froze the assets the Russian Central Bank held outside its borders. Those three decisions turned central components of the international monetary system into instruments for waging war without bombs. They built on the fundamental recognition of the infrastructural power of money for society. Harming a society could just as effectively be done by crippling that society's money.

The insight behind those actions is, in essence, one half of the argument made in this book. Money is constitutive of society. The monetary architecture steers individual behaviour, shapes economic activity and ultimately coordinates the social fabric. Change money and you would change society.

Nothing new in that line of reasoning; at least not for the monetary entrepreneurs that enthusiastically work to establish local – and less local – monies in order to transform society. It may have been more of a novel insight for mainstream economics scholars who strip their models of money.[1] For them money is neutral, its short-term dynamics inconsequential for, in the long-term, markets will always spontaneously emerge, self-regulate and self-stabilise – an imaginary they seem to hold despite overwhelming evidence to the contrary. The chronic failure of economics to predict dramatic economic events – recall Queen Elizabeth's surprise over the inability of economists to foresee the financial collapse of 2008 – is the result of a mistake of imagination, of the lack of substance in conventional ideas on money promulgated by political economists across the board, from A. Smith to K. Marx. As an academic field, it seems economics needs to clear its thinking from a few myths.

Choosing to imagine money as an artefact neutral to the economy, as the universal commodity to solve barter's double coincidence of wants, as an apolitical tool to grease the wheels of commerce, has further consequences. It stops us from opening up the sociotechnical arrangement that money actually is and, ultimately, it blinds us to the constitutive role money plays in the current state of the planet and its peoples. Chapter 3 traced the connections. The fact that the majority of today's conventional money is created by private financial actors following a profit-motive steers the direction of the economy and results in the recurring booms and busts we see across the world's economies. That money is created as a debt to be paid back with an interest firmly establishes the imperative to grow at the heart of every money-debt-related human pursuit – from those of major corporations to those of the humble student. That unpaid interests compound onto the original debt traps debtors into debt-slavery and entrenches economic inequality in society. Unfolding our conventional money was not done just for the sake of ranting on about banks and financial actors. From climate change and biodiversity loss to exploitation of the many and increasing inequality, the source of today's predicaments can be traced to the architectural design and form of governance of our conventional monetary system. Given the magnitude and the existential nature of our problems, it is then necessary we make visible, first, money's internal architecture, and, second, the direct relationship between the specific design and governance of that architecture and our many crises. The first half of the book's argument consists, simply, in adding substance and a degree of sophistication to the popular concession that money is the root of all evil. Rather than finding money, in the general, the universal culprit, the book found the root of all evil in the the specific arrangement of today's conventional money, in the set of actors, entities, imaginaries and technologies that make money and in the particular relationships among all those architectural components of money.

The second half of the argument in this book is, really, what many organisers of money already know. Money is sociality, and so, society constitutes money. Money is made out of relationships between a variety of actors, entities, imaginaries and technologies. Those relationships are not set in stone (except, maybe, on the island of Yap). That technology changes, and with it, it changes money, most are rather aware of – thereof the ardour among many a crypto-entrepreneur. What fewer seem to be aware of is that actors, entities and imaginaries, as well as the relationships among these, can change, and with that, money changes.

Put both halves of the argument together and you arrive at the conclusion that money can become an instrument for peace. If society constitutes money, and money constitutes society, then all we need to do is to assemble a money geared to peaceful society.

And free. And just. And environmentally sustainable.

An abundance of creative possibilities suddenly opens up. The first step of the book was therefore to present an imaginary of money that may enable *us* to construct better monies – better as in conducive to fairer, freer and more resilient collectives. Better as in attending to the needs and priorities of the communities that undergird the new monies. Better as in provoking the most pro-social and pro-environmental behaviours in us. Thinking money in terms of the commons has several advantages. One, it questions popular conceptions of money as the private possession of the wealthy. Two, it highlights money as an infrastructure for the common good thus highlighting the rights of the people to have a say on it. Three, it opens up the possibility for communities to govern it. In other words, a commons money imaginary has the potential to transform our collective horizons and trajectories of action.

Furthermore, a commons imaginary of money extends the possibilities for individual economic agency. In today's conventional monies, and for the great majority of us, economic agency is reduced to consume or not consume, spend or save, borrow and pay back. There is no other option for the individual citizen than to submit to the rules of a monetary infrastructure that permeates space and time. The common person is constrained to relate to the monetary system merely as a currency user, thus effectively subordinating the interest of the majority to the interests of the elite of profit-seeking bankers that do create the large majority of our conventional money. A commons money imaginary turns the table upside-down. It enables groups of citizens, cities and activists to define anew the rules of the money game and to govern the monetary infrastructure to suit their evolving priorities. From the limited role of currency user to the expanded capacity of currency issuer. An expanded room for action inheres in a commons thinking.

But reclaiming the freedom and right to assemble money anew does not necessarily translate into monies that work for the many. The second step of the book was therefore to identify what mechanism made money work for the commons. It did so by unfolding complementary monies that worked more, or less, or nothing at all, for the social body. And it found that what made monetary tokens move and work for the collective was the sense of obligation towards the community that was built into the mechanics of debt–credit monies; a sort of social responsibility, if you like, embedded in the monetary assemblage, a provocation to the individual to commit to and provide for the common good. Such sense of social obligation did not come from the values and norms of the collective alone – such over-socialised analysis of money would have blinded us to the performative effects of the (accounting) mechanics of money, to the fact that money itself shapes sociality. Rather, social obligation hinged on – indeed, it was designed into – the very architecture of money. The obligation could be either towards a horizontally organised community – in mutualist give-it-forward architectural designs – or towards a hierarchical community – in solidarity-based tax-it-forward designs. If you think about it, it is not at all strange. Saying that money constitutes and is constituted by relations – human-to-human as well as human-to-objects and objects-to-human – amounts to admitting that the sociality of monetised communities is similarly grounded in their culture and character as in the techno-economic devices they interact with. Mauss' work on the form and reason for exchange in primitive societies already recognised the central role social obligation played in instigating the parties into perpetual economic interaction. Inspired by his work, I called that sense of obligation towards the general, collective other, the *perpetuum mobile* mechanism in monetary assemblages.

We reach the same conclusion when reasoning from the entry point of commodity money. Commodity money is the property of the holder; an asset with no parallel liability; an individual right to the thing possessed without a counter-obligation towards society. With no social obligation built into that sort of money, those monetary infrastructures are deprived of any ability to align individual interests to the interests of the collective. Whether the particular money originates in a debt–credit relationship that is later commodified – as in our conventional money – or whether the money is made into commodity from its inception – as under the gold standard and in many algorithmic monies – commodified monies transform someone else's social obligation into property. Owners of those money-properties can decide to sell them forward or to hold them forward as they so please, with no need to take into consideration the effects of their decision on the borrower who initiated the debt–credit relationship – as in our conventional money – nor on the larger social order. With no symmetrical sense of social obligation built into the monetary arrangement, no reason for the holder of money to relate back to the community nor to see to communal interests. Commodification of money, that is, effectively dissociates the monetary arrangement from the common good.

In offering us a vision of a money at the service of the community behind it, a commons imaginary hopefully prevents us from commodifying money. In providing us a mechanism to make money work, the *perpetuum mobile* of social obligation enables us to claim rights and to elicit the obligations of all actors in the monetary arrangement – creditors included.[2] Now, this all sounds very well, but how do we translate imaginaries and perpetuum mobiles into plural, specific, locally responsive, inclusive monetary architectures? Or, in the more pragmatic formulation money entrepreneurs phrase the question as they go about designing, implementing and governing complementary monies: What monetary courses of action could help us advance in our efforts to build more ecological and inclusive futures?

Putting money at the service of people and planet is, really, tantamount to *securing the primacy of society throughout the monetary assemblage*. This means giving precedence to the social body in the design of money's internal architecture, in the set of rules orchestrating the production, distribution and circulation of money-tokens, and in the governance of the monetary system. Reclaiming money as a commons is synonymous to deprivatising money and contingent on some form of democratised money. Such an insight translates into a few practical guidelines:

1. Anchor the production and distribution of money in the priorities set by the community. As we saw in the previous two chapters, priorities do vary; some communities gave precedence to particular aspects of their near natural environment – recuperation of squandered urban land, local generation of energy – other communities opted to foreground their immediate socioeconomic context – economic democracy, universal employment. Yet, regardless of the issue prioritised by the community, the criteria determining the creation of money and its introduction into the community was intimately articulated with the communal priority.
2. Design financial markets away from the production of money; or, for algorithmic monies, eliminate currency markets from all code establishing how much and when money-tokens are created. This does not mean that all market articulations are to be eliminated. Markets, we saw, are, certainly, necessary places for meeting, interacting and making community. They enact spaces for social contact; intersections where members learn about each other's needs. In their role as spaces for communal interaction, markets are accessories to the monetary assemblage, not the principle determining the creation of money. To put it another way, remove financial and currency markets from the rules governing the creation of money and attach markets as appendixes to the community economy.
3. Dislodge the money-commodity fiction from any articulation in the monetary arrangement. The sole possibility to transform money into commodity directs money users onto striving for accumulation of monetary tokens which carry rights (to claim something in exchange for them) without equivalent obligations (towards the community). The commodification of money thus inhibits the possibility to align individual interests to the interests of the collective. For the individual, this results in the subordination of the general will for the sake of money income. Justice, freedom or care for nature recede from the panoply of motives directing individual action.

4. Insert a relational class of individual motives into the monetary arrangement, motives that are driven as much by individual right as by social obligation. That is, to the right to lay claim upon society that monetary tokens grant upon their holder, articulate the same individual into a countervailing obligation towards the collective (the *perpetuum mobile*). The obligation may be towards an entity representing the social body – a tax to a central authority – or towards the community in the abstract – an expectation to spend on others. It may be forced through coercion and the threat of punishment – as in state-based obligations – or through more or less formalised governance rules and social norms – as in community-based obligations. Whatever the form and reason of the social obligation, its accomplishment is to move debt from the sphere of person-to-person interaction to that of person-to-collective. In this doing, it forces individual interests to align to those of the collective.
5. Though local monies do not need the support of established public institutions to work, institutional support does however stabilise these monies, granting them more effectual infrastructural powers. This calls for experimenting with ways to embed citizen-driven complementary monies into public institutions. The municipality could, for example, act as another member in a citizen-driven mutual credit system, sourcing locally in the complementary money and accepting it as payment of certain public services – as in Turuta in Chapter 8; or it could accept certain municipal taxes be paid in the local money – as in Vilawatt in Chapter 8 and Wörgl in Chapter 5; or it could guarantee redemption of the local money into national money – as in Mumbuca in Chapter 7. Or it could, instead, offer loans in conventional money for communities to develop their productive capacity, to be paid back in the complementary currency. Public–civic monetary articulations are, however, not without risk. Their emancipatory potential is contingent upon the larger institutional context, which could co-opt – as in Yap – and even annihilate – as in Wörgl – the alternative monetary arrangement to attend interests other than those of the communities it was initially meant to serve.
6. Ensuring the primacy of society in all monetary matters requires, then, a major shift in the theory and practice of monetary sovereignty. First, it requires a shift from monetary policy devised and implemented by central banking authorities that have not been democratically elected to, instead, monetary governance in which those affected by it – citizens at large – get a real possibility to have their voice heard.[3] Second, because any society is made of multiple regions, communities and social groups, it also implies a shift from mono-currency systems that encompass whole national (and, as with the euro, supra-national) territories to monetary plurality,[4] a multiplicity of more or less local monetary systems each attending the needs and priorities dominant in the smaller territories/

groups each comprise. Multiple, at times partially overlapping, monies would free individuals to move to communities implementing monies and rules more attuned to one's ethics; it would also facilitate separate monies to adjust to changes in its proximate circumstances. Third, it involves moving from a system where a circumscribed elite of private financial actors following the market principle creates the majority of our money[5] to a multiplicity of localities adapting the creation of money to the changing conditions of their environment and their communities. Finally, because the interests of communities concern both local, regional, national and global issues, it requires the multi-scalar and complementary existence of monies, in the plural – from neighbourhood to global currencies with city, regional and national monies in between.

7. Allow for experimentation in governance forms of the local monetary arrangements. Monetary governance may be organised in many ways, some more statutory others more authoritarian, some more broadly participatory others more knowledge-elitist, some based on more direct forms of decision-making others on more representative democracy. Some, perhaps, even in ways we cannot anticipate. Autocratic or radically municipal, as a merchants' cooperative or as a civic association, inspired in indigenous pasts or in envisioned futures, one feature is however common to them all: the market principle will not govern the monetary arrangement since it was expelled from the set of rules that regulate the production of money (point two in this list).

The book set out to study seemingly innocent alternative monies; some of them, such as citizen-driven monies, appear inoffensive; others, such as algorithmic monies, are, from the outset, combative and antagonistic yet have, thus far, been similarly innocuous to the transformation of the established monetary system. By the end of the book, the study led to a defence of a plurality of complementary monies working at various territorial scales and focused in varied, at times transversal, concerns. Herein lies the revolutionary capabilities of these monies. Unoffending and peacefully working from the interstices of the dominant system,[6] alternative complementary monies carve out spaces for citizens and local authorities, activists and social entrepreneurs, civic associations and merchant co-ops, developers and grassroots groups, to experiment with and learn about the potential of these monetary instruments for recasting socioeconomic relations and refashioning individual agency. There is much possibility in their small scale: when the experiment goes awry, the consequences are limited in reach; when it succeeds, it offers lessons and inspiration for new institutional configurations.[7] Whatever the outcome, awry or successful, building alternatives on the ground serves an important function for our imagination. As a wide-ranged mix of actors get involved in envisioning and doing another economy, collective efforts to prefigure new socioeconomic arrangements erode creative constraints, open up new horizons and perform new ways of living together.

All this is, perhaps, somewhat naïve. How could small, limited, purposefully constrained alternative monies possibly address climate change, obnoxious inequality and political polarisation? Accumulation of many small acts, even if coordinated through many local complementary monies, cannot tackle dangerous heatwaves, flash floods, and mass extinction of animal species, nor can they do away with extreme poverty and the relentless erosion of democracy; all of which, the emerging consensus states, requires a shift in the way we organise society.[8] One could say that *that* is, precisely, the most important point made by the many monies analysed in the book. Politics is innate to money; and money crafts society. Collectives behind these monies conclude that a serious commitment to put planet and people at the heart of the social order demands an equally serious commitment to reclaim, reimagine and reorganise money. What does seem increasingly naïve is to expect dominant actors – central and private banks, major fossil fuel corporations and the governments the latter lobby – are going to change the monetary architecture at the root of our many crises out of their own determination. Rather than naïve, I would argue it is only hopeful to see possibility for change in the lived experiences and novel practices of those participating in alternative economic constellations. Participation in small local monies, we saw in various cases, transforms the meaning of debt and the ethics of money; it remodels social relations and one's sense of social responsibility. While we today lack the political leadership to galvanise people around a renewed democratic vision of social, economic and climate justice, still, the only thing limiting us is our will to change. Leadership and political change can emerge in small organised relational experiences that serve as grounds to new real utopias. Because imagination is always grounded in lived experience, community economies can serve as the incubators of new experiences on which to imagine novel civilisational forms.[9]

We shouldn't be naïve, but we do have a duty to hope. Despair is for better times.[10] My hope is not that implementation of many local complementary monies is going to solve our multiple predicaments. Rather, my hope is that in the lived experience of caring and equal communal relations that the remaking of money these local initiatives provoke lie the seeds of new visions for living together.[11] Ultimately, local monies advance new structures of feeling and new forms of knowledge that can project us towards many and varied civilisational futures. Because to imagine a form of money means to imagine a form of life.

Appendix

Balance sheet money mechanics

As we saw in Chapter 2, two approaches to money divide economists. The first understands money as a commodity, sees its origins in imagined barter economies, and advocates for discipline in monetary policy. This imaginary is behind monetary designs such as the gold standard. The second approach understands money as credit, sees its origins in relations of favours with concomitant promises to repay, and advocates for elasticity in monetary policy. This latter imaginary is behind the Keynesian revolution of the postwar period.

The debate between the two approaches has gone on forever, giving the impression that economists cannot agree on even the most essential matters of their discipline. Approaches to money as either a commodity or a debt–credit relationship attempt to decide the ontological nature of money – a long-standing debate that tells little of how money actually works. But there is a more pragmatic way to study money. This approach starts with the mechanics of money. It looks at what bankers – commercial and central – actually do. It approaches money from how it works, from bankers' doings, from their accounting practices recorded in balance sheets. Perry Mehrling calls it 'the money view'.[1] The money view looks at how money and its flows are accounted for in the present, it focuses entirely on the management of money as it is conducted by financial actors.

The money view builds on four fundamental methodological advices. One, it follows the money. It looks at cash flows, at payments: where do they come from and where do they go. It observes how money moves, how it circulates, and who the actors involved in that movement are. Two, the money view follows the money for everyone. All of us face the daily problems of cash inflows and cash outflows. Everyone has to meet debt and payment outflows with income inflows. Three, it thinks through balance sheets. The best way to see how money moves through every economic agent is to represent this movement through balance sheets and variations in those balance sheets. And four, it sees every economic agent – also you and me – through the balance sheet. Since everyone has to balance inflows and outflows daily, everybody's dealing with money can be represented through

Table A.1: General scheme of a balance sheet

You	
Assets (What is legally yours, what you can claim)	**Liabilities** (Your duties, your promises to pay)
Cash Bank deposits Other assets (for example, house, securities such as bonds and stocks)	Loans
	Equity (Your net worth)

balance sheets. In other words, attending to the fundamentals of money mechanics teaches us to think through balance sheets, just like bankers do when they do banking.[2]

Representing you through the balance sheet

So let's start by looking at yourself through the balance sheet (see Table A.1).

There are two sides to the balance sheet: assets to the left and liabilities to the right. The asset side records what's legally yours, your rights, your claims upon others; the liability side registers your duties, your promises to pay, your obligations towards others. On the asset side you record currency (cash in hand plus bank deposits) and other assets you may have, from securities such as bonds and stocks to a house or a car. On the liability side you record your debts; typically bank loans of various types (student loans, mortgages and other forms of borrowing). The difference between the sum of your assets and the sum of your liabilities makes your 'equity', or your 'net worth'. Looking at you from the twin perspective of your rights – what's legally yours – and duties – your payment commitments – is the start of a relational thinking of the economy – the balance between your rights and obligations.

Recording a trade on the balance sheet

A little exercise will help us see this relationality of the economy. Think of the bakery at your street corner. Imagine it needs to buy 100€ of flour from the local miller. The baker has enough cash to pay for the flour. How does the trade show in the baker's and miller's balance sheets? When the baker pays the miller 100€ from her bank account, she sees her deposits on the asset side go down by 100€ while the miller sees her deposits increase by 100€. The flour moves in the opposite direction, from the asset side of the miller's balance sheet to the asset side of the baker's balance sheet (see Table A.2).

Table A.2: Commercial trade: changes to balance sheets

Time 0 (previous to baker buying flour from the miller)			
Local baker		**Local miller**	
Assets Cash = 100€	**Liabilities** = 0 **Equity** = 100€	**Assets** Cash = 100€ Flour = 150€	**Liabilities** = 0 **Equity** = 250€

Time 1 (baker buys 100€ of flour from the miller and the trade is conducted)			
Local baker		**Local miller**	
Assets Cash = 100€ – 100€ (payment) Flour = + 100€	**Liabilities** = 0 **Equity** = 100€	**Assets** Cash = 100€ + 100€ (payment received) Flour = 150€ – 100€ (flour sold)	**Liabilities** = 0 **Equity** = 250€

One important fact coming from this little exercise reminds us of the relational nature of the economy: every transaction changes at least two ledger accounts for each of the actors involved in the transaction. When the baker paid for the flour, her cash account was marked down while her flour account was marked up. The transaction had an equal effect in size but opposite in direction in two of the baker's accounts – the double-entry accounting principle. Similarly for the miller, whose ledger records the sale – a mirror operation to the baker's buy – marking up her cash and down her flour account. Balance sheet accounting mechanics visualise both sides of the baker–miller relationship, where the baker's cash outflow is the miller's cash inflow. Or, as it is more commonly stated, *someone's spending is someone else's income.*

Representing economic actors through the balance sheet

You may not use the balance sheet to represent your economic life. The balance sheet is however the established way many economic actors visualise your economic existence in relation to them. For the various actors that will concern us when following the creation and governance of money, a simplified version of their balance sheets is represented in the following tables. For banks, see Table A.3.

In the assets side, banks hold loans, but they also hold securities as well as central bank money – reserves and currency. Reserves is the type of money banks use to settle debts among themselves. Citizens cannot access this type of money. On the liabilities side, citizens save with banks (lend to banks) and get a receipt for their savings – a 'bank deposit' in the bank's IOU, an

Table A.3: General scheme of a commercial bank's balance sheet

Commercial bank	
Assets (commercial bank's claims)	**Liabilities** (commercial bank's promises to pay)
Loans (the bank's right to claim repayment of the loan it granted you) Securities (for example, government and corporate bonds, stocks, mortgage-backed securities, and so on) Central bank reserves Cash/currency (coins and notes)	Deposits (the bank's commitment to provide your deposit on demand, either in the form of cash, or as a digital transfer of your deposit) Other borrowing

Table A.4: General scheme of a central bank's balance sheet

Central bank	
Assets (central bank's claims)	**Liabilities** (central bank's promises to pay)
Gold Foreign exchange reserves Government bonds Corporate bonds Other securities (for example, mortgage-backed securities)	Reserves Currency

obligation of the bank to give access to those deposits in the form of physical cash or digital transfer when and as demanded by the customer. Other bank liabilities include borrowing from other banks, non-bank financial institutions, the central bank and others.

Central banks hold gold and a variety of securities, such as government and corporate bonds or mortgage-backed securities. To buy these, central banks expand the liability side of their balance sheets by issuing reserves, which are recorded as commitments towards those who hold them as claims. That is in a nutshell the money mechanics of expressions such as 'expansionary monetary policy' or 'expansion of central banks' balance sheets' (see Table A.4).

Much simplified, governments hold deposits, securities and a variety of assets, and issue government bonds that investors – big and small like you and me – can hold. Though not the largest account in the government's balance sheet, the government's right to raise taxes is a crucial component of

Table A.5: General scheme of government's balance sheet

Government	
Assets (Government's claims)	**Liabilities** (Government's promises to pay)
Deposits Securities Taxes receivable Other assets (for example, land, inventory and general property)	Government bonds Other debt (for example, loans from private lenders and international institutions; overdraft with the country's central bank)

Table A.6: General scheme of private financial actor's balance sheet

Private financial actors	
Assets (claims)	**Liabilities** (promises to pay)
Currency Deposits Securities	Securities

a national monetary arrangement for it is what ultimately makes legal tender widely acceptable in payment of goods and services. Following Knapp's *State Theory of Money*, it is the state's capacity to enforce payment of taxes and to enforce the particular means of payment that grants general acceptability to that payment means (see Table A.5).

Private financial actors include hedge funds, security dealers, and the whole shadow banking sector. I won't be discussing these in the book. I just want to note that they exist and that they are a growing component of a modern monetary system. These entities borrow deposits and other short-term securities and issue other longer-term securities (lend). The degree to which they can hedge with their borrow-short-lend-long mismatch is often a function of how much speculative gains or losses they wish to forego (see Table A.6).

Balance sheet mechanics of private bank money creation

Now that we understand the basic tenets of balance sheet accounting, let's look at its role in the money creation process. Let me illustrate with an example from our bakery. What if the baker does not have enough cash to pay for all the flour she needs? Businesses deal often with this type of cash-flow problem, merchants counting on the proceedings of their sales to be able to settle debts incurred to buy their inputs. Banks can advance funding through loans. In January 2022, business loans amounted to a total of US$2.5 billion in the United States, representing 23 per cent of commercial banks' consolidated lending and 11 per cent of their assets.[3] These figures tell of the crucial function credit, and finance, plays in any economy.[4]

Without enough cash to purchase the flour, the baker asks her bank for a business loan of 50€. The bank looks at her equity, past borrowing, cash flow and business plan to assess her capacity to pay back the loan. Deeming her creditworthy, the bank grants her the loan, an operation whose mechanics consist of the bank crediting the baker's deposits account with 50€ and adding a loan account with 50€ on the liabilities side of her balance sheet (the loan-granting operation is recorded in the balance sheets as in Time 1 in Table A.7). This means the baker can now access 50€ from her deposits to pay for the flour, while at the same time owing 50€ to the bank. She can now settle her debt to the miller for the flour she uses to bake good bread to sell (payment recorded as in Time 3 in Table A.7). Hopefully, that bread will earn her enough to repay her bank loan as well as make her some profit.

Three important features of money mechanics to observe from this simple accounting exercise.[5] First, in time 1, at the moment the bank grants the loan to our baker, the baker sees her deposits – the money she can access through her bank account – grow from 0 to 50€. And yet, the local bank's balance sheet does not record an equal reduction of deposited money on its asset side. Rather, the bank's balance sheet records an equal increase in its assets. When granting a loan, the bank records an expansion of the two sides of its balance sheet equal to the expansion it records of its customer's balance sheet. This is implemented through four simultaneous accounting entries – attending double-entry accounting principle, two entries for the loan-taker and two entries for the lending bank: (1) a record of the new deposit and (2) of the new loan for the baker, along with (3) the bank's expectation of the baker making good on her promise to pay back her loan and (4) the bank's commitment to provide the baker with the new deposit on demand, the money supply in the economy expanding as the bank makes loans. That is, new money was created when the bank recorded the new loan extended to our baker.

A second important feature of the accounting mechanics of bank money creation refers to the dual character of money. The new deposit – the new money – is recorded as *both* an asset of the baker *and* a liability of the bank. That is, the baker has the right to access that deposit on demand and the bank has the obligation to provide this deposit in the form of physical cash or digital transfer when demanded by the baker. The baker's asset is the recognition of funds she can command on. The bank's liability is an acknowledgement of its debt to the baker, a promise to pay, an IOU (I-owe-you). A record with

Table A.7: Balance sheet mechanics of private bank money creation

Time 0 (previous to baker getting the loan)							
Local baker		**Local miller**		**Local bank**		**Central bank**	
Assets	**Liabilities** = 0	**Assets**	**Liabilities** = 0	**Assets**	**Liabilities**	**Assets**	**Liabilities**
Cash = 0 Deposits = 0		Deposits = 100 Flour = 50		Reserves = 200	Deposits = 100	Various CB assets = 200	Reserves = 200
	Equity = 0		**Equity** = 150		**Equity** = 100		
Total assets: 0		Total assets: 150		Total assets: 200		Total assets: 200	

Time 1 (baker gets a loan of 50€ from her bank)							
Local baker		**Local miller**		**Local bank**		**Central bank**	
Assets	**Liabilities**	**Assets**	**Liabilities** = 0	**Assets**	**Liabilities**	**Assets**	**Liabilities**
New deposit = 50	New loan = 50	Deposits = 100 Flour = 50		New loan (to baker) = 50 Reserves = 200	New deposit (baker's)= 50 Deposits = 100	Various assets = 200	Reserves = 200
	Equity = 0		**Equity** = 150		**Equity** = 100		
Total assets: 50		Total assets: 150		Total assets: 250		Total assets: 200	

Time 2 (baker buys flour for 50€ from the miller)							
Local baker		**Local miller**		**Local Bank**		**Central Bank**	
Assets	**Liabilities**	**Assets**	**Liabilities** = 0	**Assets**	**Liabilities**	**Assets**	**Liabilities**
Deposits = 0 Flour = 50€	Loan = 50	Deposits = 150 Flour = 0		Loan to baker = 50 Reserves = 200	Deposits = 150 (now all committed to miller)	Various assets = 200	Reserves = 200
	Equity = 0		**Equity** = 150		**Equity** = 100		
Total assets: 50		Total assets: 150		Total assets: 250		Total assets: 200	

two entries, money is a two-sided phenomenon – simultaneously an asset and a liability – each side recorded in the balance sheet of different actors – the loan-taker and the loan-giver. Two-sided money is but the accounting visualisation of the debt–credit relationship at the root of money creation. In other words, *money is a relational phenomenon.*

The third feature of money mechanics that can be observed is a consequence of the first two. In time 2, the baker exercises her right, and uses the bank's IOUs – her deposits – to pay for the flour. The operation of paying the miller left the baker with a zero balance in her deposits account; while the miller sees her deposits marked up by the same amount the baker's balance was marked down. The baker's debt remains though, the miller's bank account now recording the monetary units that were created through the original loan to the baker. That is, the miller's bank account is credited with an extra 50€, which is equal to the baker's debt of 50€ to the bank. Because money is a two-sided phenomenon, *someone's credit is always someone else's debt.*

A final fact worth noting concerns the nature of the monetary movements recorded in the balance sheets, what we call money transfer or digital payment. In time 2, when the baker pays for the flour with her new deposit, the bank does not send/transfer money from the baker's to the miller's account. Common language use – 'send money', 'have money' – tricks us into seeing money as something that is sent, a thing that is moved from one account to another as with the flour sold. But that is not how balance sheet money works. Deposits being a digital record, *the bank simply types the figures down and up in the respective ledger accounts* – and, voilà, the miller's account now records the digital money-tokens that were previously recorded on the baker's account.

Balance sheet mechanics of central bank money creation

QE monetary stimulus policies take the form of central banks buying government bonds which are paid for with central bank money issued for the purpose. This is carried out by means of four simultaneous accounting entries recording the creation of (1) bonds and (2) central bank money, (3) the trade and (4) the expectation of that trade being balanced by another trade in the opposite direction sometime in the future. Oversimplified, for federal government monetisation of their bonds, it looks as shown in Table A.8.

The central bank performs the same balance sheet operation for the government that we saw private banks conducted for household and firm debt.[6] Money – this time reserves or central bank money – is created through an accounting process that produces government and central bank assets *and* liabilities. Made through entering a *relationship of debt and credit*, central bank money is, again, constituted of two sides, an asset and a

Table A.8: Balance sheet mechanics of central bank money creation

Time 0 (previous to stimulus measures)			
Government		**Central bank**	
Assets	**Liabilities**	**Assets**	**Liabilities**
Deposits Securities Other assets	Government bonds	Gold reserves Government bonds	Reserves Currency

Time 1 (government issues bonds to fund stimulus measures; central bank buys those bonds)			
Government		**Central Bank**	
Assets	**Liabilities**	**Assets**	**Liabilities**
Deposits Securities Other assets **+ Reserves (or government deposits at the central bank)**	Government bonds **+ Government bonds**	Gold reserves Government bonds **+ Government bonds**	Reserves Currency **+ Reserves (central bank's IOU to government)**

liability side. The central bank records a promise – the government bond – as an asset of the central bank purchased with the new reserves, which are recorded as a liability of the central bank. Government accounting records mirror those of the central bank: the government records a promise – the central bank reserves – as an asset of the government purchased with their bonds, which are recorded as a liability it commits to honour. Central bank money is created through debtor–creditor relationships. Such quadruple entries occur regularly between parties involved in debt–credit creation.

Change the word 'government' for 'corporation' and you get the process of central bank money creation building on the relationship between central banks and big business.[7] You can similarly substitute 'government' for 'commercial banks' or 'other financial actors' and you have listed all actors through which central bank issues money.

Notes

Prelude

[1] Names have been changed for the sake of anonymisation.

[2] For a discussion of the similarity of Keynes' and Polanyi's approach concerning the power of monetary ideas in shaping the international world order, see K. Polanyi Levitt. 2013. Keynes and Polanyi: The 1920s and the 1990s. In *From the Great Transformation to the Great Financialization: On Karl Polanyi and Other Essays*. Fernwood Publishing.

Chapter 1

[1] Bible verse (1 Timothy 6:10).

[2] See, for instance, W. Goetzmann. 2017. *Money Changes Everything: How Finance Made Civilization Possible*. Princeton University Press. For a discussion on how the industrial and urban development of the European Middle Ages was accompanied by a shift from spiritual to commercial values in society, see J. Le Goff. 2005. *From Heaven to Earth: The Shift in Values between the 12th and the 13th Century in the Christian West*. Royal Netherlands Academy of Arts and Science.

[3] While such prohibitions have disappeared in countries with Christian and Judaic histories, some Muslim countries retain the approach still today. The most prominent feature of Islamic banking is the prohibition to collect interest. Its advocates argue that interest-free loans make banking practice less prone to risk and banks more stable; see, for instance, P. Abedifar, P. Molyneux and A. Tarazi. 2013. Risk in Islamic banking. *Review of Finance*, 17(6): 2035–2096. Critics, however, argue that Islamic banks have come around the prohibition by implementing other banking practices and that, as a result, Islamic banking is indistinguishable from conventional banking; see F. Khan. 2010. How 'Islamic' is Islamic banking? *Journal of Economic Behavior & Organization*, 76(3): 805–820.

[4] M. Hudson. 2002. Reconstructing the origins of interest-bearing debt and the logic of clean slates. In Hudson, M. and Van de Mieroop, M. (eds) *Debt and Economic Renewal in the Ancient Near East*, CDL Press, pp 7–58.

[5] According to Albert O. Hirschman, it was Francis Bacon who first proposed the idea of the countervailing passions. In his wonderful little book, *The Passions and the Interests*, Hirschman traces the concerns that fed discussions on the benefits of commerce and industry for the government of human passions and peoples at large. With inquisitive historical curiosity, he recovers the transformation of the sinful 'self-love' into the aseptic 'self-interest' that tamed capitalists into gentle productive men. A.O. Hirschman. 1977. *The Passions and the Interests: Political Arguments for Capitalism Before its Triumph*. Princeton University Press.

[6] A. Smith. 1776. *The Wealth of Nations*. Metalibri, book IV, ch II, p 349. Emphasis added.

[7] Another renowned analyst of capitalism, Joseph Schumpeter, similarly praised markets for their role in the betterment of the many, which he illustrated with a brief history of stockings. 'It is the cheap cloth, the cheap cotton and rayon fabric, boots, motorcars and so on that

are the typical achievements of capitalist production, and not as a rule improvements that would mean much to the rich man. Queen Elizabeth owned silk stockings. The capitalist achievement does not typically consist in providing more silk stockings for queens but in bringing them within the reach of the factory girls in return for steadily decreasing amounts of effort.' J.A. Schumpeter. 2003 [1943]. *Capitalism, Socialism and Democracy*. Routledge, p 67.

[8] Smith, *The Wealth of Nations*, p 318.

[9] The day of the year on which the world community, as a whole, has consumed an amount of natural resources equal to the amount nature can replenish arrives earlier each year. Earth Overshoot Day is the day of the year on which the world has consumed as much as the Earth can regenerate. In 2019, Earth Overshoot Day fell on 29 July. In 2022, Earth Overshoot Day fell on 28 June. For scholars relating our current climate predicament to the capitalist profit motive behind the pursuit of exponential growth, see, for instance, T. Jackson. 2009. *Prosperity Without Growth: Economics for a Finite Planet*. Earthscan.

[10] See, for instance, M. Harvey. 2019. Slavery, indenture and the development of British industrial capitalism. *History Workshop Journal*, 88: 66–88.

[11] Thomas Piketty has made this point with force. In his *Capital in the 21st Century*, he offers a detailed analysis of the development of income as compared to that of the return on capital. In a system where the rate of capital return exceeds the rate of growth, inherited accumulated wealth always grows faster than earned income. This leads to increasing levels of inequality that become incompatible with social justice and democracy. T. Piketty. 2014. *Capital in the Twenty-First Century*. Harvard University Press.

[12] Schumpeter, *Capitalism, Socialism and Democracy*, pp 67–68.

[13] K. Marx. 1976 [1867]. *Capital: A Critique of Political Economy*. Translated by B. Fowkes. Penguin Books, p 601.

[14] The latter base much of their argument on the unintended harmful effects in conditional welfare policies. See P. Dwyer's edited volume *Dealing with Welfare Conditionality: Implementation and Effects*. Policy Press. See also D. Etherington. 2021. *Austerity, Welfare and Work: Exploring Politics, Geographies and Inequalities*. Policy Press.

[15] G. Standing. 2011. *The Precariat: The New Dangerous Class*. Bloomsbury Academic. For an updated discussion of the forms and dimensions of precarity, see J. Choonara, A. Murgia and R.M. Carmo. 2022. *Faces of Precarity: Critical Perspectives on Work, Subjectivities and Struggles*. Bristol University Press.

[16] A large number of economists are raising concerns about the relationship between the large levels of economic inequality and social and political and economic instability. For some, see J.K. Galbraith. 2012. *Inequality and Instability: A study of the world economy just before the Great Crisis*. Oxford University Press; P. Krugman. 2007. *The Conscience of a Liberal*. W.W. Norton & Co; or J. Stiglitz. 2012. *The Price of Inequality: How today's divided society endangers our future*. W.W. Norton & Co. The unusual interest in an economics book such as Piketty's bestseller, *Capital in the Twenty-First Century*, attests to the extent to which inequality has come to the forefront of the discussion.

[17] Marx, *Capital*, volume 1, p 353.

[18] As Karl Marx put it in *Capital*: 'Commodities are thus sold not in order to buy commodities, but in order to replace their commodity-form by their money-form. ... this change of form becomes the end in itself. ... The money is petrified into a hoard, and the seller of commodities becomes a hoarder of money' (pp 227–228).

[19] For a development of these examples, see M. Amato and L. Fantacci. 2012. *The End of Finance*, Polity Press; C. Desan. 2014. *Making Money: Coin, Currency and the Coming of Capitalism*. Oxford University Press.

[20] Amato and Fantacci play with the dual meaning of 'end' in their insightful book *The End of Finance*. A central argument in that book is that finance – or the quick profits it rewards through the transformation of debt into assets in liquid financial markets – has become

an end in itself. They call for the end of such liquidity-based financial system and for the structuring of finance along a clearing principle. Chapter 4 of this book explains how such a clearing principle works through the example of grassroots experiments organising money along that principle.

[21] C. Desan. 2017. The constitutional approach to money: Monetary design and the production of the modern world. In Bandelj, N., Wherry, F. and Zelizer, V. (eds) *Money Talks: Explaining How Money Really Works*. Princeton University Press, pp 109–130.

[22] Desan, *Making Money*; D. Graeber. 2014 [2011]. *Debt: The First 5,000 Years*. Melville House.

[23] For an authority in this topic, see B. Eichengreen. 1992. *Golden Fetters: The Gold Standard and the Great Depression, 1919–1939*. Oxford University Press; and B. Eichengreen. 2019. *Globalising Capital: A History of the International Monetary System*. Princeton University Press.

[24] For a detailed account of the process leading to the financial collapse of 2008 and its subsequent development, see A. Tooze. 2019. *Crashed: How a Decade of Financial Crises Changed the World*. Penguin Books.

[25] For an in-depth analysis of Adam Smith's and Karl Marx's understanding of money as commodity, see G. Ingham. 2004. *The Nature of Money*. Polity Press.

[26] The fact that securities work as a special kind of money is related to the hierarchy of money. See S. Bell. 2001. The role of the state and the hierarchy of money. *Cambridge Journal of Economics*, 25: 149–163; P. Mehrling. 2013. The inherent hierarchy of money. In Taylor, L., Rezai, A. and Michl, T. (eds) *Social Fairness and Economics: Economic Essays in the Spirit of Duncan Foley*. Routledge, pp 394–404.

[27] Amato and Fantacci find in the dogma of liquidity the reason for our relation to money and securities (and other financial assets) as commodities to be sold. In *Saving the Market from Capitalism*, they argue that it is the organisation of financial markets along the liquidity principle that is at the root of capitalism's repeated booms and busts (M. Amato and L. Fantacci. 2014. *Saving the Market from Capitalism*. Translated by G. Sells. Polity Press). Hence, instead of pointing at the market mechanism for the failings of the economy, they argue that it is the extension of the market mechanism to the organisation of finance that is to be blamed. In this sense, their argument is parallel to Karl Polanyi's, who also found the root of the violent tragedies of the 20th century in the extension of the market mechanism to the organisation of money, along with the coordination of land and labour. K. Polanyi. 2001 [1944]. *The Great Transformation: The Political and Economic Origins of Our Time*. Beacon Press.

[28] For an incisive unravelling of the money commodity understanding buried in orthodox economics see Ingham, *The Nature of Money*.

[29] K. Polanyi. 1947. Our obsolete market mentality: Civilization must find a new thought pattern. *Commentary*, 3: 109–117, at p 111.

[30] Polanyi, Our obsolete market mentality. For a detailed analysis of one of the common-law texts that regulated the use of land in England until the mid 18th century, see G. Standing. 2019. *The Plunder of the Commons: A Manifesto for Sharing Public Wealth*. Pelican. Standing builds on that common-law text to develop a manifesto for protecting the natural commons in the 21st century.

[31] K. Polanyi. 2001 [1944]. *The Great Transformation: The Political and Economic Origins of Our Time*. Beacon Press, p 76.

[32] In Polanyi's own words: 'Both enclosures of the common and consolidations into compact holdings, which accompanied the new great advance in agricultural methods, had a powerfully unsettling effect. The war on cottages, the absorption of cottage gardens and grounds, the confiscation of rights in the common deprived cottage industry of its two mainstays: family earnings and agricultural background. As long as domestic industry was supplemented by the facilities and amenities of a garden plot, a scrap of land, or grazing rights, the dependence of the laborer on money earnings was not absolute; the potato

plot or "stubbing geese," a cow or even an ass in the common made all the difference; and family earnings acted as a kind of unemployment insurance. The rationalization of agriculture inevitably uprooted the laborer and undermined his social security.' Polanyi, *The Great Transformation*, p 96.

[33] Polanyi, *The Great Transformation*, p 138.

[34] Polanyi, *The Great Transformation*, p 136.

[35] Polanyi, Our obsolete market mentality, p 110.

[36] Polanyi, Our obsolete market mentality, p 111.

[37] Polanyi, *The Great Transformation*, p 75.

[38] Polanyi, Our obsolete market mentality, p 114.

[39] B. Latour. 2005. *Reassembling the Social: An Introduction to Actor-Network Theory*. Oxford University Press, p 39.

[40] Latour, *Reassembling the Social*, p 39.

[41] In choosing the verb 'provoke', I follow Fabian Muniesa's book *The Provoked Economy: Economic Reality and the Performative Turn*. Throughout that book, Muniesa explores how economic formulas and analytical tests we most often take to simply reflect reality do in fact enact the reality of which they speak. He shows performance indicators, valuation formulas, consumer tests, stock prices or financial contracts that business schools teach as ways to analyse an external economic reality do however provoke that reality into existence, actively reproducing and continuously transforming it. Far from neutral intermediaries, such analytical tools behave as mediators actively performing the economy. F. Muniesa. 2014. *The Provoked Economy: Economic Reality and the Performative Turn*. Routledge.

[42] For lists of economists and economic theories forgetting money, see, for instance, F. Martin. 2014. *Money: The Unauthorised Biography*. Vintage Books, ch 12; Graeber, *Debt*, pp 23–24. See also S. Keen. 2011. *Debunking Economics: The Naked Emperor Dethroned?* Zed Books.

[43] For some examples of this line of reasoning, see T. Skotnicki. 2021. *The Sympathetic Consumer: Moral Critique in Capitalist Culture*. Stanford University Press; Jackson, *Prosperity Without Growth*; E.F. Schumacher. 2010 [1983]. *Small Is Beautiful: Economics as if People Mattered*. Harper Perennial; A. Reichel, M. De Schoenmakere and J. Gillabel. 2016. Circular economy in Europe: Developing the knowledge base. *European Environment Agency Report* 2/2016; K. Raworth. 2017. *Doughnut Economics: Seven Ways to Think Like a 21st Century Economist*. Random House.

[44] For an example, see J. Earle, C. Moran and Z. Ward-Perkins. 2017. *The Econocracy: The Perils of Leaving Economics to the Experts*. Manchester University Press.

[45] See, for instance, Goetzmann, *Money Changes Everything*. See also Chapter 2 in this book.

[46] In building the argument of this section, I am inspired by the later Ludwig Wittgenstein's philosophy of language. He contended that many of philosophy's traditional questions are derived from language confusion. In attempting to find the meaning of a word, Wittgenstein observed, we either try to find an object in the world or a subjective reality in the mind of the speaker the word seems to point to. It is like when we teach the meaning of a word to a foreigner by pointing at the object in the world the word refers to. This amounts to a referential theory of language where words and meaning neatly correspond. But, Wittgenstein continued, language does not work like that. Think of statements like 'Water! Away! Ow! Help! Fine! No! Are you inclined still to call these words"'names of object"?' (§27). 'For a large class of cases', he concluded, 'the meaning of a word is its use in the language' (§43). More than a philosophical lesson, this is a pragmatic piece of advice for those of us trying to understand how communities are organised. Instead of looking for the thing corresponding to a name – hoping to find meaning in the outside material world or in the realities inside someone's heads – he advises us to look at the use of words by speakers in specific contexts and we will find a

form of life. He condensed the philosophical lesson in the methodological advice 'Don't think, but look' (§66). L. Wittgenstein. 1953. *Philosophical Investigations*. Translated by G.E.M. Anscombe. Blackwell.

[47] Graeber, *Debt*. For an elaboration of this topic, see Chapter 2 in this book.

[48] For a few examples, see Desan, *Making Money*; Goetzmann, *Money Changes Everything*; Graeber, *Debt*; Martin, *Money*.

[49] J.C. Davies. 2017. *From Head Shops to Whole Foods: The Rise and Fall of Activist Entrepreneurs*. Columbia University Press.

[50] P. Vigna and M.J. Casey. 2015. *Cryptocurrency: The Future of Money?* Vintage.

[51] For a couple of well-known studies of these, see P. North. 2007. *Money and Liberation: The Micropolitics of Alternative Currency Movements*. University of Minnesota Press; B. Maurer. 2005. *Mutual Life, Limited: Islamic Banking, Alternative Currencies, Lateral Reason*. Princeton University Press.

[52] J. Ryan-Collins, T. Greenham, R. Werner and A. Jackson. 2011. *Where Does Money Come From? A Guide to the UK Monetary and Banking System*. New Economics Foundation.

[53] E. Barinaga. 2020. A route to commons-based democratic monies? Embedding the production of money in traditional communal institutions. *Frontiers in Blockchain*, 3: 575851. doi: 10.3389/fbloc.2020.575851

[54] For a discussion of the difference between Polanyi's notion of countermovement and Marx's notion of class struggle, see F. Block and M. Somers. 2016. *The Power of Market Fundamentalism: Karl Polanyi's Critique*. Harvard University Press.

[55] In studying various monies as they work and are made to work, I am suggesting, as it were, a rather Polanyian approach to the study of money, one that is based on substantive analyses of the practices of those whose activities make money. As Karl Polanyi argued in 'The economy as instituted process', 'only the substantive meaning of "economic" is capable of yielding the concepts that are required by the social sciences for an investigation of all empirical economies of the past and present'. K. Polanyi. 1957. The economy as instituted process. In Polanyi, K., Arensberg, C.M. and Pearson, H.W. (eds) *Trade and Market in the Early Empires*. Henry Regnery Company, pp 243–270, at p 244.

Chapter 2

[1] B. Latour. 2005. *Reassembling the Social: An Introduction to Actor-Network Theory*. Oxford University Press, p 48.

[2] J.M. Keynes. 1936. *The General Theory of Employment, Interest and Money*. Macmillan, ch 24, section V, p 383.

[3] Because ideas of money mould relationships between trading partners as well as between people and larger sociocultural institutions, Lana Swartz discusses imaginaries of money as theories of money that have material world-making effects. As she puts it: 'Money, as technological arrangement, performs a relation between people in a moment of transaction as well as relations between individuals and the larger imaginaries we call "society", "the state", and "the economy". Money is a creature of network effects: it requires a community of shared belief to "work", to exist as something recognisable as money. These beliefs are reflexively produced in the technologies of money, which are instantiations of these shared expectations. A theory of money, then, is a techno-economic imaginary, a theory of the larger social order (or a challenge to it) and a way of materially enacting that theory' (p 623). L. Swartz. 2018. What was Bitcoin, what will it be? The techno-economic imaginaries of a new money technology. *Cultural Studies*, 32(4): 623–650.

[4] Each of the two main imaginaries of money bear an implicit division of gender roles and, even if the gendered implications of money imaginaries won't be discussed in the book, they do deserve further research. I will here have to make do with a footnote. Building on feminist insights, Ann L. Jennings argues that monetarists' understanding of money

as a veil over productive activity elevates remunerated pursuits to social contributions while finding non-remunerated contributions as nonproductive activity. Remunerated and non-remunerated activities tend to follow gender lines and thus, a monetarists' understanding of money ignores the extent to which inequality of access to money entrenches a gendered and class description of who contributes to society, who merits accumulating money, and who is granted highest social status. Jennings argues that, in their efforts to render Keynes compatible with orthodox barter models, New Keynesians commit the same mistake. And, though replacing barter models with a monetary theory of production lead post-Keynesians and Institutionalists to place money at the centre of macroeconomics, the relationship between money and capitalism's gender hierarchy goes often undiscussed. Though feminism has increasingly influenced heterodox economics since Jennings' article, there is still little written about how theories of money in capitalism contribute to encroach gendered divisions in society. A.L. Jennings. 1994. Toward a feminist expansion of macroeconomics. *Journal of Economic Issues*, 28(2): 555–565. See also R. McCaster. 2018. Does post Keynesianism need a theory of care? In Dow, S., Jespersen, J. and Tily, G. (eds) *Money, Method and Contemporary Post-Keynesian Economics*. Edward Elgar, pp 160–173.

[5] William Stanley Jevons is allegedly the first to frame the analysis of barter through the problem of the double coincidence of wants in his book, from 1896, *Money and the Mechanism of Exchange*. D. Appleton and Co, p 3.

[6] A. Smith. 1776. *The Wealth of Nations*, book 1, ch IV, p 37. Edited by S.M. Soares. MetaLibri Digital Library, 29 May 2007.

[7] Smith, *The Wealth of Nations*, p 44. Emphasis added.

[8] Smith points at the qualities that make precious metal particularly practical for use as a standard medium of exchange: portability, durability, uniformity, divisibility and malleability. Although that very passage hints at the practical and logical impossibility of barter as predecessor of money, Adam Smith seems to have been blind to the cognitive bias. The passage reads as follows: 'Metals can not only be kept with as little loss as any other commodity, scarce anything being less perishable than they are, but they can likewise, without any loss, be divided into any number of parts, as by fusion those parts can easily be reunited again; a quality which no other equally durable commodities possess, and which more than any other quality renders them fit to be the instruments of commerce and circulation. The man who wanted to buy salt, for example, and had nothing but cattle to give in exchange for it, must have been obliged to buy salt to the value of a whole ox, or a whole sheep at a time. He could seldom buy less than this, because what he was to give for it could seldom be divided without loss; and if he had a mind to buy more, he must, for the same reasons, have been obliged to buy double or triple the quantity, the value, to wit, of two or three oxen, or of two or three sheep. If, on the contrary, instead of sheep or oxen, he had metals to give in exchange for it, he could easily proportion the quantity of the metal to the precise quantity of the commodity which he had immediate occasion for.' Smith, *The Wealth of Nations*, ch 4, p 23.

[9] Smith, *The Wealth of Nations*, p 23.

[10] Smith, *The Wealth of Nations*, p 24.

[11] Charles Goodhart refers to this problem as the 'identification costs' problem. C. Goodhart. 1998. The two concepts of money: Implications for the analysis of optimal currency areas. *European Journal of Political Economy*, 14: 407–432.

[12] Smith, *The Wealth of Nations*, ch 4, p 24.

[13] Smith, *The Wealth of Nations*, pp 25–26. Seignorage refers to the difference between the nominal value of money and the cost of producing it, which, for metal money, includes the value of the material it is made of.

[14] The political stance for government to remain detached from any monetary policy is accompanied by an understanding of value as intrinsic to the money-commodity and of

markets as the natural places pricing such value. In the chapter on bitcoin, Chapter 6, we will see how these twin ideas persist in today's crypto monetary space.

[15] Smith, *The Wealth of Nations*, p 26. Emphasis added.

[16] C. Menger. 2009 [1892]. *The Origins of Money*. Ludwig von Mises Institute, p 11.

[17] G. Ingham. 2004. *The Nature of Money*. Polity Press.

[18] Adam Smith argued that the more intrinsic value a good had and the lesser its utilitarian value, the larger the agency of that good on the exchanges it enabled. The following passage is explicative: 'The word VALUE, it is to be observed, has two different meanings, and sometimes expresses the utility of some particular object, and sometimes the power of purchasing other goods which the possession of that object conveys. The one may be called "value in use"; the other, "value in exchange". The things which have the greatest value in use have frequently little or no value in exchange; and, on the contrary, those which have the greatest value in exchange have frequently little or no value in use. Nothing is more useful than water: but it will purchase scarce any thing; scarce any thing can be had in exchange for it. A diamond, on the contrary, has scarce any value in use; but a very great quantity of other goods may frequently be had in exchange for it.' Smith, *The Wealth of Nations*, p 26.

[19] For an early critique of the logical flaw of the barter story, see A. Mitchell Innes. 1913. What is money? *Banking Law Journal*, pp 377–408. He writes: 'A moment's reflection shows that a staple commodity could not be used as money because ex hypothesis the medium of exchange is equally receivable by all members of the community. Thus if the fishers paid for their supplies in cod, the traders would equally have to pay for their cod in cod, an obvious absurdity.' For a more recent staunch critique on the basis both of its logical incoherences and the lack of empirical substantiation, see D. Graeber. 2014 [2011]. *Debt: The First 5,000 Years*. Melville House.

[20] Karl Marx assumed a commodity understanding of money, but adapted the intrinsic value of money to his labour theory of value. For Marx, the value embodied in the coin resided on the labour involved in mining the gold and minting the coin. See G. Ingham. 2020. *Money: Ideology, History, Politics*. Polity Press. See also K. Polanyi. 2001 [1944]. *The Great Transformation: The Political and Economic Origins of Our Time*. Beacon Press, p 26.

[21] Frustrated, anthropologist David Graeber offers a list of current economics textbooks presenting the origin of money in make-believe lands of ancient times. Graeber, *Debt*, pp 23–24. For an overview of the controversies concerning this economics tradition, see J. Smithin. 2003. *Controversies in Monetary Economics*. Edward Elgar.

[22] Suffice to mention Christine Lagarde, President of the European Central Bank (ECB). Writing about the future of money in an article for the magazine of the French School of Public Administration ENA (École National d'Administration), Lagarde traces the emergence of money 'to overcome the limitations and inefficiencies of bartering', as an 'universal medium of exchange needed to facilitate [trade]'. C. Lagarde. 2020. The future of money – innovating while retaining trust. *L'ENA hors les murs*, 501.

[23] Graeber, *Debt*, p 24.

[24] I take the concept from John Quiggin's book from 2010, *Zombie Economics: How Dead Ideas Still Walk among Us*. Quiggin does not explicitly identify barter as one of those zombie ideas, but does identify other ideas related to that original myth of economics, such as the 'efficient market hypothesis' and 'general equilibrium'

[25] See G. Ingham. 2000. Babylonian madness: On the historical and sociological origins of money. In Smithin, J. (ed) *What is Money?* Routledge, pp 16–41.

[26] J.M. Keynes. 1930. *A Treatise on Money*. Cambridge University Press, ch 1. Emphasis in the original.

[27] In reconstructing the Babylonian origins story, I build on M. Hudson. 2004. The development of money-of-account in Sumer's temples. In Hudson, M. and Wunsch, C. (eds)

Creating Economic Order: Record-keeping Standard and the Development of Accounting in the Ancient Near East. CDL Press, pp 303–329; and M. Hudson. 2004. The role of accounting in civilisation's economic takeoff. In Hudson, M. and Wunsch, C. (eds) *Creating Economic Order: Record-keeping Standard and the Development of Accounting in the Ancient Near East*. CDL Press, pp 1–22. I also build on K. Polanyi. 1957. Marketless trading in Hammurabi's time. In Polanyi, K., Arensberg, C.M. and Pearson, H.W. (eds) *Trade and Markets in the Early Empires*. The Free Press, pp 12–26; and A.L. Oppenheim. 1957. A bird's-eye view of Mesopotamian economic history. In Polanyi, K., Arensberg, C.M. and Pearson, H.W. (eds) *Trade and Markets in the Early Empires*. The Free Press, pp 27–37.

[28] In Polanyi, Marketless trading, p 16.

[29] In W. Goetzmann. 2017. *Money Changes Everything: How Finance Made Civilization Possible*. Princeton University Press, p 34.

[30] The Babylonian story starts earlier than I have made it to start here. It could go back to the development of the cuneiform proto-writing used in the temple's clay tablets. Hundreds of thousands of small clay marbles shaped in the form of everyday objects – lambs, cows, loaves of bread, jars of oil, honey, milk, clothing, even abstract units of work – have been found throughout the Babylonian region. For long, it was unclear what they were. Children's toys? Mystical objects? Counters? Professor Denise Schmandt-Besserat's painstaking and systematic organisation of the clay marbles by shape and place of unearthing led her to the discovery of the iconographic link between these pieces and the pictographic writing in the tablets. The marbles symbolised the goods once stored in the temple of Inanna, the 'holy storehouse' in the city of Uruk, and handed by the temple to the tributing citizen as an attest of the tribute. The cuneiform script on the tablets was a written translation of the marbles into a more abstract form of recording citizens' contributions to the temple. For more detail on the fascinating history of how writing and numbers developed from the financial organisation of Babylonian temple economies, see D. Schmandt-Besserat. 2010. *How Writing Came About*. University of Texas Press.

[31] Mitchell Innes is often referred to by advocates of the credit theory of money told through the Babylonian story. Already in 1913, Mitchell Innes describes Babylonian clay tablets as the antecedent of medieval tally sticks and contemporary bills of exchange. All those monetary systems were based on the record of a debt that is to be cleared out in due time. Innes, What is money? See also A. Mitchell Innes. 1914. The credit theory of money. *The Banking Law Journal*, pp 151–168.

[32] We can recognise the Babylonian origins story in Keynes' imaginary of money when he identifies both the recording of debts and the administration of prices as enacting money. In page 3 of his *A Treatise on Money*, he writes: 'A money of account comes into existence along with debts, which are contracts for deferred payment, and price lists, which are offers of contracts for sale or purchase. Such debts and price lists, whether they are recorded by word of mouth or by book entry on baked bricks or paper documents, can only be expressed in terms of a money of account.'

[33] 'Proclamation' refers to the declaration and enforcement by the state of a unit of account for the denomination of prices and debts. The notion of proclamation acknowledges that a standard unit of account to record debts and set the value of commodities does not emerge spontaneously from the interactions among individuals seeking to maximise their utility. Rather, the standardisation and inauguration of a monetary unit of account requires a central authority enforcing it to measure and record the obligations towards the authority and their discharge. This theory was best described first by George Friedrich Knapp in *The State Theory of Money*. 1924. Macmillan and Company Limited. Stephanie Bell puts it concisely: 'What makes a currency valid as money is a *proclamation* by the state that it will be accepted at its pay offices; what makes it acceptable to its citizenry is its

usefulness in settling these liabilities.' S. Bell. 2001. The role of the state and the hierarchy of money. *Cambridge Journal of Economics*, 25: 149–163.

[34] I find inspiration for this expression in Keynes' analysis of the role of the state in the monetary arrangement: '[T]he age of chartalist or State money was reached when the State claimed the right to declare what thing should answer as money to the current money of account—when it claimed the right not only to enforce the dictionary but also to write the dictionary. Today all civilised money is, beyond the possibility of dispute, chartalist.' Keynes, *A Treatise on Money*, p 4.

[35] Long-distance inter-city markets appear to have been organised from trading ports – districts located outside the city walls with the main function of organising inter-city economic relations. Indeed, excavations reveal the structure of the cities of the Ancient Near East consisted of the town proper, the suburb and the extramural trading post. In Oppenheim, A bird's-eye view. Economic historians debate, however, on the mechanism for the determination of prices for goods exchanged in these trading posts, whether administered through inter-city treaty or formed through supply-and-demand. The first would indicate central authority assisted in the organisation of long-distance trade; the later being indicative of markets as the main organisational mechanism. Such a debate has also implications for the elucidation of motives (non-economic versus economic) guiding commercial trade. On this issue, see M. Silver. 1983. Karl Polanyi and markets in the Ancient Near East: The challenge of the evidence. *Journal of Economic History*, 43(4): 795–829; D.C. North. 1977. Markets and other allocation systems in history: The challenge of Karl Polanyi. *The Journal of European Economic History*, 6(3): 703–716. Goetzmann, *Money Changes Everything*.

[36] Though risk-free, commissioned trade was not without complexity and excitement. As Polanyi writes, '[a]lthough the principles of "fixed price," "cash delivery," "legal surety," and "commission on turnover" obtained throughout, the trader's job was far from simple: to make the right contacts among the natives; correctly to judge their requirement of goods; make his financial arrangements in time; conform strictly to rule and regulation; dispose with precision the goods entrusted to him; see to the quality of the wares, either way; procure funds with which to make advances to prospective suppliers, and for deposit with the government; as well as many other matters. Mistakes or omissions meant delay; difficulty in raising loans; small procurement; unnecessary expense; domestic unpleasantness; loss of authority in the family firms; trouble with colleagues and authorities; a reduced turnover. Yet, in this marketless trade there was no loss on prices, no speculation, no failure of debtors. It was exciting as an occupation, but risk-free as a business.' Polanyi, Marketless trading, p 22.

[37] Polanyi, Marketless trading, p 23.

[38] The existence of public and private economic spheres tells of the mixed nature of the economies of the Ancient Near East, the balance between public and private sectors shifting through the centuries. For a detailed description of the private aspects of the Mesopotamian economy, see Goetzmann, *Money Changes Everything*.

[39] D.H. Ehnts. 2019. Knapp's *State Theory of Money* and its reception in German academic discourse. Institute for International Political Economy, Berlin School of Economics and Law, Working Paper No. 115/2019. A passage that clearly shows Keynes' merging of his Babylonian interest with Knapp's state theory is found in his *A Treatise on Money*, p 11: 'The first State reform of the standard of weight, of which we have definite record, was the Babylonian reform towards the end of the third millennium B.C. But this was not the beginning. Earlier standards existed. And in the primitive age, before man had attained to the conception of weight or to the technical contrivance of the scales, when he had to depend for measurement upon counting barleycorns or carats or cowries, it may still have been the State or the community which determined what kind or quality of unit should be a due discharge of an obligation to pay which had been expressed by

the numerals one or two or ten – as when, so late as the thirteenth century, the English government defined a penny sterling to be the weight of "32 wheat corns in the midst of the ear".'

[40] Randall Wray traces the intellectual history of today's Modern Monetary Theory back to Knapp's *State Theory of Money* and sees evidence of this form of money in Babylonian temple-centred economies. See L.R. Wray. 2014. From the state theory of money to modern money theory: An alternative to economic orthodoxy. Levy Economics Institute of Bard College, Working Paper No. 792.

[41] In Mr Lowndes' own terms, 'a Policy constantly Practised in the mints of England … to Raise the Value of the Coin in its Extrinsick Denomination from time to time, as Exigence or Occasion required.' For a well-written account of this episode in monetary history, see F. Martin. 2014. *Money: The Unauthorised Biography*. Vintage Books, ch 8.

[42] For a quick overview of these debates, see R. Skidelsky. 2019. *Money and Government: A Challenge to Mainstream Economics*. Penguin Books, ch 2.

[43] For an informative book on the background, context, details and legacies of the debate, see N. Wapshott. 2011. *Keynes Hayek: The Clash That Defined Modern Economics*. Scribe Publications.

[44] In the epilogue of the well-informed and entertaining book *Money: The Unauthorised Biography*, Felix Martin similarly condenses monetary debate throughout history in two parallel questions: 'All monetary history revolves around two fundamental questions: What are the rules governing the creation of money? And who gets to decide?' (p 276).

[45] Recall the difference between intermediary and mediator explained in Chapter 1. The next chapter details today's process of bank money creation.

[46] Comparing the fixed exchange rate credo informing the gold standard and the euro, Barry Eichengreen and Peter Temin succinctly summarise the ethos of the monetarist imaginary: 'Its rhetoric was deflation, and its *mentalité* was one of inaction' (p 378). B. Eichengreen and P. Temin. 2010. Fetters of gold and paper. *Oxford Review of Economic Policy*, 26(3): 370–384.

[47] Economists have indeed made the argument that the analytical questions underlying policy disputes are closely related to the stance taken on the money imaginary. For a detailed development of the argument in relation to various contemporary controversies in macroeconomic policies, see Smithin, *Controversies in Monetary Economics*, pp 16–39.

[48] Already some 40 years ago, anthropologist Keith Hart argued the importance of seeing money as simultaneously commodity and token. The following passage illustrates his reasoning (p 638): 'Look at a coin from your pocket. On one side is "heads" – the symbol of the political authority which minted the coin; on the other side is "tails" – the precise specification of the amount the coin is worth as payment in exchange. One side reminds us that states underwrite currencies and that money is originally a relation between persons in society, a token perhaps. The other reveals the coin as a thing, capable of entering into definite relations with other things, as a quantitative ratio independent of the persons engaged in any particular transaction. In this latter respect money is like a commodity and its logic is that of anonymous markets. Heads and tails stand for social organisation from the top down and from the bottom up, epitomised in modern theory by the state and the market respectively. Most theories of money give priority to one side over the other. It is as if, not content with exploring the ambiguous unity of heads and tails, politics and markets, economists felt compelled like gamblers to toss the coin – heads or tails? – and, having opted for the one that lands up, then denied the existence of the other side, except in the minds of devil-worshippers. This Manichaean medieval impulse is deeply embedded in modern economic thought, and our century has seen the two sides inflated into an ideological struggle between state socialism and the free market that could be the death of us all.' K. Hart. 1986. Heads or tails? Two sides of the coin. *Man*, 21(4): 637–656.

Chapter 3

[1] A poll conducted by *Positive Money* in 2017 found out that as much as 85 per cent of members of the British parliament did not know who created the majority of our money, nor how money was created or what it was created for. A survey administered to 23,000 citizens in countries representing 75 per cent of the world economy – Australia, Belgium, Brazil, Canada, China, France, Germany, India, Italy, Japan, Mexico, Netherlands, Poland, Russia, Spain, South Africa, South Korea, Turkey, United Kingdom and the United States – showed the general public was similarly ignorant. To the question of who they thought created more than 95 per cent of the money in circulation, 20 per cent of world citizens compared to 15 per cent of British parliamentarians answered 'private/ commercial banks'. Financial professionals, who directly or indirectly work with money creation, knew only slightly better, 26 per cent of them acknowledging private banks' central role in creating most of our money. See D. Clarke. 2017. Poll shows 85% of MPs don't know where money comes from. *Positive Money*; Lampert, M. and van Tilburg, R. (2016). Knowledge about who creates money low amongst international population. Publication based on Glocalities Research by Motivaction International in cooperation with Sustainable Finance Lab.

[2] US: Government Printing Office. 2008. The Financial Crisis and the Role of Federal Regulators. House Hearing, 110 Congress.

[3] The large fiscal stimulus packages implemented to fight the economic crisis in the United States led to government debt rising from 60 per cent of gross domestic product (GDP) in 2007 to over 100 per cent in 2013. See M. Faria-e-Castro. 2018. What are the fiscal costs of a (great) recession? *Economic Synopses*, 22. In the euro area, aggregated governments' debt rose from 66 per cent of GDP in 2007 to 95 per cent in 2014. See P. Burial, C. Checherita-Westphal, P. Jacquinot, M. Schön and N. Stähler. 2020. Economic consequences of high public debt: Evidence from three large scale DSGE models. European Central Bank, Working Paper Series No. 2450.

[4] W. Chen, M. Mrkaic and M. Nabar. 2019. The global economic recovery 10 years after the 2008 financial crisis. IMF Working Paper No. 19/83. S.D. Williamson. 2017. Quantitative easing: How well does this tool work? *Federal Reserve Bank of St. Louis*. For a central banker's acknowledgement of the failure of macroeconomics to understand why such extraordinary injections of money were not resulting in high inflation levels, see B. Cœuré. 2019. The rise of services and the transmission of monetary policy, speech by Benoît Cœuré, Member of the Executive Board of the ECB, at the 21st Geneva Conference on the World Economy, 16 May.

[5] For a readable exposé of the extent to which macroeconomics had missed money and finance and how the crisis of 2008 prompted a rethink of the discipline, see J. Fox. 2013. What we've learned from the financial crisis. *Harvard Business Review*.

[6] The argument for government saving during economic crisis is based on a misleading comparison between government budgets and family finances. For instance, House Minority Leader Republican John Boehner opposed US stimulus plans by arguing that 'American families are tightening their belt, but they don't see government tightening its belt'. The misconception permeated not only the discourse of right-leaning politicians with a fondness for small government. It soon made it into the speeches and party programmes of left-inclined politicians. In P. Krugman. 2015. The case for cuts was a lie. Why does Britain still believe it? The austerity delusion. *The Guardian*, 29 April. Misconceiving government for household economics ignores that governments that can issue debt in their own currency (as it is the case of the United States and the United Kingdom) can fund their expenses without the need to tax (earn) first. See S. Kelton. 2020. *The Deficit Myth: Modern Monetary Theory and the Birth of the People's Economy*. PublicAffairs.

[7] See Y. Chzhen, S. Handa, B. Nolan and B. Cantillon. 2017. *Children of Austerity: Impact of the Great Recession on Child Poverty in Rich Countries*. Oxford University Press. T. Cavero and K. Poinasamy. 2013. *A Cautionary Tale: The True Cost of Austerity and Inequality in Europe*. Oxfam International.

[8] D. Etherington. 2021. *Austerity, Welfare and Work: Exploring Politics, Geographies and Inequalities*. Policy Press.

[9] With the onset of the financial crisis, the value of pension funds shrank by over five trillion US dollars. Pension funds' losses varied across countries, Irish pensions losing 38 per cent of their value, Australian pensions 27 per cent, and US pensions 26 per cent, while German, Norwegian, Spanish and Swiss pensions lost about 10 per cent. B. Keeley and P. Love. 2010. *From Crisis to Recovery: The Causes, Course and Consequences of the Great Recession*. OECD Insights.

[10] In S. Greenhill. 2008. 'It's awful – Why did nobody see it coming?': The Queen gives her verdict on global credit crunch. *Mail Online*, 6 November.

[11] In S. Keen. 2022. *The New Economics: A Manifesto*. Polity Press, p 2.

[12] Philip Arestis clearly specifies one by one the implications that the ignorance of money and financial markets by dominant macroeconomics along with its Efficient Markets Hypothesis had in the design of monetary policy. P. Arestis. 2013. Economic policies of the new consensus macroeconomics: A critical appraisal. In Pixley, J. and Harcourt, G.C. (eds) *Financial Crises and the Nature of Capitalist Money: Mutual Developments from the Work of Geoffrey Ingham*. Palgrave Macmillan, pp 196–215.

[13] In *The Economists' Hour*, Binyamin Appelbaum chronicles the rise and fall of Chicago School style mathematical economics, which regression games so contributed to give a false sense of precision to the economics profession. Appelbaum argues their reputed 'expertise' ended in the fall of 2008 with the large bailouts needed to save the banking sector from financial collapse. B. Appelbaum. 2019. *The Economists' Hour: How the False Prophets of Free Markets Fractured Our Society*. Pan Macmillan.

[14] Central banks engaged in other policies to increase the money supply. These included repo operations, lowering interest rates below the zero bound, direct lending to banks with the aim of banks lending it forward to small businesses, buying corporate bonds or lending to corporations and cities, regions, and states. For a global database of central banks' monetary responses to the COVID-19 pandemic, see C. Cantú, P. Cavallino, F. De Fiore and J. Yetman. 2021. A global database on central banks' monetary responses to COVID-19. Bank for International Settlements, BIS Working Paper No. 934. See also M.R. Grasselli. 2022. Monetary policy responses to COVID-19: A comparison with the 2008 crisis and implications for the future of central banking. *Review of Political Economy*, 34(2): 420–445.

[15] CBPP Staff. 2022. Robust COVID relief achieved historic gains against poverty and hardship, bolstered economy. *Center on Budget and Policy Priorities*, 24 February.

The rapid, robust and broad-ranged fiscal response of governments to the economic crisis brought about by global lockdowns has been credited for limiting the severity and length of the recession with the US government's response being, by and large, the most aggressive – in the United States, fiscal support amounted to about 25 per cent of GDP, compared to 18 per cent in the UK and 10 per cent in all countries on average. Such comprehensive, determined and quick government support policies have been described as 'an economic game-changer'. B. Yaros, J. Rogers, R. Cioffi and M. Zandi. 2022. Fiscal policy in the pandemic. *Moody's Analytics*, 24 February.

[16] C. Reinhart. 2022. *Finance for an Equitable Recovery*. World Development Report. World Bank Group.

[17] A.L. Jackson and J. Schmidt. 2022. 2021 stock market year in review. *Forbes*.

[18] J.E. Stiglitz. 2022. COVID has made global inequality much worse. *Scientific American*, 326(3): 52–53. V. Gopalakrishnan, D. Wadhwa, S. Haddad and P. Blake. 2021. 2021 Year in review in 11 charts: The inequality pandemic. World Bank.

[19] Two misleading views on how banks work are typically subsumed under the 'Loanable Funds' header: the financial intermediation view of banks and the fractional reserve banking theories of money creation. See M. Gross and C. Siebenbrunner. 2019. Money creation in fiat and digital currency systems. International Monetary Fund, IMF Working Paper #WP/19/285. See also R. Werner. 2014. Can banks individually create money out of nothing? The theories and the empirical evidence. *International Review of Financial Analysis*, 36: 1–19. As we saw in Chapter 2, the understanding of banks as mere intermediaries between savers and borrowers is based on a commodity imaginary of money.

[20] Students demanding reform of the economics curricula are organised under the 'Post-Crash Economics Society', the 'International Student Initiative for Pluralist Economics' (ISIPE) or 'Rethinking Economics'. Their demands centre around the teaching of an economics that is more diverse and that goes beyond the exclusive focus on free-market economics.

[21] S. Bowles and W. Carlin. 2021. Rethinking economics. *FD: Finance & Development*, spring. The CORE project is an example of a community of researchers and teachers who, reacting to their frustration over the traditional economics still taught at universities, are developing free open-access resources to transform the teaching of economics. See www.core-econ.org.

[22] An approach to money as balance sheet operations that record social relations of debt–credit follows the tradition of John Maynard Keynes, Hyman Minsky and, among others today, Randall Wray. On this topic, see P. Mehrling. 2011. *The New Lombard Street: How the Fed Became the Dealer of Last Resort*. Princeton University Press; D. Gabor and J. Vestergaard. 2016. *Towards a Theory of Shadow Money*. Institute for New Economic Thinking; S. Bell. 2001. The role of the state and the hierarchy of money. *Cambridge Journal of Economics*, 25: 149–163.

[23] D.J. Bezemer. 2010. Understanding financial crisis through accounting models. *Accounting, Organisations and Society*, 35(7): 676–688.

[24] J. Zoltan and M. Kumhof. 2019. Banks are not intermediaries of loanable funds: Facts, theory and evidence. Bank of England, Staff Working Paper No. 761.

[25] During the build up of the subprime mortgage bubble, this sort of financing operations by banks were argued as leading to the 'democratisation of finance' and the 'ownership society'. Advocates claimed that such practices reduced credit risk for banks, allowing them to extend credit to individuals traditionally deemed not creditworthy. For an early critique of this set of practices and arguments, see I. Erturk, J. Froud, S. Johal, A. Leaver and K. Williams. 2007. The democratization of finance? Promises, outcomes and conditions. *Review of International Political Economy*, 14(4): 553–575. Some have argued that, under the mantel of 'democratisation of finance', the system has actually reinforced 'the tyranny of earned income'. See J. Froud, S. Johan, J. Montgomerie and K. Williams. 2010. Escaping the tyranny of earned income? The failure of finance as social innovation. *New Political Economy*, 15(1): 147–164.

[26] See R. Wray. 2013. What do banks do? What should banks do? A Minskian perspective. *Accounting, Economics, and Law: A Convivium*, 3(3): 277–311. See also L. Fantacci. 2013. Why banks do what they do. How the monetary system affects banking activity. *Accounting, Economics and Law*, 3(3): 333–356.

[27] In *The End of Finance*, Massimo Amato and Luca Fantacci argue how the possibility banks have to sell in financial markets the loans they grant enables the rolling over of debts, constantly postponing the settling of accounts (payments in the short term) into the future (the long term). But that future is discounted onto the present based on optimistic

expectations that things won't change, that the future will be like the present. When these expectations fail to realise, debts cease to be rolled over, yet repayments are still not possible, leading to general crisis. These scholars name the logic that so organises financial markets 'the liquidity principle'. M. Amato and L. Fantacci. 2012. *The End of Finance*. Polity Press.

[28] M. McLeay, A. Radia and R. Thomas. 2014. Money creation in the modern economy. *Quarterly Bulletin*, Bank of England. See also M. McLeay, A. Radia and R. Thomas. 2014. Money in the modern economy: An introduction. *Quarterly Bulletin*, Bank of England.

[29] J.M. Keynes. 1930. *A Treatise on Money*. Cambridge University Press, p 23. Emphasis in the original.

[30] International Monetary Fund economists Marco Gross and Christoph Siebenbrunner offer a similar balance sheet example of money creation through the creation of loans by commercial banks. Gross and Siebenbrunner, Money creation in fiat and digital currency systems.

[31] The money supply is described through various monetary aggregates – M0 to M4 – each sequentially including a less liquid type of money. M0, or 'narrow money', includes the most liquid types – paper bills and coins and central bank reserves. M1 is the aggregate most used, referring to M0 plus on-demand bank deposits. Higher aggregates include assets with a longer maturity, such as saving deposits, money market funds, repo agreements and debt securities. In describing money creation through the extension of bank loans, the chapter – along with the article from the Bank of England – is focusing on M1.

For a description on what the harmonised monetary aggregates in the euro-zone include, see ECB. 1999. Euro area monetary aggregates and their role in the Eurosystem's monetary policy strategy. *ECB Monthly Bulletin*, February. These aggregates include somewhat different items in different monetary areas.

[32] McLeay et al, Money creation in the modern economy.

[33] Such ideas go under the mantel of the 'Money Multiplier'.

[34] McLeay et al, Money creation in the modern economy. Emphasis added. For a similar critique of the Money Multiplier myth, see J. Benes and M. Kumhof. 2012. The Chicago plan revisited. *International Monetary Fund*, IMF Working Paper WP/12/202.

[35] Customers' possibility to use bank's promises to pay – the bank's debt acknowledgement, its IOUs – to settle transactions defines money. As Keynes taught us, '[w]hen acknowledgments of debt are used in this way, we may call them bank money'. Keynes, *A Treatise on Money*, p 5. Indeed, Keynes anchors the distinction between money and debt in that money extinguishes debt. Accordingly, in a gold monetary system, the handing of gold cancels the debt. In a fiat monetary system, the state settles its debts in its own promissory notes (Keynes' 'proper money'). Bank deposits are a promise to convert each unit of bank money into 'proper money' at par on demand, an IOU acknowledging the bank's debt/promise to pay. Because bank deposits are accepted in payment of taxes and because their convertibility into legal tender is guaranteed by the central bank, bank deposits are also accepted to settle debts. It is in this way that bank's IOUs transform into money. See Gabor and Vestergaard, *Towards a Theory of Shadow Money*.

[36] Ann Pettifor argues that the power of the general public over the money creation process inheres in individuals agreeing to borrow. The argument implicit in this chapter is that, in the current monetary system, the will to enter a debt–credit relationship is not so much a *power* the 99 per cent wields but rather a survival *need*. Many depend on credit-granting institutions to even pay for their basic needs. A. Pettifor. 2017. *The Production of Money: How to Break the Power of Bankers*. Verso Books.

[37] G. Standing. 2011. *The Precariat: The New Dangerous Class*. Bloomsbury Academic.

[38] T. Quinsom and M. Benhamou. 2021. Banks always backed fossil fuel over green projects – until this year. *Blomberg Europe Edition*, 19 May.

[39] Hyman Minsky wrote lucidly about the credit creation process as a destabiliser mechanism endogenous to the economy that accounted for the inherent instability of capitalism. Largely ignored during his lifetime, many economists recovered his teachings in an effort to understand the process that led to the financial implosion of 2007–2009. H. Minsky. 1986. *Stabilizing an Unstable Economy*. Washington University Press. See also Mehrling, *The New Lombard Street*; Keen, *The New Economics*; P. Krugman. 2015. The case of the missing Minsky. *New York Times*, 1 June.

For a classic book on how unregulated financial markets have throughout the history of capitalism repeatedly led to instability and crises, see C. Kindleberger. 1978. *Manias, Panics and Crashes*. Basic Books.

[40] Pettifor, *The Production of Money*, p 46.

[41] On the imperative to grow and the extent to which compound interest is at its root, see M. Kennedy. 1995. *Interest and Inflation Free Money: Creating an Exchange Medium That Works for Everybody and Protects the Earth*. Inbook; B. Lietaer, C. Arnsperger, S. Goerner and S. Brunnhuber. 2012. *Money – Sustainability: The Missing Link*. Triarchy Press; C. Eisenstein. 2011. *Sacred Economics*. North Atlantic.

[42] In recent years, US-based non-financial companies have dramatically increased their cash holdings, from US$1.6 trillion in 2000 to about US$5.8 trillion. M. Faulkender, K.W. Hankings and M.A. Petersen. 2022. Why are U.S. companies hoarding so much cash? *Kellog Insight*, Kellogg School of Management at Northwestern University.

[43] This is related to the contradictory uses of money that will be explained in more detail in Chapter 5.

[44] C. Arnsperger, J. Bendell and M. Slater. 2021. *Monetary Adaptation to Planetary Emergency: Addressing the Monetary Growth Imperative*. Institute for Leadership and Sustainability, University of Cumbria, UK.

From Ancient Mesopotamia and Classical Rome to India and Islam in the 19th century, history has repeatedly shown the incompatibility between interest-bearing loans and a slow-growing or stagnant economy such as today's, resulting in high levels of unpayable debt. T. Hartley and G. Kallis. 2021. Interest-bearing loans and unpayable debts in slow-growing economies: Insights from ten historical cases. *Ecological Economics*, 188(C): S0921800921001907.

[45] Financial Crisis Inquiry Commission, USA. 2011. *The Financial Crisis Inquiry Report: Final Report of the National Commission on the Causes of the Financial and Economic Crisis in the United States* (henceforth *Financial Crisis Inquiry Report*).

[46] For a more detailed account of the role played by Wall Street firms, rating agencies and the federal government itself in the wave of securitisation of subprime mortgages, see *Financial Crisis Inquiry Report*, ch 5.

[47] For a detailed account of the role law and lawyers played in the increased complexity of financial securities, see K. Pistor. 2019. *The Code of Capital*. Princeton University Press, ch 4.

[48] In *Financial Crisis Inquiry Report*, p 68.

[49] I borrow the term to describe the monetary, banking and financial processes that coalesced in the boom first and bust later of the first decade of the 2000s from Gabor and Vestergaard, *Towards a Theory of Shadow Money*.

[50] *Financial Crisis Inquiry Report*, p 175.

[51] Stated by Robert Levin, Chief Financial Officer of Fannie Mae, a Federal National Mortgage Association in the United States. *Financial Crisis Inquiry Report*, p 180.

[52] For a detailed description of the aggressive and risky lending practices during the boom, I recommend reading Chapters 6 and 7 of the *Financial Crisis Inquiry Report*, aptly titled respectively 'The mortgage machine' and 'The CDO machine'. Hyman Minsky would have characterised these ballooning schemes as Ponzi financial structures. He distinguished

hedge, speculative and Ponzi finance as three distinct income-flows to debt-flow relations for economic actors. In hedge financing, economic actors can attend all their payment obligations (outflows) with their income inflows. In speculative financing, economic actors can only attend the interest part of their payment obligations, having to roll over their debts to attend payment of their principal obligation. In Ponzi financing, economic actors need further borrowing just to pay the interest on previous loans, their outflows surpassing their inflows. H. Minsky. 1992. The financial instability hypothesis. Levy Economics Institute of Bard College, Working Paper No. 74.

[53] Angelo Mozilo, CEO of Countrywide Financial Corporation, the biggest mortgage granting institution from 2004 until the market collapsed in 2007. Between 2002 and 2005, the company sold or securitised 87 per cent of the $1.5 trillion in mortgages it originated. In *Financial Crisis Inquiry Report*, p 105.

[54] Patricia Lindsay, a former fraud specialist at New Century, told the Financial Crisis Inquiry Commission. *Financial Crisis Inquiry Report*, p 105.

[55] *Financial Crisis Inquiry Report*, chs 4 and 11.

[56] As John Snow, former Treasure Secretary of the United States, told the Financial Crisis Inquiry Commission. *Financial Crisis Inquiry Report*, p 66.

[57] In *Saving the Market from Capitalism*, Massimo Amato and Luca Fantacci argue that it is not the market mechanism per se that is to be blamed for the recurrent crises of capitalism, but the fact that finance has been organised along a market principle. The problem, they argue, is that there is one market too many, the financial market. M. Amato and L. Fantacci. 2014. *Saving the Market from Capitalism*. Translated by G. Sells. Polity Press.

[58] In 1988, Charles Goodhart, a British economist who served as senior adviser at the Bank of England, wrote an insightful history on the evolution of central banks as the bank of banks. As the book traces the evolving role and practices of central banks, Goodhart engages with the neoliberal free-market arguments of those advocating for free-banking for whom the 'introduction of an outside agency to regulate and control the banking system represents an undesirable intervention in the otherwise satisfactory working of a free market system in the banking industry' (p 4). In contrast, Goodhart finds the non-competitive aspect of the central bank crucial for the performance of its roles as facilitator of a nation's payment system, ultimate source of liquidity and superviser of key sectors of financial markets. C. Goodhart. 1988. *The Evolution of Central Banks*. MIT Press.

[59] For a discussion of the selective introduction of central bank money, see C. Desan. 2020. The key to value: The debate over commensurability in neoclassical and credit approaches to money. *Law and Contemporary Problems*, 83(2): 1–22.

[60] Based on an analysis of Census Bureau surveys, researchers at the University of Michigan conclude the impact of the US federal government COVID-19 pandemic stimulus bills was a clear reduction of material poverty and other poverty related indicators. See P. Cooiney and L. Shaefer. 2021. Material hardship and mental health following the COVID-19 relief bill and American rescue plan act. *Poverty Solutions*. University of Michigan.

[61] Amazon has become the epitome of big business taking advantage of government financial support all while submitting its workers, at home and abroad, to inhuman labour conditions. See R. McGahey. 2020. Amazon gets billions while state and local government budgets collapse. *Forbes*, 17 December; S. Ghaffary and J. Del Rey. 2020. The real cost of Amazon. *Vox*, 29 June; D. Lee. 2020. Amazon contractors enduring 'subhuman' conditions in Philippines. *Financial Times*, 1 April; J. Greene. 2021. Amazon's employee surveillance fuels unionization efforts: 'It's not prison, it's work'. *The Washington Post*, 6 December.

[62] M. Mazzucato. 2018. *The Value of Everything: Making and Taking in the Global Economy*. Penguin Books.

[63] A. Armstrong, E.P. Davis, I. Liadze and C. Rienzo. 2013. Evaluating changes in bank lending to UK SMEs over 2001–12 – ongoing tight credit? Econometric analysis using data from the UK Survey of SME Finances and the SME Finance Monitor. Report. Department for Business Innovation & Skills, UK Government.

[64] Bank of England. 2012. The distributional effects of asset purchases. Bank of England Report, 12 July; G. Bernardo, J. Ryan-Collins, R. Werner and T. Greenham. 2013. *Strategic Quantitative Easing: Stimulating Investment to Rebalance the Economy*. New Economic Foundation. See also Reinhart, *Finance for an Equitable Recovery*.

[65] See B. Dyson, G. Hodgson and F.v. Lerven. 2016. *Sovereign Money: An Introduction*, Positive Money; Benes and Kumhof, The Chicago plan revisited; J. D'Arista. 2018. *All Fall Down: Debt, Deregulation and Financial Crises*. Edward Elgar; Amato and Fantacci, *The End of Finance*; Amato and Fantacci, *Saving the Market from Capitalism*; J. Muellbauer. 2014. Combatting Eurozone deflation: QE for the people. *Centre for Economic Policy Research*; S. Wan, E. Bartsch, J. Boivin, S. Fischer and P. Hildebrand. 2019. Dealing with the next downturn: From unconventional monetary policy to unprecedented policy coordination. *BlackRock Institute*.

[66] See L. Zelmanovitz and B. Meyerhof Salama. 2020. Central bank digital currency: The hidden agenda, *Just Money*; R. Hockett. 2020. The inclusive value ledger: A public platform for digital dollars, digital payments, and digital public banking. *Just Money*.

[67] D. Hengsbach. 2022. Monetary sovereignty in the digital age: A case of central bank digital currencies (CBDC)? Paper presented at the SASE conference, Amsterdam, July 9–11.

[68] S.L. Star. 1999. The ethnography of infrastructure. *American Behavioural Scientist*, 43(3): 377–391. See also the distinction between intermediary and mediator in Chapter 1 of this book.

[69] John Stuart Mill's discussion of money is exemplary of the invisibility of infrastructures while they work and their coming to light when they break down. Though adhering to a view of money as neutral to the workings of the economy, Mill was however keen to admit that money had an effect on the economy when it broke down. He could held this contradictory understanding within the space of two sentences. In a chapter entitled 'Of money', he writes: 'There cannot, in short, be intrinsically a more insignificant thing, in the economy of society, than money; except in the character of a contrivance for sparing time and labour. It is a machine for doing quickly and commodiously, what would be done, though less quickly and commodiously, without it: and like many other kinds of machinery, it only exerts a distinct and independent influence of its own when it gets out of order.' In other words, as an infrastructure of the economy, money is made invisible when it works, and visible when 'it gets out of order'. J.S. Mill. 1877/1848. *Principles of Political Economy with some of their Applications to Social Philosophy*, book 3, ch 7. D. Appleton and Company.

[70] CBPP Staff, Robust COVID relief.

[71] D. Autor, D. Cho, L.D. Crane, M. Goldar, B. Lutz, J. Montes, W.B. Peterman, D. Ratner, D. Villar and A. Yildirmaz. 2022. The $800 billion paycheck protection program: Where did the money go and why did it go there? *Journal of Economic Perspectives*, 36(2): 55–80.

Interlude 1

[1] I build the account of Yap from Furness' original travel-book as well as from Felix Martin's delightful opening to his insightful and entertaining book on money. W.H. Furness. 1910. *The Island of Stone Money: UAP of the Carolines*. J.B. Lippincott Company; F. Martin. 2014. *Money: The Unauthorised Biography*. Vintage Books.

[2] Furness, *The Island of Stone Money*, p 11.

[3] Furness, *The Island of Stone Money*, p 140.

[4] For both economists, fascination for Yap's stone money related to the form of rationality it was an expression of. In Keynes' words: '[The island of Yap] has brought us in contact with a people whose ideas on currency are probably more truly philosophical than those of any other country. Modern practice in regard to gold reserves has a good deal to learn from the more logical practices of the island of Uap.' In Friedman's words: 'The Yap Islanders regarded stones quarried and shaped on a distant island and brought to their own as the concrete manifestation of wealth. For a century and more, the "civilized" world regarded as a concrete manifestation of its wealth metal dug from deep in the ground, refined at great labor, and transported great distances to be buried again in elaborate vaults deep in the ground. Is the one practice really more rational than the other?' J.M. Keynes. 1915. The island of stone money. *The Economic Journal*, 25(98): 281–283. M. Friedman. 1991. The island of stone money. Working Papers in Economics, Hoover Institution, E-91-3.

[5] Furness, *The Island of Stone Money*, p 93.

[6] As we saw in an earlier chapter, seeing value in the very token that represents value defines a commodity understanding of money. Metallists see value in the content the token is made of or is made to represent. Marx adapted such idea to his labour theory of value by placing the value of the coin in the labour incurred to mine and shape the precious metal content (see Chapter 2, footnote 18). At first, Furness offers a mix of the two commodity-based understandings of value when he discusses the value of a specific *fei* as residing in its size, in its quality, and in the labour it took to quarry, shape and transport it to Yap.

[7] Furness, *The Island of Stone Money*, p 96. Emphasis added.

[8] Furness, *The Island of Stone Money*, p 92. Emphasis added.

[9] G. Simmel. 1900. *The Philosophy of Money*. 3rd enlarged edition edited by D. Frisby, translated by D. Frisby and T. Bottomore. Routledge.

[10] Furness, *The Island of Stone Money*, pp 97–98.

[11] Economic anthropologist Keith Hart reasons along these lines when he argues that '[m]oney … is an expression of trust between individuals in society, an act of remembering which allows us to bring calculation to some of our interactions and relationships. This trust is two-sided also, residing in both personal responsibility and the shared memory of communities, in personality and culture.' K. Hart. 2001. *Money in an Unequal World: Keith Hart and His Memory Bank*. Texere.

[12] Among sociologist scholars of money, Geoffrey Ingham is the first to approach money as 'a social technology' for the coordination of the economy; more specifically, as 'a specific form of social technology that accounts for abstract value and transports it through time' (p 60). G. Ingham. 2004. *The Nature of Money*. Polity Press.

[13] Elinor Ostrom showed a third alternative existed for the management of the natural commons. While mainstream economic and political theory presented the market and the state as the only actors capable of successfully managing the commons, in her travels across communities from South East Asia to Africa, from Latin America to Southern Europe, Ostrom found many an example of natural commons more productively managed by communities. For her work identifying the principles for the successful collective governance of the commons she was awarded the Nobel Prize in Economics in 2009. E. Ostrom. 1990. *Governing the Commons: The Evolution of Institutions for Collective Action*. Cambridge University Press.

For an application of Ostrom's notion of the commons to a discussion of money, see E. Barinaga, A. Honzawa, J. Ocampo, P. Raffaelli and L. Ussher. 2021. Commons-based monies for an inclusive and resilient future. In *Climate Adaptation: Accounts of Resilience, Self-Sufficiency and Systems Change*. Arkbound, pp 301–321. For an application to digital monies of Ostrom's eight principles for the government of the commons, see

D. Rozas, A. Tenorio-Fornés, S. Díaz-Molina and S. Hassan. 2021. When Ostrom meets blockchain: Exploring the potentials of blockchain for commons governance. *SAGE Open*.

[14] Furness, *The Island of Stone Money*, pp 98–100.

[15] For some descriptions of how private profiteers, supported by governments, are grabbing the natural commons to the detriment of the communities that live in and from them, see K. Lanz. 2022. *Large-Scale Land Acquisition in Ghana: Institutional Change, Gender and Power*. Routledge. J. Dell'Angelo, P. D'Odorico, M.C. Rulli and P. Marchand. 2017. The tragedy of the grabbed commons: Coercion and dispossession in the global land rush. *World Development*, 92: 1–12; J. Franco, S. Kishimoto, S. Kay, T. Feodoroff and G. Pracucci. 2014. *The Global Water Grab: A Primer*. The Transnational Institute.

[16] The example of primitive communities whose money systems were grabbed by colonising powers is not unique to Yap and recent colonial history. It appears the Inca empire partly applied its bureaucratic prowess on colonised communities by grabbing their local monetary system. Pre-existing traditional *ayllu* groups used knotted strings – *khippu* – to keep record of household's appropriations from and contributions to necessary work in the village – clearing fields, harvesting, maintaining water canals and reservoirs, porterage or repairing bridges and other communal buildings. Knots were continuously knotted and unknotted in the strings to keep track of a household's debts and their cancellation. Upon expansion, the Inca imposed labour on the *ayllus* and coopted the *khippu* to record labour debts owed to the central Inca administration. Yet, '[u]nlike the local string records, these were fixed and non-negotiable; the knots were never unravelled and retied'. D. Graeber and D. Wengrow. 2021. *The Dawn of Everything: A New History of Humanity*. Penguin Random House, p 426.

Chapter 4

[1] In G. Bazzani. 2020. *When Money Changes Society: The Case of Sardex Money as Community*. Springer VS, p 78. Subsequent quotes from Sardex are from this source.

[2] I find the following passage in Mauss' essay particularly enlightening: '[T]he system of gift-through-exchange permeates all the economic, tribal, and moral life of the Trobriand people. It is "impregnated" with it, as Malinowski very neatly expressed it. It is a constant "give and take". The process is marked by a continuous flow in all directions of presents given, accepted, and reciprocated, obligatorily and out of self-interest, by reason of greatness and for services rendered, through challenges and pledges.' M. Mauss. 2002 [1954]. *The Gift: The Form and Reason for Exchange in Archaic Societies*. Routledge Classics, p 37.

[3] Mauss, *The Gift*, p 93.

[4] Material used to build the Sardex story comes from Giacomo Bazzani's empirically rich doctoral thesis, from videos and webinars freely accessible online as well as from a couple of interviews with one of the founders. For the Málaga Común story, material comes from interviews with users and my own participation in that citizen money system.

[5] Entry in blog BlogSostenible in 2010 by one of the founders. Own translation. https://blogsostenible.wordpress.com/2010/09/05/nueva-moneda-en-malaga/

[6] Figures come from the Spain's National Institute of Statistics (Instituto Nacional de Estadística, INE). https://www.ine.es/jaxiT3/Datos.htm?t=3996

[7] See Chapter 3 in this book.

[8] From Bazzani, *When Money Changes Society*, p 35.

[9] Though economic crises undoubtedly exacerbate the scarcity of money and, therewith, the difficulty of connecting an economy – of mobilising an economy's resources to satisfy its needs – the experience is well known to regions located at the periphery of the monetary circuits of a globalised economy. Regions with little value adding industry, low rates of return on capital, and few opportunities – typically rural areas

and the global South – have few ways to attract the 'free global capital flows'. Money tends to move to financial centres with higher rates of return and economic hubs with high value adding industries. With little local production and heavily reliant on imports, communities at the margins of global networks of trade and finance see the little money they may be able to attract – through, for instance, tourism and remittances – leak out of their territory. In these regions, the scarcity of money is a constant affliction which unswervingly intensifies during global crises. In *Plugging the Leaks*, community organisers Bernie Ward and Julie Lewis build on the idea of the leakage of money to urge communities to map and identify how money leaves their territory. Such a mapping exercise would inevitably suggest lines of action to 'plug the leaks' and strengthen the local economy. B. Ward and J. Lewis. 2002. *Plugging the Leaks: Making the Most of Every Pound That Enters Your Local Economy*. New Economics Foundation.

[10] Bazzani, *When Money Changes Society*, p 35. Emphasis added.

[11] The emergence of a profusion of local currencies is a phenomenon tightly connected with economic crisis. Based on numismatic evidence, Gómez and Prittwitz revise the connection between periods of economic distress and the rise of monetary plurality for various historical episodes. See G.M. Gómez and W. Prittwitz und Gaffron. 2018. The pervasiveness of monetary plurality in economic crisis and war. In G.M. Gómez (ed) *Monetary Plurality in Local, Regional and Global Economies*. Routledge, ch 7.

[12] The estimate of the number of local complementary currencies went up to 400 if time-banks were included. Time-banks are a complementary payment method that uses hours as its unit of account and follows the principle of clearing in the dispensation and disappearance of monetary tokens. N. Hughes. 2015. The community currency scene in Spain. *International Journal of Community Currency Research*, 19: 1–11.

[13] J. Blanc and C. Lakócai. 2020. Toward spatial analyses of local currencies: The case of France. *International Journal of Community Currency Research*, 24(1): 11–29.

[14] H. Meng and A. Ueda. 2020. Characteristics of community currency that contribute to endogenous regional activation: Based on case studies of three community currencies: Ma~yu, Tengu and Awa Money. *International Journal of Community Currency Research*, 24: 54–63; Yoshihisa Miyazaki and Ken-ichi Kurita. 2018. The diversity and evolutionary process of modern community currencies in Japan. *International Journal of Community Currency* Research, 22: 120–131.

[15] I. Sotiropoulou. 2011. Alternative exchange systems in contemporary Greece. *International Journal of Community Currency Research*, 15(D): 27–31

[16] C. Thiel. 2011. Complementary currencies in Germany: The Regiogeld system. *International Journal of Community Currency Research*, 15(D): 17–21; R. Schroeder. 2006. Community exchange and trading systems in Germany. *International Journal of Community Currency Research*, 10: 24–42.

[17] J. Ryan-Collins. 2011. Building local resilience: The emergence of the UK transition currencies. *International Journal of Community Currency Research*, 15(D): 61–67.

[18] J. Mascornick. 2007. Local currency loans and grants: Comparative case studies of Ithaca HOURS and Calgary Dollars. *International Journal of Community Currency Research*, 11: 1–22.

[19] E. Gomes da Silva Hernandes, E. Souza Siqueira, E. Henrique Diniz and M. Pozzebon. 2018. A digital community bank: Mapping negotiation mechanisms in its consolidation as an alternative to commercial banks. *International Journal of Community Currency Research*, 22: 56–70; A.S. Rigo. 2020. Challenges of social currency use: A survey on community development banks in Brazil. *International Journal of Community Currency Research*, 24: 74–85; C. Place. 2011. Community currency progress in Latin America (Banco Palmas). *International Journal of Community Currency Research*, 15(D): 39–46.

[20] C. Stamm. 2021. Understanding the recent dynamics of local currency initiatives in Switzerland. *International Journal of Community Currency Research,* 25(2): 63–76; C. Place, A. Calderon, J. Stodder and I. Wallimann. 2018. Swiss currency systems: Atlas, compendium and chronicle of legal aspects. *International Journal of Community Currency Research,* 22: 85–104.

[21] G.M. Gómez. 2009. *Argentina's Parallel Currency: The Economy of the Poor.* Pickering & Chatto.

[22] I. Fisher. 1933. *Stamp Scrip.* Adelphi Company. See also J.W.C. Harper. 1948. *Scrip and Other Forms of Local Money.* PhD Dissertation. University of Chicago.

[23] For several classificatory efforts, see L. Larue. 2020. A conceptual framework for classifying currencies. *International Journal of Community Currency Research,* 24: 45–60; A. Tichit, C. Mathonnat and D. Landivar. 2016. Classifying non-bank currency systems using web data. *International Journal of Community Currency Research,* 20: 24–40; J. Blanc. 2011. Classifying 'CCs': Community, complementary and local currencies. *International Journal of Community Currency Research,* 15(D): 4–10; J. Martignoni. 2012. A new approach to a typology of complementary currencies. *International Journal of Community Currency Research,* 16: 1–17; G. Seyfang and N. Longhurst. 2013. Growing green money? Mapping community currencies for sustainable development. *Ecological Economics,* 86: 65–77; C. Meyer and M. Hudon. 2019. Money and the commons: An investigation of complementary currencies and their ethical implications. *Journal of Business Ethics,* 160: 277–292; M.J. van der Linden and C. van Beers. 2017. Are private (digital) moneys (disruptive) social innovations? An exploration of different designs. *Journal of Social Entrepreneurship,* 8(3): 302–319; L. Larue, C. Meyer, M. Hudon and J. Sandberg. 2022. The ethics of alternative currencies. *Business Ethics Quarterly,* 32(2): 299–321.

[24] I agree with French economist and scholar of complementary currencies, Jérôme Blanc, when he argues that 'attempts to construct typologies and proposals for naming moneys have generally proved disappointingly incoherent or unsystematic, as if the subject of analysis itself were not amenable to any stringent form of classification'. J. Blanc. 2018. Making sense of the plurality of money: A Polanyian attempt. In Gómez, G.M. (ed) *Monetary Plurality in Local, Regional and Global Economies.* Routledge, pp 48–66.

[25] L. Doria and L. Fantacci. 2018. Evaluating complementary currencies: From the assessment of multiple social qualities to the discovery of a unique monetary sociality. *Quality & Quantity,* 52(3): 1291–1314. Another author arguing for the particular effectiveness of mutual credit systems is T. Greco. 2013. Taking moneyless exchange to scale: Measuring and maintaining the health of a credit clearing system. *International Journal of Community Currency Research,* 17(A): 19–25.

[26] See, for instance, G. Vallet. 2016. A local money to stabilise capitalism: The underestimated case of the WIR. *Economy and Society,* 45(3–4): 479–504; J. Stodder. 2009. Complementary credit networks and macroeconomic stability: Switzerland's Wirtschaftsring. *Journal of Economic Behaviour & Organization,* 72(1): 79–95. J. Stodder and B. Lietaer 2016. The macro-stability of Swiss WIR-bank credits: Balance, velocity, and leverage. *Comparative Economic Studies,* 58(4): 570–605.

[27] J.M. Keynes. 1942. Proposals for an international currency (or clearing) union. In Horsefield, J.K. (ed) 1969. *The International Monetary Fund 1945–1965: Twenty years of international monetary cooperation,* volume III: Documents, pp 3–18. International Moneary Fund.

[28] M. Amato and L. Fantacci. 2012. *The End of Finance.* Polity Press. For a call to reform the current international monetary system along Keynes' bancor proposal, see L. Fantacci. 2013. Why not bancor? Keynes's currency plan as a solution to global imbalances. In Hirai, T., Marcuzzo, M.C. and Mehrling, P. (eds) *Keynesian Reflections: Effective Demand, Money, Finance, and Policies in the Crisis.* Oxford Scholarship Online. M. Amato and L. Fantacci.

2014. Back to which Bretton Woods? Liquidity and clearing as alternative principles for reforming international money. *Cambridge Journal of Economics*, 38(6): 1431–1452. For more on how Keynes' bancor plan worked, see L.J. Ussher, A. Hass, K. Töpfer and C.C. Jaeger. 2018. Keynes and the international monetary system: Time for a tabular standard? *The European Journal of the History of Economic Thought*, 25(1): 1–35. For a discussion of the relevance of Keynes' bancor to today's international monetary system, see P. Mehrling. 2016. Beyond bancor. *Challenge*, 59(1): 22–34.

[29] All personal names have been anonymised.

[30] Fieldnotes, 4 May 2016.

[31] Oscar. Fieldnotes, 20 February 2016.

[32] Inés. Fieldnotes, 20 February 2016.

[33] Rocío. Fieldnotes, 20 February 2016.

[34] A growing line of research within the emerging field of complementary currencies attempts to assess the impact of these local forms of money. Empathetic to the social and environmental motives that guide the monetary experiments, scholars are rejecting impact assessments that squarely focus on economic cost–benefit analysis and are instead suggesting indicators that acknowledge the social, political and environmental dimensions of local monies. Some of these indicators would be empathetic to Raquel's insight on the impact of complementary currencies on individual members' sense of belonging and emotional wellbeing. For example, see H. Nakazato and T. Hiramoto. 2012. An empirical study of the social effects of community currencies. *International Journal of Community Currency Research*, 16(D): 124–135; L. Moyer. 2015. An impact assessment model for web-based time-banks: A thought-experiment in the operationalisation of social capital. *Consilience: The Journal of Sustainable Development*, 14(2): 106–125; K. Dittmer. 2013. Local currencies for purposive degrowth? A quality check of some proposals for changing money-as-usual. *Journal of Cleaner Production*, 54: 3–13.

Some authors question the extent to which the suggested social and environmental impacts of complementary currencies suffice to stabilise these monies and compensate for their geographical limitations. In this respect, see M.S. Evans. 2009. Zelizer's theory of money and the case of local currencies. *Environment and Planning A: Economy and Space*, 41(5): 1026–1041; J. Matti and Y. Zhou. 2020. Money is money: The economic impact of BerkShares. *SSRN Electronic Journal*; L. Larue. 2022. The case against alternative currencies. *Politics, Philosophy & Economics*, 21(1): 75–93. In this line of thought, see also J. Powell. 2002. Petty capitalism, perfecting capitalism or post-capitalism? *Review of International Political Economy*, 9(4): 619–649.

[35] Conceived as values, reciprocity, solidarity and mutuality are often conflated in analysis of complementary currencies. In line with the relational approach adopted throughout the book, Interlude 2 reframes reciprocity, solidarity and mutuality as interactional patterns. The conceptual move helps distinguish the distinct effect of the three patterns on the way the monies inserting those patterns in their design work.

[36] See, for instance, E. Barinaga. 2019. Transforming or reproducing an unequal economy? Solidarity and inequality in a community currency. *International Journal of Community Currencies Research*, 23(2): 2–16; E. Collom. 2011. Motivations and differential participation in a community currency system: The dynamics within a local social movement organization. *Sociological Forum*, 26(1): 144–168; G. Peebles. 2011. *The Euro and Its Rivals: Currency and the Construction of a Transnational City*. Indiana University Press; K. Werner. 2015. Performing economies of care in New England time bank and Buddhist community. In Roelvink G., St.Martin, K. and Gibson-Graham, J.K. (eds) *Making Other Worlds Possible: Performing Diverse Economies*. University of Minnesota Press.

[37] V.A. Zelizer. 2005. Circuits within capitalism. In Nee, V. and Svedberg, R. (eds) *The Economic Sociology of Capitalism*. Princeton University Press, pp 289–322.

[38] To acknowledge the influence the work of Vivianna Zelizer has had on economic sociology, American sociologist Randall Collins remakes Zelizer's notion 'circuits of commerce' into 'Zelizer's circuits'. R. Collins. 2000. Situational stratification: A micro-macro theory of inequality. *Sociological Theory*, 18: 17–43.

[39] V.A. Zelizer. Circuits within capitalism.

[40] V.A. Zelizer. 1997. *The Social Meaning of Money: Pin Money, Paychecks, Poor Relief, and Other Currencies*. Princeton University Press.

[41] I take this expression from Nigel Dodd's book, *The Social Life of Money*. The book is a broad-ranging theoretical elaboration of what money is, where monetary legitimacy resides, and how new monies could, eventually, transform society. The book is impressive in its intellectual reach. It skilfully advances sociological approaches to the study of money and introduces much welcomed variation to perspectives on money. Yet, similar to Zelizer, Dodd falls short of recognising the determinant role social relations play into the configuration of money itself. Further, more could be done in terms of advancing an understanding of the relation between different monetary configurations and their specific performative effects on the world. N. Dodd. 2014. *The Social Life of Money*. Princeton University Press.

[42] G. Simmel. 1900. *The Philosophy of Money*. 3rd enlarged edition edited by D. Frisby, translated by D. Frisby and T. Bottomore. Routledge.

[43] Except time-banks that use 'hours' as the unit of account, most mutual credit systems use legal tender as the measure of the value of the monetary tokens they create and use. The manual for the design of LETSystems explicitly advises equalling the value of the local currency to that of the conventional national currency. The argument given is one of convenience, as the national currency is the one most users think with and thus use to assess the level of prices of the goods and services exchanged. For Michael Linton's LETSystems design manual, see https://archive.lets.net/gmlets/design/home.html. See also M. Fare and P. Ould Ahmed. 2017. Complementary currency systems and their ability to support economic and social changes. *Development and Change*, 48(5): 847–872; Seyfang and Longhurst, Growing green money?

[44] N.R. Kocherlakota. 1998. Money Is memory. *Journal of Economic Theory*, 81: 232–251. In a similar vein, British economic anthropologist Keith Hart conceives money as 'mainly, but not exclusively, an act of remembering, a way of keeping track of some of the exchanges we each enter into with the rest of humanity'. K. Hart. 2001. *Money in an Unequal World: Keith Hart and His Memory Bank*. Texere, p 234.

[45] Mike Bryan, Vice President of the Federal Reserve Bank of Atlanta, in 'Money: An Economist's Perspective. The Curious Case of the Yap Stones', a video from 2011 that explains the stone money of Yap.

[46] Recorded in the minutes to the General Assembly held on 5 April 2016. In the original, 'Tanto la parte que ofrece como la que consume aportan. Los dos aportan. Lo importante es el movimiento (circulación de la moneda)'.

[47] In *Mutual Life, Limited*, Bill Maurer attests to a similar ironic scepticism towards the local currency system he studies, IthacaHOURS. And, though IthacaHOURS builds upon a different monetary design – fiat, print-as-you-deem model – the scepticism is characteristic of the sort of critique local monetary experiments encounter both among economists and lay-people. B. Maurer. 2005. *Mutual Life, Limited: Islamic Banking, Alternative Currencies, Lateral Reason*. Princeton University Press.

[48] Limits on credits and debits is somewhat contested among practitioners in mutual credits systems. As an illustration it may suffice to mention the different views of two key figures in that field: Thomas Greco and Michael Linton. While Thomas Greco advocates the need to manage limits so as to better allocate credit, in the LETSystems manual Michael Linton co-authored there are no limits. In a recent interview, Linton goes as far as

suggesting that such 'credit limits and lots of added features [did not make] it work better, and some blocked it from working'. See Greco, Taking moneyless exchange to scale. The LETSystem design manual can be found at https://archive.lets.net/gmlets/design/home.html. The interview with Michael Linton can be found at https://www.lowimpact.org/posts/lets-origins-michael-linton-letsystems.

[49] They discussed the reformulation of many other common terms used to describe the economy and relations in it, yet these puns translate badly to English. For those readers who speak Spanish, other terms they played with were from 'tra-bajar' to 'tra-subir' or 'tra-gozar', from 'asamblea' to 'amablea' and from 'almacén' to 'alma-zen'.

[50] Dittmer, Local currencies for purposive degrowth?

[51] Evans, Zelizer's theory of money.

[52] From the meeting minutes of the General Assembly held on 8 April 2015.

[53] Bazzani, *When Money Changes Society*, p 2.

[54] From sardexpay.net.

[55] See Bazzani, *When Money Changes Society*; J. Blanc. 2021. Book review of Bazzani (2020) 'When money changes society: The case of Sardex money as community'. *International Journal of Community Currency Research*, 25(2): 77–80.

[56] From E. Posnett. 2015. The Sardex factor. *Financial Times*, 18 September.

[57] On the need to safeguard the symmetry of obligations between creditors and debtors in local mutual credit systems, see T. Greco. 2009. *The End of Money and the Future of Civilisation*. Chelsea Green. Doria and Fantacci root the particular sociality enticed by mutual credit systems in the symmetry of obligations. Doria and Fantacci, Evaluating complementary currencies.

[58] From Posnett, The Sardex factor.

[59] Bazzani, *When Money Changes Society*, p 46.

[60] Bazzani, *When Money Changes Society*, p 36.

[61] Bazzani, *When Money Changes Society*, p 56.

[62] Bazzani, *When Money Changes Society*, pp 3 and 165.

[63] From Bazzani, *When Money Changes Society*, pp 48–49.

[64] Bazzani, *When Money Changes Society*, p 113.

[65] In the minutes of Málaga Común General Assembly held on 8 April 2015.

[66] The argument that monetary configurations shape how people relate to money and to others is parallel to Michel Callon's argument that economics is performative. See M. Callon. 2007. What does it mean to say that economics is performative? In MacKenzie, D., Muniesa, F. and Siu, L. (eds) *Do Economists Make Markets? On the Performativity of Economics*. Princeton University Press, Chapter 11, pp 311–357.

Chapter 5

[1] F. Schwarz. 1951. The experiment in Wörgl. *Verlags-Genossenschaft Freies Volk*. Translated from the German by H. Martzak-Goerike and prepared and shortened for the internet by H. Eisenkolb. All figures on Wörgl come from A. Von Muralt. 1934. The Woergl experiment with depreciating money. *Annals of Collective Economy*, 10(1), pp 48–57; Schwarz, The experiment in Wörgl; and I. Fisher. 1933. *Stamp Scrip*. Adelphi Company. Michael Unterguggenberger, the mayor of Wörgl at the time, also wrote in 1934 about the dire economic circumstances in 1932. The end results of the Wörgl experiment. *Annals of Collective Economy* (today renamed to *Annals of Public and Cooperative Economics*). For background on Austria's contemporary currency policy, see H. Handler. 2016. Two centuries of currency policy in Austria. *Monetary Policy & the Economy, Oesterreichische Nationalbank (Austrial Central Bank)*, 3: 61–76.

[2] M.C. Bourdet. 1934. A French view of the Woergl experiment. Translated by G. Spiller. *Annals of Public & Cooperative Economics*, 10(1): 58–59.

[3] von Muralt, The Woergl experiment, p 55.

[4] J.M. Keynes. 1936. *The General Theory of Employment, Interest and Money*. Macmillan, ch 23, p 335.

[5] Fisher, *Stamp Scrip*; B. Champ. 2008. Stamp Scrip: Money people paid to use. *Economic Commentary*. Federal Reserve Bank of Cleveland. Today, Italian economic historian Luca Fantacci suggests Fisher's Wörgl-like stamp scrip as a monetary tool to cope with economic crises. L. Fantacci. 2013. Reforming money to exit the crisis: Examples of non-capitalist monetary systems in theory and practice. In Pixley, J. and Harcourt, G.C. (eds) *Financial Crises and the Nature of Capitalist Money*. Palgrave Macmillan.

[6] In Schwartz, The experiment in Wörgl. Von Muralt, contemporary economist and Fisher's student, reasoned against prohibition not only based on the merits of Wörgl's stamp scrip, but also the misdeeds of private bank money. In his words: 'In any case, these certificates are decidedly more harmless than the expanded credits of numerous financial institutions which have by no means been so sternly dealt with.' Von Muralt, The Woergl experiment, p 55. The prohibition of Wörgl's municipal money parallel to the legality of private bank money is testimony of the extent to which central banks prioritise the interests of banking and financial actors over those of the people and their elected officials; in the 1930s like in the 2000s. For more on this topic, see Chapter 3.

[7] Some economists and scholars of money distinguish between the medium of exchange and the means of payment functions. As a medium of exchange, cash is used to pay immediately for the goods and services bought. As a means of payment, money handed over serves to cancel an obligation. Functioning as medium of exchange, goods are sold and money acquired for the purpose of acquiring other objects through further acts of exchange. Functioning as means of payment, money is used to settle previously incurred debts – however this debt may have come about. According to Karl Polanyi, a distinguishing attribute of archaic societies is the use of different objects to accomplish the various functions of money. He gives Hammurabi's Babylonia as an example where, in general, the payment of obligations such as rents, wages and taxes was done in barley; important staples functioned as means of exchange; silver was used as the money of account (1 shekel of silver = 1 gur of barley); and wealth was stored in the form of a plot of land, a house, heads of cattle, or slaves. The introduction of markets as places of exchange led to the unification of the various uses of money into a single money-object on the basis of the exchange-use. As he writes, 'with the introduction of markets as the physical locus of exchange a new type of obligation comes into prominence as the legal residue of transactions. Payment appears as the counterpart of some material advantage gained in the transaction. Formerly a man was made to pay taxes, rent, fines, or blood-money. Now he pays for the goods he bought. Money is now means of payment *because* it is means of exchange. The notion of an independent origin of payment fades, and the millennia in which it sprang not from economic transaction, but directly from religious, social, or political obligations, are forgotten' (p 183; emphasis original). K. Polanyi. 1968 [1957]. The semantics of money-uses. In Dalton, G. (ed) *Primitive, Archaic, and Modern Economies: Essays of Karl Polanyi*, pp 175–203. Beacon Press.

In monetised societies with 'all-purpose money', the distinction between medium of exchange and means of payment can feel somewhat studious, but it carries effects. As we saw in Chapter 2, seeing money as medium of exchange is proper of the commodity imaginary of money, and directs our gaze to the assumed inherent value of money tokens. Highlighting the means of payment function is characteristic of an understanding of money as originating in a relationship of debt and credit and helps us recognise the symmetrical obligation of debtors and creditors in facilitating the repayment of the original debt.

Debtors have an obligation to pay back, and creditors an obligation to circulate their monetary tokens and ease debtors' access to a money with which to pay back their debts.

For the purpose of unpacking Wörgl's money, however, the distinction has no relevance for the stamp scrip served both to pay for goods one wanted and to discharge past debt obligations. As we will see, however, it is important to recognise the state-based debt–credit relationship (and imaginary) that anchored Wörgl's money.

8 That money serves as a unit of account to visualise economic value does however not determine the criteria on which economic value is assessed. Through his theory of labour value, Karl Marx advocated for an objective criterion that elevated the hours needed to produce the good as the basis of economic value. Mainstream economics however is aligned to subjectivist criteria where the desires of consumers for the good relative to the supply of that good determines the value of the good. For a readable discussion on the various value theories in economics, see M. Mazzucato. 2018. *The Value of Everything: Making and Taking in the Global Economy*. Penguin Books.

9 To recall from Chapter 2, the problem of the 'double coincidence of wants' is a central element of the commodity imaginary of money as it places the origins of money in a barter economy that needed of a standardised medium of exchange to address that 'when we meet, you not only have to have what I want but also have to want what I have'. N. Kiyotaki and R. Wright. 1989. On money as a medium of exchange. *Journal of Political Economy*, 97(4): 927–954.

10 C. Menger. 2009 [1892]. *On the Origins of Money*. Ludwig von Mises Institute.

11 Keynes, *The General Theory*, p 147.

12 As reported by the Spanish economic newspaper *Expansión*, based on a study by the Spanish Hospitality Federation. For a detailed report in English on the crisis in Spain written by the central bank of Spain, see F. Eguidazu. 2017. *Report on the Financial and Banking Crisis in Spain, 2008–2014*. Banco de España.

13 In 'The great slump of 1930', J.M. Keynes concisely summarises the contradiction between individual and general interest that is the defining vector of the tragedy of the commons. 'In this quandary individual producers base illusory hopes on courses of action which would benefit an individual producer or class of producers so long as they were alone in pursuing them, but which benefit no one if every one pursues them.' In J.M. Keynes. 1933. *Essays in Persuasion*. Macmillan and Co., pp 135–147.

14 Keynes identified three main reasons for individuals' liquidity preference: '(i) the transactions-motive, i.e. the need of cash for the current transaction of personal and business exchanges; (ii) the precautionary-motive, i.e. the desire for security as to the future cash equivalent of a certain proportion of total resources; and (iii) the speculative-motive, i.e. the object of securing profit from knowing better than the market what the future will bring forth.' In *The General Theory*, p 85.

15 Of Keynes' three reasons for the individual's liquidity preference – 'the transactions-motive', 'the precautionary-motive' and 'the speculative-motive' – speculation is most sensitive to changes in the rate of interest. Keynes' response to this peculiar tragedy of the commons was therefore to lower the rate of interest through active monetary policy. With it, the age of money management through interest rates began. Traditionally, monetary policy had focused on managing the quantity of money by fixing it to the gold reserves of the country, without concern or awareness of the domestic circuits through which money flowed. Keynes' suggestion to manage money through the interest rate refocused monetary policy to also consider, to a certain extent, the circulation of money.

16 S. Gesell. 1916. *The Natural Economic Order*. Translated by M.A. Philip Pye, p 11.

17 With roots in the French *demeurer* – delay – the term 'demurrage' comes from the world of chartering vessels for transportation of goods. In the shipping industry, 'demurrage' refers to the fees charged to the charterer and paid to the ship owner for the delay of the

first in loading or unloading the vessel. In the world of complementary currencies, the term 'demurrage' has kept the meaning of charges imposed on delaying circulation, this time of monetary tokens.

[18] Irving Fisher collected several of these monetary experiments in his book from 1933, *Stamp Scrip*.

[19] Gesell estimated that goods depreciated 3–4 per cent per year. To discourage hoarding and incite spending, he saw it as necessary to go beyond merely eliminating the natural advantage of money compared to the goods it is meant to buy. He therefore recommended a yearly rate of depreciation for money somewhat higher than his estimated depreciation of goods.

[20] J. Blanc. 1998. Free money for social progress: Theory and practice of Gesell's accelerated money. *American Journal of Economics and Sociology*, 57(8): 469–483.

[21] The expression 'market fundamentalism' was coined by George Soros to convey the quasi-religious certainty of contemporary advocates of the liberal market doctrine. Fred Block and Margaret R. Somers use the expression to haracterize not only contemporary neoliberal doctrines but also the spirit that dominated the years between the two World Wars and to which Keynes' and Gesell's ideas were a reaction. See G. Soros. 1998. *The Crisis of Global Capitalism: Open Society Endangered*. Public Affairs; F. Block and M. Somers. 2016. *The Power of Market Fundamentalism: Karl Polanyi's Critique*. Harvard University Press.

[22] Keynes traces the many theoretical claims of classical economics to their original assumption that demand and supply meet in equilibrium. As he writes in *The General Theory*, 'It is, then, the assumption of equality between the demand price of output as a whole and its supply price which is to be regarded as the classical theory's "axiom of parallels". Granted this, all the rest follows—the social advantages of private and national thrift, the traditional attitude towards the rate of interest, the classical theory of unemployment, the quantity theory of money, the unqualified advantages of laissez-faire in respect of foreign trade and much else which we shall have to question' (p 19).

[23] Skidelsky indeed argues that '[t]he Quantity Theory of Money continued a ghostly existence in the *General Theory*, as seen in Keynes' liquidity preference equation … where the supply of money is exogenously given, as in the quantity theory'. R. Skidelsky. 2018. *Money and Government: A Challenge to Mainstream Economics*. Penguin Books, p 125.

[24] Though John Maynard Keynes is most often thought of as a proponent of a state actively using fiscal policies, Keynes' thinking was guided by his analysis of how money works. He was a monetary economist who came to see the limits of monetary policy in promoting full employment and thus the further need for the state to spend its budget to activate the economy. In doing this, Keynes revolutionised not only the traditional understanding of money but also the traditional role assigned to the state. For a historical account of how Keynes' monetary policies challenged traditional thought in economics, see Skidelsky, *Money and Government*. For a biography that connects the evolution of Keynes' ideas to his own life experiences, see Z. Carter. 2020. *The Price of Peace: Money, Democracy, and the Life of John Maynard Keynes*. Penguin Books.

[25] Gesell criticises Marx's analysis of capitalist exploitation on the basis of money's natural advantage compared to the goods it is to be exchanged for in the market. Marx states that money is equivalent to wares in the known equation W-M-W. This leads Marx to place interest/surplus-value in the exploitation of the capitalist. But Gesell says that W (wares) is not equal to M (money) because the first deteriorate while the second doesn't. This means that the holder of M can charge an interest to buy W earlier. Gesell, that is, finds interest in the actual nature of money while Marx finds it in capitalist exploitation.

[26] Keynes, *The General Theory*, ch 17.

[27] Luca Fantacci, writing about Fisher's stamp scrip, reasons similarly. 'The money collected through the tax provides a backing to the scrip, and eventually ensures its convertibility

in actual money at a par. Moreover, the tax acts as an automatic mechanism to reabsorb idle balances: to the extent that the scrip is not spent, it is gradually withdrawn from circulation.' Fantacci, 'Reforming money to exit the crisis', p 129.

[28] J.W.C. Harper. 1948. *Scrip and Other Forms of Local Money.* PhD Dissertation. University of Chicago. See also S. Elvins. 2005. Scrip money and slump cures: Iowa's experiments with alternative currency during the Great Depression. *The Annals of Iowa*, 64: 221–245. For an in-depth account of the successes, failures, challenges and local leadership of a local scrip project in Mason City, Iowa, see B.C. Bjorklund. 2017. *Saving Local Communities Using Scrip Money to Fight the Great Depression in North Central Iowa.* Master's Thesis. University of Northern Iowa.

[29] Unemployment figures for Wörgl and Tyrol in the 1930s are found in absolute numbers. Nowhere have I been able to find what those numbers meant in terms of proportion of population of working-age unemployed. However, some studies mention that unemployment in Austria grew sharply from the beginning of the 1930s, reaching a peak in 1933–1936 with 24–26 per cent of the labour force unemployed. See P. Gerlich and D. Campbell. 2000. Austria: From compromise to authoritarianism. In Berg-Schlosser, D. and Mitchell, J. (eds) *The Conditions of Democracy in Europe, 1919–39: Systematic Case Studies*. Macmillan, pp 40–58.

[30] In the original German, 'Das grösste aller Laster, ist, Wörgl, dein Straßenpflaster'. In Von Muralt, 'The Woergl experiment'.

[31] Schwarz, 'The experiment of Wörgl'.

[32] Handler, 'Two centuries of currency policy in Austria'.

[33] The years between 1919 and 1923 are marked in German memory as the years of catastrophic hyperinflation. The exchange rate of a German mark to the American dollar went from 4.2 to one in 1914 to 4.2 trillion to one in 1923. Indiscriminate printing of money to pay war reparations to the Allies led to the precipitous devaluation of the German currency. The trauma this period left on German people facilitated the rise of anti-Semitism and radicalism in the following years, eventually leading to the Second World War. For an empathetic account of those years, see A. Fergusson. 1975. *When Money Dies: The Nightmare of the Weimar Hyper Inflation.* William Kimber & Co. Ltd.

[34] Keynes, *The Great Slump of 1930*, p 140.

[35] P. Krugman. 2012. *End This Depression Now!*, ch 2, p 15. W. W. Norton & Company.

[36] Keynes, *The Great Slump of 1930*, p 135.

[37] Keynes, *The Great Slump of 1930*, p 136.

[38] In an amusing remake of the story of Robinson Crusoe, Silvio Gesell describes the pernicious consequences of a money imagined to naturally accrue interest, suggesting the reimagination of money free of interest as the relatively simple way to move beyond economic troubles. See Gesell, *The Natural Economic Order*, part V, pp 365–370.

[39] In Schwarz, 'The experiment in Wörgl'.

[40] The text printed on the reverse side of Wörgl's labour certificates reminded its holder of the connection between slow circulation of money and unemployment. As it were: 'To all whom it may concern! Sluggishly circulating money has provoked an unprecedented trade depression and plunged millions into utter misery. Economically considered, the destruction of the world has started. It is time, through determined and intelligent action, to endeavour to arrest the downward plunge of the trade machine and thereby to save mankind from fratricidal wars, chaos, and dissolution. Human beings live by exchanging their services. Sluggish circulation has largely stopped this exchange and thrown millions of willing workers out of employment. We must therefore revive this exchange of services and by its means bring the unemployed back to the ranks of the producers. Such is the object of the labour certificate issued by the market town of Wörgl: it softens sufferings dread; it offers work and bread.' In von Muralt, 'The Woergl experiment', p 49.

[41] Schwarz, The experiment in Wörgl.
[42] von Muralt, The Woergl experiment.
[43] Calculation based on the mayor's data in Unterguggenberger, The end results of the Woergl experiment, *Annals of Public & Cooperative Economics*, 10(1): 60–62.
[44] In Schwarz, The experiment in Wörgl.
[45] Schwarz, The experiment in Wörgl, p 5.
[46] 100 groschen were equal to 1 schilling.
[47] Schwarz, The experiment in Wörgl.
[48] In its simplest form, the Quantity Theory of Money takes the form of Fisher's formula: MV = QP, where M is the quantity of money in supply, V the velocity of circulation of money, Q the quantity of goods/services exchanged in the economy and P the average price of the goods/services exchanged. The formula is by definition true for the sum total of money spent equals the sum total of goods/services bought. Quantity theorists assume V and Q to be fixed. From that assumption, the logical deduction is that an increase in M leads to an equal increase in P; that is, an increase in the quantity of money leads to an equal increase in the general level of prices, or inflation. But the assumptions need not hold true in practice; there being much slack capacity in the economy (and thus no fixed Q) and, as in Wörgl, money circulating faster than prognosticated (and so, no fixed V). A further assumption is that all M is spent and spent in the real economy, an assumption that Keynes' analysis of speculative and hoarding behaviour held to be untrue. See I. Fisher. 1922. *The Purchasing Power of Money, its Determination and Reaction to Credit, Interest and Crises*. Macmillan. For a non-formulaic critique of the Quantity Theory of Money (Fisher's as well as Wicksell's), see Skidelsky, *Money and Government*, ch 3.
[49] Unterguggenberger, The end results of the Wörgl experiment.
[50] Von Muralt, The Woergl experiment, p 52.
[51] Von Muralt, The Woergl experiment, p 54.
[52] For recent descriptions of Wörgl's stamp scrip, see Blanc, Free money for social progress; T. Greco. 2009. *The End of Money and the Future of Civilization*. Chelsea Green.
[53] Schwarz, The experiment in Wörgl.
[54] An early major critique of the euro is precisely the lack of institutions to coordinate monetary policy (orchestrated by the European Central Bank) and national fiscal and tax-raising policies (orchestrated at the national level). Given the economic disparity between the EU member states, one unified monetary policy for the euro region necessarily involves it cannot attend the various fiscal needs of all its member states. This is indeed the source of many tensions between the EU member states, economically strong countries like Germany advocating restrain in fiscal and monetary policies and peripheral countries demanding a relaxation of fiscal austerity. For a brief text that connects this tension to how we imagine money, see C. Goodhart. 1997. One government, one money. *Prospect*, March.
[55] Unterguggenberger, The end results of the Wörgl experiment, p 62.
[56] Keynes' analysis of money is one of the arguments MMT scholars use to support the validity of their description of how money works. See R. Wray. 2019. Alternative paths to modern money theory. *Real-World Economics Review*, 89, 5–22.
[57] Apart from the possibility to issue currency and impose taxes in one's currency, when considered at the national level, MMT discussions include the question of exchange rate regimes – a question that is not relevant for discussing Wörgl's labour certificates. For an introduction to MMT, see R. Wray. 2012. *Modern Monetary Theory: A Primer on Macroeconomics for Sovereign Monetary Systems*. Palgrave. For an account of MMT more accessible to the lay-person, see S. Kelton. 2020. *The Deficit Myth: Modern Monetary Theory and the Birth of the People's Economy*. PublicAffairs.
[58] Keynes, *The Great Slump of 1930*, p 135.

59 Keynes, *The General Theory*, p 325.
60 Blanc, Free money for social progress.

Chapter 6

1 M. Swan. 2015. *Blockchain: Blueprint for a New Economy*. O'Reilly.
2 S. Ammous. 2018. *The Bitcoin Standard: The Decentralized Alternative to Central Banking*. Wiley.
3 S. Ammous. 2021. *The Fiat Standard: The Debt Slavery Alternative to Human Civilization*. The Saif House.
4 For some examples of advocates arguing the utopian future guiding blockchain dreamers is already here, see C.R. Harvey, A. Ramachandran and J. Santoro. 2021. *DeFi and the Future of Finance*. John Wiley and Sons.
5 Paolo Ardoino, tweet on 2 September 2022.
6 J. Tirole. 2020. Institutional and economic challenges for central banking. In *Monetary Policy: The Challenges Ahead*. Colloquium in honour of Benoît Coeuré. European Central Bank, pp 34–40.
7 F. Panetta. 2022. For a few cryptos more: The Wild West of crypto finance. Speech by Fabio Panetta, Member of the Executive Board of the ECB, at Columbia University, 25 April.
8 IMF. 2021. El Salvador: Staff concluding statement of the 2021 Article IV mission.
9 In an interview on September 2021, Christine Lagarde, president of the ECB, put the issue adamantly: 'Cryptos are not currencies, full stop. Cryptos are highly speculative assets that claim their fame as currency, possibly, but they're not. They are not.' The assessment is based on two arguments. As the ECB sums them: 'Crypto-assets are fundamentally different from central bank money: their prices are often volatile, which makes them hard to use as means of payment or units of account, and there is no public institution backing them' (https://www.ecb.europa.eu/paym/digital_euro/html/index.en.html). The first argument, their lack of capacity to function as a medium of exchange. The second, the fact that there is no public institution backing them. While crypto enthusiasts would never accept the latter as a criteria to assess the money-ness of cryptocurrencies – their ultimate vision being a money with no need to trust a central public authority – they aim however at becoming a global medium of exchange.
10 See, for instance, P. Frijters. 2017. Why Blockchain has no economic future. *Pearls and Irritations: John Menadue's Public Policy Journal*, 13 November.
11 With 'blockchain dreamers', I am using Lana Swartz's expression to refer to those advocates, crypto-entrepreneurs and developers that exalt the technology's capacity to marshal a revolution. See L. Swartz. 2017. Blockchain dreams: Imagining techno-economic alternatives after Bitcoin. In Castells, M. (ed) *Another Economy is Possible: Culture and Economy in a Time of Crisis*. Polity Press, pp 82–105.
12 Italian economists Massimo Amato and Luca Fantacci go as far as concluding that 'the only merit of bitcoin is that it is a provocation'. M. Amato and L. Fantacci. 2020. *A Fistful of Bitcoins: The Risks and Opportunities of Virtual Currencies*. Bocconi University Press, p 125.
13 See Chapter 3 in this book.
14 L. Brainard. 2020. Update on digital currencies, stablecoins, and the challenges ahead. In *Monetary Policy: The Challenges Ahead*. Colloquium in honour of Benoît Coeuré. European Central Bank, pp 21–25. Emphasis added.
15 Massimo Amato and Luca Fantacci argue that the strong ideological underpinnings coded in the Bitcoin blockchain as well as the utopian visions hailed by enthusiasts make it a 'proposal for a new faith'. Amato and Fantacci, *A Fistful of Bitcoins*, p 97.
16 In *The Passions and the Interests*, Albert O. Hirschman refreshingly pays heed to 'unrealised intentions' as opposed to the more common focus on 'unintended consequences'.

Unintended consequences are a given outcome of any complex project and, as such, can illuminate little on the form and reason for the decisions and actions undertaken. 'Intended effects', on the other hand, act as basis for decisions with social and political consequences. While they may fail to realise, intended effects shape the course of events. In the entrepreneurial space of cryptocurrencies, intended though unrealised effects shape the design of the internal architecture and governance institutions of the new digital monies, with results, thus far, other than those originally intended. A.O. Hirschman. 1977. *The Passions and the Interests: Political Arguments for Capitalism Before its Triumph*. Princeton University Press.

[17] S. Nakamoto. 2008. Bitcoin: A peer-to-peer electronic cash system. White Paper. Emphasis added.

[18] See Chapter 3 of this book.

[19] For the earliest critiques, see J. Carrión. 2017. *Against Amazon: Seven Arguments / One Manifesto*. Biblioasis; D. Caine. 2019. *How to Resist Amazon and Why: The Fight for Local Economics Data Privacy, Fair Labor, Independent Bookstores, and a People-Powered Future*. Raven Books.

[20] Nakamoto, Bitcoin, p 1.

[21] For a similar rendition of what happens when you swipe your card as the one I develop next, see P. Vigna and M.J. Casey. 2015. *Cryptocurrency: The Future of Money?* Vintage, pp 99–100.

[22] From the ECB's payment statistics for 2020: https://www.ecb.europa.eu/press/pr/stats/paysec/html/ecb.pis2020~5d0ea9dfa5.en.html.

[23] R. DeYoung and T. Rice. 2004. How do banks make money? The fallacies of fee income. *Economic Perspectives*, 28(4): 34–51. Federal Reserve Bank of Chicago.

[24] P. Bruno, O. Denecker and M. Niederkorn. 2021. Global payments 2021: Transformation amid turbulent undercurrents. In *The 2021 McKinsey Global Payments Report*. McKinsey & Company, pp 4–13.

[25] ECB. 2019. *Card Payments in Europe – Current Landscape and Future Prospects: A Eurosystem Perspective*.

[26] Nakamoto, Bitcoin. Emphasis added.

[27] The birth of the internet has been traced back to Paul Baran's ideas on distributed networks. He developed them in the midst of the Cold War, when the United States was concerned about the possibility that a Soviet nuclear attack on a node could bring down communication infrastructures organised along centralised and decentralised models. Baran's solution was to build networks that were distributed and digital. Because in a distributed system each and every node acts as a message router, the collapse of one node would not have an effect on the overall communication capacity of the network. Though initially dismissed, Baran's ideas were after a few years tested between nodes in UCLA (Los Angeles) and RAND (Santa Monica). Within a couple of years, the network had expanded, eventually breaking off from the military sphere to become the World Wide Web.

[28] This has been simplified for the sake of clarity. In reality, nodes may leave and rejoin later, thus omitting the records of those transactions that occurred while they were out. For such cases, Nakamoto designed a method (the proof-of-work validation method, or PoW) for the nodes to accept the longest chain of blocks as 'proof of what had happened while they were gone'. For more detail, see Nakamoto, Bitcoin.

[29] Repository of all communication from Satoshi Nakamoto, https://satoshi.nakamotoinstitute.org/

[30] In the first years of Bitcoin, nodes run the blockchain with the central processing units (CPUs) of regular personal computers. As the promise of big profits started to attract investors, the technology evolved, CPUs quickly becoming obsolete. Nodes now invest

in Application-Specific Integrated Circuit (ASIC) – specialised equipment with high computer power.

[31] See S. Nakamoto. 2009. Bitcoin open source implementation of P2P currency. Blogpost at the P2P foundation.

[32] For a real-time update of the number of nodes and other figures, see https://coin.dance/nodes.

[33] For a discussion on the activity, risk profile, trust and regulatory issues associated to each of these new mediators, see M. Campbell-Verduyn and M. Goguen. 2019. Blockchain, trust and action nets: Extending the pathologies of financial globalization. *Global Networks: A Journal of Transnational Affairs*, 19(3): 308–328; as well as I.D. Motsi-Omoijiade. 2018. Financial intermediation in cryptocurrency markets: Regulation, gaps and bridges. In Kuo Chuen, D.L. and Deng, R. (eds) *Handbook of Blockchain, Digital Finance, and Inclusion, Volume 1: Cryptocurrency, FinTech, InsurTech, and Regulation*. Academic Press, pp 207–223.

[34] I. Makarov and A. Schoar. 2021. Blockchain analysis of the bitcoin market. National Bureau of Economic Research (NBER), Working Paper No. 29396.

[35] K. Finley. 2018. After 10 years, bitcoin has changed everything – and nothing. *Wired*, 31 October. For updated statistics on the number of bitcoin transactions validated per second, see https://statoshi.info/?orgId=1. For other bitcoin charts and figures, see https://bitcoin.org/en/resources.

[36] J.P. Trespalacios and J. Dijk. 2021. The carbon footprint of bitcoin. *DNB Unrestricted*. De Nederlandsche Bank. See also P. Howson and A. de Vries. 2022. Preying on the poor? Opportunities and challenges for tackling the social and environmental threats of cryptocurrencies for vulnerable and low-income communities. *Energy Research & Social Science*, 84: 102394. In an article from 2017, Zac Zimmer argues the ecological impact of bitcoin resides in the extractive logic of mining that guides its infrastructural design. To build the argument, Zimmer compares the 'bitcoin moment' we are living to the Spanish silver mining of the Potosí mountain in the New World during the 16th century. Z. Zimmer. 2017. Bitcoin and Potosí silver: Historical perspectives on cryptocurrency. *Technology and Culture*, 58(2): 307–334. Others argue that, from the perspective of the environmental damage resulting from bitcoin mining, the most apt metaphor for the cryptocurrency is not that of 'digital gold' but of 'digital crude'. B.A. Jones, A.L. Goodkind and R.P. Berrens. 2022. Economic estimation of Bitcoin mining's climate damages demonstrates closer resemblance to digital crude than digital gold. *Nature*, Scientific Reports 12.

[37] See FairCoin for an example.

[38] See B. Maurer, T.C. Nelms and L. Swartz. 2013. 'When perhaps the real problem is money itself!': The practical materiality of Bitcoin. *Social Semiotics*, 23(2): 261–277. See also Zimmer, Bitcoin and Potosí silver.

[39] Email released by Mike Hearn: https://plan99.net/~mike/satoshi-emails/thread1.html.

[40] For a detailed description of how this process unfolds, see Chapter 3 of this book.

[41] S.D. Williamson. 2017. Quantitative easing: How well does this tool work? *Federal Reserve Bank of St. Louis*.

[42] https://www.bankofengland.co.uk/monetary-policy/quantitative-easing. For data, see also https://fred.stlouisfed.org/series/UKASSETS.

[43] https://fred.stlouisfed.org/series/ECBASSETSW.

[44] The origin of the expression is attributed to a misspelling in a post in the Bitcointalk forum in 2013. The title of the post read 'I am hodling'. It was quickly adopted by the crypto community and adapted to the acronym of Hold On for Dear Life. Crypto enthusiasts cite it as a show of faith in the value and future of cryptocurrencies. For the original post, see https://bitcointalk.org/index.php?topic=375643.0.

[45] Communication between Hal Finney and Satoshi Nakamoto. https://www.metzdowd.com/pipermail/cryptography/2009-January/015004.html.

[46] G. Silverman. 2021. Crypto's wild ride raises new liquidity concerns. *Financial Times*, 11 December.

[47] http://p2pfoundation.ning.com/forum/topics/bitcoin-open-source?id=2003008:Topic:9402&page=1.

[48] P. Krugman. 2011. Golden cyberfetters. *New York Times*, 7 September.

[49] Today, the obligation of central banks is really an accounting obligation. The historical origin of this obligation is the gold standard, when central banks were obliged to covert their notes to gold upon request. This obligation ceased when Richard Nixon suspended the possibility of conversion on 15 August 1971. The event inaugurated the regime of free-floating exchange rates in which we live today.

[50] In what concerns the dual existence of today's money in the asset and liability sides of the balance sheets of various monetary actors, see Appendix.

[51] See Chapter 4.

[52] In proper, John Maynard Keynes' first reference to the barbarity of gold as a way to understand and govern money refers to the gold standard as implemented previous to the First World War. 'In truth', Keynes wrote, 'the gold standard is already a barbarous relic' for, he argued, 'actual practice has been shifting … to preserving the stability of business, prices, and employment, and are not likely, when the choice is forced on us, deliberately to sacrifice these to the outworn dogma, which had its value once, of £3.17s 101/2d per ounce. Advocates of the ancient standard do not observe how remote it now is from the spirit and the requirements of the age. A regulated non-metallic standard has slipped in unnoticed. It exists'. J.M. Keynes. 1977 [1924]. A tract on monetary reform. In A. Robinson and D. Moggridge (eds) *The Collected Writings of John Maynard Keynes*. Cambridge University Press, pp 137–138. Keynes repeated the expression in a speech delivered to the UK parliament on the topic of the International Monetary Fund. On that occasion, however, he directly called on gold as the 'barbarous relic'. https://api.parliament.uk/historic-hansard/lords/1944/may/23/international-monetary-fund.

[53] Looking back into what led to the horrid tragedies of the 20th century, Karl Polanyi identified the commodification of money as one of the reasons. It is worth re-reading his analysis in *The Great Transformation*, as it is reminiscent of the dynamics set off by a 'fictitious commodification' of money – I am here thinking of both crypto-monies and our conventional money (see Chapter 3). K. Polanyi. 2001 [1944]. *The Great Transformation: The Political and Economic Origins of Our Time*. Beacon Press. On this, see also M. Amato and L. Fantacci. 2012. *The End of Finance*. Polity Press.

[54] Sepp Hasslberger wrote to Nakamoto on 18 February 2009: 'It is important that there be a limit in the amount of tokens/coins. But it is also important that this limit be adjustable to take account of how many people adopt the system. If the number of users changes with time, it will also be necessary to change the total amount of coins.' Sepp's reasons were exactly the value distortions that we see in bitcoin and the chapter has traced to the fixed supply of money tokens. Two days later, on 20 February 2009, Sepp argued: 'The reason balance of the system is important: if it's going to be used for payments, you don't want to have large changes in the value of the coins. It would lead to distortions, I believe, by continually increasing the "purchasing power" of a single coin.' For the email exchange, see http://p2pfoundation.ning.com/forum/topics/bitcoin-open-source?id=2003008:Topic:9402&page=1.

[55] With the phrase 'code is law' Laurence Lessig neatly condensed the dangerous view that the development of protocols making up the internal architecture of the internet should be left outside the intrusion of government regulators and driven solely by the incentives igniting the functioning of free markets. The article highlighted the

danger to the freedom of the internet posed by such a code-is-law approach. As other architectures are being coded and layered on top of the original internet protocols, values other than freedom and privacy are being forced onto its users. But the coders do not necessarily abide to the original ideal of internet freedom and neutrality. Free market actors implementing identification and certification architectures are not disinterested. Their encoding of their interests, Lessing argued, was regulating behaviour on the internet. And yet, that code with those encoded interests was being created and enforced by a minority of coders. He traced the challenge to the freedom of the internet to a narrow understanding of the notion of freedom to simply indicate free from government intrusion.

It is worth quoting in full one of the paragraphs in the article for how it summarises the argument: 'Our choice is not between "regulation" and "no regulation." The code regulates. It implements values, or not. It enables freedoms, or disables them. It protects privacy, or promotes monitoring. People choose how the code does these things. People write the code. Thus the choice is not whether people will decide how cyberspace regulates. People – coders – will. The only choice is whether we collectively will have a role in their choice – and thus in determining how these values regulate – or whether collectively we will allow the coders to select our values for us.' Twenty-plus years later, Lessig's warning continues to be just as relevant both for the internet and for the blockchain technologies that similarly build on notions of distributed and open infrastructures. L. Lessig. 2000. Code is law: On liberty in cyberspace. *Harvard Magazine*.

[56] The story of one of Bitcoin's most divisive conflicts is told all over the internet, with discussion forums at Reddit, Twitter and Bitcointalk Forum, blogposts by those involved in the conflict and outsiders, and re-tellings at major crypto-news sites such as *CoinDesk* and *Cointelegraph*. The main posts from which I have built this section are Mike Hearn's letters recounting his direct involvement (M. Hearn. 2015. Why is Bitcoin forking. *Mike's Blog Plan 99*. https://medium.com/faith-and-future/why-is-bitcoin-forking-d647312d22c1; 2015. On block size. *Mike's Blog Plan 99*. https://medium.com/@octskyward/on-block-sizes-e047bc9f830; 2016. The resolution of the bitcoin experiment. *Mike's Blog Plan 99*. https://blog.plan99.net/the-resolution-of-the-bitcoin-experiment-dabb30201f7; 2020. The philosophical origins of Bitcoin's civil war. *Mike's Blog Plan 99*. https://blog.plan99.net/the-philosophical-origins-of-bitcoins-civil-war-400468335377), *Cointelegraph*'s entry (S. Haig. 2019. Bitcoin block size, explained. *Cointelegraph*. https://cointelegraph.com/explained/bitcoin-block-size-explained) and *CoinDesk*'s entry (https://www.coindesk.com/learn/2015/08/21/what-is-the-bitcoin-block-size-debate-and-why-does-it-matter/).

[57] The Bitcoin Foundation was modelled after the Linux Foundation, which maintains and coordinates updates of the open source Linux operating system. The Bitcoin Foundation however was snarled in scandal from its inception as its board members had been engaged in the online marketplace the Silk Road that enabled criminal activities, in the fraudulent bitcoin exchange Mt Gox, and in questionable behaviour in the cryptocurrency space.

[58] The mining pools were all located in China: F2pool, BTCChina, Antpool, Huobi and BW.

[59] In the crypto-world, a hard-fork refers to a radical change in the protocol that steers a blockchain, which results in branching the cryptocurrency into two. This happens when users of the cryptocurrency cannot agree on changes to the rules coded in the protocol. Hard-forks create a new blockchain, which is not compatible with the old version. Soft-forks, by contrast, do not create a new blockchain and are thus compatible with the old version.

[60] E. Smart. 2015. Bitcoin XT users allegedly suffering coordinated hack attack. *Cointelegraph*.

[61] In a Reddit post in mid-2015, Theymos, the pseudonym of Michael Marquardt, a top moderator of the bitcoin.org forum r/Bitcoin, wrote: 'Bitcoin is not a democracy. Not of

miners, and not of nodes. Switching to XT is not a vote for BIP 101 – it is abandoning Bitcoin for a separate network/currency. It is good that you have the freedom to do this. One of the great things about Bitcoin *is* its lack of democracy: even if 99% of people use Bitcoin, you are free to implement BIP 101 in a separate currency without the Bitcoin users being able to democratically coerce you into using the real Bitcoin network/currency again. But I am not obligated to allow these separate offshoots of Bitcoin to exist on r/Bitcoin, and I'm not going to.' https://www.reddit.com/r/Bitcoin/comments/3rejl9/comment/cwoc8n5/.

[62] For a simplified yet inclusive account of the various proposals set forward, see G. Caffyn. 2021. What is the bitcoin block size debate and why does it matter? *CoinDesk*, 21 August.

[63] P. De Filippi and B. Loveluck. 2016. The invisible politics of Bitcoin: governance crisis of a decentralised infrastructure. *Internet Policy Review*, 5(3).

[64] S. Nakamoto. 2009. Bitcoin open source implementation of P2P currency. *P2P Foundation: The Foundation for Peer to Peer Alternatives*.

[65] G. Standing. 2019. *The Plunder of the Commons: A Manifesto for Sharing Public Wealth*. Pelican.

[66] This wording refers to FOMO, a favourite acronym in the crypto space.

[67] Witnessed by Joseph Borg, president of the North American Securities Administrators Association (A. Nova. 2018. Desperate to get into bitcoin, investors slip into debt. *CNBC*) and reported in a survey conducted by KIS Finance. 2021. *Cryptocurrency Consumer Research and Data: Autumn 2021*. M. Brown. 2017. Some investors use a credit card to buy bitcoin and then carry over the balance. LendEDU Report; Financial Conduct Authority. 2021. Consumer investments data review April 2020 – March 2021. *FCA*; A. Perrin. 16% of Americans say they have ever invested in traded or used cryptocurrency. *Pew Research Center*; LendEDU. 2021. *Investing in Bitcoin: Survey & Report*; V. Hajric. 2021. Bitcoin's current holders are new, with 55% getting in this year. *Bloomberg*. For a contemporary critical news on this, see E. Griffith. 2021. We're all crypto people now. *New York Times*, 25 April; S. Kale. 2021. 'I put my life savings in crypto': How a generation of amateurs got hooked on high-risk trading. *The Guardian*, 19 June.

[68] For an example, see C. Reinicke. 2022. If you invested $1,000 in bitcoin this year, you'd have about $800 now. Why you still may want to buy more. *CNBC*.

[69] As Lana Swartz puts it, '[m]etallism, as a techno-economic imaginary, is a theory not just of money but of society'. L. Swartz. 2018. What was Bitcoin, what will it be? The techno-economic imaginaries of a new money technology. *Cultural Studies*, 32(4): 623–650.

Interlude 2

[1] In using the term 'entrepreneur' to refer to communities starting up their own monetary systems as well as to municipalities introducing city monies, I adhere to a broad notion of entrepreneurship – one that is not limited to ventures pursuing a profit motive. Instead, I am inspired by those Critical Management Studies scholars who go to the etymological origins of the term – from the French *entreprendre* – to refer to efforts to 'under-take', to 'set in motion' initiatives, entrepreneurship as processes of organising for change. These efforts and processes include those guided not only by a market logic of profit, but also by other logics such as a social logic of care, or a community logic of resilience. See D. Hjorth and C. Steyaert. 2009. *The Politics and Aesthetics of Entrepreneurship: A Fourth Movements in Entrepreneurship Book*. Edward Elgar; M. Calas, L. Smircich and K. Bourne. 2009. Extending the boundaries: Reframing 'entrepreneurship as social change' through feminist perspectives. *Academy of Management Review*, 34(3): 552–569.

[2] H. Minsky. 1986. *Stabilizing An Unstable Economy*. Washington University Press, p 255.

[3] For making this argument I draw on the lessons taught by the later Wittgenstein. See footnote 45 in Chapter 1.

[4] Note that in defining reciprocity on an individual-to-individual basis I am distancing myself from those that would describe a collective's giving back to one of its individual members as a reciprocal relationship. Karl Polanyi, a political economist and economic historian from whom I otherwise draw much inspiration, does follow such a broader view of reciprocity that includes collective-to-individual interactions. The reason for my different definition of reciprocity lies in our somewhat different entry points. He is concerned with the institutional patterns under which economies are organised; I am interested on the interactional patterns inhering in monetary arrangements. Though we both arrive at three patterns – he identifies reciprocity, redistribution and house-holding (autarky) – the different focus of our gaze lead us not only to define reciprocity differently but also to only partially overlapping patterns. Polanyi's redistribution is similar to my solidarity; his reciprocity is comparable to my mutuality; and instead of a counter-pattern to his autarky, I suggest reciprocity. See K. Polanyi. 2001 [1944]. *The Great Transformation: The Political and Economic Origins of Our Time*. Beacon Press, ch 4.

[5] K. Polanyi. 1957. The economy as instituted process. In Polanyi, K., Arensberg, C.M. and Pearson, H.W. (eds) *Trade and Market in the Early Empires*. Henry Regnery Company, pp 243–270, at p 250. Observe that, in that text, Polanyi reconsiders the three institutional patterns that give economies unity and stability to be reciprocity, redistribution and (market) exchange. Redistribution maintains the definition he gave in *The Great Transformation*, but reciprocity is defined as occurring between symmetrical groups, and instead of householding/autarky he identifies (market) exchange. It is Polanyi's institutional pattern of market exchange which is parallel to my interactional pattern of reciprocity. Mauss' analysis of gift economies as involving an *obligation* to reciprocate, a form of forced generosity, influences my understanding of reciprocity advanced here (for Mauss' notion of the gift, see Chapter 4).

[6] D. Graeber. 2014 [2011]. *Debt: The First 5,000 Years*. Melville House, p 103.

[7] Polanyi, The economy as instituted process, p 250.

[8] David Graeber, too, identifies three relational principles: communism, hierarchy and exchange. Because Graeber is concerned with the forms of morality that ground equal and unequal economic relations, with the 'way of thinking and arguing about the rights and wrongs of any given situation', he approaches these principles as moral principles. Somewhat provokingly, Graeber uses the term 'communism' to refer to what here I denominate mutuality; his hierarchy is Polanyi's redistribution and my vertical solidarity; his exchange is Polanyi's exchange in his 1957 text cited previously and my reciprocity. Graeber, *Debt*, ch 5.

[9] For an early description of how mutual savings and lending groups work, and the many names they receive in various low-income countries, see C. Geertz. 1962. The rotating credit association: A 'middle rung' in development. *Economic Development and Cultural Change*, 10(3): 241–263. For a recent overview of the variety of such groups across the world, see Hossein, C.S., & Christabell, P.J. (eds). 2022. *Community economies in the global south: Case studies of rotating savings and credit associations and economic cooperation*. Oxford University Press.

For a critical analysis of how the relationships of mutuality undergirding savings-and-lending groups are being embedded into a cryptocurrency with social purposes in Kenya, see E. Barinaga. 2020. A route to commons-based democratic monies? Embedding the production of money in traditional communal institutions. *Frontiers in Blockchain*, 3: 575851. doi: 10.3389/fbloc.2020.575851.

[10] Writing about the nature of money in 1913, Mitchell Innes recognised 'the sanctity of obligation' as foundational to all societies. The passage deserves quoting in full: 'We are here fortunately on solid historical ground. From the earliest days of which we have historical records, we are in the presence of a law of debt, and when we shall find, as

we surely shall, records of ages still earlier than that of the great king Hamurabi, who compiled his code of the laws of Babylonia 2000 years B. C., we shall, I doubt not, still find traces of the same law. The sanctity of an obligation is, indeed, the foundation of all societies not only in all times, but at all stages of civilization; and the idea that to those whom, we are accustomed to call savages, credit is unknown and only barter is used, is without foundation. From the merchant of China to the Redskin of America; from the Arab of the desert to the Hottentot of South Africa or the Maori of New Zealand, debts and credits are equally familiar to all, and the breaking of the pledged word, or the refusal to carry put an obligation is held equally disgraceful.' A. Mitchell Innes. 1913. What is money? *Banking Law Journal,* pp 377–408.

Part III

[1] E.O. Wright. 2010. *Envisioning Real Utopias.* Verso.

In discussing his proposal for an International Clearing Union (ICU), Keynes embraced a similar understanding of utopia as a vision that welded realism with imagination: '[The ICU] is also open to the objection, as the reader will soon discover, that it is complicated and novel and perhaps Utopian in the sense, *not that it is impracticable, but that it assumes a higher degree of understanding, of the spirit of bold innovation,* and of international co-operation and trust than it is safe or reasonable to assume' (emphasis added). J.M. Keynes. 1980 [1941]. The origins of the clearing union. In Moggridge, D. (ed) *The Collected Writings of John Maynard Keynes, Volume XXV: Activities 1940–1944. Shaping the Post-War World: The Clearing Union.* Cambridge University Press, p 33.

Chapter 7

[1] Supporters of UBI include Nobel laureates James Buchanan, Herbert Simon, Angus Deaton, Christopher Pissarides and Joseph Stiglitz; academics Tony Atkinson, Robert Skidelsky, Robert Reich, Clauss Offe and Philippe Van Paris; economic journalists Martin Wolf and Martin Sandbu. The idea has gathered other supporters who, however, defend the need for a UBI not from the perspective of deepened democracy, but from acknowledgement of the risk increased automation puts to profit due to the overall decline in purchasing power. Among these supporters we find Silicon Valley investors and tech entrepreneurs Sam Altman, Chris Hughes, Elon Musk or Eric Schmidt to name but a few. For an updated and more detailed list of supporters, visit the website of the Basic Income Earth Network: https://basicincome.org/.

[2] In G. Standing. 2017. *Basic Income: A Guide for the Open-Minded.* Penguin Books.

[3] For a thorough exposition of the main arguments for basic income – justice, security and freedom – as well as for an overview of the objections to it – mainly those concerning affordability and its impact on the supply of labour – and how to address them, I recommend reading Standing, *Basic Income,* as well as R. Bregman. 2014. *Utopia for Realists: How We Can Build the Ideal World.* Little, Brown and Company. For a discussion of UBI in relation to a reorganisation of national money along the ideas of Modern Monetary Theory see G. Crocker. 2020. *Basic Income and Sovereign Money: The Alternative to Economic Crisis and Austerity Policy.* Palgrave Macmillan.

[4] Initial studies of various UBI-type programmes in low- and middle-income countries show not only a positive impact of these programmes on the local economy (D. Jones and I.E. Marinescu. 2018. The labor market impacts of universal and permanent cash transfers: Evidence from the Alaska Permanent Fund. *American Economic Journal,* 14(2): 315–340), but also large improvements in psychological well-being (J. Haushofer and J. Shapiro. 2016. The short-term impact of unconditional cash transfers to the poor: Experimental evidence from Kenya. *The Quarterly Journal of Economics,*

131(4): 1973–2042) and health (L. Robertson, P. Mushati, J.W. Eaton, L. Dumba, G. Mavise, J. Makoni, C. Schumacher, T. Crea, R. Monasch, L. Sherr, G.P. Garnett, C. Nyamukapa and S. Gregson. 2013. Effects of unconditional and conditional cash transfers on child health and development in Zimbabwe: a cluster-randomised trial. *The Lancet*, 381(9874): 1283–1292) as well as a significant reduction in domestic violence (J. Haushofer, C. Ringdhal, J. Shapiro and X.Y. Wang. 2019. Income changes and intimate partner violence: Evidence from unconditional cash transfers in Kenya. NBER Working Paper No. 25627). These positive impacts were observable beyond those individuals and households receiving the unconditional payments, in the form of increased consumption for non-recipient households and of larger revenue for local firms (D. Egger, J. Haushofer, P. Niehaus and M. Walker. 2019. General equilibrium effects of cash transfers: Experimental evidence from Kenya. *Econometrica*, 90(6): 2603–2643). Importantly, positive impacts were sustained over time with recipients able to build higher levels of asset holdings, and maintain food security, consumption levels and psychological well-being relative to non-recipients (Haushofer, J. and Shapiro, J. 2018. The long-term impact of unconditional cash transfers to the poor: Experimental evidence from Kenya. *The Poverty Action Lab*, Working Paper). Improved impacts are proving to be resilient to dramatic shocks such as the COVID-19 pandemic (A. Banerjee, M. Faye, A. Krueger, P. Niehaus and T. Suri. 2020. Effects of a Universal Basic Income during the pandemic). Positive impacts have also been documented in high-income countries such as Canada (E. Forget. 2011. The town with no poverty: The health effects of a Canadian guaranteed annual income field experiment. *Canadian Public Policy*, 37(3): 283–305; W. Simpson, G. Mason and R. Godwin. 2017. The Manitoba basic annual income experiment: Lessons learned 40 years later. *Canadian Public Policy*, 43(1): 85–104) and Finland (Kangas, O., Jauhiainen, S., Simanainen, M. and Ylikännö, M. 2021. *Experimenting with Unconditional Basic Income: Lessons from the Finnish BI Experiment 2017–2018*. Edward Elgar, with a reduction in hospitalisations, improved mental health and increased school attendance). For an overview of impact studies of various UBI-type programmes, see R. Hasdell. 2020. What we know about UBI: A cross-synthesis review. *Stanford Basic Income Lab*. See also U. Gentilini, M. Grosh, J. Rigolini and R. Yemtsov. 2020. *Exploring Universal Basic Income: A guide to navigating concepts, evidence, and practices*. World Bank Group.

5 To name just a few: 2020 Democratic presidential candidate Andrew Yang, Indian member of parliament Varun Gandhi, co-founder of the Workers' Party of Brazil Eduardo Matarazzo Suplicy, Germany's minister for foreign affairs Annalena Baerbock, and almost half of the politicians in the Welsh and Scottish parliaments.

6 For an overview of these pilot studies results, see Standing, *Basic Income*, ch 11. For a distilling of the lessons learnt through the pilot studies into principles to design, implement and evaluate basic income pilots, see G. Standing. 2021. Basic income pilots: Uses, limitations and design principles. *Basic Income Studies*, 16(1): 75–99.

7 Guy Standing speaks of the precariat as a new dangerous class that has emerged from the demise of the traditional proletariat. The process of globalisation that unfolded with the neoliberal turn of the 1980s led to the erosion of labour rights and the weakening of trade unions. This has resulted in a change in the relations of production, a change that has been the most dramatic for the lowest income group. This group has seen its labour contracts become 'flexible', casual, part-time or intermittent – precarious. The constant change of jobs and the need to take whatever is on offer leaves the precariat with no occupational identity, forced to work for little pay in jobs that carry no pension or holiday benefits. Such structural conditions have led the precariat to feelings of anxiety, anomie, alienation and anger, turning them into a 'dangerous class', some of them united in their struggle for a progressive agenda. See G. Standing. 2011. *The Precariat: The New Dangerous*

Class, Bloomsbury Academic; G. Standing. 2014. *A Precariat Charter: From Denizens to Citizens*. Bloomsbury.

[8] The Spanish name of the movement ('Los Indignados') came from the French booklet that inspired it, Stéphane Hessel's *Indignez-vous!* from 2010. A second booklet that greatly inspired the non-violent tactics followed by the Spanish movement was G. Sharp. 2012 [2002]. *From Dictatorship to Democracy: A Guide to Nonviolent Resistance*. Serpent's Tail.

[9] For some pictures of the many occasions where these slogans can be seen on placards, see https://elpais.com/elpais/2021/05/12/album/1620811148_178548.html#foto_gal_1.

[10] Much has been written about the long-term impact of the Spanish Revolution and Occupy movements in the societies that held them. While some dismiss them as simple outbursts that left nothing but disillusion when they wore out, others argue that they transformed the political landscape, with the formation of new political parties that have changed the parliamentary game – as in Spain – the organisation of civil society to support the most vulnerable – as to stop evictions – or the reappropriation of urban space for communal use – as in the creation of urban gardens on abandoned plots. For an ethnographic account from one prominent participant in the Occupy movement, see D. Graeber. 2013. *The Democracy Project: A History, a Crisis, a Movement*. Spiegel & Grau.

[11] Graeber's formulation, *The Democracy Project*.

[12] https://monedademos.es/index.php?r=site/page&view=info.

[13] In Spanish, the term used to speak of local or community currencies is 'social currency' (*moneda social*).

[14] In Demos Manual, p 5. Own translation. (M.A. Figueroa García. 2015. Funcionamiento de monedademos.es. *Demos*.)

[15] Miguel Ángel Figueroa, interview on 12 April 2022.

[16] Mainstream economics and political science had for long argued that the only way to deal with the tragedy of the commons was through giving property of the common resource to either private owners (in whose interests it would be to manage the resource) or public authorities (who could regulate its use). That is, it was either through the market or the state that the commons could be managed. In her Nobel prize winning research, Elinor Ostrom argued there was a third way to manage the commons, one that had proven resilient to changes in the conditions of the common resource and to the passing of time. Her empirical research took her to communities that had managed water and land resources sustainably for years all over the world. She identified eight principles shared by communities that had successfully managed the commons sustainably. Summarily, well-defined communities developed governance rules fit to the local circumstances of the resource and the community, monitored the following of those rules, and developed a graded system of sanctions for those that broke the rules. Both the development and implementation of rules and sanctions worked best if they were carried out in an inclusive, participatory manner by members of the community. As we see, these are all principles Demos followed intuitively, naturally emerging from their very premise to realise economic democracy. E. Ostrom. 1990. *Governing the Commons: The Evolution of Institutions for Collective Action*. Cambridge University Press.

[17] I would like to thank Professor Eduardo Diniz from Fundação Getulio Vargas for his patience and detail in explaining the context, development and functioning of Mumbuca and its tech payment platform e-Dinheiro.

[18] D.M. Neumann. 2021. Mumbuca: Moeda Social e/ou Renda Básica de Cidadania? As narrativas sobre a moeda social de Maricá. Master's Thesis. Fundação Getulio Vargas. I have Professor Mario Aquino Alves to thank for this reference.

[19] A. Cernev and B. Proença. 2016. Mumbuca: a primeira moeda social digital do Brasil. *Revista Brasileira de Casos – Gvcasos*, 6(2), Doc 15. A. Cernev. 2019. Mumbuca e-Dinheiro. *Revista Brasileira de Casos – Gvcasos*, 9(2), Doc 10.

[20] The payment platform e-Dinheiro was developed by Instituto e-Dinheiro – formerly Instituto Palmas – a non-profit organisation that supports the development of community development banks across Brazil. See A. Cernev and E. Diniz. 2019. Palmas para o e-Dinheiro! A evolução digital de uma moeda social local. *Revista de Administração Contemporânea*, 24(5): 487–506. A. Ansonera, E.H. Diniz, E.S. Siqueira and M. Pozzebon. 2021. From community bank to solidarity fintech: The case of Palmas e-Dinheiro in Brazil. In Walker, T., McGaughey, J., Goubran, S. and Wagdy, N. (eds) *Innovations in Social Finance*. Springer, pp 251–268. For the history of Instituto Palmas itself, see C. Meyer. 2012. *Les finances solidaires comme biens communs durables: étude de cas de la Banque communautaire de développement Palmas (Brésil)*. Université libre de Bruxelles.

[21] Other cities took the step to roll out a UBI at the onset of the pandemic. The most well-known schemes are probably those of Barcelona (Spain) and Seoul (South Korea). See S. Seung-Yoon Lee, J. Lee and K. Kyo-seong. 2020. Evaluating basic income, basic service, and basic voucher for social and ecological sustainability. *Sustainability*, 12: 8348; S. Martín Belmonte, J. Puig and M. Roca. 2021. Crisis mitigation through cash assistance to increase local consumption levels: A case study of a bimonetary system in Barcelona, Spain. *Journal of Risk and Financial Management*, 14(9): 1–17.

[22] F. Freitas. 2022. Transferência de renda com moeda social em Cabo Frio, Itaboraí, Niterói e Maricá: alívio da pobreza ou renda básica? *Gestão, Política e Sociedade*.

[23] See L. Gonzalez, A.K. Cernev, M.H. de Araujo and E.H. Diniz. 2021. Digital complementary currencies and public policies during the COVID-19 pandemic. *Brazilian Journal of Public Administration*, 54(4): 1146–1160. For a discussion of digital payment technologies as instruments to implement public policies based on the experience of Maricá, see D.P. Rodrigues. 2021. Inclusão financeira e o uso de fintechs como instrumentos de políticas públicas. Master's Thesis. Fundação Getulio Vargas.

[24] https://institutoedinheiromarica.org/balanco-2018-2021-pdf.

[25] Martín Belmonte et al, Crisis mitigation through cash assistance.

[26] Up until September 2021.

[27] Gama and Costa (2021), cited in Freitas, Transferência de renda com moeda social em Cabo Frio, Itaboraí, Niterói e Maricá.

[28] A recent study conducted and co-authored by Maricá's Planning Director observed 'evidence of low currency recirculation, which limits its potential to stimulate the local economy'. To activate circulation of mumbucas, the authors discuss ways to enhance the use of mumbuca as well as mechanisms to make the city less dependent on oil royalties for the backing of the municipal currency. Among others, they discuss a more active involvement of the city in stimulating local production, thereby extending the possible use of mumbucas. See D.P. Rodrigues and D.M. Neumann. 2021. Moeda social e desenvolvimento local em Maricá (RJ). Master's Thesis. Fundação Getulio Vargas.

[29] As stated on GoodDollar's website: https://apply.workable.com/gooddollar/. Quotes in this section come from Yosi Assia's (CEO and Founder of eToro), intervention at the OECD Forum in 2019 (https://www.youtube.com/watch?v=f-iKF2rwiIl); GoodDollar White Paper: A distributed basic income (https://whitepaper.gooddollar.org/); and GoodDollar's website (https://www.gooddollar.org/). See also Y. Assia and O. Ross. 2018. Good Dollar experiment: Wealth distribution position paper, 18 April.

[30] Yosi Assia's address to the OECD Forum, 2019. Minute 2.

[31] Y. Assia, T. Barrack, T. Iron and A. Stone. 2020. The GoodDollar White Paper, p 2. For a brief, entertaining and well-informed critique of trickle-down economics, see J. Quiggin. 2010. Trickle-down economics. *Zombie Economics: How Dead Ideas Still Walk among Us*. Princeton University Press, pp 137–176.

[32] Assia, OECD Forum.

[33] Assia et al, The GoodDollar White Paper, p 11.

[34] Assia, OECD Forum. About minute 7.

[35] Assia et al, The GoodDollar White Paper, p 3.

[36] The blending of a financial logic with a logic of social good is not new. Micro-finance and social impact bonds are typically designed along both logics. On the one hand, these financial instruments attend the interests of investors so as to mobilise their resources and put them to work to achieve a social or development goal. On the other hand, there is an avowed intention to focus on satisfying the needs of more or less vulnerable groups. These are, as it were, instruments that cater to two distinct interest groups which may have conflicting interests – returns and liquidity the investors, economic development the target groups – and timeframes – the short-term dominates investors' preoccupations, while a long-term approach is central for achieving sustained socioeconomic development. As investors and financial actors ultimately hold the upper hand, the interests of investors tend to be prioritised over those of the vulnerable groups which these hybrid instruments are supposed to serve. For a critique of financial instruments that follow such a hybrid logic, see M.J. Roy, N. McHugh and S. Sinclair. 2018. A critical reflection on social impact bonds. *Stanford Social Innovation Review*, May 1. S. Yan, F. Ferraro and J. Almandoz. 2018. The rise of socially responsible investment funds: The paradoxical role of the financial logic. *Administrative Science Quarterly*, 64(2): 466–501. D. Kent and M.T. Dacin. 2013. Bankers at the gate: Microfinance and the high-cost of borrowed logics. *Journal of Business Venturing*, 28(6): 759–773.

[37] Assia, OECD Forum. About minute 4.

[38] Stablecoins emerged as a response to the volatility that characterises first-generation cryptocurrencies such as bitcoin. By pegging and backing their value to an official currency, to a basket of currencies or to an external asset (such as gold), the teams behind stablecoins aim to overcome the instability of the currency's price and thus provide a safe digital asset. DAI is a well-known stablecoin on the Ethereum blockchain backed by Ethereum-based assets deposited in the MakerDAO ecosystem. Those involved in governing DAI aim to maintain its value equal to US$1,00. Initially, much hope had been placed in the stability stablecoins promised. See, for instance, L. Fantacci and L. Gobbi. 2021. Stablecoins, central bank digital currencies and US dollar hegemony. *Accounting, Economics, and Law: A Convivium.*

The crypto-crash of 2022 has however thrown much doubt upon the reality of the backing that is to stabilise this second generation of cryptocurrencies. The implosion of TerraUSD – a stablecoin whose 1-to-1 peg to the US dollar was meant to be held by its backing in the crypto-token LUNA – was the particular event that threw the crypto world into turmoil: when LUNA succumbed to extreme selling, its value collapsed, bringing the value of TerraUSD down with it, and raising general mistrust on other stablecoins.

[39] Assia et al, The GoodDollar White Paper.

[40] Assia et al, The GoodDollar White Paper.

[41] For updated figures, visit GoodDollar's dashboard: https://dashboard.gooddollar.org/.

[42] Assia et al, The GoodDollar White Paper, p 13.

[43] Figures for the months of February, April and May 2022 are similar. For February, see https://www.gooddollar.org/blog-posts/february-2022-standing-together-sharing-the-love; for April, see https://www.gooddollar.org/blog-posts/a-record-breaking-april-as-gooddollar-membership-claiming-soar; for May, see https://www.gooddollar.org/blog-posts/up-up-and-away-gooddollar-hits-new-heights-in-may; for June, see https://www.gooddollar.org/blog-posts/june-goodupdate-advocating-for-greater-diversity-and-inclusion-in-web3-with-digital-ubi.

[44] Assia et al, The GoodDollar White Paper.

[45] G. Segovia. 2022. *GoodDAO Community Call 01: Main Features of GoodDollar V2 & Our First Governance Proposal*, 20 January.

46 GoodDollar HQ. 2021. *Introducing the GoodDAO: GoodDollar Governance.*

47 Assia et al, The GoodDollar White Paper.

48 GoodDollar HQ, *Introducing the GoodDAO.*

49 Segovia, *GoodDAO Community Call 01*, minute 28.

50 Assia et al, The GoodDollar White Paper, p 9.

51 In *Woke Capitalism*, Carl Rhodes makes a parallel argument. He discusses the extent to which major corporations set the democratic agenda through what are popularly seen as good-faith gestures. Including progressive social critique – such as denouncing racism or calling for LGBTQIA+ rights – in their marketing campaigns, corporations shape debates without the need to act on changing the very practices and structures at the root of what they may campaign for. C. Rhodes. 2022. *Woke Capitalism: How Corporate Morality is Sabotaging Democracy*. Bristol University Press.

Chapter 8

1 This is no place to repeat the environmental disasters and climate-change dynamics that are already unfolding as consequence of human action on the planet. For some of the most recent climate and environmental reports, see the Intergovernmental Panel on Climate Change (IPCC)'s *Climate Change 2022* reports. https://www.ipcc.ch/report/ar6/wg3/ and https://www.ipcc.ch/report/ar6/wg2/

2 For recent reviews of the scientific literature, see M. Lynas, B.Z. Houlton and S. Perry. 2021. Greater than 99% consensus on human caused climate change in the peer-reviewed scientific literature. *Environmental Research Letters*, 16(11); K.F. Myers, P.T. Doran, J. Cook, J.E. Kotcher and T.A. Myers. 2021. Consensus revisited: Quantifying scientific agreement on climate change and climate expertise among Earth scientists 10 years later. *Environmental Research Letters*, 16(10); J.L. Powell. 2019. Scientists reach 100% consensus on anthropogenic global warming. *Bulletin of Science, Technology & Society*, 37(4):183–184. For a list of US scientific societies issuing public statements endorsing the position that the global climate is warming and that the source of this change is anthropogenic visit https://climate.nasa.gov/scientific-consensus/#*.

3 https://www.worldbank.org/en/topic/climatechange.

4 https://www.imf.org/en/Topics/climate-change.

5 United Nations' webpage on Climate Change. https://www.un.org/en/climatechange/paris-agreement.

6 E. Masood and J. Tollefsen. 2021. 'COP26 hasn't solved the problem': Scientists react to UN climate deal. *Nature*, 599: 355–356.

7 UNEP's Emission Gap Report highlights the gap between national climate pledges and what would be needed to keep global warming below the 1.5°C that was the goal of the Paris Agreement. See, for instance, UNEP. 2022. *The Heat is On: A World of Climate Promises Not Yet Delivered*. Emissions Gap Report 2021.

8 A. Nurse. 2022. *Cleaning Up Greenwash: Corporate Environmental Crime and the Crisis of Capitalism*. Lexington Books.

9 House of Commons Environmental Audit Committee. 2005. *Corporate Environmental Crime*. Second Report of Session 2004–05. HC 136.

10 Popularised in the year 2000 by the chemist Nobel laureate Paul Crutzen, the term 'Anthropocene' – from the Greek 'anthropo' for human and 'cene' for epoch – has become a contested terrain between geologists and environmentalists. For geologists, we are in the Holocene, an epoch that started some 11,700 years ago with the end of the last major glacial period. The term Holocene does however not recognise that human civilisation has caused mass extinction of plants and animal species, altered the chemical composition of the soil, transformed the climate, and modified many of the Earth's geologic, hydrologic and biospheric processes. To heed attention to

the connection between the form of our civilisation and the health of the Earth, environmental scientists prefer the term Anthropocene. Not seeing evidence in rock strata, geologists criticise the term, arguing that there is no clear-cut proof for the existence of a new epoch and maintaining that the Anthropocene is more about popular culture than hard science. Environmentalists find evidence in the traces of radiation the first atomic bombs – those thrown on Hiroshima and Nagasaki – left in soils around the world and therefore place the start of the Anthropocene in 1945. Others place the start sometime in the 1800s, when the onset of the Industrial Revolution started impacting the levels of carbon and methane in the atmosphere. Regardless of the debates on terminology and starting date, the term clearly makes us aware that human civilisation is having an impact on the environment at a planetary scale, that the fate of the Earth ultimately hinges on the actual organisation of society and the economy. See P. Cruzen. 2002. Geology of mankind. *Nature*, 415: 23; W.J. Autin and J.M. Holbrook. 2012. Is the Anthropocene an issue of stratigraphy or pop culture? *GSA (Geological Society of America) Today*, 22(7): 60–61; W.J. Autin. 2016. Multiple dichotomies of the Anthropocene. *The Anthropocene Review*, 3(3): 218–230; J.R. McNeill and P. Engelke. 2016. *The Great Acceleration: An Environmental History of the Anthropocene Since 1945*. Harvard University Press.

[11] See, for instance, J.W. Moore (ed). 2016. *Anthropocene or Capitalocene? Nature, History, and the Crisis of Capitalism*. Kairos.

[12] For descriptions of some such initiatives, see the edited volume, published in 2021, *Climate Adaptation: Accounts of Resilience, Self-Sufficiency and Systems Change*. Arkbound Foundation.

[13] 'Prefiguration' refers to a form of citizen-driven activist politics that emphasises direct action and participatory democracy as ways to bring the future these engaged citizens call for by making it here and now. Common examples of prefigurative initiatives are workers' take-over and recuperation of factories after Argentina's economic collapse of 2001, intentional eco-villages around the world, or the community-driven organisation of the squares during the Occupy movement. On these examples, see M.I. Fernández Álvarez. 2017. *La política afectada: Experiencia, trabajo y vida cotidiana en Brakeman recuperada*. Prohistoria Ediciones; S. Clarence-Smith and L. Monticelli. 2022. Flexible institutionalisation in Auroville: A prefigurative alternative to development. *Sustainability Science*, 17: 1171–1182; D. Graeber. 2009. *Direct Action: An Ethnography*. AK Press. For recent overviews of prefiguration and prefigurative politics, see G. Fians. 2022. Prefigurative politics. *The Cambridge Encyclopaedia of Anthropology*; P. Raekstad and S.S. Gradin. 2020. *Prefigurative Politics: Building Tomorrow Today*. Polity Press. For an edited volume with contributions by leading prefigurative scholars, see L. Monticelli (ed). 2022. *The Future is Now: An Introduction to Prefigurative Politics*. Bristol University Press.

[14] R. Read. 2021. Dodo, phoenix or butterfly? Why it's time for TrAdaptation. In *Climate Adaptation: Accounts of Resilience, Self-Sufficiency and Systems Change*. Arkbound Foundation, pp 332–346.

[15] This is a reference to Bruno Latour's *We Have Never Been Modern* from 1993. In that book, Latour argues that Modernity is constituted by two processes; one hidden, the other explicit. In the explicit process, we have two separate poles. Nature is transcendent, universal, objective and general. The Society pole is immanent, contingent, subjective and specific. Between these two poles there is a no man's land. Every phenomena, every fact, is purified, analysed and classified in either one pole, never a mix of the two. In the hidden part of Modernity's Constitution, Latour finds the work of mediation, where hybrids are recognised and constructed out of both Nature and Society. Through the work of mediation Nature and Society mix in our everyday life and doing. This results in networks, connecting and mixing every point.

Moderns, Latour argues, have only seen the explicit part of Modernity's Constitution. They have always believed that the power of Western culture lies in their 'realisation' that Nature and Society are distinct and apart. Their progress lies in their belief in the independence between Nature and Society. Since they conceive time on the basis of the achievement of such distinction, Moderns classify all other cultures as Premodern. Science, Moderns argue in Latour's analysis, implies the separation of Nature from Society; no separating the two, Premoderns got Magic instead.

However, Latour continues, Moderns haven't realised that underneath the work of purification lies the work of mediation. Latour maintains that this lack of acknowledgement has enabled for the proliferation of hybrids: because Moderns believe that Nature is independent from Society, an influence on Nature wouldn't in turn influence Society. And, vice versa, shaping Society does not shape Nature. This illusion facilitated intervening on Nature or Society because, the assumption was, Moderns couldn't anticipate any bigger change on the other pole. Premoderns are more reticent to intervene in either Nature or Society because, seeing the close link between Nature and Society, they have been too afraid of undertaking any change. Hence, Latour concludes, their lack of innovation. Yet, Latour contends, the overlap of Nature with Society, what we call magic, is not a worse belief than the Modern belief of two separate poles. Rather, the reason why Moderns won over Premoderns is not the separation of the two poles, which was but a chimera, but the size of the network Moderns were embedded in. Latour maintains that we have never been Modern because, although we never acknowledged it, we have been constantly engaged in the production of hybrids, of nature–culture collectivities.

For another book about the entanglement of Nature, Society and Technology similarly building on ANT sociology, see M. Callon, P. Lascoumes and Y. Barthe. 2009. *An Essay on Technical Democracy: Acting in an Uncertain World*. Translated by G. Burchell. The MIT Press.

[16] The *Charter of the Earth* is an international declaration of principles to guide local efforts to build a just, sustainable and peaceful global society. It exhorts global interdependence and shared responsibility and calls individuals and organisations to action in restoring and caring for planet Earth. It is the result of over a decade of global collaboration between civil society organisations and was formally agreed at the UNESCO headquarters in 2000. For more information, see https://earthcharter.org/about-the-earth-charter/history/.

[17] C. Casal Lodeiro. 2015. Transició VNG y la 'turuta': hacia una sociedad diversa, sostenible y pacífica. *15/15/15: Revisit para una nueva civilización*. Empirical material for this section on the Turuta comes from a study visit in June 2016, formal presentations and debate at the Spanish National Meeting of Community Currencies in 2016 as well as at the 4th International Conference of Complementary and Community Currencies held in 2017 in Barcelona along with an interview in 2022 and several informal discussions in the last five years. Empirical material also comes from the currency's webpage and interviews with some of their members published on the internet.

[18] C. Casal Lodeiro. Transició VNG y la 'turuta'

[19] To see the land recuperation projects the Turuta is currently undertaking, see https://turutes.blogspot.com/p/participar.html.

[20] For an empirical description of a common relationship towards debt, and the resignification of debt in mutual credit systems, see Chapter 4.

[21] In personal written exchange with Ton Dalmau, co-founder and member of the Board.

[22] https://commission.europa.eu/news/focus-energy-efficiency-buildings-2020-02-17_en; https://www.resourcepanel.org/reports/resource-efficiency-and-climate-change; https://www.unep.org/resources/emissions-gap-report-2019.

[23] European Commission. 2019. *The European Green New Deal*. Communication from the Commission to the European Parliament, the European Council, the Council, the European Economic and Social Committee and the Committee of the Regions.

[24] Eurostat. 2020. Urban and rural living in the EU. See also The World Bank Data. Urban population (% of total population) – European Union, https://data.worldbank.org/indicator/SP.URB.TOTL.IN.ZS?locations=EU.

[25] The first stage of the Vilawatt initiative focused on the Montserranina District of Viladecans, with a size of 45 hectares, 20,216 residents – or 30 per cent of the city's residents – and a total of 8,026 dwellings, 6,203 of which were constructed previous to the building insulation legislation of 1976. Its residents earn an annual income 15 per cent lower than the city's average.

Empirical details for Vilawatt come from Vilawatt's webpage, the Statutes of the Vilawatt Consortia, Vilawatt currency design, operational protocols and official impact reports, the description of the project in the UIA (Urban Innovative Actions) website (https://www.uia-initiative.eu/en/uia-cities/viladecans), the UIA Case Study Viladecans, the final Journal UIA Vilawatt project, as well as a variety of pages hosted under the European Union European Regional Development Fund (see https://ec.europa.eu/regional_policy/funding/erdf_en).

[26] Vilawatt Consortium Statutes, p 3. And in Ajuntament de Viladecans. 2019. *Protocol de Funcionament Moneda Local Vilawatt*, p 4. 11/04/2019.

[27] On the politics of visibility and trust performed through numbers, see T.M. Porter. 1995. *Trust in Numbers: The Pursuit of Objectivity in Science and Public Life*. Princeton University Press. See also his post actualising the matter to today's political divide in the United States. Porter elicits the politics of numbers to deliver an incisive critique of Trump's and the Republican Party's efforts to cultivate ignorance by waging a war on accurate numbers. T.M. Porter. 2020. Democracy counts: On sacred and debased numbers. *Princeton University Press Ideas*.

[28] https://urbact.eu/networks/vilawatt/innovative-governance-energy

[29] M. Martín. 2021. Viladecans' innovative governance for Energy Transition. *UrbAct: Driving Change for Better Cities*. European Union: European Regional Development Fund.

[30] The Global Covenant of Mayors for Climate and Energy (https://www.globalcovenantofmayors.org/) is an alliance of city and local governments around the world committed to lead work towards building resilient and low-emission cities. It is interesting that cities and local governments are taking the lead in transforming the organisation of the economy towards sustainability, acting themselves while calling upon national governments to follow their lead. Emerging from cities and centred on transforming people's everyday practices, this 'new municipalism' – as this new breed of city-based policies has been called – often stems from the organisational capacities of activists and social movements to assemble actors across the board to build democratic and ecological cities. For a seminal article identifying the municipal as the spatial scale from which to develop transformative politics, see B. Russell. 2017. Beyond the local trap: New municipalism and the rise of the fearless cities. *Antipode: A Radical Journal of Geography*, 51(3): 989–1010. For an article identifying three forms of new municipalism, see M. Thompson. 2020. What's so new about New Municipalism? *Progress is Human Geography*, 45(2): 317–342.

[31] According to a United Nation's report from 2021, an estimated 12 per cent of the plastic produced has been incinerated and 9 per cent has been recycled. United Nations Environment Programme (UNEP). 2021. *Drowning in Plastics: Marine Litter and Plastic Waste Vital Graphics*.

[32] See P.S. Ross, S. Chastain, E. Vassilenko, A. Etemadifar, S. Zimmermann, S.-A. Quesnel et al. 2021. Pervasive distribution of polyester fibres in the Arctic Ocean is driven by

Atlantic inputs. *Nature Communications*, 12: 106; H.K. Imhov, N.P. Ivleva, J. Schmid, R. Niessner and C. Laforsch. 2013. Contamination of beach sediments of a subalpine lake with microplastic particles. *Current Biology*, 23(19): R867–R868; E. Genbo Xu and X. Duan. 2021. Plastic, plastic everywhere: Airborne microplastics are settling into the most remote corners of the globe. *The Conversation*; M. Bergmann, S. Mützel, S. Primpke, M.B. Tekman, J. Trachsel and G. Gerdts. 2019. White and wonderful? Microplastics prevail in snow from the Alps to the Arctic. *Science Advances*, 5(8). For impactful images showing the ubiquitousness of plastic, see the photo exhibition organised by the Basel Convention Plastic Waste Partnership, *Plastic is Forever*.

[33] J.M. D'Souza, F.M. Windsor, D. Santillo and S.J. Ormerod. 2020. Food web transfer of plastics to an apex riverine predator. *Global Change Biology*, 26(7): 3846–3857; L. Tosetto, C. Brown and J. Williamson. 2016. How microplastics make their way up the ocean food chain into fish. *The Conversation*, 1 December; M.E. Iñiguez, J.A. Conesa and A. Fullana. 2017. Microplastics in Spanish table salt. *Scientific Reports*, 7(1): 8620; G. Liebezeit and E. Liebezeit. 2014. Synthetic particles as contaminants in German beers. *Food Additives & Contaminants: Part A*, 31(9): 1574–1578; D. Yang, H. Shi, L. Li, J. Li, K. Jabeen and P. Kolandhasamy. 2015. Microplastic pollution in table salts from China. *Environmental Science & Technology*, 49(22): 13622–13627.

[34] For a swift and somber overview, see the two UNEP reports from 2021 on marine litter and plastic waste. UNEP. 2021. *Drowning in Plastic: Marine Litter and Plastic Waste Vital Graphics*; UNEP. 2021. *From Pollution to Solution: A Global Assessment of Marine Litter and Plastic Pollution*.

[35] With the infrastructure turn in urban studies, there has come a recognition of the heterogeneous nature of urban infrastructures. Building on Science and Technology Studies, urban infrastructures are conceived as sociotechnical networks, assemblages of material objects, social practices and cultural understandings that constitute and are constituted by infrastructural conjunctions. Studies that centre on the urban infrastructures of the Global South have particularly focused on how marginalised and vulnerable communities are an intrinsic element in the creation, maintenance, extension and adaptation of infrastructures across time and space. They are the human component of a continuous infrastructuring process that enables or disrupts flow of materials. See J.-P.D. Addie. 2021. Urban life in the shadows of infrastructural death: from people as infrastructure to dead labour and back again. *Urban Geography*, 42(9): 1349–1361; L. Chelcea and G. Pulay. 2015. Networked infrastructures and the 'local': Flows and connectivity in a postsocialist city. *City*, 19(2–3): 344–355; A. Simone. 2004. People as infrastructure: Intersecting fragments in Johannesburg. *Public Culture*, 16(3): 407–429; S. Graham and S. Marvin. 2011. *Splintering Urbanism: Networked Infrastructures, Technological Mobilities and the Urban Condition*. Routledge; S. Graham and C. McFarlane. 2014. *Infrastructural Lives: Urban Infrastructure in Context*. Routledge.

[36] Twenty-one is the middle point for the estimated 19 to 23 million metric tons of plastic waste that entered the ocean in 2016. That was more than a doubling for the equivalent estimate for 2010. For 2016 figures, see S.B. Borrelle, J. Ringma, K.L. Law, C.C. Nonnahan, L. Lebreton, A. McGivern, E. Murphy, J. Jambeck, G.H. Leonard and C.M. Rochman. 2020. Predicted growth in plastic waste exceeds efforts to mitigate plastic pollution. *Science*, 369(6510): 1515–1518. For exact figures for 2010, see J.R. Jambeck, R. Geyer, C. Wilcox, T.R. Siegler, M. Perryman, A. Andrade, R. Narayan and K.L. Law. 2015. Plastic waste inputs from land into the ocean. *Science*, 347(6223): 768–771.

[37] See OECD. 2022. *Global Plastics Outlook: Economic Drivers, Environmental Impacts and Policy Options*. OECD Publishing; The Pew Charitable Trusts & SYSTEMIQ. 2020. *Breaking the Plastic Wave: A Comprehensive Assessment of Pathways Towards Stopping Ocean Plastic Pollution*.

[38] In United Nations Global Compact. 2016. Banking what the sea spits back. *Breakthrough News*. Empirical details for Plastic Bank come from the website; D. Katz. 2019. Plastic

Bank: Launching Social Plastic® revolution. *Field Actions Science Reports*, 19: 96–99; a UN Global Compact brief (http://breakthrough.unglobalcompact.org/briefs/plastic-bank-sea-spits-back-david-katz-shaun-frankson/); and from Y. Gong, Y. Wang, R. Frei, B. Wang and C. Zhao. 2022. Blockchain application in circular marine plastic debris management. *Industrial Marketing Management*, 102: 164–176. Quotes also come from Katz, D. 2017. Social Plastic is a new currency. TEDx Talk (https://www.youtube.com/watch?v=tnndie-ijKs); and Katz, D. 2018. The surprising solution to ocean plastic. TED Talk (https://www.youtube.com/watch?v=mT4Qbp89nIQ).

[39] Katz, Plastic Bank.

[40] In Katz, Plastic Bank.

[41] Katz. 2017. Social Plastic is a new currency. TEDx Talk. https://www.youtube.com/watch?v=tnndie-ijKs

[42] https://www.ted.com/talks/david_katz_social_plastic_is_a_new_currency.

[43] Figures refer to 15 September 2022. For updated figures, see https://plasticbank.com.

[44] In *The Value of Everything: Making and Taking in the Global Economy*, Mariana Mazzucato engages in an accessible critique of how global capitalism and its financial markets together with mainstream economics that legitimate the system have come to understand value and organise its creation, distribution and transfer. Early in the book, she gives a swift historical overview of economic theories of value, identifying a divide between those theories that conceive value as objective and those that conceive value as subjective. Identifying where value resides is, she argues, a necessary step to sort those who create value from those that extract it without adding any. Mazzucato's book is a well-deserved staunch critique to the confusion between 'taking value' and 'making value' that pervades popular debate and that devoids big companies – such as Pharma – and financial markets of responsibility. She deplores the way mainstream economics has completely forgotten discussion on what value is. She however does not offer an alternative understanding of value that could enrich economic debate. While absent in economics, value and value-making through processes of valuation are the topic of much interest in economic sociology. See, for example, M. Callon and F. Muniesa. 2005. Economic markets as calculative collective devices. *Organization Studies*, 26(8): 1229–1250; L. Karpik. 2010. *Valuing the Unique: The Economics of Singularities*. Princeton University Press; D. MacKenzie. 2006. *An Engine, Not a Camera: How Financial Models Shape Markets*. MIT Press; F. Muniesa. 2012. A flank movement in the understanding of valuation. *The Sociological Review*, 59(2): 24–38; F. Muniesa. 2014. *The Provoked Economy: Economic Reality and the Performative Turn*. Routledge; F. Vatin. 2013. Valuation as evaluating and valorizing. *Valuation Studies*, 1(1): 31–50.

[45] https://www.ted.com/talks/david_katz_the_surprising_solution_to_ocean_plastic. Another quote from Katz that illustrates the sociomaterial nature of value is: 'If every bottle was five euros, how many would you see on the street? Zero. What did we just prove? That the question is not the bottle: it is the value that we give to it. By turning what was once waste into a resource, it becomes a way to end extreme poverty.' In Katz, Plastic Bank.

[46] Katz, Plastic Bank.

[47] https://www.ted.com/talks/david_katz_social_plastic_is_a_new_currency.

[48] Katz, Plastic Bank.

[49] http://breakthrough.unglobalcompact.org/briefs/plastic-bank-sea-spits-back-david-katz-shaun-frankson/.

[50] A most illustrative quote of Karl Polanyi's argument in this respect: 'Production is interaction of man and nature; if this process is to be organized through a self-regulating mechanism of barter and exchange, then man and nature must be brought into its orbit; they must be subject to supply and demand, that is, be dealt with as commodities, as goods produced for sale. Such precisely was the arrangement under a market system. Man under the

name of labor, nature under the name of land, were made available for sale; the use of labor power could be universally bought and sold at a price called wages, and the use of land could be negotiated for a price called rent. There was a market in labor as well as in land, and supply and demand in either was regulated by the height of wages and rents, respectively; the fiction that labor and land were produced for sale was consistently upheld. … But, while production could theoretically be organized in this way, the commodity fiction disregarded the fact that leaving the fate of soil and people to the market would be tantamount to annihilating them.' K. Polanyi. 2001 [1944]. *The Great Transformation: The Political and Economic Origins of Our Time*. Beacon Press, pp 136–137.

Chapter 9

1 For a list of economists whose models ignore money as a key element of economic dynamics, see S. Keen. 2022. *The New Economics: A Manifesto*. Polity Press.

2 In *The End of Finance*, Massimo Amato and Luca Fantacci despair over creditors/bankers' resignation of their fiduciary obligation towards their debtors. Commodifying the asset-side of the debt–credit relationship and selling it forward, bankers need no longer take care of the debtor's ability to pay back her debt and, thus, the creditor can ignore the larger effects the debtor's repayment ability – or inability – has on the larger social body. Amato and Fantacci call the create-credit-to-sell-it-forward the liquidity principle. It organises the production of private bank money, putting that principle at the root of the recurring booms and busts that have characterised economies since the 1970s. In the vocabulary used in this book, the commodity imaginary built into the monetary arrangement pushes us to relate to money as something to hold and sell, enabling individuals to disregard the larger collective and, thus, with consequences for the health of the social. Amato and Fantacci's suggested solution is to return to a banking practice where creditors have a credit-long obligation of care towards their debtors. I do admit the hurdles of implementing such solution at the national and supranational levels; after all, in the form of implementing quantitative easing monetary policy after the Great Financial Crash of 2007–2009 showed the extent to which the interests of private bankers and states are interlocked. Hence the suggestion put forward in this book to have a multiplicity of complementary monies, organised at various territorial levels and managed by actors anchored at the specific territorial/organisational level. M. Amato and L. Fantacci. 2012. *The End of Finance*. Polity Press.

3 Though I make the argument with a focus on local complementary monies, *Positive Money* makes the same argument for our conventional national monies. See *Positive Money Europe*. 2022. Democratise the European Central Bank; S. Jourdan and S. Diessner. 2020. *Strengthening the European Parliament's Role in ECB Scrutiny*. Positive Money Europe.

4 G.M. Gómez. 2019. *Monetary Plurality in Local, Regional and Global Economies*. Routledge.

5 In 2014, the Bank of England admitted 97 per cent of the money circulating in the economy was created by private banks when extending loans. M. McLeay, A. Radia and R. Thomas. 2014. Money creation in the modern economy. *Quarterly Bulletin*, Bank of England. See Chapter 3 in this book.

6 Erin O. Wright presents three strategic logics for systemic transformation, each characterised by its relation to the dominant system. Ruptural transformation involves a sharp break with the extant social order and established institutions and aims at creating institutions anew. On the other end of the spectrum, symbiotic transformation implies an extension and deepening of extant institutions to encompass those groups and address those problems currently ignored. Interstitial transformation is, in a way, unrelated to extant institutions either in an antagonistic or in a symbiotic relationship. Instead, interstitial transformative strategies work from the in-betweens, from the margins of the current social order to build new institutional forms. E.O. Wright. 2010. *Envisioning Real Utopias*. Verso.

[7] Some successful local currencies that have inspired both citizens and municipalities beyond their reach are the WIR, a mutual credit system created in 1934 in Switzerland and still functioning, which most notoriously inspired Sardex in Sardinia along with the network of similar currencies throughout Italy we saw in Chapter 4. Another example is the municipal money launched in 1973 in Curitiba, Brazil, to involve citizens in collecting garbage; it inspired the launch of Lixo in 2016 in Lisbon, Portugal, which has been replicated in other Portuguese municipalities. See S. Lima Coelho. 2019. 'E pudesse eu pagar de outra forma': o uso de uma moeda local como instrumento mobilizador de práticas de reciclageme de dinamização do comércio local em Campolide. *Analyse Social*, 233(4): 760–781.

[8] As we have seen throughout the book, voices across the ideological divide are calling for a reorganisation of societies. They differ however on the extent of that reorganisation. The more conservative call for a piecemeal upgrade of the system proposing to reimagine capitalism by giving finance a social purpose. Others conceive a complete overhaul of the system, calling for a post-capitalist future, characterised by cooperative forms of organisation and a de-growth economy. For a few examples across the array of suggestions see R.M. Henderson. 2020. *Reimagining Capitalism in a World on Fire*. Public Affairs Books; I. Ferreras, J. Battilana and D. Méda. 2022. *Democratise Work: The Case for Reorganising the Economy*. University of Chicago Press; P. Mason. 2015. *PostCapitalism: A Guide to Our Future*. Penguin Books; T. Jackson. 2009. *Prosperity Without Growth: Economics for a Finite Planet*. Routledge; G. Kallis. 2014. *Degrowth: A Vocabulary for a New Era*. Routledge.

[9] In his posthumous book, David Graeber, together with David Wengrow, looks back to the distant past to get inspiration from civilisational forms long gone. Theirs is a hopeful chant to the creativity of groups and collectives to find ways to govern themselves and do so democratically, as equals. If they could do it some 5,000 years ago, the two Davids seem to suggest, so can we. D. Graeber and D. Wengrow. 2021. *The Dawn of Everything: A New History of Humanity*. Penguin Random House.

[10] I owe this insight to Eva Álvarez de Andrés, who I only met over an intense day rich in experiences. For over a decade, she has worked with stigmatised gipsy communities repeatedly made homeless in the outskirts of Madrid, Spain. Despite the difficult conditions in which they live and the extortionist treatment they receive from employers and local authorities, they stubbornly live life full of dignity, gaiety and hope. For some of her work, see E. Álvarez de Andrés, C. Cabrera and H. Smith. 2019. Resistance as resilience: A comparative analysis of state-community conflicts around self-built housing in Spain, Senegal and Argentina. *Habitat International*, 86: 116–125; E. Álvarez de Andrés, M.J. Zapata Campos and P. Zapata. 2015. Stop the evictions! The diffusion of networked social movements and the emergence of a hybrid space: The case of the Spanish Mortgage Victims Group. *Habitat International*, 46: 252–259.

[11] The nature of hope implicit in interstitial efforts to transform society – as in Wright's 'real utopias' – differs from the nature of hope implicit in ideologies of free market or planned economies. In interstitial real utopias, hope is grounded in experiences of living differently together, in continuous involvement in making a different economy, in participation in decision-making processes concerning one's polity. Arjun Appadurai phrases it nicely when he writes: 'Hope now is a collectively mobilized resource that defines a new terrain between the temptations of utopia and the arrogance of technocratic solutions to change.' A. Appadurai. 2007. Hope and democracy. *Public Culture*, 19(1): 29–34.

Appendix

[1] Mehrling, *The New Lombard Street*. For the curious to learn more about the 'money view' and see it applied to US monetary history as well as to the events of the 2007 financial meltdown, I recommend taking Mehrling's *Coursera* free online course, 'Economics of Money and Banking'.

[2] The 'money view' builds on Keynes' and Minsky's understanding of the relation between the income flows of economic actors (households, business firms and government) and their financial commitments (or cash outflows/debt to financial actors). The following paragraph in one of Minsky's papers succinctly summarises this understanding: 'The fundamental idea of a theory that integrates the financial structure with the determinants of real income is that the various components of the real income system – household, business firms and governments – have liabilities which are commitments to make payments to financing organizations. These payment commitments on debts are supported by wage and other household incomes, gross profits after taxes for business, and taxes for governments (for simplicity we ignore international relations). These debts originate in exchanges by which the debtor receives money today and promises to deliver money tomorrow.' Minsky, *Stabilizing an Unstable Economy*.

[3] Federal Reserve Bank of St. Louis, FRED Economic Data. https://fred.stlouisfed.org/series/BUSLOANS

[4] The possibility to get credit enables the figure of the entrepreneur, which is quintessential to capitalism. As Schumpeter noted, someone 'can only become an entrepreneur by previously becoming a debtor. ... What he first wants is credit. Before he requires any goods whatever, he requires purchasing power. He is the typical debtor in capitalist society.' J. Schumpeter. 1983 [1934]. *The Theory of Economic Development: An Inquiry into Profits, Capital, Credit, Interest, and the Business Cycle*. Translated by R. Opie. Transaction Publishers, p 264.

[5] IMF economists Marco Gross and Christoph Siebenbrunner offer a similar balance sheet example of money creation through the creation of loans by commercial banks. Gross and Siebenbrunner, Money creation in fiat and digital currency systems.

[6] For a similar balance sheet example, see Gross and Siebenbrunner, Money creation in fiat and digital currency systems.

[7] In the UK, the Bank of England implemented quantitative easing by overwhelmingly buying UK government bonds from the non-bank private sector. In the US, the Federal Reserve bought both US Treasuries (equivalent to government bonds) as well as mortgage-backed securities backed by other public agencies. The European Central Bank opted to implement quantitative easing by buying banks' toxic loans. Though implementation varied in terms of what assets the central banks bought, the monetary policy results equally in the expansion of the central bank's balance sheet. See M. Joyce, D. Miles, A. Scott and D. Vayanos. 2012. Quantitative easing and unconventional monetary policy: An introduction. *The Economic Journal*, 122(564): F271–F288.

Indeed, upon their original constitution in the early 20th century, central banks soon developed into the banker's bank, commercial banks relying on the central bank to provide extra liquidity in times of trouble. It was this emergent responsibility as the banker's bank that led central banks to develop the art of monetary management. For a well-written description of the origin and development of central banks, see Goodhart, *The Evolution of Central Banks*.

References

Abedifar, P., Molyneux, P. and Tarazi, A. 2013. Risk in Islamic banking. *Review of Finance*, 17(6): 2035–2096.

Addie, J.-P.D. 2021. Urban life in the shadows of infrastructural death: from people as infrastructure to dead labour and back again. *Urban Geography*, 42(9): 1349–1361.

Álvarez De Andrés, E., Zapata Campos, M.J. and Zapata, P. 2015. Stop the evictions! The diffusion of networked social movements and the emergence of a hybrid space: The case of the Spanish Mortgage Victims Group. *Habitat International*, 46: 252–259.

Álvarez De Andrés, E., Cabrera, C. and Smith, H. 2019. Resistance as resilience: A comparative analysis of state-community conflicts around self-built housing in Spain, Senegal and Argentina. *Habitat International*, 86: 116–125.

Amato, M. and Fantacci, L. 2012. *The End of Finance*. Polity Press.

Amato, M. and Fantacci, L. 2014. Back to which Bretton Woods? Liquidity and clearing as alternative principles for reforming international money. *Cambridge Journal of Economics*, 38(6): 1431–1452.

Amato, M. and Fantacci, L. 2014. *Saving the Market from Capitalism*. Translated by G. Sells. Polity Press.

Amato, M. and Fantacci, L. 2020. *A Fistful of Bitcoins: The Risks and Opportunities of Virtual Currencies*. Bocconi University Press.

Ammous, S. 2018. *The Bitcoin Standard: The Decentralized Alternative to Central Banking*. Wiley.

Ammous, S. 2021. *The Fiat Standard: The Debt Slavery Alternative to Human Civilization*. The Saif House.

Ansonera, A., Diniz, E.H., Siqueira, E.S. and Pozzebon, M. 2021. From community bank to solidarity fintech: The case of Palmas e-Dinheiro in Brazil. In Walker, T., McGaughey, J., Goubran, S. and Wagdy, N. (eds) *Innovations in Social Finance*. Springer, pp 251–268.

Appadurai, A. 2007. Hope and democracy. *Public Culture*, 19(1): 29–34.

Appelbaum, B. 2019. *The Economists' Hour: How the False Prophets of Free Markets Fractured Our Society*. Pan Macmillan.

Arestis, P. 2013. Economic policies of the new consensus macroeconomics: A critical appraisal. In Pixley, J. and Harcourt, G.C. (eds) *Financial Crises and the Nature of Capitalist Money: Mutual Developments from the Work of Geoffrey Ingham*. Palgrave Macmillan, pp 196–215.

Armstrong, A., Davis, E.P., Liadze, I. and Rienzo, C. 2013. Evaluating changes in bank lending to UK SMEs over 2001–12 – ongoing tight credit? Econometric analysis using data from the UK Survey of SME Finances and the SME Finance Monitor. Report. Department for Business Innovation & Skills, UK Government.

Arnsperger, C., Bendell, J. and Slater, M. 2021. *Monetary Adaptation to Planetary Emergency: Addressing the Monetary Growth Imperative*. Institute for Leadership and Sustainability, University of Cumbria, UK.

Assia, Y. and Ross, O. 2018. Good Dollar experiment: Wealth distribution. Position paper, 18 April.

Assia, Y. Barrack, T., Iron, T. and Stone, A. 2020. The GoodDollar White Paper. https://whitepaper.gooddollar.org/

Autin, W.J. 2016. Multiple dichotomies of the Anthropocene. *The Anthropocene Review*, 3(3): 218–230.

Autin, W.J. and Holbrook, J.M. 2012. Is the Anthropocene an issue of stratigraphy or pop culture? *GSA (Geological Society of America) Today*, 22(7): 60–61.

Autor, D., Cho, D., Crane, L.D., Goldar, M., Lutz, B., Montes, J., Peterman, W.B., Ratner, D., Villar, D. and Yildirmaz, A. 2022. The $800 billion paycheck protection program: Where did the money go and why did it go there? *Journal of Economic Perspectives*, 36(2): 55–80.

Banerjee, A., Faye, M., Krueger, A., Niehaus, P. and Suri, T. 2020. Effects of a Universal Basic Income during the pandemic. https://econweb.ucsd.edu/~pniehaus/papers/ubi_covid.pdf

Bank of England. 2012. The distributional effects of asset purchases. Bank of England Report, 12 July.

Baran, P. 1962. *On Distributed Communications Networks*. The RAND Corporation. https://www.rand.org/content/dam/rand/pubs/papers/2005/P2626.pdf

Barinaga, E. 2019. Transforming or reproducing an unequal economy? Solidarity and inequality in a community currency. *International Journal of Community Currencies Research*, 23(2): 2–16.

Barinaga, E. 2020. A route to commons-based democratic monies? Embedding the production of money in traditional communal institutions. *Frontiers in Blockchain*, 3: 575851.

Barinaga, E., Honzawa, A., Ocampo, J., Raffaelli, P. and Ussher, L. 2021. Commons-based monies for an inclusive and resilient future. In *Climate Adaptation: Accounts of Resilience, Self-Sufficiency and Systems Change*. Arkbound, pp 301–321.

Bazzani, G. 2020. *When Money Changes Society: The Case of Sardex Money as Community*. Springer VS.

Bell, S. 2001. The role of the state and the hierarchy of money. *Cambridge Journal of Economics*, 25: 149–163.

Benes, J. and Kumhof, M. 2012. The Chicago plan revisited. International Monetary Fund, Working Paper WP/12/202. https://www.imf.org/external/pubs/ft/wp/2012/wp12202.PDF

Bergmann, M., Mützel, S., Primpke, S., Tekman, M.B., Trachsel, J. and Gerdts, G. 2019. White and wonderful? Microplastics prevail in snow from the Alps to the Arctic. *Science Advances*, 5(8).

Bernardo, G., Ryan-Collins, J., Werner, R. and Greenham, T. 2013. *Strategic Quantitative Easing: Stimulating Investment to Rebalance the Economy*. New Economic Foundation.

Bezemer, D.J. 2010. Understanding financial crisis through accounting models. *Accounting, Organisations and Society*, 35(7): 676–688.

Bjorklund, B.C. 2017. *Saving Local Communities Using Scrip Money to Fight the Great Depression in North Central Iowa*. Master's Thesis. University of Northern Iowa.

Blanc, J. 2006. Free money for social progress: Theory and practice of Gesell's accelerated money. *American Journal of Economics and Sociology*, 57(8): 469–483.

Blanc, J. 2011. Classifying 'CCs': Community, complementary and local currencies. *International Journal of Community Currency Research*, 15(D): 4–10.

Blanc, J. 2018. Making sense of the plurality of money: A Polanyian attempt. In Gómez, G.M. (ed) *Monetary Plurality in Local, Regional and Global Economies*. Routledge, pp 48–66.

Blanc, J. 2021. Book review of Bazzani (2020) 'When money changes society: The case of Sardex money as community'. *International Journal of Community Currency Research*, 25(2): 77–80.

Blanc, J. and Lakócai, C. 2020. Toward spatial analyses of local currencies: The case of France. *International Journal of Community Currency Research*, 24(1): 11–29.

Block, F. and Somers, M. 2016. *The Power of Market Fundamentalism: Karl Polanyi's Critique*. Harvard University Press.

Borrelle, S.B., Ringma, J., Law, K.L., Nonnahan, C.C., Lebreton, L., McGivern, A., Murphy, E., Jambeck, J., Leonard, G.H. and Rochman, C.M. 2020. Predicted growth in plastic waste exceeds efforts to mitigate plastic pollution. *Science*, 369(6510): 1515–1518.

Bourdet, M.C. 1934. A French view of the Woergl experiment. Translated by G. Spiller. *Annals of Public & Cooperative Economics*, 10(1): 58–59.

Bowles, S. and Carlin, W. 2021. Rethinking economics. *FD: Finance & Development*, spring.

Brainard, L. 2020. Update on digital currencies, stablecoins, and the challenges ahead. In *Monetary Policy: The Challenges Ahead*. Colloquium in honour of Benoît Coeuré. European Central Bank, pp 21–25.

Bregman, R. 2014. *Utopia for Realists: How We Can Build the Ideal World*. Little, Brown and Company.

Brown, M. 2017. Some investors use a credit card to buy bitcoin and then carry over the balance. LendEDU Report. https://lendedu.com/blog/bitcoin-and-credit-cards/

Bruno, P., Denecker, O. and Niederkorn, M. 2021. Global payments 2021: Transformation amid turbulent undercurrents. In *The 2021 McKinsey Global Payments Report*. McKinsey & Company, pp 4–13.

Burial, P., Checherita-Westphal, C., Jacquinot, P., Schön, M. and Stähler, N. 2020. Economic consequences of high public debt: Evidence from three large scale DSGE models. European Central Bank, Working Paper Series No. 2450.

Caffyn, G. 2021. What is the bitcoin block size debate and why does it matter? *CoinDesk*, 8 October. https://www.coindesk.com/learn/what-is-the-bitcoin-block-size-debate-and-why-does-it-matter/

Caine, D. 2019. *How to Resist Amazon and Why: The Fight for Local Economics Data Privacy, Fair Labor, Independent Bookstores, and a People-Powered Future*. Raven Books.

Calas, M., Smircich, L. and Bourne, K. 2009. Extending the boundaries: Reframing 'entrepreneurship as social change' through feminist perspectives. *Academy of Management Review*, 34(3): 552–569.

Callon, M. 2007. What does it mean to say that economics is performative? In D. MacKenzie, F. Muniesa and L. Siu (eds) *Do Economists Make Markets? On the Performativity of Economics*. Princeton University Press, pp 311–357.

Callon, M. and Muniesa, F. 2005. Economic markets as calculative collective devices. *Organization Studies*, 26(8): 1229–1250.

Callon, M., Lascoumes, P. and Barthe, Y. 2009. *An Essay on Technical Democracy: Acting in an Uncertain World*. Translated by G. Burchell. The MIT Press.

Campbell-Verduyn, M. and Goguen, M. 2019. Blockchain, trust and action nets: Extending the pathologies of financial globalization. *Global Networks: A Journal of Transnational Affairs*, 19(3): 308–328.

Cantú, C., Cavallino, P., De Fiore, F. and Yetman, J. 2021. A global database on central banks' monetary responses to COVID-19. Bank for International Settlements, BIS Working Paper No. 934.

Carrión, J. 2017. *Against Amazon: Seven Arguments / One Manifesto*. Biblioasis.

Carter, Z. 2020. *The Price of Peace: Money, Democracy, and the Life of John Maynard Keynes*. Penguin Books.

Casal Lodeiro, C. 2015. 'Transició VNG y la 'turuta': hacia una sociedad diversa, sostenible y pacífica'. 15/15/15: Revisit para una nueva civilización. https://www.15-15-15.org/webzine/2015/09/18/transicio-vng-y-la-turuta-hacia-una-sociedad-diversa-sostenible-y-pacifica/

Cavero, T. and Poinasamy, K. 2013. *A Cautionary Tale: The True Cost of Austerity and Inequality in Europe*. Oxfam International.

CBPP Staff. 2022. Robust COVID relief achieved historic gains against poverty and hardship, bolstered economy. *Center on Budget and Policy Priorities*, 24 February.

Cernev, A. 2019. Mumbuca e-Dinheiro. *Revista Brasileira de Casos – Gvcasos*, 9(2), Doc 10. https://periodicos.fgv.br/gvcasos/article/view/80878/77232..

Cernev, A. and Diniz, E. 2019. Palmas para o e-Dinheiro! A evolução digital de uma moeda social local. *Revista de Administração Contemporânea*, 24(5): 487–506.

Cernev, A. and Proença, B. 2016. Mumbuca: a primeira moeda social digital do Brasil. *Revista Brasileira de Casos – Gvcasos*, 6(2), Doc 15. https://periodicos.fgv.br/gvcasos/article/view/61805/63200.

Champ, B. 2008. Stamp scrip: Money people paid to use. *Economic Commentary*. Federal Reserve Bank of Cleveland.

Chelcea, L. and Pulay, G. 2015. Networked infrastructures and the 'local': Flows and connectivity in a postsocialist city. *City*, 19(2–3): 344–355.

Chen, W., Mrkaic, M. and Nabar, M. 2019. The global economic recovery 10 years after the 2008 financial crisis. IMF Working Paper No. 19/83.

Choonara, J., Murgia, A. and Carmo, R.M. 2022. *Faces of Precarity: Critical Perspectives on Work, Subjectivities and Struggles*. Bristol University Press.

Chzhen, Y., Handa, S., Nolan, B. and Cantillon, B. 2017. *Children of Austerity: Impact of the Great Recession on Child Poverty in Rich Countries*. Oxford University Press.

Clarence-Smith, S. and Monticelli, L. 2022. Flexible institutionalisation in Auroville: A prefigurative alternative to development. *Sustainability Science*, 17: 1171–1182.

Clarke, D. 2017. Poll shows 85% of MPs don't know where money comes from. *Positive Money*. https://positivemoney.org/2017/10/mp-poll/

Cœuré, B. 2019. The rise of services and the transmission of monetary policy, speech by Benoît Cœuré, Member of the Executive Board of the ECB, at the 21st Geneva Conference on the World Economy, 16 May.

Collins, R. 2000. Situational stratification: A micro-macro theory of inequality. *Sociological Theory*, 18: 17–43.

Collom, E. 2011. Motivations and differential participation in a community currency system: The dynamics within a local social movement organization. *Sociological Forum*, 26(1): 144–168.

Cooiney, P. and Shaefer, L. 2021. Material hardship and mental health following the COVID-19 relief bill and American rescue plan act. *Poverty Solutions*. University of Michigan.

Crocker, G. 2020. *Basic Income and Sovereign Money: The Alternative to Economic Crisis and Austerity Policy*. Palgrave Macmillan.

Cruzen, P. 2002. Geology of mankind. *Nature*, 415: 23.

D'Arista, J. 2018. *All Fall Down: Debt, Deregulation and Financial Crises*. Edward Elgar.

D'Souza, J.M, Windsor, F.M., Santillo, D. and Ormerod, S.J. 2020. Food web transfer of plastics to an apex riverine predator. *Global Change Biology*, 26(7): 3846–3857.

Davies, J.C. 2017. *From Head Shops to Whole Foods: The Rise and Fall of Activist Entrepreneurs*. Columbia University Press.

De Filippi, P. and Loveluck, B. 2016. The invisible politics of Bitcoin: Governance crisis of a decentralised infrastructure. *Internet Policy Review*, 5(3). https://doi.org/10.14763/2016.3.427

Dell'Angelo, J., D'Odorico, P., Rulli, M.C. and Marchand, P. 2017. The tragedy of the grabbed commons: Coercion and dispossession in the global land rush. *World Development*, 92: 1–12.

Desan, C. 2014. *Making Money: Coin, Currency and the Coming of Capitalism*. Oxford University Press.

Desan, C. 2017. The constitutional approach to money: Monetary design and the production of the modern world. In Bandelj, N., Wherry, F. and Zelizer, V. (eds) *Money Talks: Explaining How Money Really Works*. Princeton University Press, pp 109–130.

Desan, C. 2020. The key to value: The debate over commensurability in neoclassical and credit approaches to money. *Law and Contemporary Problems*, 83(2): 1–22.

DeYoung, R. and Rice, T. 2004. How do banks make money? The fallacies of fee income. *Economic Perspectives*, 28(4): 34–51. https://www.chicagofed.org/publications/economic-perspectives/2004/4qtr2004-part3-deyoung-rice

Dittmer, K. 2013. Local currencies for purposive degrowth? A quality check of some proposals for changing money-as-usual. *Journal of Cleaner Production*, 54: 3–13.

Dodd, N. 2014. *The Social Life of Money*. Princeton University Press.

Doria, L. and Fantacci, L. 2018. Evaluating complementary currencies: From the assessment of multiple social qualities to the discovery of a unique monetary sociality. *Quality & Quantity*, 52(3): 1291–1314.

Dwyer, P. 2019. *Dealing with Welfare Conditionality: Implementation and Effects*. Policy Press.

Dyson, B., Hodgson, G. and Lerven, F.v. 2016. *Sovereign Money: An Introduction*. Positive Money.

Earle, J., Moran, C. and Ward-Perkins, Z. 2017. *The Econocracy: The Perils of Leaving Economics to the Experts*. Manchester University Press.

ECB (European Central Bank). 1999. Euro area monetary aggregates and their role in the Eurosystem's monetary policy strategy. *ECB Monthly Bulletin*, February.

ECB (European Central Bank). 2010. *Monetary Policy: The Challenges Ahead*. Colloquium in honour of Benoît Coeuré. https://www.ecb.europa.eu/pub/pdf/other/ecb.20191217_Monetary_policy_the_challenges_ahead~2cac5a564e.en.pdf?6c688b33f2cc3990e816db78afce0914

ECB (European Central Bank). 2019. *Card Payments in Europe – Current Landscape and Future Prospects: A Eurosystem Perspective*. https://www.ecb.europa.eu/pub/pubbydate/2019/html/ecb.cardpaymentsineu_currentlandscapeandfutureprospects201904~30d4de2fc4.en.html

Egger, D., Haushofer, J., Niehaus, P. and Walker, M. 2019. General equilibrium effects of cash transfers: Experimental evidence from Kenya. *Econometrica*, 90(6): 2603–2643.

Eguidazu, F. 2017. *Report on the Financial and Banking Crisis in Spain, 2008–2014*. Banco de España. https://repositorio.bde.es/bitstream/123456789/15112/1/InformeCrisis_Completo_web_en.pdf

Ehnts, D.H. 2019. Knapp's *State Theory of Money* and its reception in German academic discourse. Institute for International Political Economy, Berlin School of Economics and Law, Working Paper No. 115/2019. https://www.ipe-berlin.org/fileadmin/institut-ipe/Dokumente/Working_Papers/IPE_WP_115.pdf

Eichengreen, B. 1992. *Golden Fetters: The Gold Standard and the Great Depression, 1919–1939*. Oxford University Press.

Eichengreen, B. 2019. *Globalising Capital: A History of the International Monetary System*. Princeton University Press.

Eichengreen, B. and Temin, P. 2010. Fetters of gold and paper. *Oxford Review of Economic Policy*, 26(3): 370–384.

Eisenstein, C. 2011. *Sacred Economics*. North Atlantic.

Elvins, S. 2005. Scrip money and slump cures: Iowa's experiments with alternative currency during the Great Depression. *The Annals of Iowa*, 64: 221–245.

Erturk, I., Froud, J., Johal, S., Leaver, A. and Williams, K. 2007. The democratization of finance? Promises, outcomes and conditions. *Review of International Political Economy*, 14(4): 553–575.

Etherington, D. 2021. *Austerity, Welfare and Work: Exploring Politics, Geographies and Inequalities*. Policy Press.

European Commission. 2019. *The European Green New Deal*. Communication from the Commission to the European Parliament, the European Council, the Council, the European Economic and Social Committee and the Committee of the Regions. https://eur-lex.europa.eu/resource.html?uri=cellar:b828d165-1c22-11ea-8c1f-01aa75ed71a1.0002.02/DOC_1&format=PDF; https://eur-lex.europa.eu/resource.html?uri=cellar:b828d165-1c22-11ea-8c1f-01aa75ed71a1.0002.02/DOC_2&format=PDF

Eurostat. 2020. Urban and rural living in the EU. https://ec.europa.eu/eurostat/web/products-eurostat-news/-/edn-20200207-1

Evans, M.S. 2009. Zelizer's theory of money and the case of local currencies. *Environment and Planning A: Economy and Space*, 41(5): 1026–1041.

Fantacci, L. 2013. Why banks do what they do. How the monetary system affects banking activity. *Accounting, Economics and Law*, 3(3): 333–356.

Fantacci, L. 2013. Why not bancor? Keynes's currency plan as a solution to global imbalances. In Hirai, T., Marcuzzo, M.C. and Mehrling, P. (eds) *Keynesian Reflections: Effective Demand, Money, Finance, and Policies in the Crisis*. Oxford Scholarship Online, pp 172–195.

Fantacci, L. 2013. Reforming money to exit the crisis: Examples of non-capitalist monetary systems in theory and practice. In Pixley, J. and Harcourt, G.C. (eds) *Financial Crises and the Nature of Capitalist Money*. Palgrave Macmillan, pp 124–147.

Fantacci, L. and Gobbi, L. 2021. Stablecoins, central bank digital currencies and US dollar hegemony. *Accounting, Economics, and Law: A Convivium*. https://doi.org/10.1515/ael-2020-0053

Fare, M. and Ould Ahmed, P. 2017. Complementary currency systems and their ability to support economic and social changes. *Development and Change*, 48(5): 847–872.

Faria-e-Castro, M. 2018. What are the fiscal costs of a (great) recession? *Economic Synopses*, 22. https://doi.org/10.20955/es.2018.22

Faulkender, M., Hankings, K.W. and Petersen, M.A. 2022. Why are U.S. companies hoarding so much cash? *Kellog Insight*, Kellogg School of Management at Northwestern University. https://insight.kellogg.northwestern.edu/article/companies-hoarding-cash

Fergusson, A. 1975. *When Money Dies: The Nightmare of the Weimar Hyper Inflation*. William Kimber & Co. Ltd.

Fernández Álvarez, M.I. 2017. *La política afectada: Experiencia, trabajo y vida cotidiana en Brakeman recuperada*. Prohistoria Ediciones.

Ferreras, I. Battilana, J. and Méda, D. 2022. *Democratise Work: The Case for Reorganising the Economy*. University of Chicago Press.

Fians, G. 2022. Prefigurative politics. *The Cambridge Encyclopaedia of Anthropology*. https://www.anthroencyclopedia.com/entry/prefigurative-politics#h2ref-8

Figueroa García, M.A. 2015. Funcionamiento de monedademos.es. *Demos*.

Financial Conduct Authority. 2021. Consumer investments data review April 2020 – March 2021. *FCA*. https://www.fca.org.uk/data/consumer-investments-data-review-2021

Financial Crisis Inquiry Commission, USA. 2011. *The Financial Crisis Inquiry Report: Final Report of the National Commission on the Causes of the Financial and Economic Crisis in the United States*. https://fcic-static.law.stanford.edu/cdn_media/fcic-reports/fcic_final_report_full.pdf

Finley, K. 2018. After 10 years, bitcoin has changed everything – and nothing. *Wired*, 31 October. https://www.wired.com/story/after-10-years-bitcoin-changed-everything-nothing/

Fisher, I. 1922. *The Purchasing Power of Money, its Determination and Reaction to Credit, Interest and Crises*. Macmillan.

Fisher, I. 1933. *Stamp Scrip*. Adelphi Company.

Forget, E. 2011. The town with no poverty: The health effects of a Canadian guaranteed annual income field experiment. *Canadian Public Policy*, 37(3): 283–305.

Fox, J. 2013. What we've learned from the financial crisis. *Harvard Business Review*.

Franco, J., Kishimoto, S., Kay, S., Feodoroff, T. and Pracucci, G. 2014. *The Global Water Grab: A Primer*. The Transnational Institute.

Freitas, F. 2022. Transferência de renda com moeda social em Cabo Frio, Itaboraí, Niterói e Maricá: alívio da pobreza ou renda básica? *Gestão, Política e Sociedade*. 27 April. https://www.estadao.com.br/politica/gestao-politica-e-sociedade/transferencia-de-renda-com-moeda-social-em-cabo-frio-itaborai-niteroi-e-marica-alivio-da-pobreza-ou-renda-basica/

Friedman, M. 1991. The island of stone money. Working Papers in Economics, Hoover Institution, E-91–3.

Frijters, P. 2017. Why Blockchain has no economic future. *Pearls and Irritations: John Menadue's Public Policy Journal*, 13 November. https://johnmenadue.com/paul-frijters-why-blockchain-has-no-economic-future/

Froud, J., Johan, S., Montgomerie, J. and Williams K. 2010. Escaping the tyranny of earned income? The failure of finance as social innovation. *New Political Economy*, 15(1): 147–164.

Furness, W.H. 1910. *The Island of Stone Money: UAP of the Carolines*. J.B. Lippincott Company.

Gabor, D. and Vestergaard, J. 2016. *Towards a Theory of Shadow Money*. Institute for New Economic Thinking.

Galbraith, J.K. 2012. *Inequality and Instability: A study of the world economy just before the Great Crisis*. Oxford University Press.

Geertz, C. 1962. The rotating credit association: A 'middle rung' in development. *Economic Development and Cultural Change*, 10(3): 241–263.

Genbo Xu, E. and Duan, X. 2021. Plastic, plastic everywhere: Airborne microplastics are settling into the most remote corners of the globe. *The Conversation*, 20 October. https://theconversation.com/plastic-plastic-everywhere-airborne-microplastics-are-settling-into-the-most-remote-corners-of-the-globe-168787

Gentilini, U., Grosh, M., Rigolini, J. and Yemtsov, R. 2020. *Exploring Universal Basic Income: A Guide to Navigating Concepts, Evidence, and Practices*. World Bank Group. https://documents1.worldbank.org/curated/en/993911574784667955/pdf/Exploring-Universal-Basic-Income-A-Guide-to-Navigating-Concepts-Evidence-and-Practices.pdf

Gerlich, P. and Campbell, D. 2000. Austria: From compromise to authoritarianism. In Berg-Schlosser, D. and Mitchell, J. (eds) *The Conditions of Democracy in Europe, 1919–39: Systematic Case Studies*. Macmillan, pp 40–58.

Gesell, S. 1916. *The Natural Economic Order*. Translated by M.A. Philip Pye, p 11. https://www.naturalmoney.org/NaturalEconomicOrder.pdf

Ghaffary, S. and Del Rey, J. 2020. The real cost of Amazon. *Vox*, 29 June.

Gitlen, J. 2022. *Investing in Bitcoin: Survey and Report.* LendEDU. https://lendedu.com/blog/investing-in-bitcoin

Goetzmann, W. 2017. *Money Changes Everything: How Finance Made Civilization Possible.* Princeton University Press.

Gomes da Silva Hernandes, E., Souza Siqueira, E., Henrique Diniz, E. and Pozzebon, M. 2018. A digital community bank: Mapping negotiation mechanisms in its consolidation as an alternative to commercial banks. *International Journal of Community Currency Research*, 22: 56–70.

Gómez, G.M. 2009. *Argentina's Parallel Currency: The Economy of the Poor.* Pickering & Chatto.

Gómez, G.M. 2019. *Monetary Plurality in Local, Regional and Global Economies.* Routledge.

Gómez, G.M. and Prittwitz und Gaffron, W. 2019. The pervasiveness of monetary plurality in economic crisis and war. In Gómez, G.M. (ed) *Monetary Plurality in Local, Regional and Global Economies.* Routledge, pp 223–252.

Gong, Y., Wang, Y., Frei, R., Wang, B. and Zhao, C. 2022. Blockchain application in circular marine plastic debris management. *Industrial Marketing Management*, 102: 164–176.

Gonzalez, L., Cernev A.K., de Araujo, M.H. and Diniz, E.H. 2021. Digital complementary currencies and public policies during the COVID-19 pandemic. *Brazilian Journal of Public Administration*, 54(4): 1146–1160.

GoodDollar HQ. 2021. *Introducing the GoodDAO: GoodDollar Governance.* https://www.gooddollar.org/blog-posts/introducing-the-gooddao-gooddollar-governance

Goodhart, C. 1988. *The Evolution of Central Banks.* MIT Press.

Goodhart, C. 1997. One government, one money. *Prospect*, March.

Goodhart, C. 1998. The two concepts of money: Implications for the analysis of optimal currency areas. *European Journal of Political Economy*, 14: 407–432.

Gopalakrishnan, V., Wadhwa, D., Haddad, S. and Blake, P. 2021. 2021 year in review in 11 charts: The inequality pandemic. World Bank. https://www.worldbank.org/en/news/feature/2021/12/20/year-2021-in-review-the-inequality-pandemic

Graeber, D. 2009. *Direct Action: An Ethnography.* AK Press.

Graeber, D. 2013. *The Democracy Project: A History, a Crisis, a Movement.* Spiegel & Grau.

Graeber, D. 2014 [2011]. *Debt: The First 5,000 Years.* Melville House.

Graeber, D. and Wengrow, D. 2021. *The Dawn of Everything: A New History of Humanity.* Penguin Random House.

Graham, S. and Marvin, S. 2011. *Splintering Urbanism: Networked Infrastructures, Technological Mobilities and the Urban Condition.* Routledge.

Graham, S. and McFarlane, C. 2014. *Infrastructural Lives: Urban Infrastructure in Context*. Routledge.

Grasselli, M.R. 2022. Monetary policy responses to COVID-19: A comparison with the 2008 crisis and implications for the future of central banking. *Review of Political Economy*, 34(2): 420–445.

Greco, T. 2009. *The End of Money and the Future of Civilisation*. Chelsea Green.

Greco, T. 2013. Taking moneyless exchange to scale: Measuring and maintaining the health of a credit clearing system. *International Journal of Community Currency Research*, 17(A): 19–25.

Greene, J. 2021. Amazon's employee surveillance fuels unionization efforts: 'It's not prison, it's work'. *The Washington Post*, 6 December.

Greenhill, S. 2008. 'It's awful – Why did nobody see it coming?': The Queen gives her verdict on global credit crunch. *Mail Online*, 6 November.

Griffith, E. 2021. We're all crypto people now. *New York Times*, 25 April. https://www.nytimes.com/2021/04/25/technology/cryptocurrency-mainstream.html

Gross, M. and Siebenbrunner, C. 2019. Money creation in fiat and digital currency systems. International Monetary Fund, IMF Working Paper #WP/19/285.

Haig, S. 2019. Bitcoin block size, explained. *Cointelegraph*. https://cointelegraph.com/explained/bitcoin-block-size-explained

Hajric, V. 2021. Bitcoin's current holders are new, with 55% getting in this year. *Bloomberg*. https://www.bloomberg.com/news/articles/2021-12-06/more-than-half-of-bitcoin-investors-got-in-just-this-years

Handler, H. 2016. Two centuries of currency policy in Austria. *Monetary Policy & the Economy, Oesterreichische Nationalbank (Austrial Central Bank)*, 3: 61–76.

Harper, J.W.C. 1948. *Scrip and Other Forms of Local Money*. PhD Dissertation. University of Chicago.

Hart, K. 1986. Heads or tails? Two sides of the coin. *Man*, 21(4): 637–656.

Hart, K. 2001. *Money in an Unequal World: Keith Hart and His Memory Bank*. Texere.

Hartley, T. and Kallis, G. 2021. Interest-bearing loans and unpayable debts in slow-growing economies: Insights from ten historical cases. *Ecological Economics*, 188(C): S0921800921001907.

Harvard Joint Center for Housing Studies. 2008. *The State of the Nation's Housing 2008*. Harvard University.

Harvey, C.R., Ramachandran, A. and Santoro, J. 2021. *DeFi and the Future of Finance*. John Wiley and Sons.

Harvey, M. 2019. Slavery, indenture and the development of British industrial capitalism. *History Workshop Journal*, 88: 66–88.

Hasdell, R. 2020. What we know about UBI: A cross-synthesis review. *Stanford Basic Income Lab*. https://basicincome.stanford.edu/uploads/Umbrella%20Review%20BI_final.pdf

Haushofer, J. and Shapiro, J. 2016. The short-term impact of unconditional cash transfers to the poor: Experimental evidence from Kenya. *The Quarterly Journal of Economics*, 131(4): 1973–2042.

Haushofer, J. and Shapiro, J. 2018. The long-term impact of unconditional cash transfers to the poor: Experimental evidence from Kenya. *The Poverty Action Lab*, Working Paper. https://www.povertyactionlab.org/sites/default/files/research-paper/The-long-term-impact-of-conditional-cash-tranfer_Kenya_Haushofer_Shapiro_January2018.pdf

Haushofer, J., Ringdhal, C., Shapiro, J. and Wang, X.Y. 2019. Income changes and intimate partner violence: Evidence from unconditional cash transfers in Kenya. NBER Working Paper No. 25627. https://www.nber.org/papers/w25627

Hearn, M. 2015. On block size. *Mike's Blog Plan 99*. https://medium.com/@octskyward/on-block-sizes-e047bc9f830

Hearn, M. 2015. Why is Bitcoin forking. *Mike's Blog Plan 99*. https://medium.com/faith-and-future/why-is-bitcoin-forking-d647312d22c1

Hearn, M. 2016. The resolution of the bitcoin experiment. *Mike's Blog Plan 99*. https://blog.plan99.net/the-resolution-of-the-bitcoin-experiment-dabb30201f7

Hearn, M. 2020. The philosophical origins of Bitcoin's civil war. *Mike's Blog Plan 99*. https://blog.plan99.net/the-philosophical-origins-of-bitcoins-civil-war-400468335377

Henderson, R.M. 2020. *Reimagining Capitalism in a World on Fire*. Public Affairs Books.

Hengsbach, D. 2022. Monetary sovereignty in the digital age: A case of central bank digital currencies (CBDC)? Paper presented at the SASE conference, Amsterdam, 9–11 July.

Hessel, S. 2010. *Indignez-vous!* Indigène.

Hirschman, A.O. 1977. *The Passions and the Interests: Political Arguments for Capitalism Before its Triumph*. Princeton University Press.

Hjorth, D. and Steyaert, C. 2009. *The Politics and Aesthetics of Entrepreneurship: A Fourth Movements in Entrepreneurship Book*. Edward Elgar.

Hockett, R. 2020. The inclusive value ledger: A public platform for digital dollars, digital payments, and digital public banking. *Just Money*. https://justmoney.org/r-hockett-the-inclusive-value-ledger-a-public-platform-for-digital-dollars-digital-payments-and-digital-public-banking/

Hossein, C.S. and Christabell, P.J. (eds). 2022. *Community Economies in the Global South: Case Studies of Rotating Savings and Credit Associations and Economic Cooperation*. Oxford University Press.

House of Commons Environmental Audit Committee. 2005. *Corporate Environmental Crime*. Second Report of Session 2004–05. HC 136. https://publications.parliament.uk/pa/cm200405/cmselect/cmenvaud/136/136.pdf

Howson, P. and de Vries, A. 2022. Preying on the poor? Opportunities and challenges for tackling the social and environmental threats of cryptocurrencies for vulnerable and low-income communities. *Energy Research & Social Science*, 84: 102394.

Hudson, M. 2002. Reconstructing the origins of interest-bearing debt and the logic of clean slates. In Hudson, M. and Van de Mieroop, M. (eds) *Debt and Economic Renewal in the Ancient Near East*. CDL Press, pp 7–58.

Hudson, M. 2004. Introduction: The role of accounting in civilisation's economic takeoff. In Hudson, M. and Wunsch, C. (eds) *Creating Economic Order: Record-keeping Standardization and the Development of Accounting in the Ancient Near East*. CDL Press, pp 1–22.

Hudson, M. 2004. The development of money-of-account in Sumer's temples. In Hudson, M. and Wunsch, C. (eds) *Creating Economic Order: Record-Keeping Standard and the Development of Accounting in the Ancient Near East*. CDL Press, pp 303–330.

Hughes, N. 2015. The community currency scene in Spain. *International Journal of Community Currency Research*, 19: 1–11.

IMF. 2021. El Salvador: Staff concluding statement of the 2021 Article IV mission. *IMF*. https://www.imf.org/en/Publications/CR/Issues/2022/01/26/El-Salvador-2021-Article-IV-Consultation-Press-Release-Staff-Report-and-Statement-by-the-512245

Imhov, H.K., Ivleva, N.P., Schmid, J., Niessner, R. and Laforsch, C. 2013. Contamination of beach sediments of a subalpine lake with microplastic particles. *Current Biology*, 23(19): R867–R868.

Ingham, G. 2000. Babylonian madness: On the historical and sociological origins of money. In Smithin, J. (ed) *What is Money?* Routledge, pp 16–41.

Ingham, G. 2004. *The Nature of Money*. Polity Press.

Ingham, G. 2020. *Money: Ideology, History, Politics*. Polity Press.

Iñiguez, M.E., Conesa, J.A. and Fullana, A. 2017. Microplastics in Spanish table salt. *Scientific Reports*, 7(1): 8620.

Jackson, A.L. and Schmidt, J. 2022. 2021 stock market year in review. *Forbes*. https://www.forbes.com/advisor/investing/stock-market-year-in-review-2021/

Jackson, T. 2009. *Prosperity Without Growth: Economics for a Finite Planet*. Earthscan.

Jambeck, J.R., Geyer, R., Wilcox, C., Siegler, T.R., Perryman, M., Andrade, A., Narayan, R. and Law, K.L. 2015. Plastic waste inputs from land into the ocean. *Science*, 347(6223): 768–771.

Jennings, A.L. 1994. Toward a feminist expansion of macroeconomics. *Journal of Economic Issues*, 28(2): 555–565.

Jevons, W.S. 1875. *Money and the Mechanism of Exchange*. D. Appleton and Company

Jones, B.A., Goodkind, A.L. and Berrens, R.P. 2022. Economic estimation of Bitcoin mining's climate damages demonstrates closer resemblance to digital crude than digital gold. *Nature*, Scientific Reports 12. https://www.nature.com/articles/s41598-022-18686-8

Jones, D. and Marinescu, I.E. 2018. The labor market impacts of universal and permanent cash transfers: Evidence from the Alaska Permanent Fund. *American Economic Journal*, 14(2): 315–340.

Jourdan, S. and Diessner, S. 2020. *Strengthening the European Parliament's Role in ECB Scrutiny*. Positive Money Europe.

Joyce, M., Miles, D., Scott, A. and Vayanos, D. 2012. Quantitative easing and unconventional monetary policy: An introduction. *The Economic Journal*, 122(564): F271–F288.

Kale, S. 2021. 'I put my life savings in crypto': How a generation of amateurs got hooked on high-risk trading. *The Guardian*, 19 June. https://www.theguardian.com/lifeandstyle/2021/jun/19/life-savings-in-crypto-generation-of-amateurs-hooked-on-high-risk-trading

Kallis, G. 2014. *Degrowth: A Vocabulary for a New Era*. Routledge.

Kangas, O., Jauhiainen, S., Simanainen, M. and Ylikännö, M. 2021. *Experimenting with Unconditional Basic Income: Lessons from the Finnish BI Experiment 2017–2018*. Edward Elgar. https://repositoriobibliotecas.uv.cl/bitstream/handle/uvscl/4612/%5B9781839104848%20-%20Experimenting%20with%20Unconditional%20Basic%20Income%5D%20Experimenting%20with%20Unconditional%20Basic%20Income.pdf?sequence=1&isAllowed=y

Karpik, L. 2010. *Valuing the Unique: The Economics of Singularities*. Princeton University Press.

Katz, D. 2019. Plastic Bank: Launching Social Plastic® revolution. *Field Actions Science Reports*, 19: 96–99.

Keeley, B. and Love, P. 2010. Pensions and the crisis. In *From Crisis to Recovery: The Causes, Course and Consequences of the Great Recession*. OECD, pp 68–87. https://www.oecd-ilibrary.org/finance-and-investment/from-crisis-to-recovery_9789264077072-en

Keen, S. 2011. *Debunking Economics: The Naked Emperor Dethroned?* Zed Books.

Keen, S. 2022. *The New Economics: A Manifesto*. Polity Press.

Kelton, S. 2020. *The Deficit Myth: Modern Monetary Theory and the Birth of the People's Economy*. PublicAffairs.

Kennedy, M. 1995. *Interest and Inflation Free Money: Creating an Exchange Medium That Works for Everybody and Protects the Earth*. Inbook.

Kent, D. and Dacin, M.T. 2013. Bankers at the gate: Microfinance and the high-cost of borrowed logics. *Journal of Business Venturing*, 28(6): 759–773.
Keynes, J.M. 1915. The island of stone money. *The Economic Journal*, 25(98): 281–283.
Keynes, J.M. 1930. *A Treatise on Money*. Cambridge University Press.
Keynes, J.M. 1933. The Great Slump of 1930. In *Essays in Persuasion*. Macmillan and Co, pp 135–147.
Keynes, J.M. 1936. *The General Theory of Employment, Interest and Money*. Macmillan.
Keynes, J.M. 1942. Proposals for an international currency (or clearing) union. In Horsefield, J.K. (ed) *The International Monetary Fund 1945–1965: Twenty years of International Monetary Cooperation, Volume III: Documents*, International Monetary Fund, pp 3–18.
Keynes, J.M. 1944. International Monetary Fund. *Commons and Lords Hansard*, Lords Sitting of 23 May 1944, series 5, vol 131, cc834–83. https://api.parliament.uk/historic-hansard/lords/1944/may/23/international-monetary-fund
Keynes, J.M. 1977 [1924]. A tract on monetary reform. In Robinson, A. and Moggridge, D. (eds) *The Collected Writings of John Maynard Keynes*. Cambridge University Press, pp 137–138.
Keynes, J.M. 1980 [1941]. The origins of the clearing union. In Moggridge, D. (ed) *The Collected Writings of John Maynard Keynes, Volume XXV: Activities 1940–1944. Shaping the Post-War World: The Clearing Union*. Cambridge University Press, p 33.
Khan, F. 2010. How 'Islamic' is Islamic banking? *Journal of Economic Behavior & Organization*, 76(3): 805–820.
Kindleberger, C. 1978. *Manias, Panics and Crashes*. Basic Books.
KIS Finance. 2021. *Cryptocurrency Consumer Research and Data: Autumn 2021*. https://www.kisbridgingloans.co.uk/finance-news/cryptocurrency-consumer-research-and-data-autumn-2021/
Kiyotaki, N. and Wright, R. 1989. On money as a medium of exchange. *Journal of Political Economy*, 97(4): 927–954
Knapp, G.F 1924. *The State Theory of Money*. Macmillan and Co. https://historyofeconomicthought.mcmaster.ca/knapp/StateTheoryMoney.pdf
Kocherlakota, N.R. 1998. Money is memory. *Journal of Economic Theory*, 81: 232–251.
Krugman, P. 2007. *The Conscience of a Liberal*. W.W. Norton & Company.
Krugman, P. 2011. Golden cyberfetters. *New York Times*, 7 September. http://www.sfu.ca/~kkasa/Krugman_Bitcoin.pdf
Krugman, P. 2012. *End This Depression Now!* W. W. Norton & Company.
Krugman, P. 2015. The case for cuts was a lie. Why does Britain still believe it? The austerity delusion. *The Guardian*, 29 April.
Krugman, P. 2015. The case of the missing Minsky. *New York Times*, 1 June.

Lagarde, C. 2020. The future of money: Innovating while retaining trust. *L'ENA hors les murs*, 501. [Original French version available here: https://www.serviralumni.com/fr/article/l-avenir-de-la-monnaie-un-double-enjeu-d-innovation-et-de-confiance/30/11/2020/542. Translated English version available here: https://www.ecb.europa.eu/press/inter/date/2020/html/ecb.in201130~ce64cb35a3.en.html

Lampert, M. and van Tilburg, R. 2016. Knowledge about who creates money low amongst international population. Publication based on Glocalities Research by Motivaction International in cooperation with Sustainable Finance Lab. Available at: https://glocalities.com/news/press-release-global-population-does-not-want-commercial-banks-to-stay-responsible-for-creating-most-of-the-money

Lanz, K. 2022. *Large-Scale Land Acquisition in Ghana: Institutional Change, Gender and Power*. Routledge.

Larue, L. 2020. A conceptual framework for classifying currencies. *International Journal of Community Currency Research*, 24: 45–60.

Larue, L. 2022. The case against alternative currencies. *Politics, Philosophy & Economics*, 21(1): 75–93.

Larue, L., Meyer, C., Hudon, M. and Sandberg, J. 2022. The ethics of alternative currencies. *Business Ethics Quarterly*, 32(2): 299–321.

Latour, B. 1993. *We Have Never Been Modern*. Harvard University Press.

Latour, B. 2005. *Reassembling the Social: An Introduction to Actor-Network Theory*. Oxford University Press.

Le Goff, J. 2005. *From Heaven to Earth: The Shift in Values between the 12th and the 13th Century in the Christifan West*. Royal Netherlands Academy of Arts and Science.

Lee, D. 2020. Amazon contractors enduring 'subhuman' conditions in Philippines. *Financial Times*, 1 April.

Lessig, L. 2000. Code is law: On liberty in cyberspace. *Harvard Magazine*. https://www.harvardmagazine.com/2000/01/code-is-law-html

Liebezeit, G. and Liebezeit, E. 2014. Synthetic particles as contaminants in German beers. *Food Additives & Contaminants: Part A*, 31(9): 1574–1578.

Lietaer, B., Arnsperger, C., Goerner, S. and Brunnhuber, S. 2012. *Money – Sustainability: The Missing Link*. Triarchy Press.

Lima Coelho, S. 2019. 'E pudesse eu pagar de outra forma': o uso de uma moeda local como instrumento mobilizador de práticas de reciclagem e de dinamização do comércio local em Campolide. *Analyse Social*, 233(4): 760–781.

Lynas, M., Houlton, B.Z. and Perry, S. 2021. Greater than 99% consensus on human caused climate change in the peer-reviewed scientific literature. *Environmental Research Letters*, 16(11). https://iopscience.iop.org/article/10.1088/1748-9326/ac2966

MacKenzie, D. 2006. *An Engine, Not a Camera: How Financial Models Shape Markets*. MIT Press.

Makarov, I. and Schoar, A. 2021. Blockchain analysis of the bitcoin market. National Bureau of Economic Research (NBER), Working Paper No. 29396. https://www.nber.org/system/files/working_papers/w29396/w29396.pdf

Martignoni, J. 2012. A new approach to a typology of complementary currencies. *International Journal of Community Currency Research*, 16(Autumn): 1–17.

Martin, F. 2014. *Money: The Unauthorised Biography*. Vintage Books.

Martín, M. 2021. Viladecans' innovative governance for Energy Transition. *UrbAct: Driving Change for Better Cities*. European Union: European Regional Development Fund.

Martín Belmonte, S., Puig, J. and Roca, M. 2021. Crisis mitigation through cash assistance to increase local consumption levels: A case study of a bimonetary system in Barcelona, Spain. *Journal of Risk and Financial Management*, 14(9): 1–17.

Marx, K. 1976 [1867]. *Capital: A Critique of Political Economy*. Translated by B. Fowkes. Penguin Books.

Mascornick, J. 2007. Local currency loans and grants: Comparative case studies of Ithaca HOURS and Calgary Dollars. *International Journal of Community Currency Research*, 11: 1–22.

Mason, P. 2015. *PostCapitalism: A Guide to Our Future*. Penguin Books.

Masood, E. and Tollefsen, J. 2021. 'COP26 hasn't solved the problem': Scientists react to UN climate deal. *Nature*, 599: 355–356.

Matti, J. and Zhou, Y. 2020. Money is money: The economic impact of BerkShares. *SSRN Electronic Journal*. https://papers.ssrn.com/sol3/papers.cfm?abstract_id=3732903

Maurer, B. 2005. *Mutual Life, Limited: Islamic Banking, Alternative Currencies, Lateral Reason*. Princeton University Press.

Maurer, B., Nelms, T.C. and Swartz, L. 2013. 'When perhaps the real problem is money itself!': The practical materiality of Bitcoin. *Social Semiotics*, 23(2): 261–277.

Mauss, M. 2002 [1954]. *The Gift: The Form and Reason for Exchange in Archaic Societies*. Routledge Classics.

Mazzucato, M. 2018. *The Value of Everything: Making and Taking in the Global Economy*. Penguin Books.

McCaster, R. 2018. Does post Keynesianism need a theory of care? In Dow, S., Jespersen, J. and Tily, G. (eds) *Money, Method and Contemporary Post-Keynesian Economics*. Edward Elgar, pp 160–174.

McGahey, R. 2020. Amazon gets billions while state and local government budgets collapse. *Forbes*, 17 December.

McLeay, M., Radia, A. and Thomas, R. 2014. Money creation in the modern economy. *Quarterly Bulletin*, Bank of England.

McLeay, M., Radia, A. and Thomas, R. 2014. Money in the modern economy: An introduction. *Quarterly Bulletin*, Bank of England.

McNeill, J.R. and Engelke, P. 2016. *The Great Acceleration: An Environmental History of the Anthropocene Since 1945*. Harvard University Press.

Mehrling, P. 2011. *The New Lombard Street: How the Fed Became the Dealer of Last Resort*. Princeton University Press.

Mehrling, P. 2013. The inherent hierarchy of money. In Taylor, L., Rezai, A. and Michl, T. (eds) *Social Fairness and Economics: Economic Essays in the Spirit of Duncan Foley*. Routledge, pp 394–404.

Mehrling, P. 2016. Beyond bancor. *Challenge*, 59(1): 22–34.

Meng, H. and Ueda, A. 2020. Characteristics of community currency that contribute to endogenous regional activation: Based on case studies of three community currencies: Ma~yu, Tengu and Awa Money. *International Journal of Community Currency Research*, 24: 54–63.

Menger, C. 2009 [1892]. *On the Origins of Money*. Ludwig von Mises Institute.

Meyer, C. 2012. *Les finances solidaires comme biens communs durables: étude de cas de la Banque communautaire de développement Palmas (Brésil)*. Université libre de Bruxelles.

Meyer, C. and Hudon, M. 2019. Money and the commons: An investigation of complementary currencies and their ethical implications. *Journal of Business Ethics*, 160: 277–292.

Mill, J.S. 1909/1848. *Principles of Political Economy with some of their Applications to Social Philosophy*. Edited by W.J. Ashley. Longmans, Green and Co. https://www.econlib.org/library/Mill/mlP.html?chapter_num=39#book-reader

Minsky, H. 1986. *Stabilizing an Unstable Economy*. Washington University Press.

Minsky, H. 1992. The financial instability hypothesis. Levy Economics Institute of Bard College, Working Paper No. 74.

Mitchell Innes, A. 1913. What is money? *Banking Law Journal*, pp 377–408.

Mitchell Innes, A. 1914. The credit theory of money. *The Banking Law Journal*, pp 151–168.

Monticelli, L. (ed). 2022. *The Future is Now: An Introduction to Prefigurative Politics*. Bristol University Press.

Moore, J.W. (ed). 2016. *Anthropocene or Capitalocene? Nature, History, and the Crisis of Capitalism*. Kairos.

Motsi-Omoijiade, I.D. 2018. Financial intermediation in cryptocurrency markets: Regulation, gaps and bridges. In Kuo Chuen, D.L. and Deng, R. (eds) *Handbook of Blockchain, Digital Finance, and Inclusion, Volume 1: Cryptocurrency, FinTech, InsurTech, and Regulation*. Academic Press, pp 207–223.

Moyer, L. 2015. An impact assessment model for web-based time-banks: A thought-experiment in the operationalisation of social capital. *Consilience: The Journal of Sustainable Development*, 14(2): 106–125.

Muellbauer, J. 2014. Combatting Eurozone deflation: QE for the people. *Centre for Economic Policy Research*. https://cepr.org/voxeu/columns/combatting-eurozone-deflation-qe-people

Muniesa, F. 2012. A flank movement in the understanding of valuation. *The Sociological Review*, 59(2): 24–38.

Muniesa, F. 2014. *The Provoked Economy: Economic Reality and the Performative Turn*. Routledge.

Myers, K.F., Doran, P.T., Cook, J., Kotcher, J.E. and Myers, T.A. 2021. Consensus revisited: Quantifying scientific agreement on climate change and climate expertise among Earth scientists 10 years later. *Environmental Research Letters*, 16(10). https://iopscience.iop.org/article/10.1088/1748-9326/ac2774/meta

Nakamoto, S. 2008. Bitcoin: A peer-to-peer electronic cash system. White Paper.

Nakamoto, S. 2009. Bitcoin open source implementation of P2P currency. *P2P Foundation: The Foundation for Peer to Peer Alternatives*. http://p2pfoundation.ning.com/forum/topics/bitcoin-open-source?id=2003008:Topic:9402&page=1

Nakazato, H. and Hiramoto, T. 2012. An empirical study of the social effects of community currencies. *International Journal of Community Currency Research*, 16(D): 124–135.

Neumann, D.M. 2021. Mumbuca: Moeda Social e/ou Renda Básica de Cidadania? As narrativas sobre a moeda social de Maricá. Master's Thesis. Fundação Getulio Vargas.

North, D.C. 1977. Markets and other allocation systems in history: The challenge of Karl Polanyi. *Journal of European Economic History*, 6(3): 703–716.

North, P. 2007. *Money and Liberation: The Micropolitics of Alternative Currency Movements*. University of Minnesota Press.

Nova, A. 2018. Desperate to get into bitcoin, investors slip into debt. *CNBC*. https://www.cnbc.com/2018/01/11/taking-on-debt-to-buy-bitcoin-is-a-bad-idea.html

Nurse, A. 2022. *Cleaning Up Greenwash: Corporate Environmental Crime and the Crisis of Capitalism*. Lexington Books.

OECD. 2022. *Global Plastics Outlook: Economic Drivers, Environmental Impacts and Policy Options*. OECD Publishing. https://www.oecd-ilibrary.org/environment/global-plastics-outlook_de747aef-en

Oppenheim, A.L. 1957. A bird's-eye view of Mesopotamian economic history. In Polanyi, K., Arensberg, C.M. and Pearson, H.W. (eds) *Trade and Markets in the Early Empires*. The Free Press, pp 27–37.

Ostrom, E. 1990. *Governing the Commons: The Evolution of Institutions for Collective Action*. Cambridge University Press.

Panetta, F. 2022. For a few cryptos more: The Wild West of crypto finance. Speech by Fabio Panetta, Member of the Executive Board of the ECB, at Columbia University, 25 April. https://www.ecb.europa.eu/press/key/date/2022/html/ecb.sp220425~6436006db0.en.html

Peebles, G. 2011. *The Euro and Its Rivals: Currency and the Construction of a Transnational City*. Indiana University Press.

Perrin, A. 2021. 16% of Americans say they have ever invested in traded or used cryptocurrency. *Pew Research Center*. https://www.pewresearch.org/short-reads/2021/11/11/16-of-americans-say-they-have-ever-invested-in-traded-or-used-cryptocurrency/

Pettifor, A. 2017. *The Production of Money: How to Break the Power of Bankers*. Verso Books.

Pew Charitable Trusts and SYSTEMIQ. 2020. *Breaking the Plastic Wave: A Comprehensive Assessment of Pathways Towards Stopping Ocean Plastic Pollution*. https://www.pewtrusts.org/-/media/assets/2020/07/breakingtheplasticwave_report.pdf

Piketty, T. 2014. *Capital in the Twenty-First Century*. Harvard University Press.

Pistor, K. 2019. *The Code of Capital*. Princeton University Press.

Place, C. 2011. Community currency progress in Latin America (Banco Palmas). *International Journal of Community Currency Research*, 15(D): 39–46.

Place, C., Calderon, A., Stodder, J. and Wallimann, I. 2018. Swiss currency systems: Atlas, compendium and chronicle of legal aspects. *International Journal of Community Currency Research*, 22: 85–104.

Polanyi, K. 1947. Our obsolete market mentality: Civilization must find a new thought pattern. *Commentary*, 3: 109–117.

Polanyi, K. 1957. The economy as instituted process. In Polanyi, K., Arensberg, C.M. and Pearson, H.W. (eds) *Trade and Market in the Early Empires*. Henry Regnery Company, pp 243–270.

Polanyi, K. 1957. Marketless trading in Hammurabi's time. In Polanyi, K., Arensberg, C.M. and Pearson, H.W. (eds) *Trade and Markets in the Early Empires*. The Free Press, pp 12–26.

Polanyi, K. 1968 [1957]. The semantics of money-uses. In Dalton, G. (ed) *Primitive, Archaic, and Modern Economies: Essays of Karl Polanyi*. Beacon Press, pp 175–203.

Polanyi, K. 2001 [1944]. *The Great Transformation: The Political and Economic Origins of Our Time*. Beacon Press.

Polanyi Levitt, K. 2006 Keynes and Polanyi: The 1920s and the 1990s. *Review of International Political Economy*, 13(1): 152–177.

Porter, T.M. 1995. *Trust in Numbers: The Pursuit of Objectivity in Science and Public Life*. Princeton University Press.

Porter, T.M. 2020. Democracy counts: On sacred and debased numbers. *Princeton University Press Ideas*. https://press.princeton.edu/ideas/democracy-counts-on-sacred-and-debased-numbers

Positive Money Europe. 2022. Democratise the European Central Bank. https://www.positivemoney.eu/democratize-european-central-bank/

Posnett, E. 2015. The Sardex factor. *Financial Times*, 18 September.

Powell, J. 2002. Petty capitalism, perfecting capitalism or post-capitalism? *Review of International Political Economy*, 9(4): 619–649.

Powell, J. 2019. Scientists reach 100% consensus on anthropogenic global warming. *Bulletin of Science, Technology & Society*, 37(4): 183–184.

Quayson, A. and Arhin, A. 2012. *Labour Migration, Human Trafficking and Multinational Corporations: The Commodification of Illicit Flows*. Routledge.

Quiggin, J. 2010. *Zombie Economics: How Dead Ideas Still Walk among Us*. Princeton University Press.

Quinsom, T. and Benhamou, M. 2021. Banks always backed fossil fuel over green projects – until this year. *Blomberg Europe Edition*, 19 May.

Raekstad, P. and Gradin, S.S. 2020. *Prefigurative Politics: Building Tomorrow Today*. Polity Press.

Raworth, K. 2017. *Doughnut Economics: Seven Ways to Think Like a 21st Century Economist*. Random House.

Read, R. 2021. Dodo, phoenix or butterfly? Why it's time for TrAdaptation. In *Climate Adaptation: Accounts of Resilience, Self-Sufficiency and Systems Change*. Arkbound Foundation, pp 332–346.

Reichel, A., De Schoenmakere, M. and Gillabel, J. 2016. Circular economy in Europe: Developing the knowledge base. *European Environment Agency Report* 2/2016.

Reinhart, C. 2022. *Finance for an Equitable Recovery*. World Development Report. World Bank Group.

Reinicke, C. 2022. If you invested $1,000 in bitcoin this year, you'd have about $800 now. Why you still may want to buy more. *CNBC*. https://www.cnbc.com/2022/01/24/heres-how-much-youd-have-if-you-invested-1000-in-bitcoin-this-year.html

Rhodes, C. 2022. *Woke Capitalism: How Corporate Morality is Sabotaging Democracy*. Bristol University Press.

Rigo, A.S. 2020. Challenges of social currency use: A survey on community development banks in Brazil. *International Journal of Community Currency Research*, 24: 74–85.

Robertson, L., Mushati, P., Eaton, J.W., Dumba, L., Mavise, G., Makoni, J., Schumacher, C., Crea, T., Monasch, R., Sherr, L., Garnett, G.P., Nyamukapa, C. and Gregson, S. 2013. Effects of unconditional and conditional cash transfers on child health and development in Zimbabwe: a cluster-randomised trial. *The Lancet*, 381(9874): 1283–1292.

Rodrigues, D.P. 2021. Inclusão financeira e o uso de fintechs como instrumentos de políticas públicas. Master's Thesis. Fundação Getulio Vargas.

Rodrigues, D.P. and Neumann, D.M. 2021. Moeda social e desenvolvimento local em Maricá (RJ). Master's Thesis. Fundação Getulio Vargas.

Ross, P.S., Chastain, S., Vassilenko, E., Etemadifar, A., Zimmermann, S., Quesnel, S.-A., et al. 2021. Pervasive distribution of polyester fibres in the Arctic Ocean is driven by Atlantic inputs. *Nature Communications*, 12: 106.

Roy, M.J., McHugh, N. and Sinclair, S. 2018. A critical reflection on social impact bonds. *Stanford Social Innovation Review*. https://ssir.org/articles/entry/a_critical_reflection_on_social_impact_bonds

Rozas, D., Tenorio-Fornés, A., Díaz-Molina, S. and Hassan, S. 2021. When Ostrom meets blockchain: Exploring the potentials of blockchain for commons governance. *SAGE Open*, 11(1). https://doi.org/10.1177/21582440211002526

Rubenstein, D. 2021. Interview with Christine Lagarde, President of the ECB, conducted by David Rubenstein. *Bloomberg*. https://www.ecb.europa.eu/press/inter/date/2021/html/ecb.in210916~5b06e18ebc.en.html

Russell, B. 2017. Beyond the local trap: New municipalism and the rise of the fearless cities. *Antipode: A Radical Journal of Geography*, 51(3): 989–1010.

Ryan-Collins, J. 2011. Building local resilience: The emergence of the UK transition currencies. *International Journal of Community Currency Research*, 15(D): 61–67.

Ryan-Collins, J., Greenham, T., Werner, R. and Jackson, A. 2011. *Where Does Money Come From? A Guide to the UK Monetary and Banking System*. New Economics Foundation.

Schmandt-Besserat, D. 2010. *How Writing Came About*. University of Texas Press.

Schroeder, R. 2006. Community exchange and trading systems in Germany. *International Journal of Community Currency Research*, 10: 24–42.

Schumacher, E.F. 2010 [1973]. *Small Is Beautiful: Economics as if People Mattered*. Harper Perennial.

Schumpeter, J. 1983 [1934]. *The Theory of Economic Development: An Inquiry into Profits, Capital, Credit, Interest, and the Business Cycle*. Translated by R. Opie. Transaction Publishers.

Schumpeter, J.A. 2003 [1943]. *Capitalism, Socialism and Democracy*. Routledge.

Schumpeter, J.A. 2006 [1954]. *History of Economic Analysis*. Routledge.

Schwarz, F. 1951. The experiment in Wörgl. *Verlags-Genossenschaft Freies Volk*. Translated from the German by H. Martzak-Goerike and prepared and shortened for the internet by H. Eisenkolb.

Scott, S. 2017. *Labour Exploitation and Work-Based Harm*. Princeton University Press.

Segovia, G. 2022. *GoodDAO Community Call 01: Main Features of GoodDollar V2 and Our First Governance Proposal*, 20 January. https://www.youtube.com/watch?v=HVsO9rgHyfg

Seung-Yoon Lee, S., Lee, J. and Kyo-seong, K. 2020. Evaluating basic income, basic service, and basic voucher for social and ecological sustainability. *Sustainability*, 12: 8348.

Seyfang, G. and Longhurst, N. 2013. Growing green money? Mapping community currencies for sustainable development. *Ecological Economics*, 86: 65–77.

Sharp, G. 2012 [2002]. *From Dictatorship to Democracy: A Guide to Nonviolent Resistance*. Serpent's Tail.

Shelley, T. 2007. *Exploited: Migrant Labour in the New Global Economy*. Zed Books.

Silver, M. 1983. Karl Polanyi and markets in the Ancient Near East: The challenge of the evidence. *Journal of Economic History*, 43(4): 795–829.

Silverman, G. 2021. Crypto's wild ride raises new liquidity concerns. *Financial Times*, 11 December. https://www.ft.com/content/ab2ee298-3de9-40d2-ae89-53df1ff7022c

Simmel, G. 1900. *The Philosophy of Money*. 3rd enlarged edition edited by D. Frisby, translated by D. Frisby and T. Bottomore. Routledge.

Simone, A. 2004. People as infrastructure: Intersecting fragments in Johannesburg. *Public Culture*, 16(3): 407–429.

Simpson, W., Mason, G. and Godwin, R. 2017. The Manitoba basic annual income experiment: Lessons learned 40 years later. *Canadian Public Policy*, 43(1): 85–104.

Skidelsky, R. 2018. *Money and Government: A Challenge to Mainstream Economics*. Penguin Books.

Skotnicki, T. 2021. *The Sympathetic Consumer: Moral Critique in Capitalist Culture*. Stanford University Press.

Smart, E. 2015. Bitcoin XT users allegedly suffering coordinated hack attack. *Cointelegraph*. https://cointelegraph.com/news/bitcoin-xt-users-allegedly-suffering-coordinated-hack-attack

Smith, A. 2007 [1776]. *An Inquiry into the Nature and Causes of the Wealth of Nations*. Edited by S.M. Soares. Metalibri.

Smithin, J. 2003. *Controversies in Monetary Economics*. Edward Elgar.

Soros, G. 1998. *The Crisis of Global Capitalism: Open Society Endangered*. Public Affairs

Sotiropoulou, I. 2011. Alternative exchange systems in contemporary Greece. *International Journal of Community Currency Research*, 15(D): 27–31.

Stamm, C. 2021. Understanding the recent dynamics of local currency initiatives in Switzerland. *International Journal of Community Currency Research*, 25(2): 63–76.

Standing, G. 2011. *The Precariat: The New Dangerous Class*. Bloomsbury Academic.

Standing, G. 2014. *A Precariat Charter: From Denizens to Citizens*. Bloomsbury.

Standing, G. 2017. *Basic Income: A Guide for the Open-Minded*. Penguin Books.

Standing, G. 2019. *The Plunder of the Commons: A Manifesto for Sharing Public Wealth*. Pelican.

Standing, G. 2021. Basic income pilots: Uses, limitations and design principles. *Basic Income Studies*, 16(1): 75–99.

Star, S.L. 1999. The ethnography of infrastructure. *American Behavioural Scientist*, 43(3): 377–391.

Stiglitz, J. 2012. *The Price of Inequality: How Today's Divided Society Endangers Our Future*. WW Norton & Co.

Stiglitz, J. 2022. COVID has made global inequality much worse. *Scientific American*, 326(3): 52–53.

Stodder, J. 2009. Complementary credit networks and macroeconomic stability: Switzerland's Wirtschaftsring. *Journal of Economic Behaviour & Organization*, 72(1): 79–95.

Stodder, J. and Lietaer, B. 2016. The macro-stability of Swiss WIR-bank credits: Balance, velocity, and leverage. *Comparative Economic Studies*, 58(4): 570–605.

Swan, M. 2015. *Blockchain: Blueprint for a New Economy*. O'Reilly.

Swartz, L. 2017. Blockchain dreams: Imagining techno-economic alternatives after bitcoin. In Castells, M. (ed) *Another Economy is Possible: Culture and Economy in a Time of Crisis*. Polity Press, pp 82–105.

Swartz, L. 2018. What was Bitcoin, what will it be? The techno-economic imaginaries of a new money technology. *Cultural Studies*, 32(4): 623–650.

Thiel, C. 2011. Complementary currencies in Germany: The Regiogeld system. *International Journal of Community Currency Research*, 15(D): 17–21.

Thompson, M. 2020. What's so new about New Municipalism? *Progress is Human Geography*, 45(2): 317–342.

Tichit, A., Mathonnat, C. and Landivar, D. 2016. Classifying non-bank currency systems using web data. *International Journal of Community Currency Research*, 20: 24–40.

Tirole, J. 2020. Institutional and economic challenges for central banking. In *Monetary Policy: The Challenges Ahead*. Colloquium in honour of Benoît Coeuré. European Central Bank, pp 34–40. https://www.ecb.europa.eu/pub/pdf/other/ecb.20191217_Monetary_policy_the_challenges_ahead~2cac5a564e.en.pdf?6c688b33f2cc3990e816db78afce0914

Tooze, A. 2019. *Crashed: How a Decade of Financial Crises Changed the World*. Penguin Books.

Tosetto, L., Brown, C. and Williamson, J. 2016. How microplastics make their way up the ocean food chain into fish. *The Conversation*, 1 December.

Trespalacios, J.P. and Dijk, J. 2021. The carbon footprint of bitcoin. *DNB Unrestricted*. De Nederlandsche Bank.

UNEP. 2021. *Drowning in Plastics: Marine Litter and Plastic Waste Vital Graphics*. https://wedocs.unep.org/xmlui/bitstream/handle/20.500.11822/36964/VITGRAPH.pdf

UNEP. 2021. *From Pollution to Solution: A Global Assessment of Marine Litter and Plastic Pollution*. https://malaysia.un.org/en/171922-pollution-solution-global-assessment-marine-litter-and-plastic-pollution

UNEP. 2022. *The Heat is On: A World of Climate Promises Not Yet Delivered*. Emissions Gap Report 2021.

United Nations Global Compact. 2016. Banking what the sea spits back. *Breakthrough News*. http://breakthrough.unglobalcompact.org/briefs/plastic-bank-sea-spits-back-david-katz-shaun-frankson/

Unterguggenberger, M. 1934. The end results of the Wörgl experiment. *Annals of Collective Economy*, 10(1): 60–62 (today renamed to *Annals of Public and Cooperative Economics*).

US: Government Printing Office. 2008. The Financial Crisis and the Role of Federal Regulators. House Hearing, 110 Congress.

Ussher, L.J., Hass, A., Töpfer, K. and Jaeger, C.C. 2018. Keynes and the international monetary system: Time for a tabular standard? *The European Journal of the History of Economic Thought*, 25(1): 1–35.

Vallet, G. 2016. A local money to stabilise capitalism: The underestimated case of the WIR. *Economy and Society*, 45(3–4): 479–504.

van der Linden, M.J. and van Beers, C. 2017. Are private (digital) moneys (disruptive) social innovations? An exploration of different designs. *Journal of Social Entrepreneurship*, 8(3): 302–319.

Vatin, F. 2013. Valuation as evaluating and valorizing. *Valuation Studies*, 1(1): 31–50.

Vigna, P. and Casey, M.J. 2015. *Cryptocurrency: The Future of Money?* Vintage.

Von Muralt, A. 1934. The Woergl experiment with depreciating money. *Annals of Collective Economy*, 10(1): 48–57.

Wan, S., Bartsch, E., Boivin, J., Fischer, S. and Hildebrand, P. 2019. Dealing with the next downturn: From unconventional monetary policy to unprecedented policy coordination. *BlackRock Institute*. https://www.blackrock.com/us/individual/literature/whitepaper/bii-macro-perspectives-august-2019.pdf

Wapshott, N. 2011. *Keynes Hayek: The Clash That Defined Modern Economics*. Scribe Publications.

Ward, B. and Lewis, J. 2002. *Plugging the Leaks: Making the Most of Every Pound That Enters Your Local Economy*. New Economics Foundation.

Werner, K. 2015. Performing economies of care in New England time bank and Buddhist community. In Roelvink, G., St.Martin, K. and Gibson-Graham, J.K. (eds) *Making Other Worlds Possible: Performing Diverse Economies*. University of Minnesota Press, pp 72–97.

Werner, R. 2014. Can banks individually create money out of nothing? The theories and the empirical evidence. *International Review of Financial Analysis*, 36: 1–19.

Williamson, S.D. 2017. Quantitative easing: How well does this tool work? *Federal Reserve Bank of St. Louis*. https://www.stlouisfed.org/publications/regional-economist/third-quarter-2017/quantitative-easing-how-well-does-this-tool-work

Wittgenstein, L. 1953. *Philosophical Investigations*. Translated by G.E.M. Anscombe. Blackwell.

Wray, L.R. 2014. From the state theory of money to modern money theory: An alternative to economic orthodoxy. Levy Economics Institute of Bard College, Working Paper No. 792.

Wray, R. 2012. *Modern Monetary Theory: A Primer on Macroeconomics for Sovereign Monetary Systems*. Palgrave.

Wray, R. 2013. What do banks do? What should banks do? A Minskian perspective. *Accounting, Economics, and Law: A Convivium*, 3(3): 277–311.

Wray, R. 2019. Alternative paths to modern money theory. *Real-World Economics Review*, 89: 5–22.

Wright, E.O. 2010. *Envisioning Real Utopias*. Verso.

Yan, S., Ferraro, F. and Almandoz, J. 2018. The rise of socially responsible investment funds: The paradoxical role of the financial logic. *Administrative Science Quarterly*, 64(2): 466–501.

Yang, D., Shi, H., Li, L., Li, J., Jabeen, K. and Kolandhasamy, P. 2015. Microplastic pollution in table salts from China. *Environmental Science & Technology*, 49(22): 13622–13627.

Yaros, B., Rogers, J., Cioffi, R. and Zandi, M. 2022. Fiscal policy in the pandemic. *Moody's Analytics*, 24 February.

Yoshihisa Miyazaki and Ken-ichi Kurita. 2018. The diversity and evolutionary process of modern community currencies in Japan. *International Journal of Community Currency* Research, 22: 120–131.

Zelizer, V.A. 1997. *The Social Meaning of Money: Pin Money, Paychecks, Poor Relief, and Other Currencies*. Princeton University Press.

Zelizer, V.A. 2005. Circuits within capitalism. In Nee, V. and Svedberg, R. (eds) *The Economic Sociology of Capitalism*. Princeton University Press, pp 289–322.

Zelmanovitz, L. and Meyerhof Salama, B. 2020. Central bank digital currency: The hidden agenda. *Just Money*. https://justmoney.org/l-zelmanovitz-and-b-meyerhof-salama-central-bank-digital-currency-the-hidden-agenda/

Zimmer, Z. 2017. Bitcoin and Potosí silver: Historical perspectives on cryptocurrency. *Technology and Culture*, 58(2): 307–334.

Zoltan, J. and Kumhof, M. 2019. Banks are not intermediaries of loanable funds: Facts, theory and evidence. Bank of England, Staff Working Paper No. 761. https://www.bankofengland.co.uk/working-paper/2018/banks-are-not-intermediaries-of-loanable-funds-facts-theory-and-evidence

Index

Page numbers referring to figures are *italic*; page numbers referring to tables are **bold**.

Printed and bound by CPI Group (UK) Ltd, Croydon, CR0 4YY

23/04/2025

14660718-0001